A NATURAL LIFE

Professor David Bellamy, botanist, writer and broadcaster has become one of the best-known and respected personalities in Britain. He is the author of 80 scientific papers and 34 books, many of which are bestselling children's titles. He has written and presented numerous television programmes both for the BBC and for independents. His programmes have won many national awards, including the Richard Dimbleby Award at BAFTA. He is president, patron or trustee of numerous conservation and environmental organisations and founded the Conservation Foundation in 1982.

The Bellamy Herbal is published by Century.

T0315622

Also by David Bellamy

Bellamy on Botany (1972), *Peatlands* (1973), *Bellamy's Britain* (1974), *Life Giving Sea* (1975), *Green Worlds* (1975), *The World of Plants* (1975), *It's Life* (1976), *Bellamy's Europe* (1976), *Botanic Action* (1978), *Botanic Man* (1978), *Half of Paradise* (1978), *Forces of Life* (1979), *Bellamy's Backyard Safari* (1981), *The Great Seasons* (1981), *Il Libro Verde* (1981), *Discovering the Countryside* (1982 and 1983), *The Mouse Book* (1983), *Bellamy's New World* (1983), *The Queen's Hidden Garden* (1984), *I Spy* (1985), *Bellamy's Ireland* (1986), *Turning the Tide* (1986), *Bellamy's Changing Countryside* (1987), *England's Last Wilderness* (1989), *England's Lost Wilderness* (1990), *Wilderness Britain* (1990), *How Green Are You?* (1991), *Tomorrow's Earth* (1991), *World Medicine: Plants, Patients and People* (1992), *Blooming Bellamy* (1993), *Trees of the World* (1993) and *The Bellamy Herbal* (2003)

A NATURAL LIFE

The Autobiography of
David J Bellamy OBE, Hon FLS,
An Englishman

By David Bellamy

arrow books

Published by Arrow Books in 2003

1 3 5 7 9 10 8 6 4 2

First published in the United Kingdom in 2002 by Century

Arrow Books Limited
The Random House Group Limited
20 Vauxhall Bridge Road, London SW1V 2SA

Random House Australia (Pty) Limited
20 Alfred Street, Milsons Point, Sydney,
New South Wales 2061, Australia

Random House New Zealand Limited
18 Poland Road, Glenfield
Auckland 10, New Zealand

Random House South Africa (Pty) Limited
Endulini, 5a Jubilee Road, Parktown 2193, South Africa

The Random House Group Limited Reg. No. 954009

www.randomhouse.co.uk

A CIP catalogue record for this book
is available from the British Library

Penguin Random House is committed to a sustainable future for
our business, our readers and our planet. This book is made from
Forest Stewardship Council® certified paper.

MIX
Paper | Supporting
responsible forestry
FSC® C018179

Printed and bound in Great Britain by Clays Ltd, Elcograf S.p.A.

Addresses for companies within
The Penguin Random House Group can be found at:
global.penguinrandomhouse.com

ISBN 9 7 80099414964

Typeset in Garamond by MATS, Southend-on-Sea, Essex

To the three women in my life
Rosemary Froy, Winifred May Green, Sarah Loe
and all their children.
My thanks are due to Rufus for ordering the archive.

Nature's economy shall be the base for our own, for it is immutable, ours is secondary

Linnaeus, 1763

CONTENTS

PROLOGUE

I consider myself to be one of the most privileged people on Earth. I have enjoyed family life in an affluent country, Britain to be exact, through one of the most turbulent times in the history of the living world: seven decades of destruction, during which one species *Homo sapiens*, thanks to a surfeit of prostheses – automobiles, lorries, tractors, bulldozers, chain saws and aeroplanes, all powered by fossil fuel – has changed the world and the course of evolution almost beyond recognition. Thanks to that same 'horsepower of the apocalypse' and my life as a botanist in both academia and the media, I have had the opportunity to travel the world, seeing the problems and discovering the solutions first hand. Above all else, I am an Englishman and proud of it.

1932　ROOTS AND SHOOTS　1936

1 FAMILY TREE, FACT AND FANCY

I WAS CONCEIVED in the spring of 1932, one hundred years after the passing of the Reform Act. The only reason I can say this with any certainty is that, apart from 1066, the Reform Act is one of the few dates I gleaned from some eleven years of school history lessons. I can even remember that it concerned the first major step towards universal suffrage: votes for the common man and, almost a hundred years later, for all the ordinary people. My Mum and Dad, though extraordinary to me, were just that, ordinary people. Londoners by birth and by upbringing, they were by faith devout Christians of the Baptist variety and, judged by the 'ethics' of the post-1920s, they were model middle-class citizens and lived in a rented semi, 3 Flora Villas, Brickfield Lane, Carshalton in Surrey, a county that was even then in the process of being gazumped by the suburban sprawl of the commuter belt. Having gained his qualifications in Pharmacy, Dad was climbing the ladder in the local branches of Boots Cash Chemists: Lower Sutton, Woking and Green Wrythe Lane in that order. His dream was to become manager of the Big Sutton branch or even the Kingston branch; sadly it was not to be.

These were the days before fast food, when muck and luck farming was still providing the bulk of our daily diet, and spring water that had seeped through the chalk of the flower-decked North Downs provided all our water of life. Mum, a housewife of the old 'stay at home and look after the family' tradition, kept the house spotlessly clean and the family (Granny, Dad and my big brother) stoked up with three good semi-organic meals a day. Oh, and – how could I forget – tea at teatime. Having since eaten at the best tables of the world, I still dream of hot dripping with the brown bits left in, on toast made over a coal fire on a brass Cornish Piskie holiday souvenir toasting fork. My favourite meal is still fish-shop cod and chips, or at least it was before cod became an endangered species.

So there is little doubt in my mind that during my most formative nine months I was kept well supplied with all the omega-3 and omega-6 unsaturated fatty acids needed to make up the bulk of my brain; in fact everything I required to become a man, their son. The proof is there on my birth certificate – Sex: male; point of arrival: Queen Charlotte's Hospital London. I was so heavy – at least ten and a half pounds, some say fourteen – that a home confinement was deemed to be too risky. Mum had longed for a girl, indeed I was going to be called Alice, but my sex chromosomes coded David to be more appropriate, and the complications at my birth made another baby Bellamy impossible.

It was a cold hard winter, or so my brother tells me. Indeed the newspapers of mid-January bear out the fact that there was snow on the ground and ice on the Thames. My brother looked at me enswathed in what were even then still called swaddling clothes and asked, 'Does he have feet?'

Oh, by the way, my big brother is called Gervais Thomas and he is three years older than I am. He got his Christian names from my Dad, Thomas James and, family hearsay has it, from the Reverend Jervas Bellamy who, along with his son the lieutenant, were among the first of the prisoners to die in the Black Hole of Calcutta in 1758.

I was at that time sensible of no pain, and little uneasiness. I found a stupor coming on apace and laid myself down by that

4

gallant old man the Reverend Mr. Jervas Bellamy, who lay dead with his son the lieutenant, hand in hand near the furthermost wall of the prison.

This statement was taken from an account in the *Annual Register for the Year 1758*, a copy of which is in the family archives. A leather-bound book, the *Register* also contains the poem 'Epilogue to Cleone', written by one William Shenstone Esq. and apparently spoken by a very infamous actress of the time, Mrs George Bellamy, probably at the Garrick Theatre. The poem's last two stanzas, which were addressed to the boxes, run:

> Tis yours, ye Fair! To mend a thoughtless age,
> That scorns the press, the pulpit and the stage!
> To yield frail Husbands no pretence to stray:
> (Men will be rakes, if women lead the way)
> To sooth – But truce with these perceptive leys;
> The muse, who, dazzled with your ancient praise,
> On present worth and modern Beauty tramples,
> Must own she ne'er could boast more bright examples.

Again family fable says that we are related to the said actress (who I am sure would applaud the vision of the alternative Women's Institute calendar), a not-impossible link and one given some credence by my brother's wonderful stage presence and his lifelong leanings to all things thespian. Indeed, the first memory I have of falling out with G was while rehearsing a play that he was both directing and producing and which was to be acted by the two of us in our front room. It must have been in the first year of the Blitz for I can remember cutting short the rehearsal to go out collecting shrapnel with a school friend, Alan Boris. G was not amused, although he did covet the unexploded incendiary bomb that was among our booty.

He played a great many parts from Shakespeare's repertoire, and leading roles in countless other plays. I can well remember the family christening him Grandfather Fairy when he played Oberon at the age of sixty.

Mrs George Bellamy lived part of her life in America, to which another branch of the Bellamy clan had emigrated from the uncertain future of a no-job Europe, just as, at an earlier date, our weaving dealing Flemish ancestors had fled from Belgium during the Huguenot troubles.

Another famous Bellamy living at that time in Boston was Edward, son of the Baptist minister at Chicopee Falls, Massachusetts. He became so great a reformer of the utopian type that whole portfolios of revolutionary books were styled The Bellamy Library. The first of these that came to my notice was *Looking Backwards* published in 1887, which sold more than a million copies in a world battling to overcome the effects of the Great Depression. In this Edward, through a narrator, time-warped himself forward to the turn of the twentieth century and detailed why he thought the enlightened people of that day would look with incredulity upon how society had organised itself only one hundred years before.

I did ask Dad if he had known of the existence of the writings of this once famous member of the Bellamy clan. His reply was 'yes', but sadly I never pressed the point to find out his opinion of the man with whom I like to think I share my campaigning genes.

I suppose I can only wonder what Edward Bellamy would think of the Millennium Dome as a symbol of a world in which the richest 200 people have more money than the world's poorest two billion put together. However, if our genes link us closely then I think I know.

Politics was rarely a subject of discourse in our family, although we never could understand why Winston Churchill was thrown out at the end of the war, despite the fact that Clement Atlee, who replaced him, was a practising Christian and therefore, in other circumstances, would have been our man. I was actually taken to see Atlee, complete with his bowler and rolled umbrella – the nearest politicians ever got to spin doctor attire in those days – walking to work from Number 10 to the Palace of Westminster. In later years I queued up for hours to see

Churchill lying in state at the other end of the same building.

Sydney, later Sir Sydney, Marshall, the Conservative candidate for Sutton and Cheam, was returned to Westminster for our ward with monotonous regularity. To tell you the truth, although Dad railed against Fred Pollet and his communists, I don't know which of the parties my parents voted for. I believe it would have been somewhere in the region of the Christian Democrats, if there had been such a party. So, despite my knowledge of the Reform Act, I grew up apolitical, my excuse in hindsight being that it was a waste of time when the result was a foregone conclusion, but more of that later.

To return to absolute fact, my great-grandfather John Edward Bellamy was a tobacco pipe-maker who lived at 133 Princes Road. He officiated at his son's wedding at the parish church of St Mary's Lambeth on 2 August 1891 when my grandfather married Rosina Anne Foreman, the girl who lived next door in 132. He was then a warehouseman and his wife produced a girl, my Aunt Rose. After the death of his first wife he married Sarah Loe, who was to become my Granny, on 11 March 1905 at Spurgeon's Metropolitan Tabernacle. Their place of abode at the time of their marriage was given as 18 Waleran Buildings in the Old Kent Road, the property both Granny and I would always try to buy when playing Monopoly. By the time they had moved out of the East End into Surrey he was a lay preacher of great note at the local level and even officiated at the London Tabernacle. My gift of the gab may well have come from him.

Sarah Loe was also of working-class East End stock. Her father was a shoemaker who had married the daughter of another shoemaker on 27 May 1855. Sarah went into service as a parlour maid at a very early age. She talked of working for Lord Leconfield at Petworth House, whom she always called Lord Lacking-field, much to everyone's amusement, and at Cranbrook in Kent.

Her main memory, which she shared with me, was of earning her first half-sovereign for a month's work. Apparently she walked all the way back home to London so that she could hand it over intact to her mum. Where she was working at that time I never found out. A story she saved for my Mum was that one of the extra jobs she had, as an in-between maid, was to attend to the baby of the house who was then being weaned. The nightly task was to bare her mistress's breast and apply the baby to one nipple, then the other until it was fully satisfied. The nursing mum was wont to sleep on through the whole proceeding. Granny often talked about wonderful holidays hop picking in Kent and, being a very strict teetotaller, got rather upset when I told her what hops are used for.

The history of the family on my mother's side is much more difficult to unravel. She was born at 27, Foreign Street, Loughborough Junction, in the sub-district of Kennington, London on Primrose Day, 1899, at the very end of the reign of Queen Victoria. She was a staunch Royalist all her life and so it was always very easy to choose a present for her: the latest book on the House of Windsor.

Her birth certificate gives the name of her mother as Helen Ada Green and leaves a space where a father's name should be. This probably explains the fact of her deep fear of illegitimacy, although I did not get to know about that particular skeleton in the Bellamy cupboard until after she had passed away.

One thing that we were told was that when she was a baby her nanny had accidentally dropped her down the stairs, evidently fracturing her hip. Probably not realising the extent of the damage, and fearing the loss of her job or worse, the nanny had said nothing and my mother's hip began to heal as best it could. Problems only became apparent when little Winifred May Green started to learn to walk. Sadly by then it was too late, so my mother had a childhood marred by the pain of metal and leather callipers that were meant to correct the damage to her bones that had healed very much out of place.

Her mother had by then married a high ranking police officer who evidently didn't like the idea of a lame child in his household, so Mum was sent to live with her Aunt Fan and cousins Norah and Cis in Watford. That is how the story goes, and certainly Mum was in a lot of pain and discomfort throughout her life. Despite this she was a workaholic, always ready to join in with everything. She even captained the Indian Clubs team at Mill Lane Mission. Unfortunately, when hip replacements became a possibility, X-rays revealed that her hip joint had undergone so much wear and tear that nothing could be done

Although I never met my maternal grandmother, childhood outings to Watford were always a welcome adventure. It was about twenty stops from The Elephant and Castle on the Bakerloo line, and it was on that journey that I first became acquainted with the fact that when on the way to somewhere exciting the outward journey time always seemed much longer than the return home. Dad never came with us because he always worked on Saturdays, and Sundays were the day we rested (although that actually meant going to church at least twice, and later three times, every Sunday).

Aunt Fan was the matriarch of the Watford household and a great collector of rings. Her pet macaws ruled their own roosts that were set in the magnificence of a Victorian parlour complete with antimacassars and aspidistras. When family matters were discussed, we were always sent out to play in the garden that had little to offer apart from a magnificent Bladder Senna bush, the fruits of which we were allowed to pop.

Uncle Jumbo was our favourite member of the family for he had the most amazing collection of children's toys: tops of every shape and hum and glass-topped boxes which, when rubbed with a silk handkerchief, became alive with dancing figures. Of course he also had tin toys a plenty, the most magnificent of which was a complete train set featuring a South African wood burning locomotive. We were never actually allowed to touch any of these treasures, but he would take great delight in putting each through its paces for us. He also showed us share certificates in both the Railways and the Gold Mines of South Africa and told of untold wealth awaiting the family.

His brother, who was married to Aunt Fan, was the stalwart of the family and worked in the print business. He was also a great railway buff. It was he who took me to see the Flying Scotsman steaming through Watford Junction, filling up with water en route and splashing those who stood too close. It was he who had been my mother's favourite as she grew up as part of the family. A father figure, he took her down the pub and then, because this activity was frowned on, bought her silence with a Brighton biscuit.

From all accounts Mum was the tomboy of the 'terrible three', Norah, Cis and Winnie, and got them into all sorts of scrapes, although so did Neddy Brae, Norah's toy donkey that appeared to go everywhere with them. Neddy was wont to have its nose poked into everything and on one memorable occasion fell through some railings. It looked set to be incarcerated forever in the pit down below but luckily Mum's climbing abilities came to the rescue.

Visits to Watford always ended with a sumptuous tea with real cream cakes which made the journey home somewhat hazardous. I never did understand why underground trains and stations never had toilets.

I can remember the consternation that ensued when the wrong sort of people, usually smelling of alcohol, tried to give us sweets. I can also remember the looks I got when I asked what the conductor of the bus meant when he shouted 'Bang your balls on an Elephants Arse ole, turn em green and peck em.' The lady sitting next to us said, 'Oh he's a one, don't worry dearie.' I was hurried off the bus that sped on its way to The Elephant and Castle, apparently via Bank, St Paul's and then on to Turnham Green and Peckham.

You can guess that any questions we asked about Mum's ancestry were answered with an 'Oh you would never understand.' One of the few things we *were* told, however, was that we were in some way related to John Evelyn, diarist and friend of Samuel Pepys. Evelyn's *Sylva* was the first book ever to be published urging landowners to do all they could to rehabilitate the forests of Britain. Unfortunately, try as I might, I have never been able to afford a copy of a first edition of that book, nor prove that auspicious link in my family tree. Still, I like to think that this connection, even if it was on the wrong side of the garden wall, may have accounted for the fact that I became a botanist and a campaigner against, among other things, the destruction of the world's forests.

One of my treasured possessions is a copy of *De Igne* and *De Odoribus* by the Greek father of Botany, Theophrastus. The whole, having been translated by Adrianus Turnebo and published in MDCLVI, is bound in one volume and bears the bookplates of the Evelyn Family. This diminutive book shares pride of place with *Sylva: The Tree in Britain* by Archie Miles, published in 1999. The preface I wrote for Miles's book can be found in Appendix 1, and what it says would have been equally applicable as a foreword to Evelyn's *Sylva or a Discourse on Forest Trees and the propagation of Timber in His Majesty's Dominions.*

2 ECESIS AT THE FOOT OF THE NORTH DOWNS

MY OWN FIRST memories are of the flaking yellow distemper in the scullery over the kitchen door of Flora Villas, on the lintel of which were neat piles of coins. The latter I later learned were Dad's weekly wages, each pile representing the week's outgoings: groceries, coal and gas (sustenance for the present) and weekly instalments for insurance and the church collection (succour for the future). There was also a pile of coins to pay for medical emergencies, for this was before the days of the NHS. Diphtheria, scarlet fever, pneumonia, mumps, septicaemia, mastoid, consumption and many more manifestations of the apocalypse still rode roughshod over the rapidly expanding population. A penny a week still provided assurance that a child who died of one of these many diseases could be buried with some dignity.

The garden was our playground and, although small, was full of surprises, not the least of which was that wherever you dug a hole it instantly filled up with water. Carshalton was at the foot of the chalk escarpment of the North Downs and was well supplied with springs. These fed the stream that was wont to flow across the main street, the millponds opposite the parish church (in the cemetery of which there is the Bellamy family grave) and the lake in the forbidden grounds of St Philomena's Convent. If we were lucky, water would also fill the so-called Frying Pan in the park. This provided a shallow lake with steep sides, which, when it froze over in winter, was ideal for sledging and skating. Yes, we had real good winters in the thirties; good for home based winter sports but, thanks to the almost universal burning of highly sulphurous coal in open grates, bad for everything else. These were the days when real London pea soupers and bronchitis – let alone tuberculosis – were a very real threat to the population.

We were taken to the shops, with me in a pushchair. Its wheels would scrunch along on the gravel and turn over stones, often causing water to well up. On the corner was Haydon's Butcher that had been in operation since 1652. Great carcasses hung in its window along with poultry, game and wildfowl, each in due season. On the other side of the road was the King's Arms pub, whose menu included faggots. Sadly a bomb in the war destroyed both. There was also a barber's shop where a haircut cost threepence, and if you were good you got a bar of chocolate.

Those wonderful chalk springs not only supplied Carshalton, Sutton and Cheam with the purest of water but also fed the river Wandle. It was there that we caught our first tiddlers. Placing them with care and pride in a two-pound jam jar we were mortified when they died overnight, my first lesson in aquatic ecology. The Wandle flowed on past the leather works where my grandfather had worked. This specialised in leather for making kid gloves and goldbeaters' leather that was made from the tanned lining of a sheep's stomach. Granddad must have held a responsible position in the tannery because, when my brother G got a job at Distillers Company Limited on the banks of the same stretch of the Wandle, there was an employee called Darby Allen whom Granddad had sacked. Darby had gone on to serve in the navy for twenty-one years and said that getting the sack from Tom's Granddad (G was always called Tom at work) was the best thing that ever happened to him.

Granddad's wages were £1 1s a week. The shilling was always put on the collection plate in Mill Lane Mission where he was a regular preacher on Sunday mornings. Granny told us that one day, to her horror, he put the larger coins on the plate by mistake and had to go and retrieve it at the end of the service, before the collection had been counted.

Granddad's employer soon went bankrupt with the advent of leather cloth imported from America and he died on the 10 February 1926 at the age of sixty. Despite the fact that Granddad, who I sadly never knew, became a partner in the leather business, any perforated chamois leathers were brought home for repair. Granny's nimble fingers soon made any holes invisible, so raising their value to the trade.

The pile of leathers lying in the corner was dusted with *creta prep*, French chalk to the uninitiated, and this must have permeated over the years through the wooden floorboards and wainscoting. Consequently our household spiders were something rather special, big, hairy and white. What's more, when they emerged into the room they left a trail of white footprints behind them. This always resulted in consternation because Dad was an arachnophobe and Mum, who was always up to tricks, would catch them and chase after him with them before releasing them into the garden. Why Dad had grown up with a fear of spiders I don't know; Granny would say with scorn, 'You'll never meet anyone or anything uglier than yourself' while scooping the offending arachnid up in the dustpan and hurling it out of the window.

G and I often shared our adventures with the little girl who lived in the house at the bottom of our garden. Her name was Alethea and like us she enjoyed digging the holes that would rapidly fill with water, a favourite summer pastime. Although we rarely entered other people's houses I can remember being caught short while in her garden and being ushered into their loo which to my horror sported carefully torn newspaper instead of toilet tissue. Ours was much more upmarket, with a special holder that contained flat packs of Jeyes' interleaved tissue that was shiny and not very soft and was bought at Boots of course – facts I remembered many years later when I wrote a book entitled *Poo, You and the Potoroos Loo* and did my bit advertising recycled toilet paper on television. Fortunately the modern version was 'soft on your bum, bum, bum' – not that I would have dared use such a word in my youth.

The other class distinction I remember was that we always had soap with an embossed label that started life in a special depression in the centre of the sculptured cake and ended standing proud of the last sliver of fragrant soap. To this day bathtime for me is incomplete without Imperial Leather. All this on Dad's £4 10s a week.

Oh, I almost forgot, despite the fact that my mum desperately wanted me to be a girl, my chosen name, if I happened to be a boy was going to be Lewis Edwin. The reason for that was that my dad's best schoolfriend was L.E. Holt, son of the local baker. Lewis was expected to join the family business but went on to much greater things. Although Dad did well at Sutton Grammar impecunity forced him to leave school to face a world in another deep depression. Having applied for some 600 jobs, he at last got one at the Sutton Water Company in Carshalton Road. He hated it and the job didn't last very long. Then, with the guidance of Mr Lovegrove of Mill Lane Mission, he became apprenticed to Boots the Chemist and worked his way up by going to night school with Lewis Holt. Evidently homework was done under the streetlights before Dad and Lewis parted company – Dad to bed and Lewis to work in the bakery.

The lamplit sessions after night school paid off because Dad obtained his Membership of the Pharmaceutical society and Uncle Lewis became a medic of very high standing. He worked with the team at St Mary's Paddington on the so-called chemotherapeutic revolution that was then changing the face of pharmacy from 'herbal' to what is today called 'mainstream'. We used to be taken up to St Mary's to see Uncle Lewis and we met both Alexander Fleming and Sir Ambroth Wright; in fact Gervais was used by Fleming as one of the guinea pigs for the testing of a vaccine for catarrh.

Why I ended up as David James and not Lewis Edwin is somewhat obscure, although it probably revolves around the fact that neither Lewis nor Edwin appear in the Bible. Also, David was the name of Dad's elder brother who sadly died of a brain tumour before I was born. Uncle David must have liked animals because he had a pet rabbit of which he was very fond. Returning home unexpectedly one Christmas Eve, late in the First World War, there was nothing in the larder for the festive feast, so Granny cooked the rabbit, much to Uncle's dismay. He refused to join them in the meal. Back in those days mums and grandmums were dab hands at plucking chickens, skinning rabbits, gutting fish and even wringing the odd neck when the occasion arose. They were real naked chefs, cooking from the raw, and we were expected to lend a helping hand.

Christmas 1933 saw the first crisis in my life as pneumonia struck and the congregation at the Mission prayed that the insurance money would not be needed. Back in those days treatment for pneumonia, as for many other things, was a hangover from the days of so called heroic medicine. Bowels must be opened every day, come what may, to cleanse the body of the waste products of the disease, if not of the medicines that still included arsenic, antimony, mercury and many other poisons – medicines of which Oliver Wendell Holmes had stated seventy years before that 'If all the drugs available were tossed into the ocean, it would be all the better for mankind and all the worse for the fishes.' I still wince at the thought of the taste of castor oil, let alone syrup of figs, but they certainly opened you up in an explosive way.

I don't know whether it was the drugs or the prayers that came to my rescue that Christmas, but five years later my kidneys collapsed due to acute nephritis, caused, according to *Baillier's Medical Dictionary*, 'by non-bacterial toxins as of arsenic, mercury, etc'. By then we had moved some four miles away to Cheam.

In 1901 the population of Cheam had been a mere 3,404, but by 1931, 106 new streets had been built on green fields and the population was heading for 20,000. The main redevelopment of the village, home of Cheam School of Randolph Churchill and Duke of Edinburgh fame, had begun around 1922. Dad had taken G to the village before we moved there, and could remember Cheam before the demolition of the old Harrow coaching inn. Even then everything was up to date in Cheam village for you walked on a raised pavement protected by iron rails en route from Sutton.

The dream of house ownership was realised for Thomas James Bellamy MPS and family sometime in 1936. Dad had been offered the job as manager at the Cheam branch of Boots Cash Chemists and house hunting began in earnest. Semi-detached it was, newly constructed by Potterton's the Builders: one of the Potterton brothers lived in the house two doors away, 'So they must be good,' said Granny. I later learned that Mum had yearned for a house in a more leafy part of the demesne that was then rapidly being concreted over, but this would have cost £850, over £100 more than the one that became the family home for over a quarter of a century.

Cavity walls, two reception and three bedrooms, the tiny one for Granny, an inside toilet and separate bathroom, kitchen with larder, and of course a garden back and front which came complete with a wooden shed, a bird bath and a coal bunker – all this was within walking distance of a surfeit of shops in the village, with infant and secondary schools the same distance but in the opposite direction.

Dad's old grammar school and a new Baptist church were both but a short bus ride away in Sutton. The immediate view from the front bedroom window was of disused brickfields, which had provided the bulk of our house and some of the rest of the urban sprawl that was pushing ever outwards, but that same view was also clear across to the skyline of London. On a clear day we could discern both the tower of London University's Senate House and the dome of St Paul's Cathedral. Our family telescope, which is still in our possession, gave us a grandstand view of Wren's masterpiece surrounded by the flames of the second Great Fire of London, during the Blitz.

I don't know whether there was one of those mystic Romany signs outside our gate, but we did get more than our fair share of hawkers and tramps. Mum would welcome them all with a cup of tea and let them sit on the porch from which they all admired the view. I can remember two who were regular visitors over a number of years. One was a tall clean-shaven man with very close-cropped hair. He told us of all the places he had been around the world and said he had fallen on hard times, although in hindsight he was probably a trusty who was even then allowed to fly out of the cuckoo's nest. The other was barely five feet tall, had a club foot hidden in a very large built-up boot, always wore an overcoat and carried a tray full of haberdashery suspended from a cord around his neck. We would always make a purchase and let him sit on the porch for as long as he liked. He told us that he had one room in Tooting and all he could see from his window was the wall next door and a strip of sky high above. I am sure that both of them helped put the fear of closed spaces and the longing for travel firmly in my psyche.

Our neighbours were the Bainbridges on one side and the Gruselles on the other. Uncle Bainbridge, who drove the single decker Number 213 buses that went from Sutton to Kingston had been born on Kangaroo Island off the south coast of Australia. It was the stories of his childhood that not only made me an Australianophile but were another fertiliser to the seeds of wanderlust within me. Auntie Bainbridge was the archetypal lady next door who was always ready to help if anything went wrong in the neighbourhood. She smoked Woodbines or, if Uncle had done enough overtime on the buses, the slightly more expensive Weights. We used to be sent down to Fred's shop on the corner of Fromondes and Morden Road to get them in packets of five. Our Dad smoked Gold Flake. If you had a penny, it was possible to buy a single cigarette, a Churchman's No 1 that came complete in a packet, out of a machine on Cheam railway station.

Fred's shop was also the source of ice creams and ginger beer in the summer and fireworks for the fifth of November. Only a bike ride away, it was an important part of the 'social hormone' of the neighbourhood. If anyone was ill or needed help in the home Fred would pass on the message to those he knew would lend a hand. That is how our end of society ran back in those days. Fred was just Fred, short and stocky, what hair he had Brylcreemed flat on his head. If you wanted anything he could immediately put his hand on it, and if the need arose he would wheel out an ungainly bicycle and deliver it himself.

Sweets were bought from the corner shop in Cheam Village itself. Miss Rowe ran it and at the centre of our attention were large, well-worn, once ornate, tins that contained sweets that either cost a penny, a halfpenny or even a farthing. One day, complete with a penny in hand, I rushed across the road without looking either way and was nearly run over by a car. The driver leaped out and gave me a clip round the ear accompanied by suitable expletives. Miss Rowe rushed out, sent the driver packing and led me into the back of the shop where she opened up one of the boxes of chewy delights, thus calming my nerves and stimulating my gastric juices as she told me to always look both ways before crossing. A warning that was perhaps even more apposite in those days, for although there were fewer cars on the road, they came with dumb irons sticking out at the front and very inefficient brakes.

Mr Gruselle worked in The Bank and his family, which included two girls, Joan and Ann, had a car, black as most were in those days. Their house was on the corner of Fieldsend Road and had an asbestos garage perched at the top of a little ramp, down which we used to test our home-made sledges.

Contact with our more far-flung neighbours was mainly over the fence that separated those triangular wedges of 'hanging out your washing' space that we called back gardens.

Two doors up from the Gruselles lived Mr and Mrs Pearson and their daughters Brenda and Myra. Perhaps working as a manager in a suburban shop was not quite as grand as being a City gent, but Mr Pearson was not all that keen to find us talkng to his girls. More to the point, they were never allowed to come round to play in our garden nor were we asked into theirs. However, the main thing that seemed to niggle the lesser neighbours was the fact that Mrs Pearson always appeared with a large lump of Woolworth's Brazil nut chocolate in her apron pocket. Such were the important social distinctions back in those pre-war days. Mum always said that such luxuries would be her undoing. I don't think I really understood what she meant, but certainly Mrs Pearson was somewhat on the plump side while my mum was of the leaner kind.

Mum's greatest disappointment in life was that neither G nor I had been a girl. Perhaps this was because she was a quintessential female of the 1920s sort, not pencil thin and ramrod straight like the Cindy dolls of today but a tall, loose boned almost disjointed angel of a person who, despite her lameness, moved with grace. She was always there, ready to console or praise, scold or applaud, the lynchpin of a family life that had to be contained within a strict weekly budget. It cost a lot of money to fill the shining white slipper bath with hot water, so for six days would you labour until on Saturday night you got ready for a more fragrant Sunday. G and I shared the bath, and after the tigglesome agony of having our toenails cut, Mum did her best to make her dreams come true. Both of us took turns to lie cradled on her lap as she tried in vain to train our unruly hair into a mass of ordered curls. Those were the most magical family moments, our heads being stroked into tonsorial order while listening to Mum's stories, despite the fact that most had an ultra moral tone. For her, ultra luxury and hence ultra temptation, was a blood orange with two lumps of sugar pressed down the centre. How she managed to enjoy this fruit of the devil, without slurping, I do not know and I never managed to perfect the art.

Mum always smelt the same, a mixture of Imperial Leather and hard working humanity at its best. To this day I still dream of that aroma and will awake to hear her say once more, 'Lie still, the quiff is almost there.' Then, under the magic of imaginary fingers weaving sleepy dust through my hair, I drift back into the land of nod. My favourite story, and one she told again and again, was that when we met in heaven we would be able to sit down beside the nest of an asp and put our hand on a cocatrice. The idea of heaven she wove into her stories was not unlike the pictures still found today on the tracts distributed by the Jehovah's Witnesses: Yeoman farming families living in peace with the myriad products of creation.

We lived on the crest of St Dunstan's Hill, through which the engineers had carved a cutting. After the testing of our home-made sledges on the nursery slopes of the garage ramp, this cutting presented a series of runs of increasing speed and danger. These ended up on either the cycle track or the road depending how much snow there was and how well our sledges were running.

These were the days of a brave new world that was being designed to make the garden suburbs more family saloon friendly. So it was that, not long after we arrived, the carriageway became ripe for upgrading. Not with Macadam tar but, in line with the autobahns that were even then preparing to unite Europe in the Second World War, with concrete blocks. We watched in awe as shuttering was put in place and great machines poured concrete that was smoothed by an army of workers. The navvies told us in their brogue that the black tar they also used was the soft fill of expansion joints which would accommodate the swelling of the concrete blocks, even on the hottest summer day. It certainly worked, but there was a down side for, once the work was completed, the noise of passing cars changed from a soporific swish to an annoying thump thump thump. The number of road accidents also increased and sledging became ever more exhilarating and ever more dangerous.

Nobody seemed to mind about the new Sutton Bypass; after all it was part and parcel of progress. The exceptions were the man from the United Dairy and our local rag and bone man. The latter was called 'Juggy' Hooker, although you would never have dared call him that to his face. Both men had vehicles pulled by real horsepower and so speeding cars were both a danger and a nuisance. It was one of my great childhood delights to take out lumps of sugar or apples for the horses. Of all the accidents I ever witnessed on that road – and there were many – the worst for me was when a car hit the milk float snapping its wooden shafts and mortally wounding the horse. I remember sitting with its great head pillowed on my lap as it passed away, trying to make it eat the sugar lumps and soaking it in my tears. I have always been a good crier and have come to the conclusion that I have some of the most active lachrymal glands in the animal kingdom.

Mr Hooker was the fount of everything we desired, second-hand bicycles, wood for making sledges, and pram wheels for making street carts or trolleys as we used to call them. My big brother was a handyman and a great craftsman, so his looked very professional and lasted the whole season, while mine usually fell apart on the first descent. Juggy Hooker was also our link not only with a recycling past but also with the Romanies who still used the road in force when race days at Epsom drew them to Tattenham Corner. While I never actually watched a race, the great spectacle of the crowds, gesticulating bookies and their runners, and the accompanying smelly tents labelled 'Piss or Poop 1d' is one of many that are safe in my memory banks – along with the dire warnings about the evil of gambling.

Bob-a-job hadn't really swung into action then, but grottoes on Derby Day were a local money-making tradition. A group of children would build one out of pieces of brick and clinker and coloured tile, complete with silver paper and flower heads and the strange mica that glinted in the sun on the slopes of the cutting. From all this we constructed a stupendous edifice not unlike those made by bowerbirds, beside which we sat and waited as the toffs went by in their cars en route to Epsom. I was of course reprimanded by Mum for begging in the streets and letting the family down, and the money I collected was put in the collection at church next Sunday with the homily that God would put it to better use.

I don't remember the old Baptist Church in Sutton High Street, but I do remember that Shinners, the department store that replaced it, had a curving arcade with parallel mirrors in which you could see your reflection to infinity and beyond. I also have fond memories of the new red-brick edifice that sprang up as if in defiance across the road from the Congregational church that in turn seemed to dwarf the parish church just down the hill. This was in the days of full houses every Sunday and Sutton Baptist could hold 600 souls.

I think I was about three when I was taken to the new church for the first time, with the promise of music from the fine electric organ that sported coloured lights above the keyboard. We not only had a full-time pastor, The Revd Larcombe, but also a professional organist and choir-master, Johnny Johnston. We also had our own family pew, about four from the front, directly beneath the gaze of the pulpit. Granny was my constant companion at morning services for Mum helped run the crèche and Dad the Crown Road Mission. The latter was down at the bottom of town, not far from the gas works which, apart from keeping the giant gasholders full, was the place to which those suffering from whooping cough were sent to seek a cure by taking deep breaths of the tarry air. Our house had electric lights and an electric cooker but the fires were fuelled by coal or coke and to save money we would wrap up warm, even indoors, during the winter.

One of Granny's proud possessions was a fox fur that went with a well-worn coat that had long string ties with fur bobbles on the end and which she always wore to church. The hymns were great and we all sang with religious gusto. I can to this day remember the words and tunes of many of them: my favourites are still 'There's a Light upon the Mountain', 'Onward Christian Soldiers' and 'Those Hands were Pierced'. Granny firmly believed that if she lived a devout life she would eventually climb the stairs to heaven and see angels going up and down.

Granny was a diminutive, hard-as-nails campaigner against the devil and the demon alcohol, in fact against any indulgence in all seven of the deadly sins. Her only annoying attributes were pretending to be as deaf as a post, but always hearing the slightest whisper if you were discussing a private matter, and fainting. Granny was the best swooner I ever met and the cut-glass bottle of smelling salts was never far away. Perhaps she was another source of my brother's acting genes.

The young ones were spared the long sermons, when, about a third of the way into the service, we all trooped off to Children's Church, a replica of the big one down stairs. It was situated over the Sunday school and the main assembly hall. We even had our own special blue-bound hymn books and gold-piped bags into which we put our pennies for the children served by the mission stations. 'Red and yellow, black and white all are precious in his sight. Jesus died for all the children of the world.'

This was all right in theory, but I soon found that practice could be a little more difficult. One Christmas we shared our home and the festivities with a little Indian boy called Raji. Uncle Nem, another one of Dad's schoolday friends, had given me the best present I ever had, a pedal car that had headlights that actually lit up. It was hard to be told that I had to let Raji have the first ride.

Mrs Ruth Sommer, wife of Dudley Sommer – a Deacon who was so important in the City that the Lutine Bell was sounded at his death – helped run the Children's Church. I always thought that, like my Mum, Mrs Sommer was one of the angels that had come back down the golden stairs to earth. She was very beautiful, always had a smile on her face and she drove a sports car, a little green MG.

The Sommers lived in Cedar Cottage off Cheam Road, at the back of Sutton Cricket Club. They had a large garden, complete with orchard and chicken run, and a sunken tennis lawn overlooked by a building upon the back of which was a wooden board bearing the inscription 'Ancient Lights'. Mr Sommer told us that this harped back to the days of window taxes. The windows in the building had been bricked up to save paying the tax and the sign warned would-be developers against building too close. Oh for such sense and sensibility today.

The only time that the routine of Children's Church was broken was when members of the London Missionary Society came to report on their good works in far flung places. We were then allowed to stay in the big church and listen to their stories. That is where I first learned about other countries, creeds and kinds, stories that fanned the flames of the travel bug that still burns within me. Both Mum and Dad had wanted to be missionaries, either with the China Inland Mission or the Cond Hills Mission in India, but the fact that my mum was lame precluded this, so they laboured in the home team – Dad down by the gas works and Mum in the Sunday school and as official keeper of the robes and towels used at Baptisms.

Yes, to me Mum was an angel, despite the fact that her face was wrinkled, possibly with the constant pain she had to bear – whether walking, standing or sitting in anything except a high straight backed chair. Mind you, back in those days people did seem to show the signs of age earlier; perhaps it was the smoke filled rooms, perhaps the diet or perhaps, in the absence of labour saving devices, down-on-your-knees hard graft took its toll. Whatever the reason I can remember that the first time I really lost my temper with anyone was in defence of my mum. A particularly large and nasty boy at Sunday school had shouted, 'Look, old hipperty hop, your mum looks like a witch.' I had to be dragged off him and was at a loss to explain to the Sunday school teacher exactly why I had lost my temper and let the family down, and in church of all places. But how could I tell my mum what he had said?

To me Mum was the most beautiful and kindest person in the world and, despite her lameness, a tower of strength always there when needed. Dad was seven years her junior and worshipped the ground she walked on. He called her Winnie B and she called him Jimmy B. Holding hands and a peck on the cheek when saying goodbye were the only public signs of their great love and devotion. Our upbringing was stern but overflowed with love and respect. Mum and Dad's word was our command and the thought of answering back may have entered our minds, but never came to fruition, not for fear of recriminations but out of respect for them both. I can only remember one occasion when Dad lost his cool and reverted to physical means – the end of the dog's lead across our bare legs. I think he was as surprised as we were and apologies were offered all round. I can't even remember what the kerfuffle had been about but I can remember the dog being very upset.

Between church on Sunday morning and Sunday school in the afternoon (there were Beginners, Primary, Junior, Intermediate, Senior and a Young Women's Class, so once in you were trapped for life), we all went home on the bus for the archetypal Sunday lunch. Roast beef with potatoes, greens and Yorkshire pudding and sweet treacle pudding were always my favourite. The latter came complete with a text from the Bible written on the treacle tin: 'Out of the strong came forth sweetness'. This complemented the grace at the start of the meal that always began with 'lettuce pray' which made me stifle a laugh in the summer when salad was added to the bill of fare.

On the whole, meals were a formal occasion and discussion revolved around affairs of the day from the latest epidemic of measles to the content of the sermon or the news on the wireless. You sat still, ate up all that was put before you and got down from the table only when everyone had finished. Boring it may sound, viewed from this day and age, but it was a time of real family communion, a time where good news was a cause for rejoicing, bad news was analysed and sins (like not doing your household chores) were discussed and forgiven.

On rare occasions Mum would allow me to stand up and let the golden syrup wind its way from a great height on to the steaming pudding. However, one thing that really did annoy her was if I put one of the tea cosies – and we had several, ranging from simple knitted to a sumptuous monster quilted in pink silk – on my head. Tea cosies appeared to be sacrosanct – definitely not to be trifled with.

A nice cuppa completed the meal, then Dad went to sleep in his armchair and we did the washing up in the big ceramic sink in the kitchen. With all the cutlery, crockery and cooking pans and only one large kettle of water it was a very messy business, eased only by soap flakes. G and I always fought about who did the washing and who the drying, and then about the allowed after-dinner reading material. This was housed in a glass-fronted, mahogany-veneered bookcase with a drawer and double cupboards underneath. Most of the books were concordances and reports from the mission stations, but there was also a wonderful leather-bound edition of *Pilgrim's Progress* that was full of the most gruesome pictures detailing highlights along the route. The one depicting Pilgrim being relieved of his burden of sin, which then sank into the Slough of Despond, was – and still is – my favourite.

Then there was the 1936 edition of the *Encyclopaedia Britannica* – now said to be the last edition, which could contain an adequate summary of the whole of human knowledge. The *Britannica* is the most fascinating and annoying book I have ever read, for whatever you looked up you always found something of even greater interest on the next page. This became my Bible to the real world and without it my education would have been sadly lacking.

We used to have to start back to the church early as Mum was like the Pied Piper of Hamelin gathering her flock of children along the way. To this day I regularly meet people who sing the praises of Mrs Bellamy, the lady who used to take them to Sunday school, praises that were officially recognised when she received the Maundy money from the Queen Mother, my Mum's proudest day. I wish she had been there when I appeared in the parade for the Queen Mum's one-hundredth birthday, costumed to represent the British Countryside. I am sure she would have approved of my companion Susan Hampshire who represented the English country garden but perhaps not of Jerry Hall who walked just in front of us. The Sunday school was well appointed with the chairs in each room fitted to the size of the members of each class. Bible study was the main driver, well laced with tales from the mission fields; we even took exams and got very flowery certificates. Sunday school outings were an eagerly awaited annual event.

The whole school could gather, if the occasion deemed it necessary, in the main hall that had a stage and kitchen for preparing tea and biscuits. It was here that the Girls' Life Brigade met. At the back of the church was an old drill hall that smelt of dust and sweat. It was there that the male equivalent, the Boys' Life Brigade, practised on their brass and eventually silver band instruments. They were always ready to march into cacophonous battle with the massed bugles of the Boy Scouts down the High Street. Scouts and Guides were something that happened in the Church of England while the Life Brigades were more sectarian. Yet, despite the divide in the youth groups in those days of supposed pre-ecumenism, the celebrations at the opening of Sutton Baptist Church saw a diverse range of preachers. The Bishop of Southwark, Revd D. Soper of Islington Methodist Church, Revd J.D. Jones of Bournemouth Congregational Church, Revd B.A. Nag from Calcutta's Indian Christian Church and Major Hollis of the Salvation Army all held forth from the pulpit.

The church was a community, not only of souls but of real people who had cares and worries as well as talents and ambitions. So it was that for some sixteen weeks in the year of our Lord 1937 the congregation prayed for one David Bellamy. I can remember little of the incident that primed these prayers, but family recollections tell me that it went something like this. We were on holiday at Felpham on the south coast, each of us allowed thirty minutes exposure to the sun on the first day, an hour on the second, increasing day by day until there was no more need to apply calamine lotion at bathtime. Please note that this was long before there were any worries about a tatty ozone layer. I was on the beach, sitting on Mum's lap, when she realised I was running a high temperature; indeed she claimed I was so hot she had to push me off her lap. That was the end of the holiday.

Back home and in bed in the room I shared with G, I woke up having wet the bed. Answering my call of anguish, Mum rushed in to find me in a bed awash with a mixture of blood and urine. Dr Brown, our friendly GP who always dressed like the vet in *All Creatures Great and Small*, was summoned to my bedside where he pronounced the worst: something had gone wrong with my kidneys and there was little we could do except wait and keep our fingers crossed. His prescription was water and nothing else – no food at all – so that no strain was put on the offending organs.

G tells me that I was moved into the big bed in the front room where I used to sit moaning for something to eat. Responding to my cries he evidently slipped me a Crawford's water biscuit, a taste which I still savour to this day. Dr Brown came visiting on his rounds and throwing back the sheets found telltale crumbs in the bed. My condition had also deteriorated, so off I went to Sutton and Cheam General Hospital.

One thing I do remember was Mum and Mrs Sommer standing at the foot of my hospital bed along with the ward sister. I was told later on many occasions that the sister of the children's ward had said, 'I don't think he'll be with us in the morning.' Well he was and for the next sixteen weeks I got to know Sister Needham very well.

Another child was admitted about the same time suffering from the same thing, acute nephritis. *He* was treated with the drugs of the day while I was given the starvation treatment; we both survived. The rules were very strict and if you broke them punishment was administered, so I lay there and complained that I was hungry only to my visitors who were allowed on Wednesdays and Sundays. Children visitors were only allowed on very special occasions, so I didn't have a friendly brother to slip me the odd biscuit. One consolation was that I had no operation scars to be dressed and, going by the moans from behind the screens that surrounded the many mastoid patients, I was very thankful that I hadn't. Mastoid, an acute infection of the ear, was a common affliction in those pre-penicillin days. My greatest jealousy was reserved for those who had had their tonsils out because they got jelly that slipped easily down their very sore throats.

Having read Animal Physiology in the run up to my Honours degree in Botany, I take it that either my kidneys survived the onslaught of those bacterial or non-bacterial toxins, or that I was still in possession of some embryonic kidney tissue, and so did a self-repair job. I like to think the latter, for if it is true my kidneys are younger than the rest of me. Be that as it may, after my forced anorexia I was weaned back to three good meals a day on a diet, if such it could be called, of cooked apple. This is still the only item of food I find impossible to eat to this day.

My greatest misdemeanour was forever standing up in bed to look out of the window in the hope of catching a glimpse of Mum or Dad waiting in the visitors' queue. One day I got caught and was summarily tied down in what was to all intents and purposes a cotton strait jacket. Totally ashamed and not wanting Mum to know, I lay low under the sheets and begged her to go home saying that I didn't want to see her today.

I suppose when I went into hospital I was too ill to really worry about being away from home, and by the time I was on the mend I was enjoying it: lots of other children to talk to and nice nurses and doctors young and old who would come round and have a chat. Visiting days were like mini-birthdays with little presents, something to look forward to twice a week, with postcards in between. I wish I had kept some of them, but have never been a great archivist.

I did miss G; even though there were three years between us we got on well. He was of a somewhat different temperament, good with his hands, a craftsman and an artist. If he needed something for one of his plays he would make it. In our younger days we read a lot and played games together; he always beat me at chess and I cheated at Monopoly. 'Words out of Words', a sort of forerunner to Scrabble played on a scrap of paper, was a family favourite and Granny was the champion.

Despite all the rules, regulations and cooked apple I evidently enjoyed my stay in hospital so much that I asked if I could delay my going home until after Christmas. Christmas in the children's ward was magical. Doctors, nurses and even the sisters were in festive mood and we were allowed special visitors on both Christmas and Boxing Day when I was reunited with my brother for the first time.

I don't know whether it was those Christmas festivities but from that time on my sights were set on being a doctor. This certainly pleased my Granny because that was what she had wanted Dad to be. Doctors were certainly revered back in those days, so much so that a visit to the surgery, which was always a part of a rather grand house, meant being dressed in our best clothes. What's more, we really believed that he was going to help us get well. There was also another family connection as

Dad had the job of translating the doctor's hastily scribbled pre-scriptions into bottles of medicines, boxes of pills and packets of powders and suppositories. These were all hand-made and beautifully wrapped in white paper, then sealed with a dob of red wax. Before the prescriptions were made up the scribble had to be copied in copperplate into gigantic leather-bound prescription books, complete with date and time. The need for all this rigmarole was both to keep the poisons register up to date and for use as evidence if the medicine proved a killer, the onus being on the pharmacist, not the doctor.

Dad really enjoyed the job; he was part of a real health system that linked the healer and the person being healed. His labels, though explicit in themselves, were always backed up by over-the-counter advice: 'remember after or before meals'; 'keep it out of reach of the children', and 'always finish the course as prescribed'. He was also the go-between in another way. Customers would ask, 'What do you think, Mr Bellamy, is little Johnny really bad enough to warrant the expense of a trip to the Doctor?'

He was very proud of his MPS – Membership of the Pharmaceutical Society – the grand certificate hanging, as the law demanded, in the shop for all to see. Also on show was his knowledge of a dead language and the life-giving properties of an incredible range of *materia medica* writ large in Latin on jars, bottles and rows of mahogany drawers with ivory handles. Ivory and Mahogany! Shock, horror to a modern green campaigner, but that was the way of another world as the thirties drew towards their bitter end.

In Dad's eyes Jesse Boot, once president of the Eclectic, Botanic, Medical and Phrenological Institute of Derby, had done a good job bringing the 'miracle' of medicine within reach of the pocket of the common man. Indeed, every night when Dad returned home he brought with him an enfleurage of the *materia medica*, some of which had served humankind for better or for worse, for over 60,000 years.

Dad was very derisory of 'lesser establishment' drug stores like Timothy White's and Taylor's that sold patent medicines along with buckets, mops and disinfectants. When we first contemplated writing our book 'World Medicine' we discussed the matter in some detail, coming to the conclusion that when super bugs begin to vie with super drugs it is all too easy to forget the importance of clean water and good sanitation, the twin triumphs of the Victorian era that did away with 97 per cent of all communicable diseases, at least in the towns of what we now call the first world.

My period sans working kidneys evidently left me with many problems, as I was open to infections of all sorts including boils and carbuncles and possible complications from measles and mumps. Over my head also hung dire warnings that diphtheria would be the end of me. My illness had also dumped waste matter in different parts of my body including my eyes. So I served my time suffering with the 'quiet little boy who wore glasses' syndrome at school.

In those days you could go into Woolworth's and test your own eyes on a chart and buy spectacles. Not so the Bellamys. Because we paid our money into the Hospital Fund we could go to Mr Cameron the eye surgeon. He was, even then, famed for operating and giving sight to a very young baby. His big Georgian-style house in Grove Road, Sutton was a very exciting place to visit and his darkened consulting room was full of gadgets and pinpoints of bright light. What was even more exciting was the fact that, before you went, special drops of atropine, an extract of *Atropa belladona*, Deadly Nightshade, was put into your eyes. This dilated the pupils and made your sight very fuzzy, so you could get a day off school. It was a technique used in China for thousands of years to dilate the pupils of their women. Wide-open eyes were a sign of beauty in China, but in Sutton they made it easier for the ophthalmic surgeon to see into the eye. Mr Cameron counselled that I should ask my father all about it for he had a greater knowledge of such things. Luckily, over the years, my body recycled whatever wastes my disease had left behind and my vision slowly improved. On my final visit to Grove Road Mr Cameron, knowing of my interest in biology and hoped-for career in medicine, told me that I only needed to continue to wear spectacles if I wanted microscopic vision. To this day I can still read and drive unaided, although the list at the back of the road map now does present some difficulties in poor light.

*

Meanwhile back to church. People telling us of their particular road to Damascus was a common happening which usually heralded a baptism. It was often a very emotionally charged performance focusing on the spark that ignited this fiery light, often a particular sermon, a text from the Bible, words read in a book or the account of one of the missionaries. I really believed that one day it would happen to me and I looked forward with a growing sense of frustration to that day. The feeling that I was letting my parents down was tinged with a feeling of fear: surely I must be a very wicked person and would go to hell.

The baptismal pool was at the head of the church behind the altar and the choir-stalls. Behind it was a beautiful sculpture of St John the Baptist immersing the Ethiopian in the waters of the river Jordan. This bas-relief was always said to be the work of a deacon's wife. No one could tell us exactly who was the sculptress, though rumour had it that it was Mrs Collet.

I had just typed these very lines on the afternoon of Sunday 20 November 1990 when I had to close down the computer and hurry off to Ripon Cathedral to speak at a service that was part of one of the biggest celebrations of two thousand years of Christianity. At the end of the service I was helping to distribute cuttings taken from yew trees that had been alive in Britain at the time Christ walked the Earth, a few of over 8,000 that were due to be planted out in parish churches and other sacred places across the realm. One of the lady recipients shook my hand and said, 'We used to go to the same church in Sutton, my name is Ruth Collet. We have followed your career across the years. I am an artist and greatly admire your water colours.' I told her of the coincidence and asked whether it was her mother who had been the sculptress. The reply was 'no', she too had no idea who had carried out the work. Sadly, I had to inform her that the paintings to which she referred were by another David Bellamy.

Baptisms were of course the highlight of special services.

Men would wear long black robes and women long white gowns and each was supplied with two giant bath towels. The Revd Larcome manfully struggled with even the largest of the supplicants and even Mum harboured the very wicked thought of what would happen if he either dropped one or fell over. After the service G and I used to go behind the scenes, where a nice cup of hot tea was being served to the supplicants, and help Mum to wring the water out of the robes and the towels. Even though there was a mangle for the purpose it was hard work, since often more than a dozen people had been fully immersed in the specially warmed water.

However the hardest part of all was carrying the mass of wet washing home; plastic bags were a thing of the future so each bundle was tied in the dryest towel. First, we had to haul them to the bus stop a couple of hundred yards from the church, bundle them on to the bus and then off load them at the stop at the top of St Dunstan's Hill. Finally we had to lug them over a quarter of a mile to Number 124, with Granny toddling along behind.

It therefore seemed grossly unfair to me that we should have to struggle with all those wet clothes on the bus while the deacons sailed past in their motorcars, some even in Rolls-Royces. It was this, I believe, that first stirred the campaigner in my soul and eventually made me forsake the Baptist church.

Back in those days the weekly wash lived up to the lyrics of the song 'Dashing Away with a Smoothing Iron', the first verse of which went: 'Was on a Monday morning.' Certainly if the weather was inclement the wash dragged on throughout the week and the 'linen oh' wasn't folded and put away until Friday. With twelve full-length robes and twenty-four bath towels in addition, the family wash certainly took over the entire house and the household.

It makes me laugh in these days of washing machines, tumble dryers and all the other labour saving devices when I hear people complaining about housework and finding less and less time for the family. You may of course argue that we only had two sets of clothes in those days and so, despite the smell, you didn't have to wash them every day; or that my mother, like so many other middle-class mums of the time, didn't go out to work. Both were of course true, but not only did Winifred May Green have the full-time job of looking after the family, she also found time to run prayer meetings and Bible classes, train Sunday-school teachers, organise bring and buy sales, and carry out many other church and community activities. She also helped look after a number of Down Syndrome children who were taught by another stalwart of the Church, Mrs Braddy. Of course all these things, plus the shopping, had to be done on foot or via the bus.

1937 THE SALAD DAYS 1944

3   SCHOOLDAYS

SCHOOLDAYS WERE NOT the happiest days of my life, probably because they started in a flood, not of tears but of urine. Chatsworth Road Primary School was a ten-minute walk from home, all down hill and ending with a rough grass track beside the playing field, which had its origins as a brickfield. Mrs Eastham the class teacher greeted us on our first day. All I can remember was answering the register, 'Here Mrs Eastham,' and sharing one of those double seats that were joined to a double desk, complete with holes for inkwells – although this being a primary school the inkwells were absent. Unfortunately soon after lessons started my seatmate wet herself, probably because of the stress of the occasion. She set up a moan, which was bad enough, but what was worse, owing to the lie of the seat and the floor, her puddle ended up under me. You can guess who got the blame and was made to stand in the corner.

How many times I had to stand in that corner I cannot remember but then I never was a model pupil. This fact came out fifty-eight years later when I returned to the school to re-open it in its new guise of Cheam Fields School, when I again got dropped in it. I stepped out of the car that had brought me from the station straight into a pile of dog dirt and had to disappear around the corner to wipe it off on the grass before being greeted by the headmistress. I was then introduced to a very old lady who had evidently taught me back in those days. She said, 'I don't remember you but you must have been very noisy, because you are very noisy now.' I was then led to my old classroom which looked not unlike it did in the late 1930s and was regaled with the results of research its current occupiers had done on my career.

The only other people I can remember from those schooldays were Jacky and Leonard Foster who lived just around the corner from our house. There was also the beautiful young lady from the top form who played Snow White in the school's summer pageant in which we all had to take part. I was a Robin, complete with beak and red breast and the phantom wee-er was a Blue Bird.

There were iron railings along the front of the school that separated it from an alley that ran along the back gardens of the houses in Chatsworth Road. This alley was surfaced with tarmacadam, relatively flat, car free and was therefore the best place to play marbles. We all had vast collections of these, some were clay but most were glass of a single colour. The most coveted of all contained wispy glass spirals that would have done credit to the apprentices of the glass factories of the Venetian islands. As soon as the spring days came along out came the marbles and we played along the tree-lined pavements all the way to and from school. You lost some and you won others, but every season the biggest depleters of your supplies were the roadside gutters which channelled your marbles into the drains that were, regularly cleaned out by large tankers each with a snorkel like an elephant's trunk. Though we were warned to keep away from them, in fear of noxious vapours that some still thought were the harbingers of disease, we used to watch in the hope that some of our marbles would return to the light.

If you had had a particularly bad day and had lost too many of your marbles, then it was off to the old council site next to 128 St Dunstan's Hill which we called the marble dumps. There, amongst piles of road gravel and council bric-a-brac, were a range of mountains (well they were mountains to us) made up of aeons of silt removed from the road drains. Over the fence we went armed with garden trowels and spent many happy hours digging away in the hope of finding lost treasures of past alley battles. We actually found plenty of marbles and even money, and used to cart home barrow-loads of the soft soil to sweeten the clay of our garden. Perhaps it was this that fired another bug into my brother – that of amateur archaeologist.

I can remember one glorious summer day when a band of us diggers collected elderberries for elderberry wine from the many bushes that dotted the site. I can't remember how we made it, but the effect was catastrophic for, despite the lack of sugar that was then rationed, the result was somewhat alcoholic and did us no good at all. This must have been some time around 1940 for we had Wendy Bainbridge's wind-up gramophone on which we played 'Ragtime Cowboy Joe', and a song which went something like this:

I've been in the troushca twenty days. Just twenty days ago
I met the judge, the kind old judge who was feeling fine and so
He gave me just a year in gaol, a sociable sort of a gink
All on account of a gallon of corn, which I thought I could drink.

The noise of the song, which my Mum did not like us listening to, was our undoing. We were late for tea and she set out to find us. Lured by the music she discovered our latest excavation pit and was appalled by our bacchanalian orgy amongst the drain tailings. That was the end of marble mining for that season and a good dose of castor oil made me think twice about the demon alcohol.

Gervais never went to Chatsworth Road school, for being over seven when we moved from Carshalton, he had gone straight to the big boys' school in Cheam Road. A Victorian Church of England edifice, it had windows set so high that you couldn't be distracted from your work by the world beyond the red brick of academia. It also boasted outside loos and a tarmac playground. I followed in G's footsteps some three years later to continue my climb up the ladder of learning. There I was guided through the three Rs and the history of the Indian Mutiny by Mrs Gray,

Messrs Hedges and Jamieson and the headmaster.

They all had canes, they used them liberally and they hurt, so, apart from bursts of stupidity or bravado, you behaved yourself. Mrs Gray was more lenient with the cane, favouring a carpet beater to lay down the law, but if you got your tables wrong too many times just retribution rained upon your head. You were made to stand beside her desk facing the class with your head in a net bag, the real function of which was to transport footballs to the playing field. The problem then was to stop yourself from laughing as everyone in the form knew that if you even smiled you would get your pants dusted.

After Mrs Gray's form you went to Mr Hedges'. He was the ultra fit games master who whacked you with a ruler or banged your head on the desk by catching hold of your hair. From there you had to face Mr Jamieson, not so fresh from serving in the Indian Army. From his high desk that contained his lunchtime sandwiches and two canes flexible enough to be wound up inside it, Jammy could keep an eye on everyone. However, his collection of stories, backed up by gruesome postcards of severed heads stuck on poles and treadmills worked by human beings, made history lessons, dare I say, come alive. One of his postcards was of the commemorative tablet outside the Black Hole of Calcutta that I later learnt bore the name of Bellamy. At that point in my life I didn't know the connection. If I had I would have probably kept quiet about the fact because the last thing you wanted to do was stand out from the crowd.

Mr Jamieson also tended what could only be called a large cauldron hanging over a coal fire in a grate in the corner of his classroom. In this he cooked thick soup that could be purchased in lieu of lunch for a penny a mugful. This supplemented the daily milk that was served from a full-sized churn trundled from classroom to classroom by the milk monitors. One day catastrophe struck: as the churn was negotiated around the door it fell over, swooshing a tidal wave of milk across the room. Like magic the milk disappeared down between the planks that made up the floor. The cane was liberally applied and the milk monitors were demoted, not that anyone else wanted the job. We all then set about mopping the floor with copious amounts of soapy water. This had no effect on the problem, which left a lingering smell of mouldering milk that stayed on throughout my schooldays at Cheam Road Juniors.

Jammy had his favourites who were the ink monitors, and his bêtes noires who got the cane. Ink monitors had to keep the inkwells clean and topped up from a large brown bottle labelled Stephens Blue Black. One boy who held that office for a long time was Miller, a great friend of mine who probably got his position in school life because Jammy liked to air his knowledge of English literature, by calling him Dusty. At the other end of the line was Billy Griffith, a great dodger of everything academic and Jammy's favourite whipping boy.

One day, as Billy tried to get out of the way of a stroke of the longest of Jammy's two canes, he caught it around the face. This left an ugly purple weal. That was the first time Jammy ever showed any remorse for his actions, but not so the next day when Billy's mother came in to complain about what had happened. This was done 'full frontal' in the classroom. Enter Mrs Griffith: 'If you want to cane my boy, cane him round the bum, that's what it's for.' Jammy: 'Madam I would leave immediately, unless you want one too.' Enter the headmaster who took the incandescent mother off into the corridor.

The end of that story is both sad and uplifting. Not long after that Jammy was at it again, using the cane on Billy who was laid face-down across the front desk next to Dusty's. As Jammy drew his arm back Dusty poked the thin end of the cane into the inkwell on his desk, always kept brim full. The forward stroke of the cane shot the china well across the room to smash into a thousand pieces against the wall in the midst of a gigantic inkblot. Mayhem reigned as Jammy realised who the miscreant was and it took the rest of the lesson to clean up the mess.

It is a strange thing that you always remember the worst aspects of anything, for as to my day-to-day progress through school my mind is almost a blank, except that I didn't do very well at maths. However we must have enjoyed it for there was great camaraderie and we all held the teachers, form and school in great respect.

Games occupied one heavenly afternoon each week. Football and cricket were played in Cheam Park, to which we walked in ordered rank. I must confess that I was not the greatest of sportsmen but used to enjoy the outfield from which one could take in the local countryside, especially the pond that provided us with tadpoles and frogs in spring. My first school fight, or at least the first one I can remember, was trying to stop one of the bigger boys doing unspeakable things to a frog with a straw. I came off worst but the frog hopped away into the safety of the pond. No need to tell tales; bruises and even black eyes could be explained both at school and at home by a game called busups.

Busups consisted of two or three boys linking arms behind their backs and then rushing round the playground attempting to avoid contact with the other groups who were also circulating in the packed arena. As you can guess the result was usually exactly the opposite and it was often the innocent bystanders that got hurt. I think that this game and the cane were probably the best training I ever had for both the sports field and the hard knock world of real life.

The only other exercise we got was gym. This consisted of somewhat militaristic knees bends, stretch ups and star jumps in the school hall or playground.

My first summer at Cheam Road was a hot one and truancy was a way to freedom. One day the headmaster decreed that any form that had no absentees during the following week would get an extra period of games. Mrs Gray reminded us of the fact every morning and it was the talk of the playground. As a form we decided that this was for us. Unfortunately over the weekend I started to feel somewhat groggy, yet demanded to go to school on the Monday. Tuesday was difficult with a number of trips to the outside loo to be sick. On Wednesday, although running a temperature, I again demanded to go to school. Off I went but by the early afternoon bouts of shivering warned Mrs Gray that something was really amiss and though I begged to stay, she took me to the headmaster, explained the situation and I was sent home. With no extra teachers or school taxis in those days, I had to walk. The details of the story up to this point are somewhat of a reconstruction, but that walk home is etched indelibly on my hard drive.

The pull up Cheam Road to the turning at Tilehurst Road was the worst for there was little shelter from the sun. Once into the tree-lined avenue it was better as I could sit and rest leaning against the tree trunks. The rest periods got more and more frequent and the amount of dog dirt I sat in increased. I literally crawled around the corner and up the grass bank, until I could peer over the low front brick wall behind which Dad (it was Wednesday afternoon, his half day off) and Mum were working in the front garden.

I don't remember much more except a period confined to my bed in a darkened room and a puzzled Dr Brown who couldn't quite put his finger on the problem. In hindsight it could have been a mild attack of polio, the disease that was then beginning to do its rounds with deadly effect. Whatever it was, my return to school was triumphal. Despite the fact that another member of my form had played truant, my act of gallantry had won the form that extra period of games.

Summers, when you had a whole six weeks off, are a bit of a blur. There was of course the garden, long and thin with narrow strips of grass flanking a serpentine concrete path at the end of which was an open patch. We had removed a large hawthorn tree, the last vestige of the ancient forest in our part of Cheam, in order to grow potatoes as our part of the war effort. Granny was very cross about the loss of the tree because she liked the blossom, but would never allow it to be brought into the house – bygone superstition yes, but also part of the practicalities of housekeeping for pretty as it may be massed on the tree, the smell of the short-lived flowers is like the ginger tom next door.

Over the back fence was Potterton's Yard. As mentioned, Mr Potterton had built the row of semis in which we lived and the wooden scaffolding and tiles, bricks and piping surplus to requirements were stored there in neat piles. This was our magical playground and Michael Potterton, their only son, was our key to this self-build theme park. The longest scaffold poles that protruded beyond the pile became bucking broncos upon which we became ghost riders in the sky, corralling imaginary herds. Four by four timbers could be endlessly rearranged into forts or wigwams, depending on which side we decided to be. These were the days of black and white flicks, many of which were cowboy films. The part I used to like to play was the editor of the local newspaper. He was always a goody with hidden talents in the saddle and when he did his best to shame the baddies in his columns he always got shot for his pains. I loved the part of the slowly dying hero falling off his horse. The pipes, bricks and tiles came in handy in a plethora of other ways, especially when we decided to dig a tunnel under the garden fence. This kept us busy for about a week, until the fence fell down and we spent the rest of the holidays trying to repair the damage.

Sears Park or the Rec as it was known had been transformed by the war from an expanse of well-mown playing field, into a crop of war-effort beetroot. There was a large quarry in one corner from which sand was dug to fill innumerable hessian bags. The sand pit became the territory of Beau Geste and the men of the Foreign Legion who boiled the beetroots in old tin cans over fires discreetly lit within the confines of the quarry, which we shared with sand martins. Above the quarry were the public conveniences, and it was here that I discovered to my consternation that beetroots turn your wee blood red, a fact that, given my history of Bright's Disease, scared the living daylights out of me. Luckily, as one of our pastimes was seeing who could pee furthest up the wall, I found out that we were all afflicted in the same way.

The Rec and especially the loos were the domain of Snoopy the park keeper who tried to keep an eye on everything we did. Apart from for footy and cricket, the bit of open grassland that had been spared from the war effort was pretty useless for active minds. In contrast, the broad shrubbery, which flanked the north side, was a different matter, a place for hide and seek and camps of every sort. The only problem was that in Snoopy's eyes this was forbidden territory and stopping us from enjoying ourselves appeared to be his sole reason for existence. If he thought you had stepped out of line in any way he would turn up on your front doorstep and tell your parents of any supposed mis-demeanours.

He was also wont to chase you on his bike. If escape appeared impossible you could always take the difficult way out, over the regulation-spiked railings that separated the Rec from the no-children's land of the brickfields next door. We removed two of the railings using Dad's hacksaw and soap to deaden the noise – a tip gleaned from the movies – and the gap allowed us little-uns to escape with greater ease and much less danger of impalement.

Escape, however, was out of the proverbial frying pan into the fire, an exciting landscape of old clay pits, brim full of water and old spoil heaps whose steep slopes had been colonised by scrub and trees. The kilns of the now disused brick works, which used to sport two tall chimneys, backed everything. We had watched from a distance as the chimneys had been blown up early in the war to stop enemy bombers using them as a landmark en route for London. The whole thing was hotching with wildlife; in fact this is where I first saw a cross-section of the insects, amphibians, reptiles, birds and mammals of these then still biodiverse islands. The problem was that the clay pits' fauna included amongst its number one of the nastiest primates I have ever had the misfortune of meeting. He was the caretaker of this wonderland and guarded it with a belt of leather.

It was with great care that you trespassed on his domain. Fortunately he did take holidays and as soon as the word got around our play area expanded beyond our wildest dreams. It also brought us into contact with the children from the council estate on the other side. They were a great assortment of kids from whom we learned a whole exciting vocabulary of never-ever-say-them-at-home words. It was from them I learned the jingle that went: 'I have had an invitation from the board of education to perform the operation to increase the population of the coming generation.' Thinking it very clever, not having the faintest idea what it meant, and finding Dad working in the garden shed, I repeated it verbatim. Putting on his most stentorian Sunday tone he said, 'Go and wash your mouth out with soap and water and never repeat such filth again.'

Then there was also the richer fraternity who lived on the other side of the Rec in bigger houses flanked by Boney Hole – although they called it Bourne Hollow. This was a trackway lined with mature elm trees on one side and the back garden fences of the more upmarket Quarry Park Road on the other. These kids didn't play with us and all seemed to go away to school, only coming home at holiday times. However, thanks to the elms, Boney Hole was a paradise for insects, especially may bugs and stag beetles, with which we terrified the girls, each in due season.

In bourne years (which happened back in the thirties and forties when bourne or chalk streams bubbled to the surface, flooding low-lying parts of Boney Hole) water rats could often be seen scurrying across the park. It was then that the old no-go clay pits filled up to overflowing and coalesced. This made me dream of sailing on the Norfolk Broads or even in the Lake District, dreams brought on by the books I was reading at the time. The latest Arthur Ransome was a must for Christmas and for birthdays. At nine shillings each, rising to 10s 6d, they were in the big present league. If one didn't turn up by the tree, then we could be sure of a 10s 6d postal order from Granny with which we could rush down to W.H. Smith's and buy the latest book from the then Number 1 children's author. I still have them all, most complete with well-thumbed dust jackets. The price of one represented a whole week's old age pension for Granny and we would always give her a big hug by way of thank you.

Granny occupied the small front bedroom from which she liked to look out at the passing world. By day her hair was done in a neat bun, but when she sat up in bed to receive our thanks she revealed a braid that reached down her back. Indeed I can remember her when she could actually sit on it. Granny and her bedroom always smelt of lavender and penny royal and when asked what she would like for Christmas the answer was always linseed, liquorice and chlorodine lozenges. These we could buy from a large glass jar in Dad's shop and he specially wrapped them for his mum with an extra big dob of sealing wax. It wasn't until I started to plan the book *World Medicine* with him that I realised that chlorodine was a somewhat addictive drug. It not only stopped you up, which was why linseed and liquorice were added, but also tended to give its addicts a somewhat tanned complexion.

Granny's other extravagances were buying Bible tracts from the colporteur, Mr Laughton, and paying weekly instalments to the man from the Prudential, both of whom called regularly. The colporteur, who Granny called the colpreacher, carried a little wooden box full of herbal remedies. So, apart from the tracts – some of which had pictures of Bible scenes – he also left tincture of penny royal and essence of lavender. For his part, the man from the Pru brought a sheaf of assurance certificates and collected twopence per week. Ten years on this provided each grandson with a legacy of £10 to buy something in memoriam. Granny was still doing well when the policies matured, so I decided to buy a dachshund called George to replace our old faithful black and tan Schnugg. George Red Rex to give him his kennel name was soft and silky like Granny's fur coat and my excuse was that he would remind me of her after she had gone to heaven. What is more, on Sunday evenings I then had two excuses for not going to church: George and Granny-sitting. George used to sit on her bed and join in with the odd howl as we sang our favourite hymns.

Apart from our trips to Mum's relatives in Watford, the other great treat was to go to tea at young Miss Mason's in Fieldsend Road, en route to Fred's corner shop. The older Miss Mason was very big in the Girls' Life Brigade and lived opposite Jackie Foster. Ivy Mason, the younger, was a schoolteacher, later a headmistress, and was great fun. She also enjoyed a joke, although we went too far when we sang the latest hit song, putting the emphasis on one word in the second line:

Mares eat oats and does eat oats
And little lambs eat ivy

Tea was always a bit formal, but afterwards we played all sorts of party games, a favourite being London Street Names in which the clues were on one side of a card and the answers on the other. Miss Mason should have been a black-cab driver and if you were on her team you always won. Her library was also much more exciting than the one at home, so, while Dad and Miss Mason were practising their Hebrew verbs (Dad longed to be qualified as a pastor in the Baptist Church), Mum would read to us from *Three Children and It*, *Helen's Babies*, and my favourite, *The Girl of the Limberlost* by Gene Stratton-Porter. This last book, along with the others she wrote in the same ilk, sold in their millions in the early part of the twentieth century. In hindsight I'm sure that this book set me on the road to being whatever I eventually became. Forty years before the publication of *Silent Spring* – the seminal work of Rachel Carson that questioned the sustainability of modern methods of chemical farming – Gene Stratton-Porter's books were pointing out the stupidity of the destruction of the wilderness of the USA, especially north-west Indiana where she lived. I fell madly in love with *The Girl from the Limberlost* and everything she and her swampland playground stood for. In 1997, when asked by BBC *Wildlife Magazine* to name the books that had made me what I am, I put *The Girl from the Limberlost* at the top of my list.

At the bottom of Miss Mason's road was the entrance to Nonsuch park. A favourite retreat of Anne Boleyn, it had replaced the church and village of Cuddington by the royal decree of Henry VIII. The palace had long since gone but the parkland was then still there: acres and acres of grassland, much of which became flooded in bourne years. It was a beautiful place, parkland in the true sense of the word with permanent ponds and swathes of woodland dominated mainly by elms. There were said to be secret passages under the park, large enough to take men on horseback, connecting the old Tudor houses in Cheam Village to the site of the palace. Indeed, during the war, when long trenches were dug across the open areas to stop the Germans landing their engines of invasion, the diggers cut into one such passage. Word went around the playground Mafia like wildfire and before there had been time to block up the entrances we had scared ourselves rigid by walking along the tunnel by candlelight, pretending we could hear knights in armour riding to meet us.

There were two extant buildings in the park, the smaller of which, called the Manor House, was destined to become the headquarters of the Cheam branch of Dad's Army. Nonsuch House with its beautiful walled garden was about half a mile away, at the top of a long gravel drive. Inside, an enormous wisteria had espaliered itself over the wall that enclosed a classic garden all set about with topiaried yew hedges, great cedars, and other exotic trees and long herbaceous borders. This was the place we were taken to on walks after Sunday school. Being in our best clothes, we were never allowed to walk on the greensward, let

alone explore behind the scenes. I firmly believed Frances Hodgson
Burnett's famous garden was there, waiting to be discovered. There was
a notice on the gate that warned that children under twelve years of age
were not allowed into this garden of delights unless accompanied by an
adult. I always dreamed of being twelve and so able to go and find the
broken swing.

Not far from the entrance there was the old icehouse near a large pit
screened with elm trees, which were then a dominant feature of so much
of the English countryside. The pit was the repository for all the park
rubbish, as it probably had been for centuries. We would climb about in
there amongst the mega-bric-a-brac that included fallen boughs and old
farm implements, things that I still collect to this day. Indeed, the latest
interesting item I've dragged home is a Lincolnshire chest plough, found
not in Nonsuch park but on a stall at the Country Living Fair in
London.

I can't remember the first time I was taken to London Zoo, but I can
remember going on the elephant and camel rides and watching the
chimpanzees' tea party. G and I even had our pictures taken with them,
as everyone else did. Of course, we had read books about animals and
seen photographs and films of big game taken by the missionaries in
Africa, but to measure yourself up against an elephant, watch a lion tear
its dinner to pieces before your very eyes and smell the smells was
something entirely different. Mum always said that it was cruel to keep
them in such small cages and I still hate seeing animals of any sort pacing
up and down in confined spaces. Thank God for Virginia McKenna and
Zoo Check who have today done so much to improve the lot of animals
kept in captivity.

I discussed the matter at some length with Gerry Durrell not long
before he died. We agreed that *Born Free* must be the ultimate goal, but
that in a world in which 5,000 species of vertebrate were heading for
extinction in the wild it was not enough. The only hope for the survival
of many of these wonderful animals is in properly managed populations
held in captivity. Good zoos are good news; bad zoos must be closed
down. Gerry's untimely death was a great blow to the real conservation
movement. I can only hope that the review I wrote of his official

biography (see Appendix 2) pays him and all the other people who were inspired to follow in his pioneering tracks adequate respect.

4 ROADS TO DAMASCUS

THE DAY WAR broke out I was in church. Well, it *was* a Sunday and the family were always at church on Sunday. I take it that the sermon was based on fighting the good fight and I am sure we sang with all our might. Although it was only a practice, when the sirens went off we all moved out in orderly procession to shelter in the corridors of the Sunday school where there were no windows.

Of course, the Second World War had been brewing for a long time despite the fact that, thanks to radio, Nations could by then, at the flick of a switch, Speak Peace Unto Nations. I had been taken up to Broadcasting House and shown those words inscribed above the entrance. It was much later that I began to understand that it is in the interests of the puppeteers who really make this world go round, to ensure that each fracas is followed by another.

We soon discovered the bad side of war: that your Dad and, if you had some, your elder brothers and sisters had to leave home to fight and perhaps die in foreign fields. Moreover, as this was the first war in which the aeroplane really figured both in attack and defence, the home front often had a ringside seat to the battles.

It must be said that the war did produce some positive side effects.

The local enclaves, especially in the large towns, found a cause which welded them together into what can only be called village communities. The main catalyst for this new social hormone was a heady mix of fear and national pride, a mixture that was, understandably, tainted with the worm of prejudice against those who were not called up. This hit our family to a certain extent because Dad – being the only young pharmacist in the community – was deemed by the powers that be, vital to the health of the local village. He was therefore put on the reserve list and it wasn't long before I learned the term 'conscientious objector' and had to campaign for my family's honour.

If the local veterans of the last débâcle were deemed too old for the Home Guard then they became air raid wardens, firewatchers or a combination of both. Every family unit became part of the home front war machine and everyone had an identity card. Most of us didn't have telephones in those days so the first complex number I could recall was CNKM 1885. Being the youngest in the family I was number 5, Gervais 4, Granny 3, Mum 2 and Dad, the head of the family team, number 1.

We were presented with a brand new stirrup pump, but we had to use our own buckets. We were also issued with a tin hat for Dad, directions to the local control centre in the village hall and an All's Well sign. Our first test run was to extinguish an imaginary incendiary bomb at the base of the pillar-box that stood outside our house. It was great fun because we all had a turn at pumping and squirting. Things became a bit riotous, but were soon dragooned by Mr Kemp the warden into some semblance of regimental order. Gervais lay flat on his face, right arm above his head and directed the stream of water at the imaginary bomb, while Dad pumped slowly and surely, never allowing the jet to show any signs of incontinence. Mum, Granny and I kept the buckets full and I had to report the progress of the battle to the control centre. We were so good in practice that we were presented with a long metal pole with a hook on the end to remove incendiary bombs out of gutters before they set the house on fire.

Much more ominous was the fact that the top of our now extinguished pillar-box had been painted a sort of orangey yellow. We were told that this would change colour if the unspeakable Germans sank low enough to use mustard gas. We certainly knew something about that gas for we had met hospitalised veterans of the 'Great' War (great for those who owned the armament factories), out for rare constitutional walks on Belmont Downs. As far as I can recall it was one of these lone figures in powder-blue uniforms who had first shown me a frog orchid growing in the well-cropped grasslands near the railway cutting. While that old soldier is long gone, the orchids were still growing there last time I looked.

So it came to pass that we all trudged to school shouldering our new burdens of defence, a loop of cord attached to a cardboard box that contained a gas mask. Regular gas mask practices became part of the school curriculum and woe betide anyone who had replaced the mask with their lunchtime sandwiches.

Despite all the practice, mayhem reigned when the first stick of incendiaries – along with a couple of oil bombs – splattered St Dunstan's Hill. Fire fighting teams streamed from their homes, each staking out their crop of bombs, and set to work with a will. Problems came thick and fast: how, for instance, do you get a flaming bomb out of the gutter when your pole isn't long enough? Answer: lean out of the upstairs window and do your best, but make sure you are not directly beneath its trajectory.

We were all on fast learning curves as I was to find out when I set off through St Dunstan's Churchyard to report to the control centre. Sheer bravado soon turned into terror as the white light of incandescent magnesium lit up the whole scene, making devil's fingers stab upwards from behind gravestones, which themselves appeared to sway and dance in the light. I ran like I have never run before – or since – only to find the village hall closed and so made my way back home the long way round to be greeted with Horlicks and bed.

Next morning, All's Well signs greeted us from many windows as we did the rounds, satisfied with a great haul of tail fins and even one unexploded incendiary which we added to our collection of shrapnel in the garden shed. A mixture of a good job done by the local fire fighters and a bad job done by the Luftwaffe left our locale slightly singed but still smiling, except for one household that had received a direct hit with an oil bomb. Despite the mess, camaraderie did its best to cheer them up as we all helped clear up the oil.

The sky at night was spectacular with searchlights picking out the enemy for all to see. The best and most expensive firework display (so far) in the world lit up the London skyline at night and we had a grandstand view from 124. We would turn off the lights and watch from behind windows, which, being of the leaded light variety, didn't need the extra protection of sticky tape to trap the flying glass. Although on the nights we had big mobile guns parked on the opposite side of the road, banging away at the enemy directly overhead, we needed all the protection we could get.

Mr and Mrs Sommer had three dogs all named after lesser potentates of the Asian world. Negus was my favourite, a sealyham that would lick you to death. The others were spaniels, Rajah and Sultan. When the Sommers went away in their Railton down to their country retreat we not only helped look after the dogs but also had permission to use their sumptuous air raid shelter that had been built within their house. When the sirens sounded the whole family would lock up 124, and traipse off across the Rec and down Boney Hole towards the safety of Cedar Cottage. Sleeping on the bunk beds in the Sommers' shelter was very exciting and certainly, once inside, we felt much safer than we did under the dining room table back home. Long before the sirens went, we enjoyed the spectacle of an aerial battle of a different sort: bats chasing a myriad flying insects including privet hawk moths and death's head hawk moths, across the local airspace. We knew a lot about privet hawks because their handsome caterpillars used to help us keep the hedges around the front garden well trimmed. What's more there was a great kerfuffle in the newspapers when someone found a Siamese twin hawk moth of the death's head sort in their garden and mistook it for a butterfly bomb. These anti-personnel bombs did turn up on occasions, but, being well warned by pamphlets and the radio, we didn't intend to add one to our collection. The nearest we ever got to one of these fiendish contraptions was when one became stuck in the tarmac beside the post box at the top of Sutton Common Road. A policeman and a couple of wardens guarded it until the army came and clipped its wings.

This must have been in autumn because we were on our way to help harvest the fruit in the grounds of the large house on the corner. The lady of the house was unable to climb all the trees so we were called in. Our reward was to eat as much fruit as we liked while we were picking. It was quite a small orchard but the variety of apples, pears, plums, greengages and quinces was amazing. My favourites were the russets with their brown skins and waxy texture. Quinces were a challenge and everyone dared everyone else to sink their teeth into the fruit's cloying flesh. The main problem was that we always ate too much, not a good thing to do on wartime stomachs that were always somewhat empty. However we were allowed to take home a basket of windfalls for making jam, which helped eke out the weekly ration.

Rationing was a pain in the neck, eased by very rare food parcels from abroad and by reconstituted eggs. The latter, though much maligned, made super omelettes and Spam fritters. We also became addicted to Cod Liver Oil and Malt; I still hanker after both tastes. Not a scrap of food went to waste and those precious ration cards helped to bring the community together. When a near neighbour's daughter decided to get married while her fiancé was on leave we helped out with clothes coupons for the something new, and cooking fat was offered to help make the cake for the homecoming and the celebration. Other celebrations like Christmas also took a lot of planning. Plums from the autumn harvest were stored away wrapped in newspapers ready for the Christmas pudding which was cooked in the copper that was usually used for washing clothes. It seems amazing now, but in those days chickens were a luxury and were usually the crowning glory of Christmas dinner. What's more you had to baste them while cooking. This was before the days of breeding for weight and battery farming and the hens were used to running wild and flying up into trees to escape the attention of foxes. Fit and healthy, they were free of those now dreaded saturates that erupt from every overbred, fast food capon.

Although the pace of wartime life was much slower and you couldn't travel far from home, we were not battery people living caged in houses and cars. We walked everywhere and there was always lots to see in the way of wildflowers and wildlife and lots of people to talk with en route. An after Sunday lunch walk could take well over an hour.

Another great treat, courtesy of the Sommers, was holidays in their country cottage on the Whispers Estate near Midhurst. Taking the train from Cheam Station, we changed at Petersfield and were soon on a magical branch line, passing the stations of Fittleworth, Petworth and Midhurst – not that any of the stations were labelled, nor were there any road signs to help enemy spies on their way. However, Granny knew the route well and pointed things out as the steam train chugged along between well-coppiced woodlands. In spring these were awash with primroses and cowslips and in summer bluebells then campions pink and white. Vistas opened all along the route revealing glimpses of distant villages each set in a knot of topsy turvy fields. Beech hangers climbed the steepest slopes, above which rooks rode the thermals while herons hunted the banks of the streams. Then it was a short taxi ride along lanes overarched with trees and finally down a cart track into our own secret valley.

On arrival, our first holiday task was to man the pump in the kitchen and fill the water tank from the spring that gave the cottage its name. Beside the house was a pond backed by rhododendrons and part choked with waterweed beyond which stretched woodland drained by a gurgling stream in which we spent hours exploring and creating pools for bull heads and midge larvae. The lane in front of the cottage swung up past a real wooden Romany caravan and then on through heathland. It was here that Granny 'came into her own' and showed her prowess at collecting brambles and whortleberries. She also warned us about getting lost in the bracken, the fronds of which were certainly taller than all of us. The whole valley was ours for a week, and, what with building rafts to cross the pond, damming the stream and getting lost in the bracken, the weeks we spent there were certainly the happiest and, in my mind, some of the most formative of my life.

One of the books in the cottage was *The Gamekeeper at Home* by Richard Jefferies. As I write this chapter I can lift that copy down from a very special section of my library. It is inscribed: 'For David Bellamy in remembrance of Dudley Sommer'.

Mr White, who was gardener and gamekeeper, was always on hand to explain the mysteries we discovered and to show us the ways of country life. I well remember the day that Granny emerged from a patch of blackberries brandishing something in her hand and saying, 'Look at this pretty stick!' Having read *Swallows and Amazons* I suggested she put it down seeing, with horror, that it was not a stick but an adder. Having trapped it in our blackberrying tin for return to the cottage we proudly showed the find to Mr White. I was appalled when without hesitation he cut its head off with the garden shears. When I remonstrated with him over killing a living thing he said, 'You would have thought different if ee ad bit you.' He then went on to tell us that it would continue to wriggle until sunset, which it did.

Another time we had crossed the pond on a carefully constructed raft made of an old door lashed on to two petrol drums. We regarded this as a rather perilous journey but it gave us access to the rhododendron thicket on the further shore. Crawling about in the dense shade of the rhododendrons was always somewhat scary but that day I was stung by what I thought was a wasp. As if by magic Mr White, who was setting traps in the woodland, came to the rescue and pointed out that it must have been a bee for the sting was still stuck in my arm. Carefully unscrewing it, he made sure not to squeeze the poison sacs and so inject any more venom and, after hurrying me back to the cottage, he applied the 'blue bag' borrowed from the scullery sink. The next day he took us out to the hedge bank at the bottom of the garden and showed us the entrance to a wasp nest. This he treated with poison and later dug it up so we could see the great nest ball made of 'wasp paper' as he put it. He also showed us other wasps hard at work rasping away at rotting wood to make the paper to build their own homes.

The countryside was a wonderland and every turn of every walk brought new excitement. However the wet woodland at the back of the cottage was always my favourite. In my mind the stream was the river Amazon, full of wonders waiting to be discovered, and it was here that, in hindsight, I believe I found my road to Damascus. It was in a glade in this woodland that it happened. Whenever I went there I felt overwhelmingly at ease, at home with nothing but, yes, creation all around. Drifts of flowers surrounded me, especially in the springtime – I now know that they were early purple orchids and opposite-leaved golden saxifrage – while powder-puff pollen exploded from great tassels of catkins that hung down from the hazel trees. This glade became my favourite private corner, somewhere in which I could sit all alone, be myself and say thank you to someone I still call God for being, and for allowing me to be part of something so full of wonder. I returned to that glade many times and to this day find total peace and sacredness in all such places.

It's easy to say now but I suppose that that was it. I never have enjoyed the formality of dressing up in my best clothes and sitting sweating out a service in church. I hate shopping, committee meetings are my anathema, the thought of keeping a diary – even a dive log – drives me to distraction – so much so that I am convinced that I have some form of autism that makes me look sideways at every situation in which I find myself. I hate being hot, I love being cold and wet. I hate tarmacadam and concrete but I love walking on soft wet earth, wading in wet places and swimming in lakes, rivers and the sea. I hate centrally heated bedrooms, sleeping behind shut windows and being anywhere without the freedom of escape. Of all the characters of fiction, I want to be Tom Bombadil, Tolkein's green giant whose very existence revolves around the wonder of being part of the forest. This is why, until the day I become part of such a forest, I will campaign to halt the destruction of all such natural places and do my bit to help heal the Earth by recreating such sacred spaces in which others can find peace.

Back home during the glorious summer of the Battle of Britain, we had a ringside seat as Spitfires harassed the Messerschmitts in RAF-blue skies. This was stunning stuff until they headed our way and came too low; then we would all rush into the house to take shelter under the table. One day we were watching a particularly good dog fight with Schnugg – our dachshund – from the bank in front of the house. Suddenly the whole mess of planes swooped in our direction and we went diving in to safety. The smell was awful and we all thought the enemy had deployed a new secret weapon – 'ze stink bomb'. This wasn't the case, but rather, in our haste to reach safety, we had all walked in Schnugg's most personal offering to the war effort.

Taking our German sausage dog for a walk in the park raised derisory remarks from the occupants of Manor House, 'here comes Adolf's secret weapon', but the members of the Home Guard would always share their sandwiches with the wursthund. This motley crew would also demonstrate what weaponry they had, which included pitchforks and broomsticks – strictly for practising drill we were told. It was in the open field where they drilled that I had my closest shave of the war. We were making our way home across the park when the sirens went and a German plane appeared, flying low overhead, dumping its bombs and with its guns crackling away. We dived for cover and lay down beside the fence. Once over the shock, we collected cartridge cases from the flowerbeds and continued home. The reception when we got there was in some ways even fiercer, for we had earlier filled the Anderson shelter in Geoff Stevens's garden with water to make a pond for sailing our boats, and on hearing the same siren Mrs Stevens unsuspectingly leapt in.

The most spectacular fire of the war was of course on the night of 10 May 1941. Sirens wailed as searchlights, tracers and flak lit up the London sky and we sat and took turns with the family telescope, an instrument with which Leonardo Da Vinci himself would have felt at home. All brass and polished wood, it allowed us a close-up view of the flames lapping around the dome of St Paul's. A photograph of that same scene was to adorn a wall in the Baptist Church where on the following Sunday we all gave thanks – during all three services – that Wren's masterpiece had been spared.

This was certainly a high spot of the war and the point at which I think Londoners believed that God was on our side and we were going to win. This was in marked contrast to the days after Dunkirk when special trains brought the wounded and the dead back from the coast through Cheam Station on their way to the hospital or to Brookwood Cemetery. William, the errand boy from Dad's shop, died on those beaches and we all cried openly at the news.

Although one didn't think about it then, we, like the boys and girls on the front, all lived under the constant threat of injury or death, yet we somehow got on with the day to day job of living. We were all heroes and heroines in our own right, a fact brought home so well in the recent BBC production, *The Last of the Blonde Bombshells*. I watched it – as I do most films I see today – from the discomfort of a long-haul flight across a world still troubled with wars and rumours of peace, and remembered those days of my childhood with relish. It was a childhood spent outdoors, not stuck in front of the telly or computer. My Play Station was the freedom of the parks and the informal greenspace which included bomb sites in which nature had held its breath or found new habitats.

Our favourite hidey-holes and hidden campsites were also the chosen spots for assignations when boyfriends came home on leave, and watching their goings on completed our sex education full frontal. One day, on returning to our most secret camp, we found a wallet stuffed with pound notes and containing an identity card, leave passes and a packet of frenchies. We took it to Sutton police station and handed it over to the arm of the law. It was all very exciting, filling in the forms, being congratulated for our honesty and being told that if it wasn't claimed it would be ours. A few days later a bobby came to our house with a letter of thanks and a ten bob note, riches indeed.

The radio was a godsend and kept our morale as high as possible. There were no complaints that official secrets kept the truth from us and we revered every speech that Churchill made, laughed at Lord Haw Haw and of course with Tommy Handley in *Itma*. I reckoned that Mrs Mop deserved a Victoria Cross at least, while Jack Warner's 'mind my bike' always brought William to mind. William was very proud of his shop bike emblazoned with 'Boots Cash Chemist' complete with the original Swoosh and a big square wickerwork basket. It was in part the memories of Mrs Mop that made me accept the Presidency of The British Institute of Cleaning Science many years later.

Monday Night at Eight not only stopped the roar of London's traffic but also brought the whole family together to enjoy Miss Frain and tricks such as Arthur Askey making the station announcements at

Victoria. *Children's Hour* with Uncle Mac, Norman and Henry Bones and Larry the Lamb, Dennis the Dachshund and Mr Grouser were all part of our regular sessions at the wireless. Then there was the *Blue Door Theatre*, the story of a family with thespian bones and *Ballet Shoes*, the story of a girl that wanted to be a ballerina. I had long been in love with Peggy Blackett, mate of the good ship *Amazon*, but here was a new star in my life, so I became a nascent balletomane and borrowed books from the W.H. Smith's library that happened to be beside Dad's shop. There were plenty of Biggles and Enid Blyton of course, but the few books on ballet had me hooked for life.

If those summers were hot – and they were – the winters were cold and, as everyone was burning highly sulphurous coal in open fires, peasoupers were something to be reckoned with, adding to the death toll of the Blitz. Smogs were really an accepted part of British life until 1957 when the Clean Air Act began to clear the atmosphere and reduce the toll of winter deaths.

For me, the highpoint of this pollution menace was the day we went to see the show at Cheam Century Cinema and got our money back. On the best of days the air inside the cinema was full of cigarette smoke, but on that occasion it was so thick with smog that the picture could barely reach the screen. Our tickets were refunded and by the time we got outside it was so bad we had to walk from one lamp post to the next in order to find our way. The pollution did, however, bring one boon with it, no air raids so we could all sleep safe in our beds.

It was at about this time that both G and I were becoming somewhat disenchanted with the aura of Sutton Baptist and its Sunday schools and, much to our parents' dismay, we started to drift away from it. We had both tried the Boys' Life Brigade and certainly benefited from the experience, but for me it was all too militaristic and however good a Christian soldier you wished to be, marching up and down in a dusty hall and saying yet more prayers at the beginning and end of every meeting was – to use modern parlance – not that cool.

Late in 1944 G and I joined the scouts and enjoyed a few happy years trailing trek carts and learning the skills of woodcraft and camping, despite the fact that we were members of the First Belmont Air Scouts.

Our headquarters was in the old school in Belmont Village and we went camping either near Box Hill in Surrey or on Sid Marshall's farm: 'First Belmont Camp at Basing Farm, that is the place for me. Down in deepest Sussex, Altogether now.' We found ourselves riding along on the crest of Baden-Powell's wave and all took part in our own Gang Show each Christmas.

Basing Farm was full of land girls and prisoners of war and, as food rationing was still firmly in force, some of the patrol leaders who, in those wartime days ran the show, became dab hands at catching rabbits for the pot. I used to go along and let the little ones out of their snares, although, I must admit I'd tuck into rabbit stew with a will. One day, as we were doing the rounds of the field, we found a fox dead in one of the snares and took it along to the POWs working in the fields. We wanted to ask how to skin it, so that we could make very special woggles. No sooner had we produced our prize exhibit than its skin was off and the gutted carcass was in their cooking pot. Well they were hungry too, despite the Geneva Convention.

There was also a very old house on the farm which had been empty for a long time and in which we developed a novel game. After dark one patrol would provide the farm with a pack of ghosts and the other would then have to walk through it to be haunted. The only problem was that members of both teams would end up with a bad dose of goose bumps followed by horrendous nightmares, and eventually our leaders banned the game.

Our other campsite was near a lake and a highlight of each visit was to be allowed to fell a large tree and use the wood for various forms of construction – spanning the local streams with intricate bridges or even building a tree house. We paid for our campsite by helping the gamekeeper coppice the woodlands on the estate. He was our fount of all wildlife knowledge and would show us the nests of dormice and the drays of red squirrels. He would also proudly point out the variety of varmints on his many gibbets, each of which occupied a prominent position around his patch. He explained that unless he kept the carnivores, including stoats, weasels and crows under control there would be less in the way of wildlife and fewer pheasants and partridges for the gentlemen to shoot, and it was the shooting that paid his wages. In his own way he also explained that coppicing provided a continual cycle of change and a patchwork of different habitats, each one ideal for different sorts of flowers, insects, birds and animals. Even the gigantic hooves of the horses that dragged the big logs out of the forest produced depressions in which rain collected and midge larvae could find a home, while the part-digested grain in the piles of horse droppings was an extra source of food for some of the seed-eating birds.

Many years later I returned to the area as President of the Surrey Wildlife Trust which had taken over management of the same woodland as a nature reserve. Memories came flooding back as I watched the great draft-horse scatter orange tipped butterflies as he pulled the logs along the rides which had been reopened as part of a new programme of coppicing designed, in part, in the hope of bringing the dormouse back. Two ladies who had lived on the estate all their lives came and enquired about my connection with the woodlands. I told them my story and asked if they could remember the name of the gamekeeper? 'Mr Bridle', was the answer; how could I ever have forgotten that?

It was at this point in the war that the Pearsons were evacuated and we inherited their Morrison table shelter which was re-assembled in our front room. Although it didn't leave much room around the edges, this metal monstrosity was an ideal size on which to play ping-pong, or to arrange our toy soldiers in battles in which the British always won. Henceforth each wail of the siren signalled our retreat into this metal cage, our fortress against the Hun. Sunday lunch was also taken around this makeshift table and woe betide you if you used your knives as drumsticks on its reverberating surface.

5 DOODLEBUGS AND
GRAMMAR SCHOOL

SCHOLARSHIP EXAMS WERE in the offing. These would allow me, the family hoped, to follow in my father's footsteps to Sutton Grammar School. I am afraid I didn't make the scholarship grade, and so became one of the last fee-paying boys at the school in which Thomas James Bellamy had been one of the first scholarship boys some thirty years before. Of course, since his day, the school had moved to new purpose-built premises complete with a playing field at the back with a once-hallowed cricket square in the middle. I say 'once-hallowed' because the whole thing had by this time been knocked about a bit by the construction of underground air raid shelters just outside the boundary line. The year was 1945, doodlebugs were in the air, and as they flew themselves by day many lessons were taken underground.

Our first fracas caused by these new-fangled, pilotless flying bombs came when the latest consignment of Cod Liver Oil and Malt was smashed by the blast from a near miss. Dad had been on firewatching duty, stationed high in the tower of the Century cinema which commanded a view clear across the village. On the way home he went in to check the shop and found the stockroom swimming in the stuff, well laced with broken glass and straw packing. So, after a very early breakfast, the whole family trooped down and got stuck into the job of putting the shop back into working order. Then it was off to school.

J.A. Cockshutt, Jacko the Headmaster, masterminded assembly in the great hall. A magnificent stuffed barn owl (the school emblem) gazed down from a glass case on the wall. Nat Coult, chemistry master was at the organ and the boys were arranged in ascending age, new boys at the front, sixth formers at the back, all under the watchful eyes of the whole staff, each bedecked in academic black. 'Keep Faith' was the school motto and from the moment you joined until the day you left you tried to do just that – keep faith with the principles of the school as the brain you had inherited from your family tried to keep pace with the talented few. Of all the parables I had heard at church or read at Sunday school, the one about the talents was now the most difficult to swallow. I seemed to have entered a world of super people whose talents in every subject on the timetable were an order of magnitude greater than mine and indeed those of my brother G who was three forms up. The only good thing about assembly was that on the last day of each term we sang 'Lord dismiss us with thy blessing' – but not before the exam results of each person in each form had been read out. G and I came close to bottom with monotonous regularity. So it was that one had a clique of best friends who were also counted among the less talented; my best friend was Chris Toole, one of a family of three Catholic brothers and one sister.

'Why was the man with only one talent thrown into outer darkness?' I asked my Granny who knew all the parables off by heart. 'Because that's the way it is,' came the reply. 'Whatever talent you have you must use it in God's name in the service of your fellow men.' The trouble was I never did find my talent. So I privately hated people like John Blatchley, always top of the form, the Gilham brothers who always won the music competitions and Gerry Worsell who, though a bit of a bully, shone in every aspect of sport. He went on to be head boy and then to captain the England water polo team. These boys seemed to speak fluent French from day one or got 100 per cent in algebra, geometry and trig every time. You couldn't even call them swots because they appeared to do very little work at all. They just soaked it all up. In the academic race I seemed to be always puffing away at the back.

Perhaps it was G's theatrical leanings or the *Blue Door Theatre* serial on BBC radio, but, for whatever reason, I had fired myself up to believe that my only talent lay in classical ballet. I bought books on the subject and would practise positions and pliés in my bedroom when no one was looking. It became my absolute obsession and I really believed that I would eventually dance at Sadler's Wells. Nobody else at school seemed to have any interest in such an outlandish subject, indeed it wasn't a subject you talked about in a school where sports were worshipped. I couldn't even discuss it at home where dancing of any sort was a frowned upon frivolity.

Unfortunately my career in the ballet was not to be. From my reading and the pain in my legs I soon realised the limitations of my weight to ankle ratio and dropped the idea. I think it was my frustration at being unable to join the ranks even of the corps de ballet that led me into a period of academic doldrums – as my school reports of the period show only too well. I have no other excuse, Sutton grammar was a damn good school and my parents were 100 per cent behind me. My explanation has always been that I grew too big – my mass exceeded my aspirations – and so eventually I chose science or, as you are about to discover, science chose me.

At that time my only academic prowess appeared to lie in English, thanks mainly to Danny Sayer, a wonderful Welshman who did his best to allow us to find inspiration within our own language. In hindsight he was a bit like a character from *Under Milk Wood*, a mixture of one of the sailors that would gob at a gull for luck and Dylan Thomas himself. It was in his lessons that Shakespeare came alive as we each had to play a part: 'All men are actors Bellamy, go on put your soul into it, hell man you are Lady Macbeth, let it out' – and much to my surprise I did: 'Come ye spirits that tend on mortal thought, unsex me here and fill me from top to toe with direst cruelty'. Despite the sniggers, that speech even got a round of applause at the end.

Inspiring he certainly was, but he was not that good at discipline and we played some awful tricks on him. One of these was to rig up a fully-wound record player on top of a classroom cupboard. A long bit of string allowed it to be turned on at the most appropriate moment. As the record started to rev up, Danny went to investigate, saw the string, tugged it and almost brought the record player down to the floor. Admonishing us for the fact that the record was now broken, he asked who had had the bright idea and banished the culprits, myself included, to the corridor for the rest of the lesson. This was a very dangerous position to be found in if the headmaster was on his rounds and we waited in trepidation. Fortunately for us, the headmaster didn't appear and Danny's bark was worse than his bite. At the end of the lesson he called us back in and, after making sure that the gramophone was still in working order, let us go. On the way out he took me aside and said, 'You ought to have been a Welshman Bellamy, you have a wonderful command of your language but for God's sake, learn to spell and use punctuation.'

He was right of course and when I first took O Levels I did very well in English literature but failed in English language. To this day I can still remember poems like 'The Old Vicarage, Grantchester' and 'The Pied Piper of Hamelin' and still surprise myself as I did at the Wildlife Photographer of the Year Awards in 1998. The winner was a picture of a polar bear so I threw away my prepared speech and quoted 'The Ice Cart' from 'Perched on my city office stool,/I watched with envy while a cool/And lucky carter handled ice' right up to the end: 'The carter cracked a sudden whip./I clutched my stool with startled grip/ Awakening to the grimy heat/Of that intolerable street.'

French, mathematics and geography were my real hates, along with art. The former hurt because Mr Lloyd taught it. He had become fluent while serving in the army as a trooper in the Tins, a chapter in his life about which he had written a fascinating book. However, those who weren't very good at the subject came under the deadly aim of his own brand of 'drumming it in'. This was a long piece of quarter-inch rubber, the sort used to arm catapults, and Lloyd used it to thwack your ear with deadly accuracy. Ouch! 'Non, mon ami le mot pour vous est stupide.'

Mr Lloyd also ran the school boxing team and if two boys were found fighting in the playground they could finish the job in the gym under Marquis of Queensberry rules. Towards the end of my school career the house of which I was a member had no one in the twelve stone plus bracket, so I got roped in to defend the honour of the Blues and found myself up for three rounds against the captain of Red house. I'd never worn a pair of boxing gloves before, so it came as a bit of a surprise that a left, or was it a right, to the head hurt so much. I don't remember much of the bout except that I was cross and must have given almost as good as I got. The bout ended with a lot of mixed blood on the floor and a win for Red house on points.

Our maths master was called Squeaker, sorry Captain Waller, who also commanded the Cadet Force. He was not the largest of men and his parade ground voice, 'To the right, salute!', crescendoed into a high-pitched squeak. I never did understand why anyone would want to carry water in a leaky bucket to fill a bath at the top of a hill. Maths was not my forte and lessons were a constant battle to find excuses for why I had not done my homework. It all came to a head one day as I slumped in my seat asleep. Squeaker roared, 'Look at him'. Waking with a start I sat up. 'No, back you go,' said Squeaker, pushing me back into my recumbent position, 'Just like his brother and father before him.' Something must have snapped for I replied, 'You can say that about my brother, but not my father, he did very well at maths when he was at this school.' 'Insolence,' squeaked Squeaker and I was summarily carted down to the headmaster's study where I had to explain the whole thing in detail. Having dismissed Captain Waller back to his class, Mr Cockshutt gave me a real dressing down for being rude to a master; but I was spared the cane because he agreed that he should not have said that about Dad.

It wasn't long before I found myself up in front of authority again. One of the windows had been broken in the gymnasium, and the stalwarts of our form, refusing to identify the actual culprit, were told that we must collectively pay for a replacement – about two shillings each. When the time came I refused to pay, and in front of the deputy headmaster I explained why: two of my friends had measured it up, gone down to the builders' merchants in the High Street and found out how much it would cost to replace the pane – a figure much less than the school was demanding. So it was agreed we could get the glass and do the job ourselves and share the cost between us. For me the school was a great school, in part because of things like that, things I could keep faith with – and I only hope I have.

As I have already said, my life at Sutton Grammar began during the era of the flying bombs. During that time great lines of barrage balloons were stationed at the bottom of St Dunstan's Hill in an attempt to deflect these jet-propelled harbingers of destruction from their flight paths into central London. By this time all our windows had been blasted out of existence, and replaced by wooden frames fitted with roofing felt, good for the blackout but not very helpful during the daytime. If you were lucky you eventually got a white, cotton-like material that let in some light during day but had to be blacked out by night. We used the tiny diamond panes from the broken windows to build mini-greenhouses to protect our efforts at digging for victory. We melted the lead down over campfires and then poured the molten metal into makeshift moulds of all shapes and sizes. This technique came in useful many years later when I took up skin diving, but my weight belts were the roughest in the Durham branch of the British Sub Aqua Club, for I never did perfect it.

By this stage of the war we had got used to rationing as well as the blackout, but one day when I was en route to the depot to collect a new roll of the white blackout material, I found a block of sweet coupons outside the posher tobacconist's on Cheam Road. Sweet coupons! My mouth watered as the devil reared his ugly taste buds. I kept them for almost a week, waiting for my pocket money, but good would out; repenting I took them back and handed them into the shop to be told, 'Oh those belong to old Mrs Nelson. She doesn't eat sweets.' Next day, I was called into the shop and given the coupons. For the next two weeks we ate our fill.

Sunday was always sweet day. We were given chocolate at breakfast and Sundays still don't seem the same without it. Dad shredded his on to bread to make a sandwich and we hoarded ours to be savoured later.

Then, after lunch, we were given sweeties of our choosing. My favourites were and still are dolly mixtures, liquorice comfits and Jap lumps; the latter tasted of carnations and if you sucked them with care you could make them last for almost half an hour.

The worst thing about those long hot nights of the wartime summers was being put to bed early and having to lie and listen to lawn mowers whirring up and down the lawns. There was also the smell of tobacco, as everyone except Mum seemed to smoke. One sultry night, Friday 16 June 1944 to be exact, I had just got to sleep when I was woken not by the wail of the siren but by the drone of a doodlebug low overhead. It went past us on its way to London, but then the sound of its engines became louder once more. One of its stubby wings had evidently hit the wire of a barrage balloon, reversing its course, and it was on its way back. Dad shouted, 'All downstairs.' As we all rushed to obey we heard the engine cough and stop and in the silence that followed we could hear the swish of the bomb as it glided down. By this time I was beside Schnugg who was still fast asleep in his basket. Turning, I saw the French windows that separated the dining room from the best back parlour slowly begin to move across the room. The next thing I remember was struggling to my feet with the blackout frames around my neck. G was running round with our goldfish cupped in his hands, their bowl broken in the blast. Mum checked that we were OK and was just filling the sink with water to house the flapping fish when the Revd Larcombe's face appeared at the window to enquire if everything was all right. He then pedalled away on his bike around the corner to Miss Mason's house where the doodlebug had made its landfall.

We were OK but where was Granny? We all rushed upstairs in great apprehension and opened the door of her room, fearing the worst. Granny was nowhere to be seen, but we could see up into the roof space and through several gaps in the tiles out into the moonlit sky. At about chest height was the remains of the ceiling that had descended, almost intact, to rest on top of the chest of drawers. We held our breath and didn't dare to look, but amazingly Granny was all right – still snug in bed with a couple of inches of headroom. Despite all our cajoling she was determined to stay where she was and so, after making the house as safe as possible, we hung up the All's Well sign and went off to the nearest shelters in the grounds of Nonsuch Girls School.

While I was returning home early next morning the large bulldog that lived in Park Road, not far from Truelove's the Undertaker, greeted me. It came lolloping out of the front gate as it always did and knocked me flat on my back. Its owner came out all of a twitter asking, 'Are you all right?' I was; the only problem was that I was being licked to death to the accompaniment of Alvar Liddell reading the news on the wireless. Once home we found Granny, still fast asleep, and made her a cup of tea.

The bomb had indeed fallen in the garden of the Misses Mason in Fieldsend Road, who after having been dug from the ruins of their house were taken off to hospital along with others from the less damaged properties opposite. Our house had lost most of its windows and several patches of tiles, so we all set-to, trying to repair the damage.

A few days after this first near-miss, a gang of Italian prisoners of war were brought in to help clear up the bombsites and put roofs back on damaged houses. I suppose this was the first time I ever met foreigners. They weren't the strange 'Waps' lampooned in the comic strips, they were of course, real people, just like us, and told us about their wives and children back home in Italy. One even had photographs of them and they all looked forward to the end of the war when they would see them again. It was fun trying to make yourself understood in sign language with a bit of schoolboy French thrown in for luck. They all seemed to come from tiny mountain villages and could tell us little about Rome or Pisa. We soon made friends with them and they in turn found us bits of the bomb among the rubble.

So it was that on Saturday 8 July we shouted 'arrivederci' to two of the gang high on the roof of one of the houses under repair and set off down to the Park to play tennis. The game was in full swing when the siren went. This was followed very rapidly by the appearance of a flying bomb. Its engines cut out right over the top of the church spire and we watched in awe as loss of momentum caused it to sideslip down exactly in the direction of our house. Racing out of the courts, past Fred's shop and up Fieldsend Road we headed for home. Speeding round the corner we found our house still standing. Unfortunately all the newly replaced roofing felt had gone and a number of the inside doors had been split off, leaving only a couple of inches of wood still joined to the hinges. We knew Mum was out shopping with Granny, so the only member of the family unaccounted for was Schnugg. We searched everywhere to no avail until we realised that his basket was missing too. Then, lifting the bureau, the door of which had miraculously flapped open as it fell, we found the dog curled up in his basket safe and sound inside.

The bomb had fallen almost exactly in the same place as the last, but this time it had killed two of our Italian friends; they were still lying there amongst the rubble and an ambulance had arrived. The blast had also blown another of them clean off the roof, but deposited him so gently on the ground that he was unhurt. The shoppers returned home in time to find us with the kettle on and about to take cups of tea to those of our friends still left on the rebuilding site. I can remember asking the air raid warden how long it would be before the families of our Italian friends would learn that they were not to see them again. He didn't seem to know. The only counselling we got was a trip back to the depot to beg some more felt to start the patch up job all over again.

Friends disappeared from school for a number of reasons; we said prayers for those who got killed in the Blitz and said farewells to those who were evacuated. Although we didn't live in central London, Boots ran a scheme whereby children could be sent on holiday with families of other members of staff who lived out of the danger area. Perhaps two near misses were enough so on 22 July 1944 we were told that we were going to the countryside for a holiday with the manager of the branch in Wisbech. Off we went on the 23rd with a very tearful Mum on the train. It was an exciting journey that ended in fond farewells at a nice house with a big garden on the outskirts of the town where, I learned much later, one of my heroines Octavia Hill had been born. Mum left us with a 10s 6d postal order. That night the air raid siren sounded, a rare occurence in Wisbech and we were looked on with some awe as we hardly batted an eyelid.

Next day our host, who was very proud of his garden, went off to work with the suggestion that we dig his vegetable patch ready for planting. This was a job we hated doing at home. However the first spadeful revealed several bits of the stems of clay pipes. This discovery aroused not only the amateur archaeologist in G, but also newfound pride in the profession of our grandfather. The more we dug, the more we found: plain bowls, bowls decorated with crossed swords, even ones with initials. This was almost as exciting as the collection of shrapnel we had left at home. When our host came home for lunch he was horror struck at the state of his garden. We were sent to the shed to clean the spades while he set about repairing the damage. We were forbidden to set foot in his garden again.

The local newsagents presented us with the ultimate problem: there on sale was an array of sweets but also an Arthur Ransome book we didn't have in our collection, *Pigeon Post*, the price marked on its dust jacket as 10s 6d. The sweets looked ultra tempting but in the absence of any coupons we blew our worldly wealth on the book and carried this prize back to our digs, where G read it to me from beginning to end. I can't remember much more about the visit but very soon we were on our way home. This is my fondest memory of Mum from my childhood days: her hair flowing free as together we sped along, carriage windows wide open on the train that was taking us back to London, the sparks from the locomotive threatening to set fire to the bone-dry summer countryside. We had read about just such a fire raging across High Topps in the Lake District in our Ransome storybook. Our mum was at that moment just like Mrs Walker, mother of the Swallows. Oh how we longed to go to the Lakes and see it all for ourselves.

Dad's garden shed was the repository for all our shrapnel and dud incendiary bombs. Some of the latter had notes in them from the forced labour who had risked their lives to make sure the bombs never went off. We always hoped we would find the tail fin or something else recognisable from a doodlebug, so when we found a whole one that hadn't exploded on impact we were overjoyed. Although it hadn't gone off, its chambers had burst open so we carefully removed some of the explosive, filling our supply of two-pound jam jars ready to make fireworks. Our supply of explosive was of course a very well-kept secret, even from our best friends.

The man who lived across the road and whose garden backed on to the brickfields had dug a hole for his shelter. This regularly filled with water after heavy rain and he had a foot pump with which he used to try to keep it dry. When he got fed up with standing pumping it himself, he used to let us have a go. It was during these episodes that we had discovered a rusting motorbike behind the hawthorn bush that flanked the shelter. It was, to be exact, a 1913 Douglas 500cc flat twin with a belt drive. The owner of the shelter had a new Beezer Bantam. He said that the old Douglas would never go again and that we could have it for a quid, hence our collection of jam jars which, when sold back to the shop provided us with a halfpenny for a pounder and a penny for a two-pounder.

G and I, along with our friend Geoff Stevens, became dab hands at making fireworks. Bangers were our speciality and they tended to get bigger and louder thanks to our ample supply of explosive.

Geoff, a year older than G, was tough as nails, the son of a builder and a wizard at all things electrical back in the days when radios were anything but wire less and the bigger the aerial the better the reception. I can remember a very angry neighbour, whose pride and joy was his ten-valve communications receiver, bursting into Geoff's garage to complain that our latest gadget was blocking his reception. On seeing the work bench festooned with wire and glowing with valves of every shape and size he settled down to a complex discussion of baffles and tuners until his wife turned up to say that dinner was on the table.

School meals were taken either in a room that half-filled the top floor of the school (the other half being occupied by the very well lit Art Room) or at the so-called British Restaurant in Sutton High Street. The food at both was unappetising, but made more bearable on Fridays when the sweet was either spotted dick or jam roly-poly. Both came or, rather, went with custard. The staff, clothed in their black gowns, sat at a sort of top table on a raised dais and we all sat below in hungry ranks. Every week a different form had the job of serving. This consisted of passing plates from the hatch along a line of waiting hands to a lucky recipient at the other end. The servers were rewarded with second helpings – if there were any, so you can guess that Friday was the favourite day to be in the serving line up. The quicker you could get the job done, the warmer were the seconds. One memorable day we were whizzing away on the serving line when, horror – as I passed an overfull plate of roly-poly and custard to the next in line, the pudding shot off its plate and hit the back of a master's gown. Down it slid, leaving a yellow and red trail in its wake. The food was caught before it hit the floor and the plate was passed on in a somewhat strained silence. The master and the rest of the staff never knew what happened and we all got second helpings.

Although it is said that Britain's wartime diet was the healthiest we ever had, it did leave growing youngsters feeling hungry and so we found ways of alleviating the pangs. If you fed at the British Restaurant, there was an Italian café next door that had specialised in ice creams before rationing came in. These were, of course, now in short supply, milk being strictly limited. However Del Remo appeared to have an endless supply of cones, which you could buy in stacks of however many you had the money to pay for, so the less fortunate who had to go out of school for lunch were plied with orders for crunchy cones. One day I was turning the corner with a stack of three-dozen in each hand when I met Jacko coming the other way. Because my hands were full I found it impossible to raise my cap in the time-honoured greeting. So I just inclined my head and said 'Good afternoon, Mr Cockshutt.' 'Bellamy, where's your cap?' came the response. 'On my head,' said I, not realising that my hair was so long that it hid that most important article of uniform. The reply came, 'Take a detention and get your hair cut.'

Another of our ploys for supplementing our food intake was even more risky since it meant breaking bounds at morning break and legging it up to Woolworth's. There we would buy bread rolls for waiting customers back at school. This presented two main dangers. If members of the local secondary modern who referred to us as Sutton County Closet Cleaners caught you, then you got debagged and lost not only your respect but also your rolls. If a member of staff found you, then it was Saturday detention time. However most of the prefects were on our side, for they were hungry growing lads too.

Playground games were more varied than those at junior school and the most energetic was hijimmanacker. One team bent down, head between the legs of the person in front to form a snake-like series of backs and back sides. The other team then had to vault on to the line of backs until one team was piled high on the other. If the bottom team could bear the weight while the top shouted 'Hijimmanacker 123, hijimmanacker 123, hijimmanacker 123, all over', then they had won the round. The teams then changed places and roles. Team selection was crucial, the more weight you had the better chance your team had of winning. However, you needed some wiry athletic types so that they could vault far enough to allow all of the team members to gain a place on top. One memorable session of this game was played against the top post of one of the long air raid shelters. Number two of the jumping team took off in the most tremendous leap. Sadly, he totally misjudged it and shot off the side straight through the shelter door, which was unfortunately at the bottom of concrete steps. Mr Bibby, the school's official first-aid man, and who had taught my Dad chemistry when he was at the school, was rushed to the scene. The patient ended up in hospital and the game was outlawed, which simply meant that it had to be played on the other side of the shelters, out of sight.

Apart from sports days, the only other time I can remember Mr Bibby in first-aid action was one winter when the members of the art school challenged us to a giant snowball fight. It was one hell of a battle and such fun that when the end of breaktime came few took heed of the bell. At that point it began to get dirty and our side found themselves under attack with bricks lightly disguised as snowballs. However, the leader of the art school mob came off worst and we were ordered to carry his prostrate form into the prep room. Mr Bibby looked in disgust at the semi-bearded object and told us to wash our hands before we returned to our classrooms.

Eventually I saved enough to buy the motorbike from the man who lived beside the brickfield. We wheeled it in triumph to Jackie Foster's house and set out with a will to put what was, to all intents and purposes, a mass of rusting scrap, back on the road. Our first mistake was to remove the petrol tank for as we laid it on the ground the iron oxide that was holding it together collapsed. Our second was to swathe the whole thing in oily rags and set it on fire. The idea was to remove as much of the oil and grime as possible in order to see what was underneath. The result was that a great cloud of oily smoke billowed in through the open window of the kitchen, ruining Mr Foster's newly painted ceiling. This set the job back a bit but at last, after several weeks' hard work, we got it on the road, complete with a two-pound golden syrup tin in lieu of a petrol tank.

Petrol was still on ration so we filled it with lighter fuel and off we went. We each took turns at the handlebars while the rest pushed. After several dud runs, it was Mike Foreman in the saddle when the engine roared into life. He took the straight part of the road in his stride but catastrophe struck as he tried to turn the corner. Mrs Foster was standing on the pavement, watching the spectacle, as the smoking velocipede shot behind her and crashed into the wall, shedding its fearless driver but not before the external fly wheel had taken a chunk out of his leg. Perhaps it was fortunate that the end of the holidays came before we repaired all the damage to the bike.

1945 OUTWARD BOUND 1960

6 THE DAY THE WAR ON THE EARTH BROKE OUT

YES, WE HAD a street party. Back in 1945 you could have such things for there were very few cars and not that much dog dirt to worry about; what's more we knew most of the people in our neighbourhood. Living perched on the side of the first really unlimited bit of road out of London we couldn't have ours in the middle of the carriageway, so made do in a side street and even had a band in the village hall. I can remember Nigel Spong, son of our new neighbours in 122, whose name today appears on the credits of *Mr Bean* videos, standing beside the band doing a sort of jig throughout the whole proceedings. I can also remember that the compere gave each of us our chosen present. To my horror he made a great point of the fact that I had requested a copy of *Baillier's Medical Dictionary*, and why should a little boy want that?

We also had a firework display. Good old Fred at the corner shop had saved the stock of fireworks he had laid in back in 1939, safe in large biscuit tins, and now he cashed in on his investment. They were all Brocks of course; their factory had been at the bottom of our road. We also added our own homemaders to the display. Of these we were extremely proud and the making of fireworks could have become an obsession if catastrophes hadn't ensued.

We borrowed Brocks' own *Book of Pyrotechnics* from the library and so knew a thing or two about big bangs, although we were never very good at getting stars to fly out of our exploding rockets, despite sitting for hours with a file, turning incendiary bomb cases into magnesium powder, the stuff pyrotechnic stars are made of. Our workshop was in the front bedroom of Geoff Stevens's house, although jumping bangers were finished off in our kitchen. Once the mixture was complete, the crafting of the fireworks began. In these days of political correctness the formula must remain a secret, for fear of litigation after a series of washroom catastrophes, although, as you are about to learn, it would be very difficult to accomplish with a spin dryer. The technique was simple: long thin tubes were carefully rolled out of newspaper; these were then filled, very very carefully, with the explosive kept slightly damp, and were then compacted by rolling the whole thing through the kitchen mangle, ever so gently. What would have happened if we had got that bit wrong I dread to think, for Mum's mangle with its giant wooden rollers made of sycamore was her pride and joy. Finally the long flattened tube had to be bent into the form of a cracker and tied with string. As we perfected the process our jumping bangers got bigger and bigger; if there had been one in those days, I reckon they would have made it into the *Guinness Book of Records*.

Then it happened coming home one day we found a large tube made of one of the new fangled plastics (I think it was paxelin) on the rubbish pile outside what must have been one of the first plastics factories. Ideal for making a really big bang, it was duly packed with our number one mixture and carried in triumph to the far side of the marble dumps to be stuck in a heap of road gravel. The detonator was one of the halfpenny bangers we had got at Fred's, so, lighting the blue touch paper, we all retired as quickly as possible. The effect was a spectacular small bang followed almost immediately by a ka-boomp as a fountain of gravel flew skywards, showering us and breaking Mrs Potterton's kitchen window. Thank goodness she was out, but unfortunately our Aunt Rose Haydon, a stentorian battle-axe of a woman if ever there was

one, had come to tea. The meal became a sombre affair with dire
warnings that we would all come to no good and would be the death of
our poor mother.

This was of course just a prelude to the real day, the fifth of
November. In order to put the final touches to our party Geoff, G and
I met in Geoff's upstairs laboratory to use what remained of the
explosive and craft a few big bangs. The most delicate part of the
operation was mixing the two main ingredients by pouring them from
one container to another. G was on the floor rolling tubes, I was holding
a mortar full of the finished product and Geoff was doing the delicate
work. The next thing I remember was a room full of acrid smoke and a
burning sensation all over my face. The curtains were on fire as I tried
to open a window to get some air. The problem was there was no
window; it had been blown out by the blast and there, gesticulating in
the street below, were all the neighbours looking up at me. At that point
the fleeing Geoff and G realising that I was still inside the room, came
back, fearing the worst. G, having been on the floor, had missed the
blast but Geoff was in a real mess: the bulk of the boiling tubes were
either in his arms or chest. I had received bits of the mortar in my face
and was bleeding badly. Geoff dragged me out and tried to mop me up
but only succeeded in adding his blood to my own.

At this point Dad turned up on the scene closely followed by Mum,
then the Fire Brigade. Dad took charge and, finding that most of my
wounds appeared to be superficial, turned his attention to Geoff who
was rapidly carted off to hospital. G and I escaped and with our tails
firmly between our legs walked up the hill towards 124. Granny, all five
feet of her, was standing like a black bee at the door. I got a sharp clip
around the ear and we were both ordered to bed, which I must say was
the only place I wanted to be at that moment. My head felt not unlike
a wasps' nest and I knew when our parents returned from the scene of
the disaster that a complete explanation would be required, so it was
heads down.

The light went on as two very large policemen entered the bedroom,
neither being our local friendly Bobby. I was nearest to the door, and
reading from his notebook, the largest of the policemen said, 'You are –

err – David Bellamy.' I nodded painfully. 'What's your name and address?' Even in my befuddled state that did seem a bit of a daft question, but G and I both tried to explain what had happened. Dad and Mum then returned, telling us that Geoff was going to be OK, and Dad checked me over, finding that some tiny bits of the mortar were embedded in the wounds on my face. He cleaned them up a bit more and then said good night.

Next day was November the fifth and we had our fireworks, although it was a somewhat subdued affair for most of our homemades had gone up in that one big bang. After several minor operations to remove the bits of ceramic I was sent back to school, my head swathed in bandages. The hero's welcome (I had got my name in the paper for the first time) ended with me being hauled up on stage in assembly at school and reprimanded for the stupidity of making fireworks. On my way back to the steps through the serried ranks of the 'men and one woman in black', I heard Nat Coult, the chemistry teacher, whisper as I passed him, 'You'll make a scientist, yet.'

Apart from fireworks, our other post-war delight was visiting Proops Brothers, purveyors of ex army, navy and air force equipment, situated near Kingston upon Thames. We always dreamed of being able to buy a Spitfire but in our impecunity settled for a radar set that cost thirty bob. It took us several trips to wheel it home in an old pram, then we set to work with a will. Dad had always been a communications freak, indeed he had had one of Logie Baird's original licences to construct a television set; based on a dismembered aluminium saucepan polished to make the revolving mirrors, a Meccano set and some very expensive valves, it worked and received that first broadcast from Alexandra Palace. With our radar set and Dad's help we went into production and amidst tangles of silk-covered wire and glowing valves got our first pictures: four, all on the one green screen, all at once and all upside down, great for watching cricket especially from Australia.

As one passes from form to form your coterie of friends changes. Mickey Foreman and Sam Alwyard formed the Red Arrow Cycle Club whose sole aim appeared to be to own a bicycle with a hand-made frame and ride it down to Brighton to camp for the weekend. Mickey got his hand-made bike and we all cycled to Brighton and the freedom of life beside the sea. My most memorable trip was on the back of a very heavy tandem with Jacky Foster up front. Off we went after school on Friday and enjoyed the trip, which is mainly downhill, in the cool of the evening. The journey back was not as pleasant for the two steep downhill stretches became Hands Cross and Reigate Hills respectively, which in the heat of Sunday afternoon, with all the badly tuned cars of the 1940s belching out black smoke, was a nightmare. Still it was a great experience.

Brighton gave me what I have always claimed to be my first real job, collecting deck chairs at ten shillings for the weekend. I would travel down to Brighton by bike, sleep under the Palace Pier and, after a long two days out in the sun, (you always remember sunny days), cycle back home on Sunday evening. Sadly I didn't get paid until Sunday as we left for home, a fact that led to my first and last felony. On Friday evening I had seen a gaggle of full milk bottles outside a house. They were still there on Saturday evening, and being both hungry and thirsty I stole a bottle. Removing the cardboard cap I took a large swig, much larger than I had meant to for the congealed mass wouldn't stop coming. It must have been on the step for days and I learned a very sour lesson that taught me not to steal and gave me a wary respect for yoghurt when it eventually came on the market. It's strange to think that in those post-war years soup was always tomato, milk was full cream and butter was good for you. Our only 'super' market was in the open air, a tuppenny bus ride away in Croydon, a journey we took most Saturdays to stock up on fruit, veg and dairy goods, almost fresh from the farm gate. These you then lugged home in a variety of wicker baskets and canvas shopping bags. How things have changed.

Things were certainly changing for me as Scouting for Boys rapidly metamorphosed into Youth Hostelling, each of them providing ever wider horizons of adventure and discovery. As the war ended a new aid to learning began to explode across the British scene, it was called *I-SPY*, a series of great little books, which in their time sold over 40 million copies. For many years the books were backed by a regular column in the *Daily Mail* and mailbags overflowing with letters, many written in the special code were delivered to Big Chief I-Spy. Yet when *Little Chief Willy Feather's I-SPY Cyclopaedia* was published in 1993 it was at his own expense and I wrote the following words as a forward to the book: 'I suppose like many others of my age I grew up with the concept of I-SPY as almost part of our British Heritage. "I Spy with my Little Eye" was one of the first games I ever played with Mum and Dad, and then the books were a must in family journeys long or short. I can remember when, as a young University Don, taking a group of students on a field trip in Cumberland, I pointed out a Clapper Bridge and said, "That's worth ten in my *I-SPY* book." They all understood exactly what I was talking about. I am sure that those little books have over the years opened many similar eyes to the world around them. That's why I was delighted and honoured to serve as Big Chief I-SPY and update and write some of the books.'

In hindsight I can say that they came to raise awareness just in time, because the end of the Second World War left society with a surplus, not only of Spitfires and radar sets but of bulldozers, chain saws and a fricassee of novel chemicals, many designed to kill. These weapons of destruction were rapidly redeployed in what has come to be known as the 'War on the Earth', a war that would rapidly and catastrophically strip 130,000 miles of hedgerows from the face of Britain and wipe over 98 per cent of our flower rich grasslands from the face of this formerly multicoloured and pleasant land. All this raised the score of many of our common plants, birds and animals ever upwards on the scale of rarity as small fields became chemical-drenched, broad-acre mono-crops and vibrant villages became sleepy dormitories. At the time, of course I did not even understand that it was happening, I was but one of the pawns caught up in the game of urban sprawl and economic change. I had no expertise in botany, ornithology, entomology, economics or sociology and so had no baseline understanding against which to compare the past, or predict the future.

If only I had been a better archivist I would still have my *I-SPY* books and my Youth Hostel Cards, and so could give a better account of a

Britain that even then still burst with biodiversity. The cards were my first passports to the wider countryside, each one completed with great care and stamped at every hostel. Tanners Hatch was my first, then Elam Hall, the centre spot on what later became the Pennine Way, and my all-time favourite, Hindhead, nestling below the rim of the Devil's Punch Bowl in Surrey. Stamps with pictures were in great demand, for each had a story to tell. Winchester's waterwheel recorded the fact that ablutions could be carried out on the end of a rope dangling in the millstream. Not that you wanted reminding of that in winter, when it would've taken a mallet to tuck frozen blankets around your regulation sheet sleeping bag. The wardens and the veteran hostellers were always a fount of local knowledge interpreting not only the hostel rules but also the things you had missed or that were a must to see en route to the next hostel.

Routes followed well-worn tracks skirting small fields overflowing with wildflowers and wildlife. Yeoman farmers (our home bred heroes) and their hard-working families and farmhands were always about, ready with a word of welcome, a farm tea or even a place to camp. Then, as heavy working horses were finally relegated to the refurbished stables of heritage museums the Ferguson Tractor, towing an ever-increasing complexity of gadgets, began to reign supreme.

Lest we forget, the end of the First World War had seen troops returning from all fronts to begin the search for peacetime jobs. Many were given parcels of land which, in a subsistence economy, could have provided an adequate sustainable living, but even then heavy horses were becoming a thing of the past and steam had already given way to petrol and diesel in the ever more glossy catalogues of farm implements. Sustainability, at least in terms of keeping people down on the farm and rural communities in 'good heart', whatever that is or was, began to disappear off the face of Britain. The spectre of starvation that had driven people out to the colonies was still there, but was being rapidly replaced by science-based chemical farming. We could at last make use of the inert gas that makes up 76 per cent of the atmosphere by weight and put it to work down on the chemical-drenched farm. Yes! nitrogen could be turned into fertiliser with the potential of unbridled harvests.

The exploding human population could be fed. The so called Green Revolution, eutrophication and genetic modification were but another, even more science-based, war away. Then after that Second World War, a series of civil wars began to engulf the planet, sending ever more species to the wall of extinction, while at the same time writing ever more people out of the equation of productive livelihood.

Sarah Loe had of course lived through both world wars, and though scarred she had come through smiling, thanks in all probability to her simple faith that there was a better land and one day she would live there, in peace. It was one of those hot summer days when school had been a bit of a drag that I stepped down from the bus at the top of St Dunstan's Hill and there, in the shade of a magnificent yucca plant growing in the adjacent garden, stood my Granny, dressed as she always was in Sunday black. On the way to and from church we had always liked to see the yucca with its magnificent spike of creamy white flowers. Dad told us that they were perfect examples of the *Lilliaceae* and we discussed the fact that they looked like the folded wings of an angel. Granny turned towards me, smiled my Granny's smile and disappeared. It couldn't have really been Granny for she had been housebound for a number of years. Indeed it was an accepted family joke that David would come home from school and, lifting George up on to her bed, would enquire, 'Still with us Granny?' To which she would reply, 'You little tinker, when the time has come I will be ready', but there she was and I knew her time had come.

I hurried home and, entering the front door, saw Mum and the Revd Larcombe standing there. I said, 'Granny's dead isn't she?' I didn't need an answer and ran upstairs to my bedroom. There was no need to cry for she had said her own personal goodbye and was on her way to heaven. I retraced my steps down the stairs to join the gathering throng of neighbours who had heard the news. We had tea and biscuits and as people trooped upstairs to pay their last respects I demonstrated my collection of sundews, all in flower under a glass cloche on the front room windowsill. When I was asked if I wanted to see Granny for the last time, I declined the offer. We had already said goodbye and I wanted to remember her smiling at the bus stop on her way to heaven, but that was our secret.

It was this incident that made me want to believe in ghosts and some time later, when I had forsaken Sutton Baptist and was doing the rounds of other religions, I went to the Spiritualist meeting hall in Sutton, seeking help. Seeing my Granny's ghost had been a very personal thing, but the conjuring up of spirits for mass consumption, though fascinating, smacked too much of other people's failed attempts on the road to Damascus.

The nearest I ever came to conversion was to the Roman Catholic faith. I had been to the Catholic church in Cheam to attend the funeral of my long-term schoolfriend Chris Toole, who drowned while swimming in a flooded quarry. The pomp, the flowing robes, the incense and the circumstance certainly lifted me above the humdrum of the everyday experience and made me really *feel* that there was a God up there. I felt very sad for all the family, especially his younger sister Liz whose tearful eyes looked bigger and more beautiful than ever.

Much later I was invited to the Catholic church in Kingston by Moira Murphy, one of the assistants at Dad's shop and the youngest of six equally beautiful sisters. The first time was a catastrophe for feeling pretty macho I followed them all down the aisle and, while taking in the scene, almost fell over the diminutive genuflecting form of Moira who was leading the way. We all filed sideways into the overful pew where Dad and Mum Murphy were already kneeling and I found myself attempting to sit on the wooden knob that surmounted the arm. Certainly worship appeared to be much more part of everyday existence for them, part of family – a very large family – life. Yet I felt it was all too centred around the church and seemed to have nothing to do with the other aspects of creation. So I remained in a self-imposed spiritual limbo for many years.

I can't remember when Dad bought the book *Science and Music* by Sir James Jeans, the man who actually dreamed up the idea of continuous creation. In simple terms, this little book explained how the vibration of strings, reeds or simply air flowing through wood or metal pipes could be made to produce music. The *Encyclopedia Brittannica* had elegantly supplied the bits and pieces for me to think about, but here they were all joined in a union of purpose linking science and the arts. I reckon that it was reading this book and going to the Proms for the first time that began to turn me into a scientist. On one occasion I remember the consternation of the conductor as the orchestra leader's bow began to disintegrate. At last I could link those rather boring experiments we did with Kund's Dust Tubes to the production of music; suddenly science began to make sense. I loved the Proms and made it to the last night on one glorious occasion. I sang 'Land of Hope and Glory' and believed every last stanza of it – a truly exhilarating experience. Strings, wood-wind, brass and percussion all working together with people of every creed, colour and kind, here was science and arts, yes creation working in grand harmony.

Although I couldn't be a ballet dancer my love of the ballet never waned. For me there was and still is nothing that can equal the wonder of a 100 per cent fit athlete being trained in the perfection of making his or her body carry out impossible feats of great beauty and technical virtuosity. I saw Anton Dolin dancing at the local Gaumont Cinema and then made as many trips as I could afford to Sadler's Wells. It only cost 3s 6d in the gods and I was fortunate to see Margot Fonteyn dance the lead part in *Ondine*. Like the Proms, these were evenings of total and absolute magic.

For those of us, like me, who did not shine in any of the sports, the cross country had to be the highlight of the sporting year as you stretched every muscle, many of which you didn't know you had, in the pursuit of points for your house. Everyone without a medical certificate had to take part in this circuit around the periphery of Banstead Downs. I am sure it didn't always rain, but the stretch up the aptly named Piggy Lane was always deep in mud. If you were one of the more tardy ones in the junior group the fastest of the seniors who started much later would plaster you with the stuff as they splashed by. At regular intervals non-combatants of every house were posted to urge you on to ever-greater things, until exhausted you ran in an alleyway of white tapes to be clocked in by Mr Scobell. Then you had to get your school uniform back on and, oozing with mud, make your own way home. The same was true after sports afternoons for although there were hot showers in the gymnasium in Sutton, there were none at the sports field in Cheam which was only equipped with a ramshackle wooden changing room. Mind you, as it was next to Nonsuch Girls' School, it did have its compensations.

At about this time my best friend was Mike Slann, a cricket fanatic who was heading for a career in the Air Force. We decided to go on holiday in the Lake District and, having accumulated the requisite 13s 6d for the return fair, we set off by coach to Keswick. The English lakes lived up to everything Arthur Ransome had cracked them up to be, although I don't remember him writing all that much about rain. We chose a campsite in a Swallowdale setting not far from a small beck that tinkled its way down towards the lake, which we had decided to circumnavigate on foot. It is a long way around Derwent Water and we arrived back very late, just as it started to rain. The sleep of two tired teenagers came very quickly, but not for long as we were soon woken by the waters of the swollen beck pouring through the tent.

There was nothing we could do except evacuate ourselves and all our belongings and head into the town where we found an already overful drying room in the retort house at the gas works. It rained for the next few days and so this became our home base. It was here that we met a group of Scousers who were up doing all the peaks. Their gear, like ours, was flimsy in the extreme – plimsolls or at the best ex-Army boots studded with hob-nails, cycle capes or cut-down raincoats, and what was in all probability washing line belayed around their waists with a variety of knots straight out of *Scouting for Boys* – a far cry from the high-tech stuff we had to provide for our children when they took to the hills on school trips. Yet it sufficed to get us everywhere we wanted to go, even to the top of Scarfell Pike where we emerged above the clouds to bask in the summer sun that had seemed to bless every move of the Swallows and Amazons. Perhaps it was warmer and dryer earlier in the century, before global warming raised the temperature of the atmospheric greenhouse and began to evaporate more water to make sunshade clouds before falling upon the earth beneath.

Despite all the rain, it was a wonderful holiday, and one I was reminded of years later when I led one of the early groups of tourists back into the Tibetan plateau after the cultural revolution in China. One highlight was a visit to an intact monastery of the orange order of Buddhism. There I was welcomed into the cell of the chief monk who proudly showed me a very faded picture of Derwent Water pinned up on the wall and said that before he died he wanted to go to see the English lakes, 'the most beautiful place in the world' – the exact same excuse I had used to lead the party to the Himalayas.

My matriculation and first year of O level results had left a lot to be desired, but by then I had found two new interests: biology and rugby. Biology had turned up as an adjunct to physics and, apart from the day that Mr Lorimer caught his ear on a piece of wire attached to one of the terminals on the Wimshurst Machine while at full rev, biology seemed much more exciting.

As for rugby, well it was a new sport at school, a sport of which the headmaster did not really approve. However some stalwart sixth-formers decided it should be on offer and one day, as I was sitting in the school library, the putative rugby captain breezed in and whispered, 'How much do you weigh?' 'Twelve and a half stone,' was my surprised answer and I found myself playing for the first team the next Saturday. Thence followed innumerable black eyes, dislocated joints and the great camaraderie of some twelve seasons – school, local club and university, second row, right hand side. Although I had to learn the rules as I went along, my self-respect grew week by week. I am sure that it was the rugby field that actually woke me up to the reality of what life was all about, not that final wow on the road to Damascus but the ouch of hard work in the rat race of survival. My school reports bear witness to the fact that from this point on I was putting more effort into all aspects of school life, and at last I made it into Room 17, the hallowed sanctum of the Science Sixth.

To prove our prowess in the arts we scientists had our own feature in the school magazine, the much-lauded 'Chronicles of Room 17'. We also had a hand built radio, its case crafted in the woodwork room. It was on this that we heard of the death of King George VI and alerted the headmaster to the fact that we now had a Queen about to take the throne. My stint at writing the Chronicles coincided with a new master appearing on the scene to teach religion and run the debating society. A Roman Catholic by calling he was immediately christened Pope Forkenburg (that was his name) the First. As even the Gentlemen of Science had to dabble in Religion I wrote: 'and Pope Forkenburg 1st descended upon the Land of Room 17 leading some of us to Mass and others in Debate'. I evidently satisfied the editors that there were no hidden innuendoes in the text and it duly appeared in the *Suttonian.*

The female of the species was now part of school interest if not life and we all hoped that we would obtain a part in the annual Gilbert and Sullivan opera, always a joint production with the Girls' High School, thus side-stepping the problem that the girls' uniform was purple and ours was pillar-box red so normally a couple together stood out in any crowd. It was even worse when you were a prefect because your cap was braided with silver. I never made it even into the chorus of the opera. However, with school dances in the offing, a group of us decided to sign on at Doreen Fretter's School of Dance so we could get to grips with the whole thing. One main attraction was Jill Dee, who lived almost opposite the school and held parties at which you played sardines and postman's knock, overseen of course by her mum. Doreen Fretter had a shock of bottle-blonde hair and our partners were mainly members of her tap class. Doreen obviously recognised the undoubted talents of Eggy Giles, Alan Sheppard and me and we were soon part of the chorus line, appearing alongside the Bradbury Girls at the Fairfield Hall in Croydon. This, my first stage appearance, involved singing and dancing to 'We were walking in the park one day' and 'John took me home to see his mother'. The Bradbury Girls were somewhat older than us and were part of the workforce of a local factory which bore that name.

It was at a subsequent charity performance in Sutton Public Hall that I was truly taken by surprise by a pair of very lovely and familiar eyes looking up at me from the audience. They belonged to my mum. Thank goodness we were well rehearsed for I didn't miss a step, although my voice might have wavered as I intoned: 'then she shook her head, looked at me and said'. The family knew I was learning to dance, but I had mentioned nothing about a dance troupe, and when I got home later that night, I was more than a bit worried about what she would say. Greeting me with what I can only describe as her wickedest smile she said. 'I did enjoy it, you and your friends were really very good. Who was the pretty little girl you were dancing with?' I was flabbergasted, this was my mum speaking and she approved of me dancing on stage! I had to pinch myself, hard. If only I had shared my dancing dreams with Mum years before, I thought, perhaps . . . but no, I have to be honest, it was my bulk that overcame my balletic aspirations.

In those days ballroom dancing was, as the music-hall joke said, 'a naval encounter without loss of seamen'. This was a decade before flower power blew middle-class morality out of the school chapel window. I don't think I was more naïve than my children when they reached that age: we knew a lot about the sexual side of things, matters that were discussed not only in the biology classroom but also in the playground. Soho, with its one or two highly-disguised sex shops, was but an underground ride away and *Health and Efficiency* and the *Red Light* were on sale in more and more outlets. Page-three girls began to appear and were stuck up in our desks, but there was a certain code of morals that still, in many people's minds, demanded wedlock to legalise the lusts of the flesh. Sadly, as A levels called, we lost touch with the members of the Fretter Academy and I can only wonder what happened to most of them – although Jill Dee turned up, as beautiful as ever, when I was the celebrity in *Class Mates* in the late nineties.

Having been to the Schoolboys Own Exhibition in Olympia, where you could meet top scientists, engineers and others who were paving the way to our science-based future, the men of Room 17 decided to put on our very own Science Exhibition. Having got permission, we set about it with a will and wrote to ICI, Wedgwood and every science-based industry we could think of to ask for help with material or even stands. Our prime exhibit was to be a replica of Foucault's Pendulum strung down the stairwell inside the front entrance of the school. Then disaster almost struck. We were called into the headmaster's study to explain why we were planning to turn the school into a commercial exhibition. On informing him that I had written to HRH Prince Philip, asking him to come and perform the opening ceremony, the head had a change of heart. Prince Philip declined the offer, but the Science Fair went on, minus some of its more commercial exhibits. My part in it was a demonstration of pond life in a range of aquarium tanks that purported to show the evolution of the animal kingdom and the food chain. I stood beside the last tank, a large china sink containing a school of sticklebacks and adorned with a label saying Frying Tonight. It was a great success and all was forgiven, despite the fact that the bit of the Earth under our Foucault's Pendulum refused to show its paces.

The biology group, though much looked down upon by the purist mathematicians, physicists and chemists, was held together by Mr Hutchings. He was the first teacher I had ever met who made learning fun and his sense of humour was a match for any of ours, so lessons and especially practicals were great occasions, even plant anatomy. During these we learned how to sharpen and strop the cut-throat razors with which we prepared sections of stems, roots and leaves of a whole cross-section of the plant kingdom. The collection of beautifully prepared slides against which we tested our expertise was Hutch's pride and joy and was not to be tampered with. So it was that we decided to add a very special specimen to the collection while the boss was out of the room. At last it was complete, the special round coverslip sealed on with Canada balsam and two labels, one on either side of the specimen. The first read 'Transverse section of Hutch dead from the neck up', the other 'Stained with safranin light green in cellosolve and a lot of patience'. As we were reviewing our handiwork, Hutch returned to see us messing about with his cherished box of slides in which we had just secreted our masterpiece. Its still-wet Canada balsam was our undoing for the offending slide came out stuck to his fingers. Wild with righteous indignation is perhaps the best description of him, but on taking a closer look he beamed, 'A beautiful preparation, well stained and you chose a section of oak, our hardest native wood.'

In the absence of an official biology laboratory we were nomads carrying our microscopes and part-dissected dogfish from pillar to post. One of the microscopes was of the brass Victorian variety and that was always my favourite. Dad, with his upbringing in *materia medica*, had always hankered after owning such an instrument and together we found a lasting interest in microscopy, which culminated with Dad becoming a member of both the Queckett Microscope Club and the Royal Microscopical Society. This also fanned the flames of my lifelong interest in the history of science.

Two glorious years under the tutelage of Mr Hutchings, who was a stalwart of the Congregational church, was all a budding biologist could ask for, and once our A levels were over we decided to take him to the zoo to say a big thank you. What a day it was, the highlight being when the camel decided to empty the contents of its scoop-like tongue over poor Hutch. We helped dry him off, and to complete our round of thanks took him to Drury Lane to see *Oklahoma*.

Hutch certainly kindled the flame, but it was trips to Haslemere with the Poveys that moved me one step along the way to a life steeped in field botany and ecology. We stayed in Fernhurst, a large rambling guesthouse with an elegant sitting room scattered with cushions and an assortment of books and magazines. It was here I could steep myself in *Country Life* and added another favourite book to my list, *The Broom Squire* by Sabine Baring-Gould. I have never been a great reader of newspapers or magazines, but *Country Life* has been an obsession ever since, always there, in the doctor's or dentist's waiting room and on display in W.H. Smith's at railway stations and airports. It still gives me great pleasure when returning to my home in the north-east to buy a copy on King's Cross, sit in the train and dream that one day I might be able to afford to live in one of the great houses advertised for sale. The sad thing is that whenever I have thought I could afford to make my dream come true the prices have doubled. Fortunately the editorial and countryside articles still keep me up to date with the nation's real economy, and my finger on the pulse of what really matters in what's left of our countryside.

The guesthouse was run by the Hutchinsons whose paternal father had been the founder of the Haslemere Education Museum. From my earliest days I must have been a bit of a museum freak because when it came to closing time at the end of my first visit to the Natural History Museum I lay down by the great Diplodocus and screamed. In truth I can't remember the incident, but I have had to re-enact that tantrum for the television cameras on three occasions – with dire results the last time when no one had informed the security guards. For me Haslemere museum was my favourite. It had stuffed animals and birds in plenty, dioramas, geological sections, man traps, scolds' bridles, well-stocked aquaria and vivaria, and a wildflower table that was replenished every day. If you could find a flower that was not already on the table, it would be given pride of place.

In order to try to get a specimen on the wildflower table I scoured the countryside. The setting of *The Broom Squire* was the perfect place for a plant safari and there we discovered not only dodder, a parasitic plant swarming over the heather, but also the diminutive Youth Hostel and the warden who lived in Gnome Cottage and was a great fount of local knowledge. From the depths of the Punch Bowl it was a wet walk to Thursley Common, which was still getting over the effects of being a tank training ground during the war. Large areas of bare sand and deep ruts where the tanks had sunk in and got stuck were being rapidly colonised by heath and bog vegetation. This was the first place I saw sundews, our most abundant insectivorous plants, growing in situ, but both the long-leaved and the round-leaved were already in the museum display. Then, in a lesser rut, I found what at first sight looked like a green caterpillar crawling across the bare ground. Returning to the museum with my find, I was rewarded with a place on the table while at the same time being warned about picking rare plants. I had found the marsh clubmoss, a relative of the giant clubmosses whose remains helped make the coal in the carboniferous period. I was taken and shown their fossils.

That was great, but the best bit for me was out at the back of the museum, where a series of small lakes had been created by impounding the stream to provide homes for a collection of exotic waterfowl, now long gone. The lakes were then a profusion of water plants and aquatic insects, and John Clegg the curator would come down, armed with nets and enamel trays, and lead us in a spot of pond dipping. I was hooked especially when we carried our catches back to the big lecture room, placed them under the projection microscope and saw them on the big screen. There were things which I had only read about in books: hydra banging off their stinging cells to poison water fleas, before dragging them down into their one-way gullet; dragonfly larvae using their masks to trap sticklebacks and then tear them to pieces; and, with the microscope on its highest power, a staggering array of plankton, desmids and diatoms, mating *Chlamydomonas* and spring-loaded *Vortichella*. It wasn't a film but a real live show before your very eyes. When we were all satiated, even with the most gruesome bits, at the command of Mr Jewel, the assistant curator, we would carry our living treasures out and put them back into the pond. I was hooked, and years later was able to relive the whole thing miniaturised down in *Bellamy's Backyard Safari*, thanks to the BBC.

On Sundays, during these trips, we went to church in Lynchmere and were told in hushed tones that those were Richard Dimbleby and his two sons, David and Jonathan, sitting in the pew in front. I never did speak to Richard, although I am sure it made me feel much prouder when I received the award that bore his name at BAFTA in 1978. The television series that got the award was *Botanic Man*, 'The Story of Evolution' as I had first seen it set out on the walls of that wonderful museum. The making of it took me around the world no less than four times.

By this time my brother had been called up and was a proud member of the Ordnance Corps in which he learned exactly what had gone wrong on the night of our big bang. He had bought a motorbike and, after our débâcle with the Douglas, while he was away at Aldershot, I decided to try my skills on it in the back garden, almost writing myself off over the rockery. G's father-in-law-to-be was John Wright, master plumber by trade, who not only had a very beautiful daughter called Audrey but owned a motorbike with a sidecar in which he carried all his tools. His pride and joy was, however, an ex-police Wolsey that was kept tuned to perfection. Audrey's cousin was destined to marry Damian Hill's Dad. Her brother Ron was then just getting over a terrible motorbike accident, so Pop Wright, as he liked to be called, warned me off bikes and pointed me in the direction of cars, fast cars. Pop was a great companion, with the strength of a bull and muscles of steel, and I soon found myself caught up in a new world of plumbing and motorcars. The whole family was mad on them and I was off to Silverstone to take in the spectacle of motor racing: real motorcars, belching Castrol R, and drivers like Prince Bira of Siam, Fangio, Farina and of course Mike Hawthorn and Stirling Moss. In those days you could actually hang around the pits and, if you were lucky, talk to them in between the races. I started to dream of being at the wheel of one of these machines.

Saturdays at the Wrights were very different from those at home, for Auntie Vi, as I called her, was a great exponent on the piano and we had great singsongs. As I come from a teetotal background, the fact that both Heineken's and gin flowed free was a novelty, although I declined to partake. Home from the rugby field on Saturday, a quick bath then it was round to the Wrights, where tea came with lashings of fatty cakes straight from the oven, and then the singing began. Aunt Flo and Cousin Gladys were always there, and so was Ron with his very beautiful wife Pat. We all had to do our bit and, fired with my success on the local stage, I did a passingly good imitation of Danny Kaye singing 'Manic Depressive Pictures Present, Hello Fresno Goodbye' and Rose Murphy's intonement of 'I Put a Nickel in the Telephone' and 'Me and My Shadow'. Another of my party pieces was my imitation of Dame Clara Butt's rendition of 'The Better Land'. I was rather ashamed of this because the original was a family favourite in the Bellamy household; indeed it was the first record I ever bought, HMV Black Label no less.

They were carefree days and my world, the post-war world, was changing very quickly. The fact that G was away in the Army and that I was no longer a regular churchgoer must have hurt Mum and Dad, but there were never any recriminations. Though steeped in the values of their age, they realised that another generation must be allowed to make their own way in life.

School holidays took on a new dimension as I became a plumber's mate, learning to talk a new language of two-inch barrel, plumber's tow and stilsons. I helped Pop put in pigswill boilers in a farm at the Ewell end of Nonsuch Park and install and service tack-room heating in some very famous stables in Epsom. I also learned to wipe a lead joint using a blowlamp and a moleskin. I even met the man who kept the lawns in Nonsuch Park free of moles and hence the local plumbing trade supplied – a trade that once provided the greatest number of members of the House of Lords, such was the importance of a pure supply of water. Many years later I was proud to agree that my face could appear on water bills in the north-east, extolling the cause of 'Water Aid', a charity that helps to provide poor communities across the world with this essential of all life.

I was taken on a trip up Teeside where the Wright family had its roots at Kirkleatham twixt the North York Moors and Redcar. Little did I realise that it would be on a sewer pipe, in this jewel of northern resorts, that I would make my debut in the world of television, and that a building in the village would one day become the headquarters of the Cleveland Wildlife Trust and bear my name. Here I was in for another culture shock: the reality of heavy industry, the pollution it caused and yes, even in the 50s, barefoot children playing in the streets near the transporter bridge which crossed what was then one of the hardest working and most polluted rivers in the world.

Cars became an obsession and Gordon Polson and Brian (Rollo) Rawlings – left-hand prop in the school rugby team – decided to build and race a 750 Special. We bought all the books and found the perfect base in the *Exchange and Mart*, a 1932 Austin 7 on sale in East Finchley. Off we went to collect it. Rollo's father, Detective Inspector Rawlings, had agreed to tow us home around the North Circular. All went well until we slowed to a halt at the traffic lights at Hanger Lane, Ealing. Our brakes were not as good as his and so, unbeknown to any of us the towrope got around our front axle. Going on green meant that we shot sideways towards the people waiting at the bus stop. Over came two local bobbies: 'Here, here, what's all this?' An identification card handed out of the front car soon had them helping unwind the rope and we were on our way.

We had decided to work on it in our back garden and the only way to get it in was by dismantling part of the back fence. It wasn't too difficult as we chose that section which had borne the brunt of our tunnelling activities. We were just easing it through the gap when Dad arrived home from work and joined in with the final push. We celebrated with one of Gordon's parties to which everyone brought some food. As usual we ended with far too much, including mountains of Iced Gems, our favourite biscuits at that time, and so the party went on for three days, each night in a different house, the diminishing pile of food being wheeled to the next party in a barrow. In between the parties we started to strip the car down before strengthening the chassis prior to reassembly.

Another attraction was the Festival Gardens in Battersea Park. A great crowd of us would go up on the bus, stay late, and then walk home to Cheam: there were no late night trains and buses in those days. On one of those memorable evenings, we all got on the Rotor together and formed a pile of bodies too heavy for the centrifugal force to hold high up on the wall. As we descended very rapidly into a heap on the floor the seat was ripped out of my trousers, great fun for the crowd who were waiting their turn at the top.

Sadly, we never completed the rebuild of the car; those carefree days were coming to an end as we all drifted away in search of gainful employment. Mike Slann, Gordon Polson and his cousin Derek, on whose Matchless I first travelled at 100 mph, went into the Air Force and Rollo and P.G. Harris to the Army. Conscription was, of course, then still firmly on the cards and at the command, contained in a brown envelope labelled OHMS, off I went for selection. Secretly I had hoped to get into the Guards so was very glad when I got full marks in the aptitude test, part of which was putting a complex lock back together in record time. All I actually did was bung all the bits inside and screw the faceplate on. However, I was more than a bit miffed when at the end of my medical I was turned down, not on the grounds of flat feet and dandruff, but due to the fact that I had had Bright's Disease. On questioning, the doctor explained that it would be too much of a risk in training, as I really should never allow myself to be put into a position in which I would be cold and wet. No amount of cajoling would make him change his mind so I never took the Queen's Shilling.

By this time I had said goodbye to school, still without the requisite four A levels needed to get into a good medical school, for I still thought that I wanted to please my parents and become a medic. So, while I had another go at the exams, there was a living to be earned. Jobs there were in plenty at the Labour Exchange and, apart from working as a plumber's mate with Pop Wright, I painted white lines down the roads around Carshalton, inspected sewers beneath the streets of London, worked in a variety of departments at Paynes Poppet Factory in Croydon, and helped make plastic at Vinatex on the banks of the river Wandle. Each job taught me something new. Working with Pop and playing rugby every Saturday, I probably got as fit as I ever managed to be. At Paynes I discovered that girls were as interested in boys as vice versa, and if they managed to catch you en masse they had some very sexciting habits with molten chocolate; thank goodness I was fit. While working as a binman, I learned all about recycling, for it is strange what people throw away or indeed what gets into London's drainage system. At Vinatex in Carshalton, not far from the place where pollution from my grandfather's tannery must have tainted the river, I did the night shift while working days in the sorting office of the Royal Mail. Fortunately I never got caught sleeping on either job. I also worked with a number of firms on the Festival Site, so, when invited to the Festival Hall to launch a film I made for the Royal Society for the Protection of Birds, I was able to stand up and say, 'The first time I appeared here was as a tea boy for a building firm.' Perhaps that is why I have never been offered a post, even on the committee of that august body which is to this day the upmarket end of conservation. I finally applied for a post at Ewell Tech in 1953. The whole family agreed that it was the ideal place to brush up my academic credentials.

7 *ROSMARINUS OFFICINALIS* AND

FRANCIS ROSE

EWELL COUNTY TECHNICAL COLLEGE, which had opened its doors on the corner of what had, in those pre-Common Agricultural Policy days, been the largest field in England, needed a lab boy. Geoff Stevens suggested I apply and after an interview with the head of the science department, Frank Dearnley, one of the nicest men I have ever met, I got the job. Geoff had already got the position as Laboratory Technician, and I take it that the staff of this shining new establishment of learning, who were being recruited from all over the country, were not aware of our explosive association.

They were heady times. The college had been set up with the express aim of supporting the new science-based industries that were beginning to service the high-tech future that was looming on the horizon. The principal, Buchanan by name, was ex-Army, as were many of his staff. They came from those heydays of University when the portals of higher education, though still redolent with *Doctor in the House*-type departments of all sorts, were invaded by men in demob suits and women who had already served in all walks of civilian and military life.

Three of these were to have a profound effect on my future: George Fluck, a not so distant relation of Diana Dors, and Ned Norris, both not long out of the Army, and Margaret Cornish, a still-blushing graduate from Bedford College for Women.

George was out of Army stock living in Fleet in Hampshire, not a sergeant major's bellow away from Aldershot, where my brother and so many others learned the basics of everything the Queen's Shilling held in store. George was at a school that was local to the crash site of the prototype Meteor, the first jet plane that was to change the face of warfare and speed the way to package holidays. On finding that much of the wreckage was missing, and knowing that boys would be boys, the authorities did the rounds of the local schools and got it all back, and assembled it in the playground. That is probably the reason why George had wanted to go into the Air Force. However, not fit enough to fly a plane, he was taught to drive a tank instead. Queen Mary College in the Mile End Road became his alma mater where he graduated in Zoology under the tutelage of Professor Newell, co-author of the then best selling A level text, Grove and Newell.

'Laid back' was a concept still waiting to be invented but George was the role model. However, Ned Norris, or Ikker as he liked to call himself, was frenetic, the best lecturer I have ever had the pleasure to learn from, let alone work alongside. He came to head the Ewell Biology team from the King's Royal Rifles via Exeter University. Having been among the first liberators into the death camps of Nazi Germany his lectures on animal physiology pulled no punches. His practicals, however, were a joy to take part in and even better to be part of. The subject was then in rapid transition, from do-it-yourself Manometric Van Slykes (complex quick fit and quartz apparatus used for the accurate measurement of gas volumes) to the paper, column and gas chromatography that would eventually allow the mapping of the human genome. His was the world that spawned James Lovelock, mastermind behind both modern gas analysis and the Gaia Hypothesis. Any new technique that appeared in the literature, we tested in the prep room before it was wheeled out into the teaching laboratories.

The prep room was our holy of holies and only certain people were allowed within its portals. A large jar of liquorice comfits was always kept topped up, as were the blood sugar levels of the favoured few. Anyone taking a sweet had to announce the fact with the words 'Sweeties, nick, nick'. String and sealing wax were the essence of success in laboratory practice. In the absence of instruction manuals you really had to understand the nuts and bolts of apparatus and methodology. All of a sudden learning was fun again and I found myself on the steepest of learning curves as I helped put biology on the Ewell map.

Equipping the laboratories and making them work was all part of each long day's work, a working week that often spilled over into the weekends. One Sunday I can remember being dragged out from under a bench, where I was bashing a hole through the new laboratory wall, by an irate Principal. 'What the hell is your car doing parked in my place?' 'Well,' said I, 'it's Sunday and I didn't think you were coming in.' 'And why are you bashing a hole in the lab wall?' 'To get three phase mains through to supply a new centrifuge; we need it for tomorrow's lab.' 'Good man, get on with the job.' But I did go out and move my car.

At last I was earning a wage *and* owned a car. The one that had annoyed Buchanan was a soft-top Morris 8 two seater with a fold down dickey. I bought it from Ron Wright at the garage he helped run in Balham. He had just got it in part exchange and he let me have it for £27 10s. I drove it home, neither of us knowing that the only thing connecting the steering wheel to the wheels themselves was a bent nail hammered in to the splined cog at the bottom of the steering column. No MOTs then, you could buy an old banger, put it on the road and learn by your mistakes. What is more, when you opened up the bonnet there was an engine that looked like an engine: four spark plugs, an alternator, a coil and a carburettor. If it went wrong you could fix it. My new car didn't, however, stop me ogling the vehicles in Jack Bond's Motor Emporium, a showroom packed full of the most tempting horseless carriages. You name a classic car and it was there waiting to be bought, Isotto Franchinis, Buggati Royales, Type 35 Cs, Cream Cracker MGs. Such wonderful machines were but dreams in a lab boy's eyes.

*

Physiology was raw in tooth and claw back in the days when microscopes were still made of brass, as were the clockwork chymographs that recorded the twitching of a frog's muscles and the tone exercised by the gut of a rat. Was it because we still had the excuse of the horrors of war redolent in our minds, and that counselling was but a clip around the ear by the local bobby, that we appeared to be less caring? I don't know, but as we dissected our worms, dogfish, frogs and rabbits, I don't think we were any less humane than those who today rail against such practices. Over the years I have given this a lot of thought and have come to the conclusion that in many ways we were perhaps much more humane, able to make decisions for ourselves and terminate the sufferings of a myxamitosed rabbit, an oil-soaked sea bird, a mouse or songbird part-chewed by a pet cat, or a fox or badger part-squashed on the road, with one swift blow. I hate having to do it, but can summon up enough courage if the occasion arises. Surely this is better than passing by and pointing fingers of scorn while other people do our dirty work for us.

One job I had was to go to the local slaughterhouse and search the guts of the animals for tapeworms to demonstrate to the students. A brutal place, yes it was, but most of the men who worked there had a compassion all of their own and did the job as humanely and as quickly as possible. They were each zoologists in their own right with an intricate knowledge of anatomy and physiology. It was there that I first learned that cows were in reality not herbivores, but omnivores. I saw the contents of their second stomachs and was told that it was the seething mass of tiny living animals that digested the tough cellulose of the grass, turning some of it into protein, which the cows could digest along with the contents that spilled out of the plant cells.

It was the misapplication of such knowledge that later led to the BSE or 'mad-cow disease' débâcle. Ground-up waste animal offal, including tissue from the nervous system, was fed to cattle and the disease organisms it contained were thus passed on. In terms of agricultural practice it may have appeared to be the best way of dealing with the problem of all that waste offal but, like eating people, forced cannibalism is surely wrong, a point I made some twelve years later when invited to the Agricultural Department of Reading University to discuss the possibility of being offered the newly-created post of agricultural ecologist. They showed me all sorts of bizarre experiments in recycling wastes of all sorts by feeding them to chickens, pigs and cows. I had my say, pointing out that such work had but little relevance to real ecology, only to be told that it did away with a lot of potential pollution and helped increase the profits of farming. I was not asked to apply for the job.

With Distillers Company Limited not far away and Beecham's Research station within an easy bike-ride, the jobs were waiting for our ex-students. It was an exciting place to be and every day brought something new to think about. My mind was in turmoil, deciding what I wanted to do with my life.

Rosemary Froy officially became Mrs Rosemary Bellamy on 3 January 1959 – but I am jumping ahead of myself. I had first seen her across a crowded room, the teaching laboratory at Ewell Tech to be exact, in October 1953. She was one of the first influx of pre-nurses shepherded into the aegis of the biology department by Mrs Dearnley, wife of the head of science. Among a fantastic bevy of talent, three stood out, Angela Fairbairns with a shock of golden curls, Mary (Pussy) Cat, and Fluff, as Rosemary became known, for she then had a very striking angora jumper. The prep room gang soon put names to faces as we helped them buy lenses and dissecting kits, and ensured that they were properly attired in regulation white lab coats.

They were soon persuaded to take part in the Christmas pantomime 'Robin Would but Maid Marion Wouldn't' or 'A Jerk in Lincoln Green', and it wasn't long before those favoured few, which included Fluff, were allowed into the prep room and to even partake of our Liquorice Comfits. The pantomime, in which most of the biology staff either took part or were lampooned, was a great success. However it was in Love Lane in Cheam Village that it happened; I fell in love. It was the Saturday before Christmas and Fluff was working, as most students did in those days, on the Christmas post. It was one of those cold, mizzly

December days; I turned out of Spring Close into Love Lane and there she was wearing her russet brown St Philomena's uniform raincoat. Wow! And I have been saying Wow! ever since, so much so that when asked to write this autobiography I said to the publisher, 'I fell in love forty-six years ago and I am still happily married to the same young lady, what have I got to write about?' Well, you are now both the judge and the jury.

I fell hopelessly in love, not with the angora jumper or the russet brown raincoat, but with the amazing young lady who wore them with style on the catwalk of life. From that moment on I was hooked, in a total dilemma of what to do, so as not to ruin my chances with her. Christmas was a nightmare of despair, wondering how to make my approach, and then, in the new year, I found myself working in the conservatory at the top of the main stairs in the college, when George and Ikker sent Rosemary up to get some plants to take down to the laboratory. Here was my opportunity, nothing shatteringly romantic, a simple 'How about coming to the pictures?' She said, 'yes', and blushed as deep a red as the pelargoniums she was carrying.

The rest of the year buzzed with activity, mainly botanical, but my whole existence revolved around Fluff. A regular feature of weekdays would be to meet at Cheam Baths to go for a pre-breakfast swim and then off to Ewell together. It was on one of these idyllic mornings that I plucked up enough courage to introduce her to the family. Apart from the fact that Mum plied her with the full monty – eggs, bacon and fried bread – it all boded well for the future.

A regular earner now, I could do more than cast my eyes over Jack Bond's Emporium near Tooting. My dreams came true when a French Salmson that had held the lap record at Brooklands in 1924 came up for sale at £30. The Morris went the way of a trade-in and three of us pushed it home all of six miles. Twin overhead cams, a float chamber the size of a bucket, we just had to get it on the road although it was minus a petrol tank and had a completely worn out universal joint on the transmission. A trip to the scrapyard in Merton solved the petrol tank problem; it came off a Ford and was installed suspended just above the driver's knees. Gravity did the rest. Armed with a large lump of phosphor bronze, a drill and some files it took the whole weekend to complete the job, then with a loud bang and a puff of smoke we were off down the road, much to everyone's surprise.

It was not the easiest car to control, a fabulous machine with an A cut box, three forward gears and a penchant for using petrol very fast. I could fill the tank for a pound, but public transport was a lot cheaper. However, I did drive it to the Tech as often as I could, mainly to impress Rosemary and also to use up waste lab alcohol and other flammable chemicals which added a bit of oomph and produced a lot of smoke. On one occasion I approached the roundabout just past the Glynn Arms pub a little too fast and had to do a handbrake stop on the grass. 'Here, here, what's all this,' said the bobby as he parked his bike and came over to admire the car.

I was exceptionally lucky back in those days to be rubbing shoulders with so many practical teachers and scientists. One part of the job I really enjoyed was working with R.R. Fowell who came down the hill from Distillers Company Limited to teach us the intricacies of handling fungi in pure culture. Under the best microscopes of the day he showed us the structure of yeasts: little blobs of life budding off their offspring and leaving scars that to the expert eye gave them enough character to allow identification. Once they were named and isolated there was the possibility of hybridisation; the goal was to breed a super yeast that could tolerate living in more of its own waste than its parents. The waste product in question was of course alcohol. Mr Fowell was a key part of a team that succeeded in doing just that and so disappeared from the Ewell scene to higher things in Distillers Company. If this had not happened I might well have ended up as a mycologist.

My parents still vainly hoped that I would head for medicine. I realised that I had already let them down abominably. At school I had never got a prize of any sort on speech day, which we were duty bound to attend, and my termly reports were so bad that I had often felt like throwing them away before I got home. So, in an attempt to get that elusive A level in chemistry and make it into medical school I went along to classes in between my work. However, a medical career was not to be. Despite gaining at last, those four A levels and an interview at Westminster, the living world was calling out too loud.

If any one person was really to blame for my final choice of career it was Margaret Cornish. The simple reason was that it was she who gave me the opportunity to discover my one real talent. One of my jobs was to accompany the A Level botany class on their summer field trip to the Peak District in Derbyshire. Margaret was in the middle of completing her MSc on the invasion of chalk grassland by a tough grass called the erect brome and she chose the location. Our base became Ravenstor Youth Hostel and that is where I became a botanist; there is even a plaque commemorating the fact, unveiled not long after I took up the Presidency of the YHA many years later.

Out we went on the first day, complete with quadrates and transects, into unknown terrain all set about with wall to wall (dry stone of course) plants, each one of which had a Latin name, enunciated to perfection by Margaret. I was captivated and, instead of just carrying the gear as a lab boy should, I was down on my knees soaking it all up. The fact that plants, like animals, lived in a constant state of siege and war, and that a change in grazing regime or a subtle change in climate could tip the balance of survival was something I found fascinating. That evening, I walked down the sloping meadow in front of the hostel hand in hand with Rosemary, putting Latin names to the plants and found I had remembered them all. At last I had discovered my one real talent! Even if there had been career advisers in schools back in those days, I don't suppose the list of possible jobs for budding field botanists would have been very long. However, as A Level botany was still a requisite for medical students, the teaching profession offered a distinct possibility of gainful employment and so the die was cast. An honours degree in botany became my aim in life.

Not long before that fantastic trip, George and Ned had persuaded Rosemary that *her* talents perhaps lay in a degree course and that she should follow in George's footsteps to Queen Mary College. They had also taken me aside in the prep room and said, 'You have got a brain between those two ears, for God sake use it.' I can't say that Granny's remonstrations concerning the Parable of the Talents were uppermost in my mind at that moment, but I did know that if one day I was ever going to be able to ask Fluff to marry me, I had to get to university too.

It's amazing what a woman can do to you. I even let her drive the Salmson, my most prized possession, which was by then more firmly on the road. It was not the easiest thing to coax between gears, and Rosemary soon managed to get the A cut gear teeth irrevocably stuck somewhere between second and third, so we ended up having to push the car all the way back to base on its front wheels. On reaching home and while sorting the gearbox out, I was well and truly under the bonnet when she pressed the starter button, which I had recently fitted for convenience. The mag-dyno did nothing to the engine but it chucked me flat on my back, and there she was sitting in the driving seat, as she has been ever since, grinning from heavenly ear to heavenly ear.

Another Rose was also at that time beginning to influence my life – Dr Francis Rose to be exact, lecturer in plant ecology at Bedford College and Margaret Cornish's research director. A walk anywhere in the countryside with Francis held me spellbound. From a hundred yards he would extol the Latin names of mosses and lichens growing on the distant tree trunks. Then it would be down on his knees in the mire, demonstrating the wisps of leafy liverworts growing on his beloved *Sphagnum*, then off again into the local thicket to show us some diminutive orchid.

Suddenly I was caught up in another world, the world of field naturalists. I met characters like Jim Bingley and John Sankey, both wardens at field centres set up in the post-war years by a group of natural historians concerned at the rape of the British countryside, caused by changing methods of agriculture and management. I had of course witnessed this. I knew that the may bugs and stag beetles had all but disappeared from Boney Hole as the mighty elms were reduced by Dutch elm disease. I had watched as the urban greenspace of my childhood, where I had picked wildflowers for my Mum, was covered with concrete, as hedgerows were torn down to make way for ever larger reapers and binders. Bluebell woods, but a cycle ride away from central London, became part of a drab grey-green scene of open fields drenched with fertiliser. All this was happening but, without any expert knowledge, I had been unaware of the gravity of the situation. All of a sudden I was mixing with experts in every walk of natural history, some of whom were starting to do something to try to stop the rot.

I found myself at a meeting of like-minded people who were then setting up what is now called the Surrey Wildlife Trust. Today it's one of a partnership of forty-seven such trusts, which covers the whole country and of which I am proud to be President. Likewise, during a walk with Francis and John Sankey over Juniper Top on the north-facing slope of Box Hill, we met members of the first working party of the Conservation Corps. They were clearing the scrub from the slopes of the hill to protect the habitat of the rare orchids that can only live in open lime-rich grassland. Thanks to their dedication and hard work, the descendants of those orchids are still there to be enjoyed by all discerning visitors.

At Box Hill I learned first-hand that chalk downland was a man-made habitat, as were so much of the so-called 'natural' habitats of the British Isles. When people had first turned up in force on the English scene most of it, including the southern chalk, was covered with ancient forest. To be able to make a living they cleared the trees and began to graze cattle and eventually sheep, the constant nibbling of which kept the trees at bay, providing an open habitat for a myriad wildflowers, including the orchids first made famous by Charles Darwin. When the sheep were removed to make way for holiday makers, a healthy population of rabbits (a non-native species introduced by the Saxons) continued the job of mowing the downland lawn. However, catastrophe loomed for the orchids, the glow-worms and all the other plants and insects that went with them as myxomatosis wiped out the nibblers. The Conservation Corps, which metamorphosed into the British Trust for Conservation Volunteers, just had to be invented. The day after I started writing this book I was back on Box Hill, celebrating forty years of their dedicated service to the biodiversity of Britain.

The British Bryological Society and the then embryo Lichen Society were another great source of inspiration, and trips with Wallace and Boniface – the former worked for W.H. Smith's and the latter was a plumber – introduced me to the very special world of the amateurs, an enormous band of unsung heroes and heroines, the real mainstay of natural history in Britain, each of whom has become expert in their own particular field in their spare time. I also came face to face with the arrogance of mainstream academia which is wont to dismiss the often superior knowledge of the amateur in the absence of paper qualifications.

It was Francis Rose, however, who was my main inspiration, as he was to thousands of others. We were often taken for close relations, even father and son, both being bearded and of much the same build. I knew that I was never going to be as good as him, but I filled innumerable notebooks and wore out a couple of hand lenses trying. So it was that, from that point on, every spare moment was spent in the field, attempting to make up for over twenty wasted years.

That summer saw another dream come true, my first trip abroad, across the channel to France. I had hoped that Rosemary would have been allowed to come with me, but her mum said an emphatic 'No'. Mums were like that in those days and not to be disobeyed, so it was off with another student from the tech called John Raybould. John was hoping to go to university to read biology and he was great company. Being something of an esoteric with Buddhist leanings he set my mind on things much further afield than France.

Memories of war were still strong and the Union Jacks on our rucksacks meant the hitching was easy. Our entry into Paris was almost triumphant, for we had been given a lift in one of those Citroën vans that looks as if it was made of corrugated tin. It was owned by a larger than life local village butcher and his tiny assistant, both of whom were proud to have been members of La Résistance, a fact they rubbed home with multiple embraces. They and their van smelt of clean sawdust and their breath of fresh-brewed coffee which they shared with us out of a gigantic thermos as we trundled into Paris, the meat hooks clanging on the overhead gantry from which hung spotlessly white aprons.

We found ourselves honoured guests, on show at the meat market where Les Anglais were asked to choose 'le boeuf pour le village'. At last I had met real people who actually used the verbs we had tried to conjugate. Having been shown how to check the teeth and feel the firmness of the flesh we, after much prodding and vive la France-ing, chose a small white bullock. Our choice went down well and, as it was led away to slaughter, we drank to its demise in Dubonnet. Our new-found friends wanted us to go back to their village with them to continue the celebration, but our sights were set on the Côte d'Azure.

Late that evening, we took the metro as far south as it went, picked up a short hitch and then set off down the road into a pitch-black countryside. Our progress was not helped by a thick mist rising from la campagne, and the after effect of several glasses of vin ordinaire that had followed the Dubonnet. We finally parked ourselves in what we thought was a wooded glade in a field and immediately fell asleep. Awoken by the roar of early morning traffic, we discovered that we had pitched tent on a large island in the middle of a main road junction.

Hitch after hitch sped us along la route bleu, in actual fact along any route the drivers appeared to be taking, but they always assured us that it was south towards what, sadly, became an elusive goal. Lorries, tractors with trailers, ex-Army jeeps, Renaults, Citroëns, Fiats, even a Chevrolet and a giant Mercedes Benz, each had a proud owner with a story to tell and an immense knowledge of the local terrain. The fact that we never made it to the Med was simply because the Massif Central got in the way.

We were picked up by an ultra-careful driver and were tootling along at about 25 kph down a very steep gradient when all of a sudden we realised that the car had lost its brakes. Thank goodness the driver was au fait with the fact before we were, and as we gathered speed he did the only thing he could to save the day. He chucked the car into a thankfully deep ditch: the only thing between us and a several-hundred-metre drop into oblivion. A local gave us a lift into the nearest village where I came abruptly to my senses as the local doctor did his best to sew the skin, upon which grew my left eyebrow, back on to my forehead, his very pretty daughter ooh la la-ing outside the surgery window with a bottle of Cognac. The driver paid the doctor's bill and out we walked into a blazing hot sun, my head swathed in bandages, to continue our journey. I think John and I were more than a little concussed and lay down to sleep in a shady ditch.

John did his best to console me with the fact that, if we had been killed in the crash, it would have been but another step on the route to Nirvana, and that we might have been recycled next time round as Frenchmen. All the way along, I found he had a very different way of looking at things, well not really looking but trying to be part of another philosophy of life, a philosophy in which what you did do rather than what you didn't do really mattered. I refound that philosophy many years later as a part of village life in Sri Lanka.

I was soon woken from my sleep by an all-enveloping munching noise and, looking over the low hedge, found a field full of Colorado beetles; there were so many of them you couldn't see the potato plants. Both of us were feeling somewhat groggy so we decided to head for the nearest town and using our best French enquired, 'Où est la gare, s'il vous plâit?' Looks of blank amazement had me chugging up and down enunciating 'Chemin de fer, choo choo.'

We did better once we reached Roanne and were directed towards the camping place. A winding path threaded its way past the town's rubbish dump, which was gently smouldering in the gathering dusk. A notice pointed towards a café with tables gathered around a central grassy patch. 'Camping?' 'Dans le parc' was the reply, indicating the open gravel-covered space which doubled as a dance floor. So we joined the locals in song and dance, and when the last had wobbled off back through the dump we unrolled our bags and lay down, dans le parc. Extinguishing the lights, the patron introduced us to two gigantic 'chiens méchants' and wished us bonne chance. I lay there terrified while both dogs tended my bandages with lolloping tongues.

I am not blaming the dogs, but next day my stitches were in a suppurating mess and, with insufficient money to pay doctor's bills, we decided it was time to head back home. The Paris train was jam packed full and we got two places sleeping against the door – a precarious way of travel for when the door opened at a station we tended to fall out, and

French stations don't have platforms. As both of us were determined at least to see the Mona Lisa at the Louvre we did just that before leaving for home, but not before some Americans demanded to take our pictures while mumbling something about apaches.

8 THE DISCOVERY OF MY DAD

HAVING AT LAST got all four A levels, I started to apply for a place at university to read not medicine but animal physiology, zoology and honours botany. Rosemary got accepted by Queen Mary College in the Mile End Road to study biology and I got a place at Chelsea College of Science and Technology, just off the Kings Road, which in those days came complete with Mary Quant and everything her special breed of chic stood for. We may reminisce about the swinging sixties but the fifties had a special sort of magic too.

So began three hectic years, commuting up to London with all those bowler-hatted businessmen, some of my old schoolmates among them. Saying fond farewells at Victoria Station, Rosemary and I went our own ways, she on the underground, me on the most gregarious transport, the Number 19 omnibus. Chelsea College was as different from QMC as Kings Road Chelsea was from the Mile End Road, the former full of art students and budding pharmacists, the latter a bastion of the male of the species, groaning with engineers and physicists. On rare occasions I would meet Rosemary at QMC and walk back down the Mile End Road past one of London's seven great cemeteries that was even then coming to the end of its life. Despite the pollution, lichens grew on the myriad tombstones which conveniently bore dates from which you could get some idea of the rate of growth. It was also a great place to hold hands. After the closure of the cemetery, the trees took over, shading out the lichens but still providing a convenient, shady space – a green lung for the people of what became the infamous Tower Hamlets.

I first recounted this story when asked to open the field studies centre at the old cemetery, the only one I know in which the classroom is purpose built to contain an arm of the pond, so that even the heaviest rain need not stop a lesson in pond dipping. The first class I ever took on a nature ramble through the cemetery was as much fun as it was multi-ethnic. Most of the kids had never seen an earthworm before, let alone the large carabid beetle we discovered crawling across a tombstone. There were screams of horror and delight as one student asked 'Where do you put the battery in?' Despite a certain amount of vandalism their cemetery became a proud possession of the community, a focal point of pride. After much hard work it was eventually given the status of a local nature reserve. What a celebration there was, at which I was given a picture of a spotted woodpecker flying past a tree trunk on which there was a love heart inscribed with the letters DB and RF.

The Chelsea College botany class of 1954 was very small: myself, Ed Cossins and Ann Wood; and the staff wasn't any bigger. Comyns J.A. Barclay, who had served in the Fleet Air Arm and was one of the first to land a plane on a converted trawler, headed the team; a wonderful Welsh miner, H. Duerden, had dug himself out of a life down the pits and encouraged in us a love for the fossils and John Vaughan was an expert on the anatomy of fruits and seeds.

The zoology department was led by Dr Henschel, ably supported by Dr Margaret Brown, an expert on the fishes in all their diversity, Muriel Sutton, who sported a glass eye and was wound up in the world of the Salps – free floating distant ancestors of we humans – and Dr John Mortimer, fresh from Queen Mary College, whose pride and joy was an Austin 7. How it ended up parked on the lecture bench in the Zoology Lab, on the second floor he never knew, but he made quite sure that it came to no harm as we carried it back to street level. They really were the great days of university when students and staff had a mutual respect for each other based on a love of their chosen subject.

Chelsea being a member of the even-then gargantuan London University, we had access to a multitude of libraries and intercollegiate lectures. The learning curves were steeped in the joy of discovery and it was here that I became a workaholic. The sharing of knowledge was fun, and has been ever since, and there was also the challenge of a degree to be won. With the Natural History Museum but a walk away, wet days would find me with my sandwiches (prepared fresh every day by Mum) among all those 'lonely' people who seemed to spend such days just sitting in the museum. Some would talk and share the great knowledge they had gleaned from that great cathedral about the process of creative evolution. Others just sat like the statue of Darwin and smiled far away smiles.

On fine days a walk in the other direction took me to Chelsea Physic Garden where the bell pull at the side gate summoned a gardener, complete with green baize apron, who would let bona fide students in to wander among the ordered beds or keep warm in the stove houses in winter.

Bentham and Hooker wrote their *British Flora*, first published in 1800, as a pre-breakfast relaxation, but by the 1950s, the hefty Clapham, Tutin and Warburg *Flora of the British Isles* was the standard work and, along with Rosemary, became my constant companion. At last Rosemary's mum had given her permission for us to holiday together, youth hostelling of course with no possibility of hanky panky in non-wardened situations, and so it was that the three of us set out on a Scottish trip that was to seal my fate as a field botanist and ecologist.

We took the train to Spean Bridge, went on by bus and then started to walk under angry skies to Balmacara Hostel twenty miles away. Arriving soaked to the skin, way past check-in time, and used to the ultra strict regime in English establishments of the same sort, we entered with trepidation, but there was no need to worry. A ceilidh was still in full swing, led by a kilted warden. The drying room was a rack over the cooking range and the dormitories were Nissan huts made of corrugated iron. These also served as an alarm clock of ear shattering proportions, as we discovered at seven the following morning when the warden ran the length of the building dragging his stick along the roof.

Our first tin of Ambrosia Creamed Rice was washed down with smoky tea and we were on our way, discovering that along with the flora came that most irritating part of the ecology of Scotland, midges. Despite them, and the rain, the next ten days were a voyage of total bliss and discovery. We were in love and we fell in love with the landscapes of the west coast. Every mile of the way had something new to offer and there was the clearest of water, clearer than anything we had ever seen before. This was before the days of plastic rubbish, and no fish farms or overfishing had marred the interest of the strandline and the rock pools. Likewise overgrazing by sheep was a thing of the europhile future.

Craig Youth Hostel was a long walk from the nearest road, mile after glorious mile across rolling bogland, replete with a wonderful leafy liverwort *Pleurozia purpurea,* that typified what I later learned was one of the world's rarest types of vegetation. Here in the wettest part of Britain the whole landscape was swathed with a magical coat of many colours. A living tapestry was nurtured by the rain and woven by *Sphagnum*: a group of bog mosses in which my life's work was about to become immersed, and a Latin name that would one day become my e-mail address. I can think of no more beautiful place in the world: mountain peaks and headlands swathed with *Sphagnum* and collaged with bog rosemary, deer sedge and sweet gale, with distant views of white horses on a dark blue sea.

Ullapool Hostel was a spotlessly clean white-washed building on the quayside with a welcome, though stern, as great as the vistas to the Summer Isles. The vision of the founders of the YHA must not be underestimated; they not only opened up the wonders of the world to people young and old but gave them the privilege of staying in buildings that were a key part of the landscape heritage. We sat on the bench beside the entrance, enveloped in each others arms and the presence of the highlands and islands. On we went to Stac Polidah, where we climbed with golden eagles, to Loch Sciornascaig to witness great herds of deer swimming from island to island, and finally across the Tralagil

Limestones towards Cape Wrath and the western expanses of the Flow country. We held hands and learned plants every step along the way and would have carried on forever. Despite the fact that those particular holidays came to an end, we have continued to do that for almost fifty years.

Apart from his brass microscope – a Ross no less – one of my dad's most prized possessions, and one of the books we had been allowed to read on Sundays, was *The Wonders of Creation*, a series of travelogues by famous explorers. So, when a College prize of £30 was offered for an essay on 'to where would you travel if you had that sum to spend', mine soliloquised on the fact that I would follow in the footsteps of Lord Dufferin to discover the wonders of Iceland for myself. To my surprise and delight I won and set to planning the itinerary. A stern 'no' from Mrs Froy scuppered the idea that Rosemary would accompany me, but she lent me her Girl Guide tent and, as John Raybould had expressed a desire to come on the trip, I booked two tickets on the MV *Gullfoss* from Leith to Reykjavik. John had been great company on our French trip and I was looking forward to seeing the wonders of creation through his Buddhist mindset. Sadly, poor results in his first-year exams meant re-sits, and made the month-long trip impossible for him. I thought I was going to be on my own, and then the bombshell came. Dad arrived home from the shop and announced that he had got an extra two weeks' holiday and was coming with me. If it had been Mum, it would not have been a surprise, but it was an entirely different matter with Dad, who as a schoolboy was wrapped in brown paper underneath his school uniform to keep him warm in winter, and had never before ventured outside England.

I must admit that I tried to put him off; the thought of my always precise, besuited, hair-never-out-of-place Dad walking across Iceland just didn't bear thinking about. I tried all ploys: what about Crown Road Mission? – don't you think you should take Mum away on holiday? – you will get soaking wet and freeze to death – all to no avail. Mum was even on his side: 'It's your father's fiftieth birthday soon, time he did something he really wants to do.' How could I say no? So, it was off to Black's of Greenock to buy boots and a Grenfell jacket, and to Proop's for an ex-Army rucksack, and then there we were standing in Princes Street in Edinburgh, both wondering what we were about to let ourselves in for.

The Pentland Firth in approaching gale force winds soon sorted the wheat from the chaff and, as we were in steerage class, there was no hiding the fact. I retired to my top bunk followed by fatherly remonstrations that 'sea sickness, it's all in the mind'. Ten minutes later a very green face appeared over the end of the bunk and a sickly voice said, 'No it's not.'

Morning broke with the sea still doing its unlevel best to sink the ship, but up we went to be faced with our first smorgasbord breakfast. To be honest there were very few other people who had made it and some of the crew were not in the best of shape, but Dad and I were determined to do the banquet proud. One of the other diners at that gargantuan feast (roll mops, salmon, smoked lamb, cheeses, black pudding, eggs boiled, fried, scrambled and poached, breads the taste of which we had never before enjoyed) was Mac, a plumber from Airdrie. He had been given his ticket by a friend who had had to pull out of the trip only a few days before and so he was on his own. We all tucked in with great gusto. Dad was a little more restrained in his choice of fare but stuck into the boiled eggs. Half an hour later Neptune got his share as we both fed the fishes somewhere off the coast of the Orkneys.

Meals came and went in quick succession as the *Gullfoss* made her way towards our goal. Our first glimpse of land was of the Westmann Islands from which a swarm of small boats appeared like magic to trade duty free wares. Then, as we moved into the lee of the Reykjanes Peninsular, we saw the first signs of volcanism, steam rising from the ground, one of the many wonders of this land of ice and fire.

Reykjavik was, from the distance, a skein of coloured clapboard houses separated from the black beach by the dark green of the maritime fringe vegetation. The magnificent backdrop was the Eskjanes volcano, rising black and white like some gigantic Orca beached by tectonic forces of the past and left fresh frozen to protect the capital from the icy winds of the north.

As we stood on the top deck, with the ship slipping through the dead calm water of the harbour, that skein of colour slowly resolved into a busy port for trade, fishing and whaling. Today, having been on more anti-whaling rallies than I care to remember, it seems strange that in the fifties Pathe Gazette regularly screened news of the modern-day Ahabs who braved the dangers of the deep on factory ships to win the rich harvest of oil and spermaceti.

After signing in at the British Embassy we walked around the town to try to buy some paraffin for our primus and found the language quite a barrier. Even at the chemist's, where Dad came into his own, we were first offered castor oil, but eventually, all fuelled up, we set out on the road towards Thingvellir. There was no need to hitch, for the first lorry that came along stopped and we were invited to climb up on the back. At a turn in the road the driver stopped again and, pointing us in the right direction, rumbled off on a side road. By then dusk was gathering, so we decided to pitch tent and brew up for the night.

Sleep was not far away and I soon joined in with Dad's sonorous snores, but a few hours later, I was awoken by a different noise, the chattering of his teeth. Despite the fact that he had a blanket held in with blanket pins, his sleeping bag was too thin so I peeled mine off and made him use both of them. He slept like a log and I, well, I got up early, and it was as I was making a cup of tea that a tousled head of hair appeared at the tent door. I had of course known him for twenty years, but it was the first time I had ever realised that his hair was naturally curly. He explained that, when he joined Boots such frivolity was frowned upon, so he had conjured up his own hair oil in the dispensary and always toed the straight line.

The rising sun soon warmed us up as we made our way to the valley that had been the site of the Althing, the first parliament in the world, perhaps the only real parliament in the world, one of complete democratic subsidiarity, for the whole population were expected to attend to discuss the problems and work out the solutions. A day was not long enough to explore that seat of ancient wisdom, with its deep volcanic cracks filled with the crystal clear water into which aeons of travellers had tossed coins for luck. We did our best to do justice to it all, and pitched camp that night in the shelter of the scrub birch. The only other person we saw was the local priest who came over for a chat and, taking pity on our meagre fare, departed to return with a gigantic cod. Fresh it was, but not the easiest thing to cook for breakfast in a billy can.

Then it was off towards the interior. The first time the path crossed a stream, Dad sat down and removed his boots and socks and paddled across, drying his feet with care on the other side. Two or three crossings later he just waded in without a grumble and carried on. A wider river appeared to be a little more of a problem because Dad couldn't swim, but a local complete with two ponies came to the rescue. Indicating that we should wait, he disappeared across the river, returning about half an hour later with another pony which ferried Dad across, leaning into the current. The farmer then led us back to his substantial farmhouse, set in the bright green homefield with his sheep still grazing out on the hills. There we were treated to a great meal of smoked lamb and black bread and given the barn in which to sleep. The farmer's wife was German and so we could communicate a little and were told how, by manipulating the water table in the meadows, they could coax a better crop from the land.

Mac had by then caught us up and from then on, we were a threesome. We planned to go to the Great Geyser and then on to climb Mount Hekla. As we walked I would point out the flowers that lined our route and Dad would tell me about their uses in herbal medicine: bear berry was for menstrual pains, ergot, infecting some of the sedges, was a potent abortificant, things that were never mentioned at home. We even talked about perhaps one day writing a book about it all. All of a sudden my Dad was talking to me man to man. He told me of his disenchantment with the way the role of a pharmacist as part of the National Health Service was changing, relegated to one of routine management, the downhill slide towards the anonymity of the drugstore and beyond. To my amazement he also told me of his disenchantment with the sectarianism of Christianity, saying that he longed to be able to worship anywhere he chose. It was there and then that I confided the fact that the wonders of creation had both lined and paved my road to Damascus and wondered why there was any need for so many branches of one religion. I also said that when I got married I wanted a church ceremony and he suggested that I joined the Anglican Church, which I did. In actual fact, and much to my surprise, Dad and I were confirmed together.

Once at the Great Geyser, which is still for me one of the most strangely beautiful places in the world, we immediately went to the Strokkur and, as Lord Dufferin had advised, threw in a clod of turf to make it erupt. To our chagrin nothing happened, so we dangled our can of baked beans into the gently simmering water as a voice from behind us announced itself as belonging to Helgi Frau Brenner, an amiable Icelander who seemed to be a fount of knowledge about all local matters. Among other things he told us the Strokkur had not worked for many years having been blocked up by idiots like us chucking things in. He also told us that the next day the Great Geyser was going to be doctored to make it perform for the Bolshoi Ballet, who were on a visit.

The next afternoon, lo and behold a coach arrived in a cloud of dust to disgorge the Bolshoi who disappeared into the hotel for lunch. As the whole company were swathed in fur coats with hoods that hid their faces from public view, it was impossible to recognise them. We lesser mortals stood in the wings as enormous bags of what looked like soap flakes were then poured into the bowl of the Great Geyser and as soon as the water retreated down the funnel the Corps de Ballet were called to witness the spectacle. Three times this happened in vain before the imminence of the evening performance back in Reykjavik stopped play and the bus whisked them off. No sooner had their dust settled in the distance than the water retreated down the funnel and this time she started to blow; we had the full performance all to ourselves.

Our main objective was to climb Iceland's most famous volcano Hekla and so the three of us set off further into the interior, taking in the pounding majesty of the great waterfall Gullfoss en route. Though cold at night the autumn weather was kind to us and we made good speed, Mac and I lending a helping hand to Dad who was not used to walking so many miles every day. After many detours along the route, at last we made it to a magical hanging valley within easy reach of the summit route. 'Magical' is an inadequate word; there towering above us the majesty of tectonic forces in the raw were enough to take your breath away. Cinders and scoria spilling down from the summit had created a harsh desert of new rock and debris waiting to be colonised by plants or reshaped by the next eruption, only time would tell. Apocalypse and resurrection, a wrap-around picture book of revelation – fresh lava flowed like gnarled fingers of destruction, reaching down from the mouth of hell itself, cradling this green and pleasant land in which sheep were safely grazing and in which we would sleep that night.

As the evening drew to a close our valley was filled with cloud spilling down from the volcano, enveloping us in a soggy blanket. The last red-gold rays of the sun lingered on, lighting up the droplets, bejewelling the gossamer strung by a myriad spiders between the autumn tints. We decided to sleep in the hayloft of a nearby barn, the main floor of which was already filled with sheep bedding down for the night. With a couple of hundred woolly radiators below us our stone walled bedroom soon became a sauna and we dropped off to sleep. Sometime in the early hours Dad woke me up in a bit of a panic, saying that something was crawling over his face. The beam of the torch revealed a mass of tiny spiders doing just that. Knowing his horror of arachnids in any shape or form, I switched off the torch and assured him there was nothing there. He turned over and went to sleep.

The morning dawned bright and still, so Dad, perhaps fed up with walking many miles each day or entranced by the wonders of creation, decided to stay put and enjoy it while Mac and I set off for the summit. We were very low on food so our rations for the day were one large Spanish onion each. Dad was left with what remained of the porridge oats.

The higher we climbed the better the view – glaciers carving up the mountains that flanked the black cinder plains, themselves crossed by ancient lava flows with wisps of steam marking out the thinnest parts of the Earth's crust. The wind was getting up over the summit as we took shelter in the crater and ate our onions gazing down in awe at the great hollow left by the most recent cataclysm. The view from the top was primaeval in the extreme, volcanic peaks hidden by glacial ice which took on the colour of the sky in its daily round of moods – a wind-blown kaleidoscope of blues of every hue, greens, greys and, as the day drew on, silvers, golds, pinks and reds. Then, with the sun sinking towards the horizon, we turned and ran all the way back down the screes, braking in the sand and cinders when the going got too much out of control. Dad was waiting, tea on the boil, and I have never seen him looking happier and in better health. His Bible lay open on the ground and I am sure that he had found here the sacredness of natural places; his only regret was that Mum had not been with him to witness this heaven on Earth.

Perhaps more than any other, that well-worn Bible made me keep faith with the roots of my religious upbringing. On the way home I found it lying on his bunk on the ship. It was Mum's Bible he had carried with him and inside was a slip of paper on which were written special verses.

With no food left in our rucksacks, we tore ourselves away from the magic of that valley and started the long trek back to Reykjavik, following the stragglers of the autumn bird migration on their way to warmer climes. They appeared more sensible than we, for they only flew when the wind was helping them along. Hunger is a strange thing and we soon found that tightening your belt does help. However, the best thing was to do your best to think about anything other than food and there was a lot to keep botanical minds engrossed. The long silvery plumes of the fruits of mountain avens were everywhere and the dwarf willows were in full fruit. Soon we came across great swathes of bilberries and down on our knees we went to browse their tart goodness. Whether it was simply eating too much on an empty stomach or whether there were crow berries in the patch I don't know, but in a bitter wind we found ourselves with rampant diarrhoea and no shelter. Our saviours were some local fumaroles puffing warm steam out into the cold night air, nature's own self-heated bidets, which turned this mal de terrain episode into a bottom warming experience.

With two days to go before the *Gullfoss* was homeward bound, we were strapped for cash except for a £5 note. We decided to seek the shelter of the Salvation Army Hostel where we were made very much at home. The luxury of a hot shower allowed me to soak off my string vest, which I had slept in for far too long – heaven indeed. Knowing that hard foreign currency was a very sought-after commodity in Iceland, Mac and I decided to try our luck at the nightclub and see if we could find someone who would enter into a little bit of foreign exchange. Just as we were about to sell to the highest bidder an enormous Polish fisherman lumbered into sight, screaming 'Juden' while gesticulating at me. It was no time to try to explain my distaste of apartheid of any sort and, as all routes of escape were blocked by a seething mass of humanity, the time had come to stand up and fight with this drunk armed with a bottle. Suddenly, an even larger apparition appeared behind my would-be assailant and, twisting his arm behind his back, frog-marched him to the door. It was the nightclub bouncer and when he had dealt with the fisherman he returned and politely introduced us to the official moneychanger – himself.

The night was still young and with some local currency in our pocket we took in a little more of the scene before making our way back to the hostel which we found was all locked up for the night. It was by now very cold and the only lighted doorway was that of the police station. Mac led the way in and did his best to ask if we could stay there in the warm until morning. To our surprise we were ushered into a cell, which contained two bunks and a spittoon. Even more to our surprise, the snoring form of the Polish fisherman occupied one of the bunks. We shared the other bunk and hoped that our companion wouldn't wake before 7 a.m., the time our hostel would be open for breakfast. Thank goodness he didn't. Likewise, Dad had had a good night's sleep and hadn't even missed us. The journey home was again full of smorgasbord delight in the company of a bevy of Peter Scott fans, bird watchers on their annual migration back to Britain.

It wasn't all work at Chelsea and I quickly became involved with the entertainment department of the students' union and found myself on stage once again as the Mermaid of the Lamp in the Christmas pantomime. Well I did write the script. It must have been a success for

I was press-ganged into standing for a position on the students' union.

The hustings not only took over the college but also much of Kings Road, and we got Jimmy Edwards of *Whacko* fame, who lived just around the corner, and Tony Armstrong Jones to sign our campaign posters. I ended up on the entertainments committee and treacled and feathered in the fountain outside Peter Jones in full view of a London bobby who, spotting my semi-naked state, signalled that I immerse myself immediately, before going off to get help. I then became perhaps the original Chelsea Streaker as, shedding feathers, I ran back to college.

My highlight in the entertainment world came at the summer ball when, running short of funds, we overstretched ourselves by booking Chris Barber and Humphrey Lyttelton with the Temperance Seven filling in. We saved the day by closing all the windows and made a roaring profit on the bar, eventually selling the water that the beer glasses were rinsed in.

Intercollegiate war was mainly on the rugby pitches and on the river. The Chelsea eight's boat had become a little warped with time, and in consequence our team usually corkscrewed in last. However we did play our part in the great rag that was filmed by Granada, the then new ITV. It was a daft idea fraught with all sorts of problems from the start. Chelsea was going to pinch Battersea's mascot and vice versa, and then they would be returned in neutral territory on the middle of Chelsea Bridge. Of course, by the time the handover was scheduled, Sir John Cass College had stolen Battersea's mascot from us and so the handback descended into mayhem. I, along with a number of others, ended up in the river and then got roped into the taskforce who were going to uphold Chelsea's honour by pinching Cass's mascot, a large fossil fish. Unfortunately, it was kept on the second floor and was joined to a large block of concrete. The A team got access to the treasured object and the B team waited in the road to catch it, the engine of the get-away car all revved up. Thank God they didn't throw the mascot out of the window, but, as that was their only escape route, out they came minus certain articles of attire having been debagged in traditional fashion. Some of the Cass students must have thought that we had got the trophy for a chase ensued which ended up in a fracas with a taxi in Parliament

Square. Names were exchanged as the policeman explained to by-standers that students would be students.

Terms flew by and the time came when I had to decide on the topic of my research project, an important part of an honours degree in botany. Under the growing influence of Francis Rose, and in the light of a summer walking around Scotland, I decided to look at the ecology of one of Britain's rarest plants, the Rannoch rush.

The following summer, Dad joined Rosemary and me to stay at Loch Ossian Youth Hostel where from the nearby station we could take the high road south to Rannoch Moor, the home of this elusive plant. The waiting room at Rannoch station came complete with a harmonium, for it doubled as a refuge for the soul on Sundays. The Rannoch Arms close by was a welcome refuge of another sort, well stocked with warming spirits for when the rain, lifeblood of the acid bogland, became too much for mere lowland Londoners.

Day after day we charted the distribution of *Scheuchzeria palustris* and measured water tables and water flows across its last-stand habitat in Britain using an old barograph specially modified for the purpose by Dad. The ever-changing pattern of clouds and the light on distant Schehallion and across the Black Corries almost made me throw in the academic sponge and take on the job of local barman.

There was a train back to Ossian in the late afternoon but, if we missed it, it was a pleasant walk along the rail track, although the midge population in the shelter of the snow sheds that protected the most exposed parts of the line could be murder. It was on such peregrinations that I came to realise the wealth of life, both plant and animal, that enjoyed living on and along the track. Indeed the cuttings and embankments had themselves added variety to the terrain, creating new habitats for a great variety of wildflowers and wildlife, and even the Rannoch Rush had benefited where the embankment had helped to keep the mire even wetter.

Ossian Hostel was a great place, marred only by the job of emptying the chemical toilet. As the handle of the receptacle had long since rotted away you had to clutch it in both hands as you staggered across the uneven peat to deposit its contents into the aptly named bog hole.

Evenings were spent collating the day's data, chatting with other hostellers and taking part in long singsongs. All too soon the end of the vacations loomed and it was back to college and into top gear, for finals were only two terms away.

The terms of our university grants did not allow undergraduates the privilege of being married, but by mid-1957 the possibility was only a year away, so I went shopping for a ring. Shopping of any sort has always been anathema to me, so it was with great trepidation that I set out on a tour of relevant establishments in the West End. What is more, with only £28 in the bank, the prospects seemed somewhat limited. However, having decided to blow the lot, I asked the assistant in a shop just off Oxford Circus to show me rings within my stated range of £30. A tray was set out on the black baize cloth and I immediately chose a gorgeous single diamond. With profuse apologies I was told that it had got in the wrong tray and its price was £900, so I settled for a zircon set on a simple band of white gold.

I had already worked out the place where I was going to finalise the proposal – in the middle of a sphagnum bog on Thursley Common, at Thor's Stone which had played a very special part in *The Broom Squire*. I wanted it to be a complete surprise so on 3 November 1957 we set off on a sunny but cold day to do a little bit of botanising in one of our favourite places.

The heathland was in its autumn perfection with a backdrop of pines loaded with cones and the Devil's Jumps, from where old Nick himself had removed the stone from his shoe and flicked it into the bog. Having completed our list of plants, I suggested that we traversed the bog to see the famous stone that was meant to turn round if ever the local church clock struck thirteen. I had planned to sit Rosemary on the stone and pop the question, all very romantic – and it was, except for the fact that heavy rain had swollen the bog waters, making the approach to the chosen trysting stone even more difficult than usual. I did eventually lift her on to the stone, but only because I had to, because at that moment she had stepped into the even deeper pool that surrounded it. 'Please will you marry me?' said I, proffering the ring in its now soaking cardboard box. She smiled her angelic smile and we kissed. I don't know how long that particular kiss lasted, but the next hour of our engaged life was spent with me rushing up and down trailing her jeans in the heather, in an attempt to get them dry enough for the homeward journey.

Once home, I had to ask Mrs Froy formally if I could marry her daughter and I was not looking forward to it. Rosemary's aunt Jane and cousin Audrey were firmly of the opinion that she should marry into the professions, a medic or a vet at least. Fortunately Rosemary's Granny was firmly on my side, so the answer was 'yes'. It seemed ridiculous to go on calling her Mrs Froy, and I could never bring myself to call her by her Christian name, so she became 'Other Mother'. We celebrated the fact with a beano – spam fritters toasted in Harvey's Bristol Cream.

Although they must have known that we would get married one day, my Mum and Dad did question the wisdom of what they called 'rushing into important things'. How could we make ends meet on two research students' grants? Rosemary, the business woman that she still is, came to my rescue with a cash flow plan in which even Dad could find no flaw.

By now our dreams of a life together were beginning to gel. School teaching seemed a distinct possibility and we dared to visualise the day when our combined salaries would top the £1,000 per year mark and we would be able to start to travel, even go skiing. There were also other possibilities if we got good enough degrees: research at home or in foreign climes. we were very excited, the world was ours as we scanned the job adverts in *Nature* and were both agreed that I should try my luck at the post of forest botanist in Brunei.

I was interviewed and offered the job, which I accepted with great jubilation. We were sent reams of instructions about what married couples should expect of life in the tropics and what we should plan to take with us, including a wickerwork perambulator and supply of terry towelling nappies. There is no getting away from the fact that we were excited, but it was not to be. Trouble in Indonesian waters brought a letter from the Foreign Secretary, stating that all luxury postings in the area had been cancelled. I never could understand how a forest botanist could ever be considered a luxury in what was, even then, an oil-rich country covered with pristine rain forest that included the most important swamp forests in the world.

Another application went in to the Nature Conservancy Council, for the post as Regional Officer for the South-East of England. Even though I was a recent convert into the field of plant ecology, I had cut my teeth in the region, knew the area well, and really wanted the job. The interview was impressive, with the legendary figure of Max Nicholson in the chair. An argument broke out in the ranks of the panel concerning the role of snails in the ecology of bogs. I suppose my remarks that most bogs were too acid to support a diversity of molluscs didn't help my cause too much, and, much to my annoyance, they offered the job to another candidate, fresh back from a spell in Africa, who didn't even know the region. I was even more annoyed when, out of the blue, they asked me to apply for a similar post in the west Midlands, about which I then knew little or nothing. I declined the offer in a somewhat acerbic manner, but became great friends with the guy who eventually applied and got the job, Tom Pritchard, who became a visionary leader of Nature Conservation in Wales.

Our three undergraduate years had flown past and the agony of finals was upon us. The vivas were bad enough, especially when my interrogator Roy Clapham said that I had spelt *Scheuchzeria* wrong in my dissertation. The only answer I could come up with was, 'Well, I copied it out of your *Flora*.' The idea of being able to do justice to all you had learned over three years' hard study in just a few hours was ludicrous in the extreme.

The examination halls were furnished with skylights and the heat inside was tropical, so the final bell, that summoned you out of this ultimate of academic hells into the cool heaven of the gardens of the Natural History Museum, just around the corner, was more than welcome. Lying on the grass, I contemplated my now official place in the Natural History scene and hoped that gainful employment was lurking somewhere within its aegis. Ed Cossins, Ann Wood and I, the only three Honours Botany candidates from Chelsea that year, celebrated the end of our last six hours of torture by going to see the film *South Pacific*. Although we kept in touch, in effect we then went our own ways: Ed to do research that led to an academic career in Canada, Ann to be a highly successful teacher and a fantastic Mum and, well, you are reading all about what happened to me.

The agony of waiting for the results was tempered only by a lovely summer and a trip to Flatford Mill on fieldwork. Returning to the lawn flanked by Willy Lot's Cottage of Constable fame, I found that there, taking tea on the greensward, was a cross-section of the hierarchy of British Botany: Professors Clapham and Tutin and Hef Warburg, co-authors of that *Flora of the British Isles*, and Harry Godwin, the father of plant ecology and the study of the history of vegetation. It was in that august company that Francis Rose told me, off the record, that I had got a good enough degree to get a grant to do research with him at Bedford College for Women. Rosemary had by then already got her results and a place to work with Maud Godward at QMC, so our lives were set for another three years commuting up to London.

First, however, it was off to the Suffolk–Norfolk border for detailed study of a series of fenland remnants that were even then losing all their rare plants. Was this the natural process of succession that would eventually turn the open fens into alder carr and woodland, or was there some other reason for their rapid drying out? Using the same apparatus we had employed on Rannoch Moor, we recorded the changing levels of the ground-water table in the Redgrave, South Lopham fenland complex. These showed strange fluctuations that appeared totally inexplicable, until we discovered that a borehole owned by the Essex and Suffolk Water Company was on the edge of the fen. After asking them to shut down the pumps, our recorder responded with a rise in the fenland water table. The results were published by the Suffolk Natural History Society – my first scientific paper: '*The Waveney-Ouse Valley Fens of the Suffolk-Norfolk Border*' by David J. Bellamy and Francis Rose.

Towards the end of the paper we wrote, 'What of the future? We cannot rely on the Coypu already established at Weston to keep the fens open; conservation and a well-executed management plan is the only answer.' The thought of ever closing the borehole never entered our heads, and we certainly couldn't rely on the depredations of that introduced rodent, for a well-organised eradication programme was then underway to remove its presence from the face of Britain. Little did we think that forty-one years on, the once-native Taipan horse would be reintroduced from Poland to help clear the trees from those fens – the first step in a visionary management plan, instituted by a partnership of the local Wildlife Trusts, English Nature and the water company – let alone that I would be invited on 7 June 1999 to turn off the pumps for the last time, before the borehole was relocated at the expense of the European Union. This was the first time that a public water supply had been moved in the cause of conservation. You can guess that I had my fingers firmly crossed as I turned the tap. If the conclusions of our research were right, the recently gazetted National Nature Reserve was about to get a new lease of life. Thank God, it worked.

I had my degree; I had a grant to read for a PhD to be entitled 'Ecological Studies on some European Mires', under the tutelage of Francis Rose at Bedford College. All I had to do was go along for an interview and impress L.J. Audus, Professor of Botany. I had already heard him lecture on his adventures on the Burmah Road, where, along with another prisoner, a mycologist, he had helped keep their platoon moderately healthy by using some of their meagre rations to culture vitamin rich yeast to supplement their diet. However, as the Professor was away I found myself being interviewed by Douglas Spanner, reader in plant physiology.

I walked in, wearing my one and only all-purpose suit, and was immediately handed a large transformer brimful of oil to hold as we got down to the real point of my visit. This truly amazing man had just taken delivery of a second-hand electron microscope and was busy servicing it, hence the transformer. I must have made a good enough impression for I was shown into the lab in which I would work, a lab occupied by a multinational group of research students, all working on some aspect of growth hormones. I was going to be the odd one out, a mere ecologist.

Professor Audus was an inspirational team leader and put up with me in his lab until my efforts overflowed my bench space. At that point I was relegated to the lab in the corner of the botanical garden where I could spread ecological pandemonium, to the amusement of the local population of mallards. An important part of my sojourn in the garden was scooping baby ducklings out of the ornamental pond and returning them to worried mums waiting on the big lake in the park.

My new routine was set: up on the train from Cheam to be joined by Fluff on Sutton Station, then fond farewells at Victoria as she headed once more to Mile End Road and I to Regent's Park. There I was very soon met by several hundred ducks that all knew I arrived with lots of bread. At that time Rosemary and I looked in vain at a super three-storey house with an iron balcony on the corner opposite the park entrance. The price tag of £13,000 was impossible, even on our combined grants embellished by payment for demonstrating practical work to the students. In hindsight what an investment that would have been.

As soon as the college students' vacations came, which meant no more demonstration duties which were so crucial to our cash flow, my great see-the-world travel plan was put into action. The title of my PhD included the words 'some European Mires', so it was off on fieldwork along two transects: one, which, at least in my mind, stretched from the far north of Scotland to the south of France, the other from the far west of Ireland to the borders of Russia. I don't suppose I realised it at the time, but I was becoming one of those dedicated academics who would spend his life being paid to follow his hobby – a play-as-you-earn workaholic whose ambition revolved around one thing: the ecology of wetlands. Fortunately for me, I could and still can look at the world through rose-coloured spectacles. What more can anyone ask of life? But, I don't think at that time either of us knew what we were letting ourselves in for.

9 HONEYMOON WITH NATURE

THE PHOTOGRAPHS IN the official album are perhaps the best way of remembering a wedding because they miss out all the preparations. Ours are dated 3 January 1959, and suffice to say it was a great day. Families and friends joined us in that communion of faith in Cheam Parish Church and then ate and drank well, before waving us off to the challenge of a new relationship. George Fluck, who had officiated as best man, then drove us to Haslemere where we were to spend the first two days of our honeymoon. We went via the Royal Hospital and Home for Incurables at Putney to visit Rosemary's father who was in the final stages of a life blighted by disseminative sclerosis. He was sitting up in bed, working on an intricate piece of basketwork with which he passed his time. We handed over flowers from Rosemary's bridal bouquet and some of his favourite pipe tobacco and were on our way.

Not long after leaving Guildford our car was enveloped in a pretty impressive snowstorm and at one point we thought we wouldn't make it, but George delivered us safe and sound to the hotel. Next day, the whole of the surrounding countryside was buried in a deep blanket of snow. We walked out across Hindhead and down into the Devil's Punchbowl, leaving double tracks in the pristine white, then on to

Thursley Bog and Thor's Stone; this time the going was easy for everything was frozen solid.

On the Monday we set off by train to go on the honeymoon proper among the bogs of western Ireland. Arriving in Killarney, we took a taxi to the Muckross Park Hotel, where we were the only guests. What a welcome; roaring fires in the dining room, hot water bottles in the bed (not that we needed them for we were just getting used to double occupancy) and the luxury of linen sheets. I was hooked, so much so that many years later, when asked by Roy Plumley what luxury I would take along with my chosen discs on to the desert island, my answer was 'a pair of linen sheets', and I meant it.

Despite the sheets and the legality of cohabitation, we were up early to walk to the Meeting of the Waters, a magical spot for tourists but for two botanists a wonderland of plants of every shape and size. What's more we had it all to ourselves and everything was covered in frost, a very unusual occurrence, despite the fact that then most scientists were beginning to talk about the next ice age being on its way. The most famous plant in the area is *Arbutus unedo*, the strawberry tree, which finds its only natural Irish stronghold here. It is a member of the heather family, and ranges all the way down the western seaboard of Europe into the Black Sea, sticking close to the wet, warm, maritime climate. It was along this essentially frost-free highway that the Celtic people travelled to discover and develop the riches of Hibernia.

The natural riches of temperate rain forest dripping with woody lianas and epiphytes were there to greet us. The lianas are only honeysuckle and old man's beard and the epiphytes mainly mosses, liverworts and lichens, but what they lack in size they certainly make up for in luxuriance. Every trunk, bough and branch is festooned and even the twiggyest of twigs are etched with a tiny lichen aptly called *Graphis scripta,* for its tiny black thallus looks like ancient hieroglyphics standing out from the bark.

Tiny pieces of each were collected for identification as we made our way among the oak trees and on into the dark shade of the yew woods for which the area is also famed. Many agree that the name Eire has its roots in the Yew Isle and at least two of the five great tribal trees of

Ireland were said to be yews. What is more, many of the earliest wooden artefacts found preserved in Ireland's famous peat bogs are made of the hard durable timber of this tree. It was a wonderful experience and we could have spent the whole fortnight wandering through the Muckross Woods, searching out the tiny mosses and liverworts, some of which rank among the rarest plants of Europe, but there was work to be done. After all I was meant to be studying the peat bogs of Europe and here we were among some of the most famous of them all.

Ryan's Car Hire got us mobile, although the car in question was a not-so-new Morris Minor and the icy state of the roads did their best to keep the secrets of the bogs safe with the little people. At one point we found ourselves going backwards with the brakes full on as we tried to negotiate the bends up to Ladies View. The plan was to go from the very wet coast of Kerry, inland to the drier areas, looking at the flora of the famous red or raised bogs. These have some of the strangest and rarest types of vegetation to be found anywhere in the world, much rarer than the tropical rain forests, the destruction of which we were only then beginning to worry about. Each bog was a great dome of peat rising up many metres above the local ground-water table. In consequence the plants that grow upon the surface are isolated from the mineral rich soils beneath and so have to rely on minerals supplied by the rain. Close to the coast the rain is charged with sea spray and so is richer in sodium, magnesium, calcium and chloride than it is further inland, a fact that was thought to determine some of the differences in the floristic make-up of the unique bogs of Ireland. Well, that was the theory, so off we went, notebooks in hand and a goodly supply of plastic bottles in the boot.

The bottles had been specially cleaned with deionised water so that I could collect samples of water from each bog ready for chemical analysis. Catastrophe – at the first stop we found that our supply of bottles had been got at by our wedding guests. Each one was full to the brim with confetti. So we sat on a bog hummock, still fresh frozen in the morning rime and emptied out the confetti, burying it carefully in the peat. I didn't note down the exact location of that particular bog but the evidence of our presence will be there forever, a cache of coloured paper flakes preserved in the peat. I have often wondered what some future peatland archaeologist would make of it when the radiocarbon tests date this particular find to circa AD 1959.

Sadly, the peat from many of the raised bogs which even then stretched from the Shannon clear across Ireland, almost to the outskirts of Dublin, has been, to use the proper word, won – cut away to be burned and turned into electricity, won for short-term warmth but lost to posterity. The more we travelled, the more we came across signs of this new phase of massive destruction. Bord na Mona's giant machines were everywhere, and railway tracks criss-crossed the moonscape cut-aways, carrying the dried peat to strategically placed power stations.

Our honeymoon bedroom was soon so full of drying specimens and labelled bottles waiting to be filled with water that the hotel gave us the one next door as well. As our store of empty sample bottles came to an end we knew it was time to return to London, where a short paper was written and submitted to *Nature*. It was titled 'Occurrence of *Schoenus nigricans* L. on Ombrogenous Peats'. This may not sound very romantic to the untutored ear but in today's speak, it would be equivalent to getting your wedding reported in *Hello* magazine, at least for a budding botanist. It was at this juncture that, for better or worse, I set myself a goal that one in ten of all the papers I ever published would be in this prestigious journal. I did write another much more important paper about these experiences, a letter to the *Irish Times*, setting out the fact that these were unique types of vegetation and that key habitats like Clara bog should be set aside for posterity as reserves. I don't think that my letter ever appeared in print, and it took a number of decades of indiscriminate destruction before Clara was sold back to the people of Ireland as a reserve, thanks to many other people who championed the cause of peatlands, including many people from Holland who, having destroyed all but one of their own raised bogs, took up the cause.

Rosemary and I were enjoying ourselves, we had lived within the aegis of our parents and the suburbs of London all our lives and, despite the fact that we loved and respected them dearly, the cork was off the bottle and the prospects of a lifetime together bubbled out. We had a home base of our own now, an upstairs flat almost opposite the swimming baths in Throwley Road, Sutton. Rosemary wanted to teach and the potential of an academic post at university was there for both of us. All that stood in the way was a PhD, the highest of academic awards.

Easter in the Cairn Gorms is always magical, but Easter there in 1960 was very, very special. Having decided that the best way to succeed in anything was to get a lot of practice, I had applied for a lectureship at Durham University – impossible I thought, but worth a try. To my surprise I got called for an interview and was of course very excited. Still the PhD had to be completed, however, and so it was we went into the field in Scotland over the holidays. Rosemary and Dad had joined me as field assistants again and we were staying at Killin Youth Hostel. Leaving them to enjoy the countryside for a day, I boarded the train to Durham via Edinburgh. In my mind's eye Durham was a big industrial city and so I arrived early in the morning to something of a shock. I asked the porter, 'Where is the University?' He led me out to the front of the station and waving his arm in the grandest of arcs across that fantastic heritage skyline said, 'There.' On my enquiring where I might be able to get a wash and brush-up and change into my interview suit, which was neatly folded in my rucksack, he suggested the Swimming Baths.

Off I went and got ready to give it my best at the interview. Of that actual event my mind remains a bit of a blank, except for being asked to explain my research and whether I would be willing to run field trips and teach courses in plant anatomy and biochemistry. I was told to wait after the interview, as we would be told the results there and then. I must have made the right impression for I was called back in and told that I had got the job, with a salary of £850 per annum. Evidently there was a long pause because Professor Valentine then asked, quite pointedly, 'Do you accept the post?' Scout's honour, I had not expected to get an interview let alone be offered the job, so I was in somewhat of a quandary. I was halfway through my PhD and so was Rosemary, and I was a Londoner through and through. 'Eerrr,' I said, 'yes please,' and shook hands.

I was then whisked off and introduced to the staff and research students, all ten of them, having tea in the herbarium. Jack Crosby was a geneticist and expert on the evolution of the primroses, Min Chalklin, an algologist with a passion for seaweeds. Geoff Banbury was a plant physiologist, and Pauline Watson a mycologist who studied the ecology of dung once it had been deposited on the ground. Of the research students, two became great friends, Trevor Elkington and Joe Harvey who were working on the flora of Upper Teesdale, which was even then under threat of a reservoir to slake the thirst of Teesside's heavy industry. It was like being reunited with a long lost family, a family all of whom shared one major interest, the wonderful world of plants. The father figure was David Valentine, an ex-Cambridge botanist of the old school who came complete with a pipe and a large family all of his own. I owe a great debt to those people, for not only did they make me welcome but broadened my horizons as to the fascination and the importance of being a botanist and eventually a father.

My excitement grew on the train journey back to Killin; I had got a job with a pension, I was a lecturer at a highly respected university and, despite the fact that I was on a sleeper, I lay awake all night. The attendant knocked me up as we steamed out of the stop before Killin and there I was bursting with the news. Dad was quite ecstatic and Rosemary seemed excited too as we drank to Durham with our cups of tea in the hostel kitchen. Then it was back to work on the PhD.

Things had of course changed dramatically. I was going to have to finish my doctorate from within the harness of a full-time teaching post. As for Rosemary, well she made the final sacrifice and decided to dump the call of a PhD and go straight into teaching. We talked endlessly about what sort of house we would be able to afford and what life would be like in Durham. Dad swelled with pride at the fact that I had a university post with a pension. It was all above our wildest dreams. En route home we drove our Austin A35 van down the east coast and visited the city that was to become our home for over twenty years. We sat in the lay-by on the old A1 and reflected on our future together as our lives moved into top gear. I had said yes, there was no looking back, and there was a lot of hard work to do before moving north.

At this point a fairy godmother came into my life in the guise of the British Council. My whole PhD had begun to revolve around the work of Stanislav Kulczynski, a Polish professor of geography, who had published a book about the Prypet Marshes in 1942. Thank goodness it had been translated into English. It seemed to answer many of the queries I had concerning the ecology of wetlands, and so I applied to the British Council for a scholarship to go and work with him. Lo and behold I found myself on a train with slatted wooden seats on a long-haul journey from the Hook of Holland to Poland. On arrival I was met by the Council's man in Warsaw, backed by a large black Warszawa car with chromium-plated flagstaffs on each side of the bonnet. To my amazement I was told that this was my car and my chauffeur for the duration of my stay and was whisked off to the Hotel Bristol. A hotel right out of an Agatha Christie novel, it had a glass lift and a concièrge with a stiff, though not so white collar. After checking in, I was introduced to Krzysztof Bitner, who was to accompany me on my travels, and we sat down to a breakfast of scrambled eggs and what I took to be a small glass of mineral water but it turned out to be vodka. I was going to consume a lot of both over the next few weeks as I very rapidly got used to Polish coffee and the pungent smoke of papariska.

Our travels took us first to Szczecin where we met Michael Jasnowski, another of Poland's great peatland experts. While studying the diverse estuarine wetlands which flanked the local shipyards a young man was pointed out by the name of Lech Walesa, who was even then creating waves around the port. Our main study was of the peatlands on the island of Wolin. Kulczynski joined us for a day and while the chauffeur collected wild strawberries for tea, we discussed my research programme in a mixture of very broken botanical German and English. Then it was on to Ruchiane in the Mazurian Lake district where work began in earnest.

Krzysztof was not only a mires man but also a keen fisherman, and so some of our work was carried out from a canoe, at one time towed along at great speed by a very large pike. I can tell you it was very large, for a great crowd of us dined well on it that night. The mires were absolutely classic and we had soon accumulated a great amount of floristic data ready for analysis once the maestro had rejoined us, but before this it was Midsummer's Night, a night that turned out to be a real Bacchanalian orgy which went on far into the next day. As far as I could understand the reason for all that happened was steeped in the heritage of man's relationship with Mother Nature.

The night started in a very noisy nightclub in Ruchiane, where we got into trouble with the landlord because our host accused him of adding water to the vodka, proving his point by failing to ignite it with a match. Emerging in an inebriated state, we wended our noisy way through the forest and sloshed our way through the wetlands. Then, at the witching hour, all the young ladies lit the candles that adorned their floral head dresses and floated them on to the surface of the lake. In went all the men, young, old and in-between, who all did their best to emulate Mark Spitz as they swam to retrieve their chosen's floral tribute. Why no one was drowned I do not know, but a good time was had by all.

The next day I met someone who spoke fluent English, a school-teacher from Cracow. We had a long talk about England, which he wished to visit, and about why I was in Poland. Halfway though the conversation he said, 'I don't think you know whose car you are riding about in.' 'Yes,' said I, 'it belongs to Stanislav Kulczynski, Professor of Geography at the University of Warsawa.' 'Yes,' came the reply, 'but he is also one of the Vice-Marszalek, Sejmu. Sejmu is the name of the Polish Parliament.' There was still a blank look on my face, so he translated, 'He is Vice President and Chairman of the Democratic Party, and that's his car you have been riding about in.' From then on I treated my mentor with even greater respect.

On our return to Warsaw I was told to take my passport along to the police station where they would issue an extension to my visa. Evidently the Professor was either enjoying himself being a botanist again or he was not satisfied with my progress and had arranged a trip to Zakopane on which he was going to join me for several days. I had to phone home and break the news to Rosemary who began to get some inkling of what the rest of her life was going to be like – Rosemary Bellamy, not a grass but a *Sphagnum* widow, or to bring it cruelly into modern perspective, though happily married, the hard-working head of a single-parent family. It sounds awful, but at that point I don't think either of us gave it a thought; we were beginning to live our lives together with a capital L for Love.

The Tatra Mountains were everything I had read about and more and with Kulczynski as my guide we soon amassed enough floristic data to demonstrate his method of statistical analysis, called Kulczynski Squares, a technique he had perfected while in prison during the war. Even then he was regarded as such an important man in Poland that, instead of sending him to the work camps, the Germans allowed him to continue to analyse the botanical data he had collected over a period of years working in the Prypet Marshes.

At last, satisfied with my progress, we ate a hearty dinner of venison and scrambled eggs and drank each other's health – and that of Tolpa, the father of the study of the ecology of mires in Poland, and just about every other famous botanist we could think of – not in common or garden vodka but in Warnolty, the spirit of the landscape, redistilled through Holy Grass, *Hierochloa odorata,* the favourite food of the bison I had been taken to see in the Bialoweja Forest.

1960 THE DECADES OF
INSTRUCTION 1980

10 FLOWER POWER AND THE
DURHAM COLLEGES

I HAD PROMISED Professor Valentine that I would return to Durham in the summer and help run the field trip, which I duly did. Arriving for our first real look round, we found St Mary's College full to overflowing so ended up in the sanatorium. We were getting ready for bed when the door opened and a tall young woman, one of the college's moral tutors, appeared asking what a man was doing in the room. Explanations followed and it was the first time I remember saying, 'I am a Don.'

This was also the first time I ever saw Holy Island and Upper Teesdale and I began to realise just how much I had to learn about the subject I would be teaching in just two months' time – two packed months, for I had a big field programme to complete in Germany as well, before the move up north.

By that time we were proud owners of a little grey Austin A35 van and it successfully carried us, our luggage and field equipment around the continent. Dad and Mum came out to help in the field and we stayed at the Hotel Hirsch Post in Kislegg while we were surveying the local mires. One fantastic day we left my mother labelling water bottles in the shade of the pines and surveyed our way across the dome of peat. Looking back we saw her surrounded by a herd of red deer. On our return, she showed us a trail of ants she had been watching and asked how it was that they knew biscuit crumbs were good to eat? She had been totally oblivious to the presence of the deer, in her own heaven on earth, sitting not beside the nest of an asp but not far from a nest of *Formica rubra*. We even got her up to the summit of the Nebelhorn, Germany's highest mountain, and took her to see Oberammergau before they had to return home.

Then it was in at the deep end, as I got down to teaching a full lecture load. Not finding the time to complete my PhD was perhaps the silliest thing I ever did because science, yes even the science of plant ecology, was beginning to change gear, thanks to the computer revolution that was sneaking around the corner. At that time, all I really needed to complete my research was my field and laboratory notebooks, a European Flora (Professor Valentine was a stalwart of a committee that was even then writing one) and, with Kulczynski's technique under my belt, a hand-cranked calculating machine. I should have got on with the job of finishing the thesis there and then, but life was full of new challenges: a new crop of some of the country's best young brains to bounce ideas off, every year, all in a bite sized university in which you had a fair idea who every one was and what they did. In the early sixties the whole faculty of science met for morning tea in a room in the West Building that housed the main lecture hall and Bill Fisher's department of geography. The whole science lab complex was then administered by one remarkable lady called Beatrice Hollingsworth, who later had a room with a blue ceiling decorated with gold stars just inside the main entrance. From there she kept an authoritarian eye on everyone, and the whole place ran on wheels oiled by her complete command of everything that was going on. When I joined Durham the main characters were Charlie Holmes of St Cuthbert's Society, Professor Hutchings, head of the music department and Geoff Banbury, botanist extraordinaire. Geoff's research focussed on the way moulds, mushrooms and toadstools orientate themselves with respect to gravity, light, humidity and sound. He was a gadgeteer and handyman without equal and so, if he wanted equipment, he simply got on and made it himself.

For the first three months of our sojourn in Durham we had a flat in Geoff's house, which we shared with him, his wife, four children and another lodger, an Icelandic librarian who aspired to be an opera singer. Thus we were thrown into academia at the deep end, removing soaking nappies from the one bath, waiting impatiently for some aria to grind to a climax in the toilet, and being called out to help fix the roof or the drains. The most hairy occasion was when a couple of slates came off the roof three storeys up and, being the tallest, I found myself swaying at the top of one ladder lashed to the top of another fully extended double ladder with a borrowed clothes line. My only comfort was that Derek Wilson from the maths department was wrapped around the junction of the two ladders, giving me a running commentary on what was going on down below.

On another occasion, when the sewers broke higher up Claypath, we had all Geoff's family and a number of students manning the manholes along the main road while Geoff poured a large quantity of vegetable colouring in at the top of the street in an attempt to track the exact source of the leak, which was flooding our cellars. We never did find out exactly where it was coming from, so we just pumped the cellar dry and plastered the floor and walls with waterproofing. Later, there was the time that we were invited to dinner to celebrate the installation of a sunken bath in the room above. Spectacularly, Geoff had omitted to complete the plumbing. Halfway through the meal the ceiling gave way with the weight of soapy water. Unruffled, Geoff's only remark was that it saved doing the washing up.

Before coming up to Durham we had scanned the Ordnance Survey map, seen the name Pity Me atop a small village to the north of the city, and decided there and then that it must be an ideal place in which to put down our roots. Closer inspection of the locale showed that it was slap bang on the Great North Road, and its name was appropriate, although it was reputedly derived from Petit Mere. We looked a little further afield, a few hundred yards to be exact, at 6 Witton Grove, a fully detached 3-bedroom bungalow, almost new, up on the market for £2,750, just on the outskirts of the city with open countryside at the back and the maternity hospital just down the road. This was just what the doctor ordered, for Rosemary and I dearly wanted a family of our own, and Dad and especially Mum couldn't wait to be grandparents. We had discussed the matter and decided in the cold light of Malthusian fact, that we would have two of our own and, if my career prospects lived up to expectations, we would adopt perhaps two more.

Having arrived at this milestone in our lives, we went with trepidation into the offices of the Halifax Building Society and intimated that we wanted to buy this choice little number. 'How much deposit do you have?' came the question; 'Nothing,' went the answer. 'Do you have a job?' (I was wearing the tartan lumberjack type shirt I had worn for much of my student life.) 'Yes,' said I, 'I have recently taken up a lectureship at the university.' We walked out with a 100 per cent mortgage, ready to move in a few weeks later.

Wages were paid two months in arrears and so we borrowed an electric ring from the labs and settled down on our double Lilo in well-worn sleeping bags. The only inconvenience was that, having no curtains, we had to switch off the lights before undressing to go to bed. The next salary cheque saw us at Fowler's Auction Rooms for the whole day, during the course of which we furnished much of our new home for around £16. That included an antique armchair and an American rocker, which are still prized possessions, although the grandfather clock unfortunately was so riddled with worm that it fell to pieces on delivery.

Rosemary had got a job at Shield Row Junior School in Stanley. She used to travel there either on the bus or, if I didn't have an early lecture or afternoon practical, I would take her there or collect her in our little grey van, which we fondly called Wormy Wagon. I don't think she really understood the children's broad accents for several months and the feeling was mutual. Nevertheless, they got on with each other like a house on fire and I soon found myself borrowing the department mini-bus to take some of them on an outing to High Force. Most of them had hardly ever left the mining village, not even for a trip to nearby Newcastle, let alone to a local beauty spot. So, instead of coming dressed for the countryside, they were all in their best, some even with party shoes. They were all super kids who took it all in their high-heeled stride and even made it to the top of the waterfall and stood on the dizzy heights to have their picture taken.

Everything was rapidly changing; King Coal was beginning to come to the end of his reign and the sun set on the steel works at nearby Consett, following the fate of the shipbuilding industry that had once helped Britain rule an empire, let alone the waves. However, the whole of County Durham was still redolent with the magic of hard-working communities with great pubs and clubs that sold real beer. I soon joined the ranks of the Department of Extra Mural Studies with classes in both Hartlepool and Sunderland, each with a hard core of Golden Oldies who stayed with me over many years, before succumbing to the earth-to-earth syndrome that eventually gets us all. Some had been regular attendees, since the heyday of extra mural education when the most popular WEA (Workers Educational Association) classes had waiting lists of hundreds. I was taken firmly under their wing and shown the ropes of completing registers and the exact length of regulation tea breaks. They not only taught me a lot about the urge to learn but also became my guides and mentors regarding all things local, and especially the best sites for wildflowers.

The secretary of the Hartlepool class was Arthur Lambert, an engineer by profession, who made the most wonderful working models of old steam engines. My star botany pupil was Miss Appleyard, a local schoolteacher, who one day arrived at the class with a specimen that she wanted identified. When I told her that it was the burnt tip orchid that had not been seen in Durham for almost 100 years, she almost fainted away at the thought that she had picked such a rare thing. We changed location of the field trip that evening to visit the cliff top where she had made the find. There it was, five tiny spikes of this strange little flower, blooming at the northern limit of its distribution in Britain, almost exactly where it had been known all those years ago.

It was on another field trip that I first met Derek Hall, one of the north-east's most remarkable artists. At that time he was scouring the rocks of Cassop and other fossil-rich locations of the Magnesian Limestone, and turning his fossil finds into pictures of the reptiles as they probably were when alive and eating each other. On hearing me enthusing about the totally unique type of vegetation, his direction in art underwent a radical change. He started to paint not just flowers but vegetation in all its intricate detail, bloom-by-bloom, leaf-by-leaf and, whenever necessary, root-by-root. Among my most treasured possessions is a picture by him of a tiny patch of vegetation, life-size and so good in every detail that any phytosociologist worth their salt would immediately be able to give it its proper Latin name, *Seslerietum courulea* Shim. The 'Shim' after the Latin name lets the world know that this was first described and named by David Shimwell, the best field botanist I ever had the pleasure to help tutor through a degree and a PhD.

Another was the Revd Gordon Graham, vicar of Wheatley Hill. Like John Ray and Gilbert White before him, Gordon found the wonders of creation within the parish which he served, Bible and field notebook in hand. Avidly he went on every specialist course on offer and signed up with me to study for a MSc on the scraps of woodland in Upper Teesdale. It was on a course at Slapton Ley Field Studies Centre that Gordon found his match, a field assistant called Paddy who filled his every thought, so much so that he began commuting to Devon between Sunday services, weddings and funerals, until she said 'yes'. They got married, and in due season Paddy and Gordon could be seen pushing prams and push-chairs along the highways and byways of the parish, noting down the names of all the plants growing in or around the very special limestone that allows montane and even sub-alpine plants to grow almost at sea level. Gordon went on to write the *Durham Flora*, the cover illustrations of which were by Derek Hall. Derek also started on the mammoth task of illustrating the vegetation types of Britain, county by county. Sadly he was called away in his prime to paint angels in heaven.

I soon got caught up in the Northern Naturalists Union, championed by the redoubtable Mrs Gibby, wife of Dr Gibby who was not only on the chemistry staff but an expert on local history and, long after he retired, guided tourists around Durham Cathedral. On one occasion, when filming for the BBC, I had climbed up one of the towers that flanked the famous rose window. The pointed top had been removed for repairs and I was standing in its place. Along came a Gibby group, mainly Japanese, and he gave his spiel about the famous window, which everyone was happily snapping. I stood quite still and was amazed when they all walked off, leaving me wondering who would be the first to notice a strange figure in their holiday snaps.

Two other stalwarts of the NNU were Old Man Heslop Harrison (not that you would have dared use that title to his face, but he did have an equally brilliant son, Jack), legendary professor of botany at Newcastle, and Tommy Dunn, biology master in Chester le Street. I don't really know if learning curves had been invented in those days, but on a day out with either of those, mine was vertical. Mind you, you had to be one of the inner cliques to be taken to the most special spots, like Thrislington Plantation. Everyone whispered in awed tones about the richness of the flora and fauna, which included a major colony of the unique Durham Argus butterfly. As all these treasures and the local steel industry depended on the purest deposits of Magnesian Limestone in the country, it was under threat of becoming part of a very large quarry. I put all my best students on to the job of recording in detail what was there. Then, when the time came, I worked with Steetly Magnesite (now part of Laffarge Redland), to lift sixteen acres of the soil and its vegetation, piece by piece, before moving it a few hundred yards to a safe site that had been specially prepared and landscaped. There, the biggest jigsaw in the world was put back together. Steetly, who were very good at moving earth, designed and built a special soil slicer and vegetation transporter which would even carry the ants (so important in the life cycle of the Argus) in safety and all the work was carried out in the winter when everything was in a dormant state, work overseen by David Park and Ken Foster.

I did do a lot of worrying about setting a future precedent for moving very rare vegetation out of the way of development. However, back in the sixties there was no option, and the thought of closing down a major local industry in the cause of conservation was a decade of destruction away. All I can say is, thank God it worked, and the cost was not much more than the normal process of stockpiling the soil and rehabilitating the site at the end of the quarry's life.

Thrislington Plantation and the other jewel in the local crown of lowland vegetation, Cassop Vale, are today National Nature Reserves, in part because of the very special type of vegetation that Derek, David, Gordon and Paddy recorded for posterity. I was very sad when pressure of work made me give up my extra mural tuition, and I was very proud when I was later made Honorary Professor of Adult and Continuing Education by the university.

They were very happy days despite the fact that each one brought a new challenge. One of the first was where to carry out large-scale research and class experiments. Taking a leaf from Geoff Banbury's book, I ordered a large build-it-yourself clear span greenhouse kit, duplicated the instruction manual, and presented it all to my first year students for their next week's practical. Apart from carrying the heavy bits myself, I gave a running commentary on the fact that wood is not only a renewable resource but also nature's own fantastic plastic.

Then there were field trips to be organised. Every new intake of students was taken on a day trip during which they walked across the Pennines from Cow Green to High Cup Nick and down to Dufton, taking in the delights of Upper Teesdale, one of Europe's most important botanical sites, en route. The whole area was then being annexed into what is today England's largest National Nature Reserve.

At the beginning of the spring term, which back in those days was still in the depths of a real winter, there was a weekend trip to climb Britain's most important botanical mountain, Ben Lawers in the Breadalbanes of Scotland: off on Friday night, sleep on the Gypsy Queen coach, breakfast in Killin, then up the mountain where you really found what it was like to be an arctic alpine plant, Saturday night in the Youth Hostel, with haggis cooked by me on the menu, and then, after a quick look at Britain's oldest tree, a Yew in the churchyard at Fortingal, a morning's botanising in the Spey Valley before it was back to Durham.

Easter saw us studying ferns, mosses and liverworts in Wales, based at the University college of Aberystwyth, and staying at a most wonderful bed and breakfast run by the redoubtable Mrs Evans, whose husband was the porter at Aberystwyth railway station, and who did eggs, bacon and laver bread if you asked for it. I did and my mouth still waters.

The crowning glory of the fieldwork year was a two-week trip to southern Germany to study the wetlands in the foothills of the Alps near the Bodensee. Then it was on to Cortina d'Ampezzo in northern Italy, there to revel in the high alpine flora growing on the most spectacular outcrops of Magnesian Limestone in Europe. I would always make sure that we arrived there in the first light of dawn, so all could enjoy the wrap-around spectacle of what looked like cardboard cut out mountains.

The only reason that the latter trip was possible was that we had a departmental van and, as the years went along, a motley collection of ageing tents and eating irons. My colleagues and I did the driving and the catering while the students did the washing up. As the years went by, and those trips went on for twenty-two years, the camping sites and the local hostelries we used to frequent got to know us well. Our beef stroganoff, which was cooked, as were all the meals, over a Primus stove, was renowned in the campsite at Cortina and the regular Italian campers used to queue up with the students for second helpings.

To highlight any one incident from those many field trips is difficult, for each and every one provided many stories to tell. I will however afford myself the luxury of just one and will not mention the student by his real name for he may well have gone on to great things. Let's call him Mel. I trust you are sitting comfortably for here is the tale of Mel's coming out party.

He was the strangest of students, nearly impossible to communicate with, almost autistic. Tutorials with Mel appeared to be a complete waste of time and his college reports confirmed much the same. However, his academic record was good enough for him to make the grade in the first year. En route to Cortina I did my best to coax him into conversation, but failed. He just sat huddled in the back of the mini-bus in two overcoats, completely self-contained. At meals he ate his fair share, and he helped do the camp chores and silently took part in all the field work, still wearing his heavy coats. His day, or rather his evening, dawned on our first night in Italy. Our favourite bar was close to the trampolino, a one-time olympic ski jump and on its bill of fare it offered the strongest cheese sandwiches I have ever tasted and a phenomenal array of different flavoured schnapps ranged along three shelves. Every time we visited this establishment we would sample another flavour. That night it was Enzian, and we had decided to take Mel along. Placing a glass in front of him, I said, 'This is how we do it,' banging the glass on the table, 'One, two, three.' Down went the schnapps and to our surprise Mel smiled. Bang bang bang, down went the second glass. Then, even more surprisingly, Mel leaped up on to the table and shouted, 'Up the botany boot boys!' He joined in with the festivities until, very late, we had to carry him down to his tent, a reformed student. I can't claim that he was totally cured of whatever it was that had locked him up in two overcoats, but from that point on he was much easier to teach and went out into the big wide world with a Durham degree.

During the two weeks we had one day off and that was usually spent on a day trip to Venice for a little bit of culture. One day, as we were proceeding along the side of the Grand Canal someone spotted Sophia Loren in a motorboat. In his excitement he fell in. We soon found Lambrusco followed by Grappa Ruta is just as effective and a lot more pleasant than a stomach pump.

I always tried to make the homeward journey coincide with the Beer Fest at Murnau, not far from Wolfratshausen, a favourite watering hole of the German botanist and poet, Goethe. Botanical German was still on the syllabus in those early days and everyone soon learned the meaning of 'eine beer bitte '. We would then spend our day floating down the Isar, a process fraught with some danger due to the rapidity of the river's flow. We'd haul out like a pod of beached whales to study the alpine flowers, including great drifts of lady's slipper orchids, which found an open habitat on the shingle banks. Sadly, all this began to change very rapidly as more and more fertiliser spewed out of the Common Agricultural Policy, so enriching the habitat that ranker weeds took over. We call it eutrophication, while the Germans have a much more apt saying, which translated means 'the devil always shits on the largest pile'.

The Beer Fest has also changed. In the early days it teemed with families and good cheer and all ladies were sent home at 23.00 hours. We were always made welcome with the cry 'Wilkommen die Botaniks' and were expected to stand up on the benches and sing while clashing our steins. One memorable night Tony Peabody, later of forensic medicine fame, was on the outside of a particularly rowdy line up and was shot off through the side of the tent to roll down the railway embankment. Over the years some of the good cheer factor began to disappear as our campsites, chosen for their floristic diversity, became hemmed in with trim tracks, tennis courts and other sorts of 'Das betreten ist verboten' Keep Out signs.

We worked hard and we played hard, the only problem was that all too often in their vivas the students would extol the virtues of their 'holiday'. This did tend to get up the noses of certain members of the hierarchy whose practicals were tied to the laboratory and so moaned that it was all a waste of departmental money. I pointed out that one of my field trips cost less than an ultra centrifuge and that the day my students had to pay to do my practicals I would resign, and I did.

11 MEANWHILE, BACK AT THE BEGINNING

TALK ABOUT IN at the deep end – with no teacher training whatsoever I had to face my first students with courses on plant anatomy, a subject guaranteed to turn most people off. Classes included Judith Hann, destined for *Tomorrow's World*, Neil Cleminson, who also went into television on the production end, and Maggie Dalpra and Ba Carter, a sort of female Laurel and Hardy act, the life and soul of every party.

Somewhere in my psyche there was a nagging truism that you couldn't really call yourself a botanist until you had seen a tropical rain forest. So, right from the start, I laid plans for a student field trip to Sierra Leone, where Durham had a sister university at Fourah Bay. I even joined the staff committee of the Durham Colleges Exploration Society (Newcastle was then still part of the old joint establishment, but was about to become a new red-brick institution of its own), in an attempt to find out what running a real scientific expedition was all about.

I soon found myself leading a weekend training course to camp at High Cup Nick up in the Pennines. It seemed like a good idea; we were going to walk in from Wemmergill carrying an immense load of gear, just to prove how fit we were, and meet a party coming from the RAF Search and Rescue Mob in Northumberland who were walking in from Cow Green. Mother Nature decided that we should really be put to the test and dumped several feet of snow over the area. Led by Peter Pearson, then a student doing a PhD on dog daisies who went on to be a leading light in the human genome project, we made it, just about, and tried to erect our tents in a force 10 gale. Though old, as most of the Explor. Soc. equipment was, thank God they were of the sleeve type made famous in Antarctic expeditions – great for withstanding gale force winds, but not so easy to erect while they are still blowing. I remember hanging on to our tent like grim death as we were being blown at ever increasing speed towards the edge of the famous Nick. Finally, having made it safe by piling snow on the skirt, we crawled inside, where we all huddled together and tried to cook 'goulash a la Cleminson' on a Primus in the middle of the tent.

I had already fallen foul of the College system, so I wondered what the college authorities would have said about me allowing the co-habitation of male and female students, all eating from a billy can with one spoon. My first fracas had occurred when, returning late from my class in Sunderland, I had come across a lady student weeping outside St Hild's College. When I enquired as to her plight, she replied that she was locked out without an exeat. 'Never fear,' I said, 'I know the way in,' – as did most other real members of the university. Easing her up through a ground floor window, always left ajar, I felt the not so gentle touch of the vice principal on my shoulder. My explanation, that it was stupid to lock young ladies out in the street just after closing time, didn't go down too well.

Now, snug in my sleeping bag, I consoled myself with the fact that I was not at that time a moral tutor (at that point no college was willing to take the risk with this new boy on the block) and fell into an untroubled sleep. I woke up next morning welded to Maggie Dalpra's sleeping bag with the remains of the goulash, which had tipped out of the billy and frozen solid. Fortunately, the storm had abated and we were greeted by duck egg blue skies. The RAF team turned up later that day; having fallen into the Maize Beck, they had sensibly camped for the night. It was on this trip that I tried my feet at skiing for the very first time. It was a catastrophe, and I concluded that the tropics were a must. I had just read a series of papers on salt balance in tropical mangroves, as I decided to learn the then quite new techniques of using a Self Contained Underwater Breathing Apparatus. Rosemary also decided that scuba was for her.

I can't say that the Durham branch of the British Sub Aqua Club made it easy; the training schedule was, as far as I could see, guaranteed to put you off, with dire warnings of the bends and air embolism. However, with the help of Jim Barnes, our friendly washing machine supplier and maintenance man, we succeeded. Jim was a real pioneer; having followed the drawings of Cousteau and Gagnan, he had built his own scuba set using a Calor gas bottle and regulator. With the gadget firmly strapped to his back, he had disappeared into the sea on a family holiday at Whitley Bay, much to the consternation of his family who didn't understand that it allowed him to breathe under water.

Being very claustrophobic, I soon found that I was never going to be a natural diver, and can remember with terror my first open sea dive at Souter Point. Visibility was as usual nil as I did my best to follow Harold Wardropper down until I collided with the bottom. Apart from the soft and, as I was later to find, highly polluted silt, the only way I knew which way was up and which down, was by feeling the dangle of my weight belt. Thanks to Jim who became my diving mentor and later buddy on a number of expeditions, I made the grade of third class diver, as did Rosemary

Rosemary had by then joined the staff of Durham School where all the boys called her Rosiebell. Observatory Hill sloped up behind the school, at the top of which was an old tractor winch, operated by Thomas de Winton (who also masterminded school skiing trips) as a ski and sledge tow in the winter. As soon as there had been a decent fall of snow, and there were lots in Durham back in the sixties, the whole school took to the slopes. The popular scientific journals of those flower power years were full of prognostications regarding the next ice age. Many scientists argued that the last ice age hadn't really come to an end, and that we were enjoying but the brief respite of an interstadial. Others feared that a nuclear winter was but a cold war away. However it wasn't our skiing but our diving antics that caught the imagination of the local papers, and a picture cutting of Rosemary adorned the inside of many desks at Durham School.

When we reached Sierra Leone, we were amazed to find the same picture in the prep room of Fourah Bay College. Miraculously, with a lot of help from Professor Valentine and Mr Redhead, the department's chief technician, we had got our act together and there we were, diving among the coral reefs that fringed the mangroves: Sam Hill, Maurice Kirman and Jim Hunt, three of my undergraduates, Joe Harvey, one of Professor Valentine's research team, and Anna Thomas, who had been with me at Bedford, to keep Rosemary company. We had booked our passage on a cargo ship with passenger accommodation called the *Onitsia*. It was everything an into Africa experience should be: deck quoits, swinging darts and a sort of golf amongst enormous wood and brass reclining chairs scattered in an orderly fashion around the deck, and enormous meals, served with elegance four, or was it five, times a day. It was like a large slice of Edwardian England in a floating gentleman's club, where one presumed that you might meet Dr Livingstone himself, sipping pink gin. The only thing that spoilt it was the smell of diesel – if only it had been steam. Then reality hit as we stepped out of the cool safety of the ship into the blazing bustle of full frontal Africa. Sweat, turned on like a tap, soaked us from the skin outwards as we were led by porters down the quay, which itself staggered under the weight of goods on their way to or from somewhere.

Our sojourn in the university was long enough to learn that the large royal python in the cage on the veranda was friendly as long as you fed it, and there were plenty of large rats about. It had once escaped to freedom, causing great sighs of relief among all snakeophobes, but as soon as the rainy season began it came back to roost, demanding to be fed. Every day someone would turn up with an animal in a sack and try and sell it to anyone in the building who was stupid enough to say yes. The most infamous occasion was when an excited local turned up with a writhing sack and the message, 'very good snakey, thirty shillings'. When, on opening the mouth of the sack, he was told that it was a Gaboon viper, he dropped the sack and fled, leaving us with one of the world's most poisonous snakes. We were also there long enough to hear the screams of girls undergoing ritual initiation by clitoral mutilation.

Mangroves and reefs were fascinating enough, but the main quest of our expedition was to study real tropical rain forest, so it was off up country in the Extra Mural department's Land Rover. Our back-up vehicle was a Peugeot that belonged to Dr John Harrop, one of the botany lecturers, who was on his way back for a holiday in Britain. He also lent us Abdullah, his cook boy, who left his two wives at home to become our travelling companion and guide in all matters of local protocol.

Our first stop was the rice research station at Rokupra where we arrived very late, thanks to torrential rain which, apart from making travel on the dirt roads ultra hazardous, at least got us used to the stuff that makes both rice and tropical forests grow. The staff made us at home and were full of stories, possibly apocryphal, about a recent visit of Her Majesty the Queen and Prince Philip. A brand new loo had been installed for royal use, with all the junk hidden away in the other, ready for the great day. After lunch one of the more junior scientists had found himself on royal duty and ushered HRH into the wrong room. Prince Philip emerged completely satisfied, drying his hands on part of yesterday's washing, a bra. We too were royally welcomed at the station and, after learning a lot about the agronomy of rice production, continued, two days later, on to our final destination.

We were lucky to be staying in the luxury of the circuit house that came complete with a night guard who slept in a chair under a very tatty umbrella on the leaky veranda. On arrival, we immediately lit the flame in the kerosene fridge that was gently rusting away in the corner of the main room. Half an hour later our preparations for supper were interrupted by a great scuffling noise and, on opening the fridge door, a whole army of disgruntled cockroaches rushed out across the floor.

After eating our evening meal of rice and chicken – our bill of fare for the next few weeks – we showered under a broken down pipe in the midst of a phenomenal electric storm, which washed a startling array of spiders down the spout, and started to retire for the night. Our room had two two-foot-wide camp beds, each with mosquito net. We were soon joined by Abdullah, shaking with fear as he told us that the local people were cannibals and could he please sleep in the house, not in the hammock on the veranda. Rosemary and I gave him one of the beds and doubled up on the other one.

Some hours later I woke to the sound of a mighty rustling. Grabbing my torch, I found not only that our net was covered with whip scorpions, busy eating up all the visiting insects, but there was a trail of driver ants on a route march under our bed and out into the next room. I then did a very stupid thing. Instead of leaving them in peace to make their way to wherever they were going, I squirted them with insecticide. This caused instant social pandemonium; instead of being an ordered procession following their pheromones, they broke ranks, rushing all over the place, which included us. So, despite the local cannibals, we *all* spent the night out on the veranda.

At last we were standing in real tropical rain forest, ready to get down to work delving into its biodiversity, not that the word had been invented at that time. As a self styled phytosociologist, that is someone who attempts to classify and hence gain some understanding of vegetation by its floristic make-up, I found myself in at the deadest of ends. I had read so much about this type of forest in accounts written by my heroes, Henry Walter Bates and Alfred Russel Wallace, and here I was – David James Bellamy, wallowing in their footsteps. The trouble was that none of us had the faintest idea of the Latin names of most of the trees, let alone the plants growing beneath their shade. Fortunately help was at hand. The local people, including the kids, made use of many of the trees, lianas and herbs not only for fuel but also in the construction of their houses, furniture, utensils and toys, and as food and even medicine, and so they knew all their local names. All we had to do was check the names they used against the Latin ones in the floristic lists and we were in business.

So it was that we used to travel with an entourage of kids, all singing 'We are the Boys from Kamabai. Riding along. Singing our song.' They became our friends and forest botanists. One day travelling back from a village about fourteen miles from base, we overtook a lady with an enormous tin bowl, piled with all her belongings, balanced on her head. One of our helpers said that it was his auntie, on her way to stay with them, and suggested we gave her a lift. Stopping the Land Rover, I offered to take her load and nearly fell over with the weight. She was too polite to laugh, though not so the boys from Kamabai. Wherever we went, we became objects of great curiosity, especially among the women. Approached by a truly statuesque lady, the sort that tribal wars must have been fought over, Rosemary was asked how two such skinny women could satisfy so many men.

A highlight of the trip was when Rosemary and I set out to scale the Rabbit's Back, a local mini Ayers Rock that was said to be unclimbable. Because it was made of exfoliated granite covered with a jelly-like layer of blue-green algae, we found it lived up to its reputation and started to retrace our steps down through the gallery forest, botanising as we went. On the way up we had seen a long green snake sleeping in a bush and had given it a wide berth. It was still there, and not far away from its chosen spot I could see a beautiful white ground orchid, somewhat out of reach up a cliff, which I decided to add to our collection. Unfortunately it was the private property of a large spider – and I mean large – which didn't like the intrusion. The pain it inflicted was excruciating, not unlike plugging into the mains electricity. The real problem was, there was no way of turning it off. Rosemary hadn't seen the spider scuttle off and, thinking the snake had bitten me, leapt up brandishing a knife, ready to let my blood, and a handkerchief for a pressure bandage. Well, she *was* a Queen's Guide with hundreds of badges, including one for first aid. Rapidly I explained what had happened and sank to the ground so that I could dangle my wounded arm in the cool water. The fang marks had already turned into a red-blue weal and my whole right side began to seize up.

I eventually got back to the circuit house, part crawling and part being floated down the river. Thankfully the pain had by then subsided somewhat and I felt a little better. But not for long. We had been invited to dinner that evening by one of the local missionaries and towards the end of the meal I started to shiver uncontrollably. On being told of my adventure, she said nobody had ever lived after being bitten by a bush spider. This was probably true locally, for the level of malnutrition there was very high, so I turned into bed, hoping that her prognostications didn't apply to a fourteen-stone well-fed Brit. In the middle of the night the shivering bout started again and Rosemary, coming to my rescue, shone the torch across the bed into a blanket of steam rising from my overheated body. Having lost so much water, when I tried to move, every muscle in my body went into paroxysms of cramp. I sat up for the rest of the night, drinking tepid water well laced with effervescent salt tablets. The moral of my tale is: however ill you feel, always take your anti-malarials; I forgot and so got a dose of malaria as well.

Of course most of the locals couldn't afford the luxury of western drugs, except for the few who had got jobs working in the logging camps, plantations or on the diamond fields that in those days allowed Sierra Leone to rank among some of the richer nations of Africa. The rest, well, once their tropical rain forest had gone, they either headed for the shantytowns around the capital, looking for work, or succumbed to other diseases exacerbated by malnutrition. I had to attend the funerals of two of our little helpers, and so came out of Africa a campaigner for intellectual property rights and the wise use of all of Earth's natural resources.

All this happened in the same year that saw the publication of Rachel Carson's *Silent Spring*, and eight years before Friends of the Earth was formed. Forty years on, I must apologise for not having done too well, for today Sierra Leone is reeling from the effects of an horrendous civil war and is one of the poorest countries in the world. I can only wonder how many of the children of my Boys from Kamabai were part of its piteous children's army.

12 WHY DIDN'T I KEEP MY MOUTH SHUT?

IT WAS GOOD to get home and get back into real harness once again, a harness that included a new slant to some of my lectures and a growing number of research students. My first was Jack Reiley, who arrived from Glasgow with a wife, an Alsatian and a research grant, so it was off to Lloyds to introduce my bank manager to my first protégé. Jack wanted to buy a terraced house in the middle of the city and needed £650. After an interview, which highlighted the great expectations of a future PhD from Durham, the manager said he would be willing to give him a loan to cover the cost, but first Jack would have to open an account in his bank. Yes it really did happen like that, back in those pre-credit-card days when bank managers were part of the social hormone of the locale in which they were situated.

Jack was soon joined by Jenny Dodd and Wendy Tickle, both ex-Bedford College, Keith Thompson, one of my own graduates, and Peter Holland who had been at QMC with Rosemary. They were all working on wetlands of one sort and another and all were welcomed into the family home at 6 Witton Grove.

Just along the old A1 from our bungalow was Brown's County Hair Salon, which perhaps above all showed the spirit of the sixties. Flower power may have been sweeping the more affluent south but the north-east (though in the main phase of the destruction of its heavy industries and the close-knit society that went with them) was fighting back, planning a brave new era that would create real jobs and help keep more of the affluence, if not the profit, in the hands of the locals. A new Technical College was being opened at Framwellgate Moor and one of the lecturers was Jacky Brown, a great entrepreneur, son of the man who had started the family business in a tin hut with nothing more than a basket chair and a pair of scissors, back in the days when miners had tramped along the road to the local pit. The new shop was a cathedral to the tonsorial arts with the latest reclining chairs, hair dryers, sterilising kit and a range of hair care products administered by pretty girls and well-groomed young men, all in a row. They would even serve you a cup of coffee while you were being transformed from a scruffy young lecturer into a latent star of the television screen or, as the *Northern Echo* put it, 'A Real Gone Don'. I think Jacky really despaired of ever making me shed the mad scientist image. However, he was such an entrepreneur that when the World Cup was being fought out in Britain he invited the Russian team to the shop for a free haircut before a crucial match played in the north-east.

The other local entrepreneur was T. Dan Smith, whose battle cry was North-east Redevelopment. His face was always in the papers and on the news. He, like Jacky Brown, had known the best and the worst of the past and dreamed of a much brighter future. Both knew that if that brightness were ever to shine, then the drive had to come from within, not from without, the region. If coal, shipbuilding and steel making were forsaking County Durham so were students forsaking botany, a subject that still had connotations of pressing flowers, a pastime more fitted to young ladies from St Aidan's than rugby-playing members of Hatfield College. So it was that at a Board of Studies meeting I suggested that we should run a weekend course for local sixth formers called North-east Development and the Plant Sciences. T. Dan Smith even came and opened it for us.

Each member of staff held forth on their favourite topic: Professor Valentine on the famous Teesdale flora, Jack Crosby on the evolution of primroses, Min Chalklin on seaweeds, Geoff Banbury on gravity and toadstools, and Pauline Watson on spore dispersal in the fungi. It was a great success and got good coverage in the local media. I talked about our work on the blanket bogs that used to cover the Pennines but were now falling into sad array because of the lack of good moorland management. Thanks mainly to the inspiration of Howard T. Odum, an American ecologist, these were the days of production ecology, so called because all around the world teams were attempting to measure the productivity of natural vegetation. One of these teams was at Moor House National Nature Reserve in the high Pennines where a whole portfolio of research on moorland management was in full swing: research that was emphasizing the importance of such peatlands in upper catchment management and the key role of good gamekeepers in getting the formula right. I waded in, saying that if we only got the management of our uplands right, then we would have better, more regular flows of water down the Tees, Wear and Tyne and the effects of pollution in the estuaries and adjacent coast would not be as bad. That one statement was to transform my life.

One of the audience, I don't know who, must have reported the fact in high places and a few days later I received a telephone call. The voice at the other end of the line said, 'This is the Department of Scientific and Industrial Research.' I sat to attention beside the phone. The voice went on, 'You have a grant of £3,000 and two years to produce a report on pollution along the north-east coast.' My rather lame reply was, 'But I am not a marine biologist.' To which came the reply, 'Well you shouldn't have opened your bloody great mouth.' It wasn't the last time I was going to hear those words. With that, the phone was down at the other end and I had got my first official grant for a programme of research.

I remember sitting there, somewhat nonplussed; £3,000 seemed a lot of money in those days, but mission impossible stretched before me. How the hell was I even going to attempt to do that? The idea of the scoping study hadn't even been thought of and the concept of ecologists as environmental consultants was but a twinkle in Max Nicholson's eye. Here I was, in at the deep end of some of the most polluted seawater in the world.

Jacky Brown came to the rescue. He was one of the hierarchy of the Durham branch of the British Sub Aqua Club, which was always looking for things to do, and so together we dreamt up the idea of harnessing the club's expertise to expedite the job. Access to a brand new inflatable Zodiac dive boat would work wonders, so we were off: a motley bunch, with an assortment of wet and dry suits, although the dry suits were in the old sense of the word, a selection of old pullovers and trousers. They were dry until you got in, but did at least trap some warmer water around your body, allowing a little longer immersion in the cold North Sea.

The idea behind the study was to check the effect of pollution on the most obvious marine systems, the beds of seaweed that grew along the rocky shores, comparing their make-up, depth range and productivity in places affected by and free from pollution. Of course everyone wanted to take part in the clean waters of the Farne Islands and St Abb's Head, but the volunteers fell off, as did the seaweed, in the most grotesquely polluted areas like Souter Point and Seaham Harbour on the Durham coast. The more stalwart members even braved the waters in the Tees estuary which was doing its best to deal with the untreated effluent of the hundreds of thousands of people drawn to its banks by the affluence of the chemical industry. Before the industrial revolution had appeared on the scene, its limpid waters had acted as the 'kidneys' of the Tees catchment and the 'ovaries' of this stretch of coast. Together gigabillions of tiny creatures living in amongst the silt and sand kept the waters clean, their abundance feeding a complex food chain enjoyed by visiting birds that used the estuary as a stopover on their long migration flights. Marine plants both large and small kept the waters charged with oxygen, making them ideal nurseries for a multitude of fish and shellfish, even for seals that hauled out on the many acres of pure, clean mud at low tide. Back in the sixties all that had gone, replaced by some of the most polluted waters in the world.

I well remember surfacing near some rocks, to be hailed from a boat which bore the letters ICI. When asked what we were doing in that filthy water, I replied, 'Trying to find out what you are chucking into it.' From that point on we remained in contact with ICI's Brixham laboratory, where they were also engaged in research on their own pollution record. Yes, industry was even then beginning to try to change its spots, from the 'muck and brass' syndrome that is still doing so much harm to the world's environment to the 'duty of care' prescription. However, it is still being diluted by the greenwash of the vested interests of the quick profiteers.

It was at that point in my career that I began to wonder why we were wasting money trying to find out the *effects* of pollutants but could get little in the way of information about *what* was being disposed of in the sea in the first place. There was little doubt that the fathers of the chemical industry had found tidal estuaries very convenient dumping grounds for a fricassee of waste, and their sons were still following suit. Likewise the collieries and coal washing plants had not done much for the beaches and poor old Seaham Harbour, having survived that infamous pit disaster in 1871, was getting much more than its fair share of pollution of all types and from all directions. Centred on the three estuaries and Seaham Harbour, the Durham coastline was a stinking, filthy mess. The stink came mainly from human sewage and the effect of this and the industrial waste appeared to have taken its toll. Thanks to the friable nature of the Magnesian Limestone rock, the most polluted coastline of County Durham had always had more turbid waters, thus reducing the depth range of the beds of seaweed. However, it wasn't only their depth range, it was the whole make-up of the systems that appeared to have changed.

At first our research certainly took some flak, especially from the local marine biologists who looked on seaweed as their own preserve. Who could blame them? Certainly not this upstart on the marine scene who used amateur divers to collect his data. Still, the fact that human activity could pollute the sea enough to cause discernible ecosystem changes on the macro level was firmly on the research agenda and, with quite a lot of my grant left, we dreamed up Operation Kelp. The idea, to put a massive task force of sport divers around the British coast, was advertised in *Triton*, the official organ of the BSAC.

One of our unused teaching laboratories was fitted with racks and blow heaters for drying large amounts of kelp. The age of each individual plant had to be determined so that we could get some estimate of productivity. To do this we had to cut the holdfast (whose branches held the kelp on to the rock) vertically into two halves so that we could count the annual growth rings. It also soon became very obvious that the multitude of animals sheltering among the branches were very different in polluted and non-polluted waters. The most obvious pollutant was human sewage and the most obvious effect was an increase in abundance of filter and detritus feeders, mussels and sea urchins and the like. The old adage 'where there's muck there's opportunity' is equally as true in the marine environment as it had been in the industrial conurbations that had provided much of the pollution. The local fishermen of course knew this already, and so did the sea birds who congregated downstream from the sewage plume, living on rich pickings or, as the locals called it, 'worms and weeds'. Green seaweed, to be exact the aptly named *Enteromorpha intestinalis*, dominated the rocks in all highly polluted waters. We soon found that the best way to map the course of the polluting plumes was to count the fishing umbrellas and the bird watchers' binoculars on a sunny weekend. Another method was to dangle a hydrophone over the side of the Zodiac and listen in to the clicking of gangs of sea urchins, happy in their work of gobbling up the nutritious sludge.

On the long journeys in our old diesel long-wheelbase Land Rover we dreamed up all sorts of schemes on the way to and from the dive sites. One of these was to build cages over Sunderland's long sea outfall and fill them with happy pollution-eating *Echinus esculentus*. We did realise that we might have PR problems, persuading people to eat the potential crop of edible sea urchin, so this fast food idea never came to fruition.

Operation Kelp did as advertised and our results were reported in *Triton* and in lots of other magazines and newspapers. It called on all BSAC branches to get out and survey the kelp beds at their favourite dive sites, checking depth range, age, length and dry weight. The latter made me somewhat unpopular with the families of the divers because it necessitated drying the seaweed in the oven and then weighing it on the kitchen scales. The smell of drying kelp wafting through the corridors of the university was bad enough, but the same smell emanating from home kitchens was a different matter. Still, it worked, and over a couple of weekends, thanks to the hard graft of hundreds of amateur divers, we got a base line picture of the clarity of British waters.

It was at about this juncture that I was summoned by Bernard Eaton, editor of *Triton*, to speak at the Diving Congress in Brighton. Bernard was and still is a visionary and the list of lecturers at the gathering was to say the least fantastic: Emil Gagnan and Jacques Cousteau, Hans and Lotte Hass, Jacques Pickard, Ed Link, who invented the Link Trainer and was deeply into submersibles, and Arthur C. Clarke, who had just found a massive treasure trove on Lighthouse Reef in Sri Lanka. He had some of it with him and said, 'Anyone who can pick up this suitcase that's full of concreted silver coins, can have them.' Oscar Gugen, director of Lillywhites and chairman of the Club, Kendal McDonald of the *Evening News* and John Meridith of Compton Electric organs were also there. I was ecstatic.

The nightmare came when my lecture was moved into the number one slot next morning and I had to talk to 900 sport divers, all of whom had been well tanked up the night before, on the subject of Marine Pollution. Falteringly I started, 'I have a little green book that tells me that if you have to give a public lecture, always start with a quotation. If you don't know a good one, you need look no further than the Bible. So here goes: "Men who go down to the sea for whatever purpose are likely to see their own business in the great waters."' Roars of guffaws. Despite the fact that I can't remember exactly what I talked about, I must have warmed to the occasion because, for better or worse, I was credited with such corkers as 'we live in an effluent society' and 'you can't swim from Palace pier, you can only go through the motions'.

Descending from the platform to rapturous applause, I was accosted by the media, all of whom wanted me to repeat it, especially the lavatorial bits. One reporter shoved a microphone under my beard and said, 'Please vil you speak to the German people about zee shit in zee sea?' It wasn't until some time later that Nick Fleming told me that this had been a hoax, but it didn't matter, I was on my way. Requests came to lecture all over the place, and I was put on the Committee Mondiale des Activides Subaquatique, meetings of which I could never attend for they were held in Monaco and I had a full teaching schedule at the university.

What a summer it was, diving all over the place, and the summer field trip was to Poland to retrace my student years with Kulczynski. To cap it all, a letter came from the British Council, containing an invitation to go as visiting Professor to Dibrugah University in Assam, followed by a lecture tour across India. This sent me scurrying to my beloved *Britannica* and to the papers of Heinrich Walter, which contained his very useful climatic diagrams. Not far from Dibrugah was Cherrapungee, reputedly the wettest place in the world, a location where trees and acid bog land lived together in constant battle. It was going to be a busy year.

Perhaps our exploits in Sierra Leone had prepared us well. Our visit to India could have been a culture shock, but instead it became the grandest of grand tours and we talked on numerous occasions about the possibility of moving there. The downside was that it was very hot, and even in the cool shade of the Fairlawn Hotel, where the waiter would change into a fresh pair of clean white gloves to herald every course, I sweated like the proverbial pig. This hotel appeared to be an elegant transit camp for those engaged in Voluntary Service Overseas. It was great to talk to these youngsters of their hopes and fears for the future of themselves and of that still storybook country, the population of which, as I write, has officially topped the one billion mark.

It was then on to the Great Northern Hotel in Calcutta where, at the end of a long arcade lined with fascinating craft and antique shops, there was a barber who gave me the best beard trim I have ever had. Calcutta in the sixties will always remain my favourite city – a place so full of people that you could begin to understand what it might be like to be an ant or any other social insect. Each individual, cast in the mould of a life, struggling to survive as part of a successful whole that wove order out of chaos.

The carts went round each morning, carrying the mortal remains of both rich and poor who hadn't made it through that particular sultry night, taking them off to the burning ghats. Yet everywhere there were the smiling faces of the poor trying to make a living. You can't call it begging when two urchins with grins from ear to ear persuade you that your shoes need cleaning for the twentieth time that day, or when they find, to their amazement, that you don't have a watch whose glass they are willing to polish free from dust and scratches, they summon a gaggle of their more upmarket pals who try to sell you one. 'A real Timex,' they cajole, following you to the edge of their territory, extolling the virtues of always being punctual. They were not willing to sit in some hostel of whatever denomination, waiting for free handouts; they were, of necessity, too caught up in the business of living.

When you asked where they lived, the answer was always a sweep of the hands indicating the street, grimed with good honest grime and the pats of sacred cows, which contained everything from very well-digested food through to cardboard and plastic, nuts and bolts. Some boys took us and showed us the endless jumble of shanties, crafted from the waste of the more affluent end of their society, with their younger brothers and sisters in spotless white uniforms going happily off to school. Education – a way out of all this? To what? A ladder to be climbed? To where? Time and again Kulczynski's words, that the thing that was ruining Britain was the welfare state, haunted me, as they have done ever since.

Then there were the dhobi men, washing an endless stream of saris, chirwanees and little white socks, in what in effect was a gigantic settling pond for the sewage of many thousands of people. *Eichornia crassipes*, with its hyacinth-like sprouts of mauve flowers and strange leaves each with a swollen float, covered the surface of the water as far as the eye could see. For years I had taught my first year undergraduates that the internal structure of the water hyacinth (a noxious weed which was then beginning to run riot across lakes and reservoirs around the world) was nature's own green print of the geodesic airframe, Barnes Wallace's invention that had allowed us to get to India so quickly, the miracle of modern airliners. Seeing it en masse for the first time, rocking gently in the wake of a tiny fishing boat, as it pumped oxygen both up into the foetid air and down into the deoxygenated water. I could no longer regard it as just a pest – an aquatic weed to be got rid of – for here it was providing tertiary treatment and nutrient stripping for Calcutta's waste water. Yes, it did block up the waterways, and its dying remains could strip the oxygen from the water, but, harvested at regular intervals, it provides a rich source of organic fertiliser for a myriad small vegetable plots.

It was here I decided upon some of my Assam research programme and began to wonder why we in the west use detergent, which was even then causing pollution and enrichment of the waters back in Britain, much to the annoyance of our sport fishermen. The local fishermen in Calcutta had no need to worry for beneath the water hyacinth's oxygenating blanket there were fish in abundance, vital supplies of protein for the inhabitants of the shanty towns. Each dhobi man used only a smidgen of soap flakes and an average of forty-nine slaps on a well-worn stone to get the washing clean enough to be spread like sails, across the armada of water hyacinth. There the nascent oxygen from below and the sun from above finished off the job, producing whiter than white tablecloths, in good time for a fish supper harvested from the same ponds.

Punctuality at the airport was certainly advised for the formality of boarding a plane consumed as much time as it did paper. We had a good view of the great delta as we swung north away from Calcutta – thousands upon thousands of tiny fields growing food to be consumed by the locals or sold to the people of that metropolis, a jigsaw puzzle scene, full of individual pieces, full of future problems, but vibrant with answers for those who would take a sideways look. I have flown across that delta many times since then. In a good year, when more nutrient rich silt has been dumped by the river, adding a little bit more to this 'head, just above water' land, more people move in to claim it for their own. In a bad year, when the monsoons push the sea back up against the flow of the river, catastrophic floods bring erosion, cholera and death in their wake. The fields get more numerous, but each is just a little bit smaller as the ebb and flow of humanity tries to make a living off what is best called 'unreal' estate. Those who believe in the worst scenarios of global warming, worry that, if the sea levels rise too much, millions of the world's poorest people will not only lose their homes but their source of sustenance as well.

The greeting at Dibrugah airport was effusive and we were both covered in garlands of flowers as we were introduced to Dr Baruha and his wife Parrakutty. We were welcomed all over again at the university, before being ensconced in the guesthouse, shaded by a large lychee tree with crotons and hemp bushes in profusion. Our bed was a sort of four-poster, all hung about with mosquito nets which stretched up to the corrugated iron roof. The only thing that left a little to be desired was the shower, for it was a nice, cool, always-damp habitat for legions of land leeches. We soon learned to stand in the centre of the shower, out of reach of even their most ductile advances. This gave us very good practice familiarising ourselves with these truly obnoxious creatures, for we were going to help feed many hundreds of them over the next few weeks. We also shared the bedroom with a very large female toad who, along with assorted geckos, helped to keep the insect hoards in control. We tried but never got her to eat the leeches. She demanded to be let out of the house when it was raining gently, but would not budge off the veranda in a downpour, especially if there was thunder and lightning.

Between the guesthouse and the university buildings were a series of disused paddy fields full of water lilies and other aquatic plants, including a few patches of water hyacinth. These fields stretched on beyond the campus towards the town. Wherever the irrigation channels or the flooded fields were affected by sewage, they were completely smothered with this invasive plant, so, between us and the town was a perfect gradient from unpolluted to polluted water and it was here that Rosemary and I started our research on 'The Depth Time Scale in Ephemeral Swamp Ecosystems'.

The idea of people wading into these swamps was of course nothing novel, for those without the luxury of a shower were used to bathing in them. However, the sight of two white-skinned academics not only wading in but also collecting great bags of the water plants was too much. That evening, as was my wont, I sat leaning against a particularly friendly sacred cow who parked herself there every night and lay down whether it was about to rain or not. As I began to write up the day's notes, along came a bevy of female students in their finest saris, followed by a group of men all in spotless white. Settling themselves on the benches they didn't ask what I was doing but why I was leaning against the cow and why we didn't employ some one to do all that hard work for us. I don't think that either of my answers – 'because it is more comfortable' and 'because we enjoy doing it' – really made much impression, but I think I did motivate some of them to realise that there was more to academia than reading books. I also suggested that, if the water hyacinth could be harvested and put to good use at the end of its oxygenating life, some of the problems it caused could be alleviated if not solved. After that, in order not to offend their religious sensibilities and to help provide much wanted local jobs, I always sat on a bench, and employed someone locally to help collect our specimens.

Our trip up to Cherrapunji was a pilgrimage into one of the most special places in the world: a forest of oak and giant rhododendrons bedecked with *Tarzan* type lianas, all of which were draped with epiphytes of every size and description. Orchids, large and small ferns, mosses, liverworts, lichens and my favourite plants, the bog mosses called *Sphagnum*, carpeted every available surface to a depth of a foot or more. We had of course set out with grandiose ideas of a study of the phytosociology (biodiversity in modern day speech) and even of getting some idea of the productivity of this the wettest forest in the world. The impossibility of doing this in the time scale left us with no option but to collect our specimens, rather as we had done in Ireland, for future reference. As for productivity, well we counted the number of leeches that had got through our considerable defences to suck our blood.

Of course, even in the mid-sixties only scraps of the original forest, the so-called Sacred Groves, were left. The rest had long since gone, turned over to acid heathland thanks to the leaching power of over twenty metres of rain per year, and relentless cycles of slash and burn. In my lecture to the local Rotary Club I tried to put over the importance of rehabilitation of large areas of the forest as a key to good catchment management, but I don't think I got that point over either.

Our base was in the circuit house, which was like something straight out of medieval Shropshire: mock half-timbered with chimney pots each leading down to a fireplace, one to each guest room, with really big grates in the dining, smoking and other public rooms. The one in our bedroom burned night and day, banked up by an always cheerful man whose job was to do just that. He and his fires came in very handy when Rosemary went down with a raging temperature and a malady not unlike malaria, except that her temperature stayed up very high all the time. They were horrendous days and both of us thought she was going to die. We sought the best medical advice we could, and both herbal and modern medicines were prescribed and administered. The whirling fans did overtime and ice, soda water and tonic supplied from the bar did wonders. At last her temperature began to fall and rejoicing we weaned ourselves back into the reality of active life by eating corn on the cob, dry-fried by two diminutive girls in a wok-like receptacle over a charcoal fire which they tended at the street corner.

With no more than a water buffalo and a wooden plough, the locals were precision farmers. They knew every inch of their land and didn't waste lime or fertiliser on those areas of soil that wouldn't turn it into profit. They also hedged their bets by planting a diversity of each crop, so that whatever the environment threw their way, they could reap some sort of harvest and save some of the crop for next year's sowing. In this time honoured way they were carrying on age-old traditions of plant breeding, always selecting the best seed of each variety that had been created by their forefathers.

Like the food, the coal was locally produced and was very smoky and sulphurous, which made mosquito nets obsolete. The bar in the smoking room served the local whisky, which had a kick not unlike the smoke, and the menu in the restaurant boasted a wine list, so one evening, to celebrate Rosemary's return to health, we plucked up courage and asked for wine, starting at the cheapest end of the list. With some embarrassment the wine waiter explained, pointing to the top of the list, that they only had the most expensive (about £1) left. When he brought the bottle, the tattiness of its label belied its age. What had we discovered? Whatever it was it had not aged with grace. Still, we drank the bottle dry.

Two courtesy calls were laid on for us during our stay; the first was to take breakfast with the then owner of the tea estate that produced Assam Golden Tips. Rumour had it that this venerable old man had started life as a tea boy on the estate and then worked his way ever upwards. Over breakfast (which included an astounding range of western dishes and even apples, Cox's Orange no less, straight out of the fridge), discussion revolved around the future of the university and the sort of new courses and departments that should be developed. Evidently our host was a great benefactor of the institution. Having just got my third paper 'The Use of the Term Base Rich in Ecology' published in *Nature*, I was talking pompously about biophysics. I hope he never took my advice. We left with two miniature tea chests, perfect in every detail, containing the very best of this champagne among teas.

We were then taken in an air-conditioned Rolls-Royce on a tour of the Assam oil fields. The shock of leaving this personal refrigerator and stepping out on to the platform of a drilling rig in the heat of the midday sun is one I will never forget: one small step into the light for an individual, but a giant leap in the dark for humankind, from the heaven of 'sustainable' cultures to the hell of a non-renewable future.

On our return to the university some students came to ask us how to build air raid shelters. There was a lot of sabre-rattling going on between India and Pakistan and the doomsters were warning that China was thinking of joining in, via the Sikkim corridor. To rub it in, a cable from the British Council suggested that we should leave Dibrugah as soon as possible because the railhead was a likely avenue of attack. Drawing on our experiences of the Second World War, we suggested that they dug trenches and roofed them over, thereby having a safe place away from flying glass. This would have been a sensible suggestion in London – not so in Assam where the trenches rapidly filled with water, becoming highly efficient snake traps, and the only roofing material readily available was banana leaves. Tension mounted and news of anything like an aeroplane in the vicinity triggered the wail of the sirens, a noise that still sets my stomach all of a quiver. One bright spark with a prominent house at the edge of the campus switched on all his lights, locked the door, and took his family away for the night. As soon as the sun went down, off went the sirens and all hell was let loose. I don't think there was an enemy plane in the skies, but every gun started firing skywards. With shrapnel falling on the corrugated iron roof, we retreated under the bed where our pet toad squeezed herself between us. Rosemary asked, 'What the hell are we doing here?' 'Looking after the toad,' was all I could muster.

A few days later we were firmly told that it might be best if we took the train the next day; aeroplanes were out of the question and there was every possibility that the railway line might be cut. So, with fond fare-wells, we were packed into a first-class carriage equipped with six fold-down bunks and a toilet and shower out the back. Our companions were a local businessman and an Italian engineer and their wives. With the windows open it was a very pleasant journey, the whole pageant of Assam displayed in continuous though jerky motion, not unlike an early movie.

As we waited for refuelling at a large station, dinner was served through our carriage door and a sumptuous one it was. The guard then told us to keep the windows closed for safety and locked the door from the outside as the great engine pulled the train out of the station. Not long after there was a great rattling of the door and we all thought the enemy were upon us. The rattling continued and we could hear a sort of moaning noise, 'Pani pani' repeated again and again. Plucking up courage, I opened the shutter to reveal a boy from the restaurant car holding six glasses and a large thermos of pani, water, hanging on like grim death. We let him in through the window and he begged forgiveness. He had forgotten the water with the meal and had been sent along the running board outside the train to deliver it. We washed the curry down with tepid water, tipped him handsomely with those wonderful polo-mint-like coins which he threaded on his string belt, and off he went back to the kitchen. Good food and a sort of 'what the hell can we do anyway' resolve, gave us a good night's sleep and by morning we realised that we were through the Sikkim Gap and safely trundling towards Patna, the first stop on our lecture tour. We arrived about 5.30 in the morning, dead on time as the Indian railways always appeared to be.

Our hosts took us on a visit to the local hot springs, which had been channelled through waterspouts each shaped like an animal's head. The whole series appeared to have been engineered so that the water emanating from each successive spout was hotter than the last. You bathed beneath each in turn in readiness for the final plunge down into a bubbling pool at the bottom of a flight of stone steps. The surface of the water was covered with floating lotus petals and there, on the wall, was a statue of the elephant god Ganesha. The heat of the water made you wish you too were a pachyderm, and when you splashed the statue the water flowing back into the pool felt refreshingly cold. A series of lectures and meetings completed our stay then it was back on the train to go to Benares.

We were greeted by Professor Misra, India's leading plant ecologist, and two coach loads of students and set off on a field trip which, I soon learned, I was expected to lead. This was not easy for this was my first time in the field on the Indogangetic Plain and every plant was new to me. Thank goodness we headed to the river, to an area below a waterfall whose splash zone supported wetland communities, a little more in my element.

Lunchtime came and the field assistants gave each one of us a cotta plate piled with enormous helpings of curry and vegetables. The food was good, and so were the plates, each one with a slightly different pattern. At the end of the meal they were smashed and left in a heap. On my commenting on the fact that it was a waste of resources, the students told me that it was a very hygienic practice, that clay was in abundance and that potters needed work. They showed me other piles marking past picnics, all rapidly crumbling away to be resorbed back into mother earth from whence they had come.

A visit to Benares would not be complete without coming face to face with the ultimate example of recycling: the burning ghats, where the faithful are brought with all the pomp and ceremony their family can afford to be sent on their way to Nirvana. It is an awesome sight, not because of the bodies but because of the total devotion to spirituality which is, I believe, within each and every one of us. It was awesome too for an ecologist whose calling would seem to want to replace that spirituality of being with hard statistics about what a waste of wood it was, and think of the problems of pollution of the sacred river by all those ashes. The freshwater fish on sale in the market answered the second of those points, at least in part, and the fact that India was then heading to become the largest producer of tropical hardwood in the world (80 per cent of which is burned to keep body and soul together or apart) answered the first. Earth to earth, ashes to ashes: dust was revived by the water of life to form earth that would produce more crops to feed another generation, a continuous cycle of being and believing in a better future. The press of people at the ghats on an ordinary day is bad enough, but on the main Holy Days, this is the one place in the world where you can witness four million people on the move. An unstoppable force of faith moving to bathe in the holy waters of the Ganges, which carries the dust of humanity to enrich those connurbations of tiny fields we had seen as our plane left Calcutta.

Benares is one of the world's great wonders and our stay was far too short. However, on one of our last evenings there, a student came to collect us and took us on a magical mystery tour by tricycle rickshaw. As he pedalled us along he sang us Indian songs telling us that we were lucky to be so happily married. We certainly were, for all the evidence points to the fact that it was in this fair city that Rufus, our eldest son, was conceived.

Just as we parked the rickshaw the air raid sirens sounded and, although we were assured it was only another practice, the whole city was thrown into darkness, stygian being the apt adjective, especially in the narrow streets through which we were making our way, apparently against a constant stream of people and sacred cows. Perhaps they knew something we didn't, but we went on anyway to reach our destination, which turned out to be the silk warehouse of our friend's father.

We were greeted at the door and taken into a large well-lit room, much of which was taken up by a slightly raised dais covered with spotlessly white cloth. Sitting on one corner we were served with what appeared to be sweet yoghurt and betel leaves, well laced with lime. Suddenly the electric lights went out again, plunging us into complete darkness. There was no sound of bombs exploding or even anti-aircraft guns so we sat tight and with nothing better to do, we ate yoghurt and chewed betel. What do you do with all that red saliva when surrounded by spotlessly white cloth? You use your yoghurt bowl and your handkerchief.

At last electricity was restored and, before we had time to check for red stains, silk merchants entered and literally threw their wares into the air until they covered the white arena. We had never seen cloth like it and when we were told how it was made we understood the high price: sari lengths had taken families large chunks of their working lives to gather, spin, dye and weave, the techniques and patterns having been handed down only through the male of the line. There were of course some lesser cloths, and from these Rosemary was allowed to choose a sari, not a sales pitch but a gift.

Next stop on the broad-gauge line was Lucknow where we were guests both of the university and the Botanical Institute – a purpose-built centre for research into, amongst other things, the canons of Arduvedic herbal medicine. An oval mural depicting Mahatma Gandhi, walking away into the distance occupied one wall of the entrance hall. It reminded me of the Pathe Gazette news films I had seen as a child: that tiny dynamo of a man pleading the cause of 'small is beautiful, hand looms' with the buxom workers in the dark satanic mills of Lancashire.

Our host was Professor K.N. Kaul who invited us to a high society wedding and suggested that I should go to the local tailor to get the proper attire, which included a Nehru cap. The immaculate suit was ready in six hours and the wedding, which commenced with the spectacle of the groom riding into the compound on a great white horse which appeared to be almost encased in gold, lasted three days. The procession was flanked by what seemed an endless stream of men bearing Tilly lamps festooned with crystal lustres. As honoured guests we were introduced to the bride who was sheathed in silk even more wondrous than that which had been blown across our minds in Benares. The food was an endless array of gourmet dishes served with all the ceremony they deserved. The only sign of the twentieth century was Coca-Cola. The young men showed their daring by piling on the hot chilli pepper to every curry on the menu.

Despite all this pomp and circumstance, the most impressive thing we saw during our visit was the work of Professor K. N. Kaul on the rehabilitation of the hyperalkaline soils that had been produced by recent changes in farming practice. His method was to plant local trees, so providing shade and putting organic matter back into the soil, all this backed by research on the use of traditional crops and traditional herbs which together would provide a healthy diet and an affordable herbal health service for the exploding population.

The last leg of our journey was overnight into Delhi. Despite my A level in physics, I will never understand how diminutive and aged porters, with legs and arms like bean sticks, could carry cases we could hardly lift. Defying the laws of gravity up these went on their heads and stayed there as they waited patiently in the glaring sun to load them into your carriage. As night came the smoky light of thousands of paraffin lamps and cooking fires picked out villages and small towns, a twinkling concatenation that coalesced as the train approached the capital. Sunrise woke us in time to see the world's greatest lesson in wise use of resources as every field left between the houses was scattered with squatting men, each doing their daily duty of recycling while sharing the daily news by word of mouth, no need for newsprint. Each had a brass or aluminium pot of water, one hand being used for wiping, while the other was reserved for eating. A good job done, for them it was but a short walk back home to enjoy breakfast gathered fresh from last season's shitting fields. As we prepared for home I wondered what chance the wildlife of India had of survival in the face of a then exploding human population. Could the then still nascent World Wildlife Fund ever save the tiger?

Landing at Heathrow we went back to reality of another sort, with a battle hotting up on the local horizon. Cow Green in Upper Teesdale had for some time been under the threat of a large reservoir, designed to supply water to industrial Teesside. Battle lines were drawn: jobs and prosperity for some in the north-east, against the survival of one of the most important sites for the wildflowers of Europe.

A message from the Teesdale Defence Committee of the Botanical Society of the British Isles says it all.

> MORE FUNDS ARE NEEDED URGENTLY. Although the response to our appeal has been magnificent (£9,000), it is not enough to match the massive resources of the Water Board backed by ICI. This is an unavoidably expensive battle. For the present commitments, and for the petition to the House of Lords, the Committee estimates that a further £7,000 will be needed.

An article from *The Times*, suggesting that atomic powered desalination plants might hold the key to freshwater supplies in the future, indicates what the new conservation movement was up against.

I was called out by a local news crew to cover the story and in driving rain did my best to try to demonstrate the reasons for our concern, the very special plants of Teesdale. Sadly they hadn't brought their close-up lenses and wanted to know if there were any bigger orchids to film. The problem of making the general public understand the importance of conservation was even then beginning to raise its difficult head. 'Jobs versus flowers', is what the media said. Despite the fact that heavy industry on Teesside was entering a state of rapid decline, its pundits, managements and unions were demanding more water.

Eventually we lost the battle and the reservoir was built, erasing the wheel of the Tees from the face and the map of the dale, and taming the two great waterfalls that attracted tens of thousands of visitors every year. The huge body of dark, peat-stained water was also a threat to the unique communities of arctic alpine and alpine plants that wove their magic along the north-facing slopes of Widdybank Fell, the rising bulk of which used to trap the cold air draining down the valley from the high Pennines. The idea of global warming was still decades away, but the replacement of a frost trap by a heat store was not likely to improve matters, especially the chance of survival of these unique plant communities.

While certain voices welcomed the idea of a large body of water to attract more species of birds to their National Nature Reserve, ICI supplied some of the money for a research programme to record what would be lost as the reservoir went ahead. Margaret Bradshaw, a tireless worker with the Extra Mural Department, got the job, and between them she and her assistant and loyal volunteers from her evening classes spent thousands of hours, come rain or shine, down on their knees, recording the exact position of all the rarities for posterity. Margaret Elizabeth Bradshaw was awarded a well-deserved MBE for her Trojan work, and I dedicated my book about the dale, to MEB-MBE. It was called *The Great Seasons* and was eventually turned into four documentaries of the same name.

At that time the local papers were also full of plans concerning a group of hand-picked boy scouts from the north-east who were going to provide support for a scientific expedition that planned to study the vegetation of north-west Spain, from the top of the Sierra Cabrera to the depths of the kelp forests off the famous fishing port of Vigo. Having been a scout, and knowing of their insatiable desire to camp in strange places, I had thought it seemed like a good idea when I'd had it some eighteen months before. Now, however, with an increase in family size at last coming to fruition, I was a worried man.

13 Family Matters

I MUST CONFESS that this was the chapter I really didn't want to have to write, not because I didn't want a family but because, in hindsight, when it comes to family matters the most complimentary description of me, would be 'absentee father'.

To go back in time a little, once we had a house of our own and had decided to let nature take its intercourse, problems dogged our family planning: the little Bellamys-to-be didn't feel inclined to stay the course. We were both distraught and so were the grandparents, waiting in the wings with knitting needles at the ready. Miscarriages in the early stages are bad enough, but when a child is born and lives only for a few hours the pain for both parents is appalling. To compound the problem, whenever a family crisis loomed I was all too often away over the horizon.

Timothy was born on 26 January 1964 and lived almost a day. Fathers were not allowed at the bedside in those days, but I saw this tiny scrap of a thing and was allowed to cradle him in my arms. Biologically I – or rather we – had filled our sole biological function. For better or for worse we were now a 100 per cent living partnership, having passed on a mixture of our genes to another generation. For a few hours we were the proudest of parents, and Rosemary, who had always wanted a boy first, was overjoyed. Then all our dreams were shattered when the light, which had for a few hours lit up a new future, was gone.

Phoning round to tell our parents the news was the most difficult thing I ever had to do. How do you soften the blow of 'Rosemary has had a boy, his name is a good biblical one, Timothy, but he's gone to live with Jesus.' I couldn't even say that 'Dad' was doing fine because mental anguish is a terrible thing. I left Rosemary in the care of Dryburn Hospital and went to record both the birth and the death of our first born son in that order. Forms are easy to fill in, but talking about it, even to a kindly official who congratulated me for becoming a father before he heard the worst, tangles you up inside. The whole Botany department and all our friends rallied round, but the sight of a tiny coffin disappearing through the automatic doors in the crematorium was too much; perhaps sorrow is best borne in solitude. I went back to the hospital to be with Rosemary.

We sought the best advice we could from Mr Williamson, Dryburn's resident obstetrician, who advised us to try again as soon as we felt able. On 26 November in that same year, Samantha, who had been born the day before, followed the same route as Timothy to heaven. Both had been christened in hospital as was then usual if a baby was in any risk. I had already been planning our trip down to Liberty's to buy her first frock, just like Mum had planned to do if I had been a girl. I understood the sorrow of the parents of the children we had helped bury in Sierra Leone, but at least they had a grave that they could tend until it was swallowed up by the regenerating forest. So it was that we went to see the Church of England Children's Society and started down the long road to adoption. Much later, I joined the Bishop of Ely and the Arbory Trust to help make official woodland burials possible, blessed by the Church of England.

Back from India, and having already used up our favourite names, we spent many hours going through those fascinating but frustrating books of lists to have some new ones at the ready. Rufus appeared on 8 June 1966. Martin Williamson had given permission for me to be at the birth. I was of course very excited and sat with Rosemary in the hospital for most of the afternoon and evening. As all appeared quiet, I was sent home just before midnight, only to be phoned a few hours later to be told that a baby boy had been born at 2 a.m. and both mother and son were doing fine. Despite our preparations, he got his name from the fact that when I first saw him his chin was covered with reddish down. He was premature by some five weeks and we were very worried. The whole Bellamy clan had their fingers very tightly crossed as he was transferred to the intensive care unit. There, under the ever-watchful eye of Sister Holland, he went from strength to strength.

Four weeks later we went to collect Rufus in my then most prized possession, a self-build Lotus Super Seven. I had already got used to people saying rude things about it: like the policeman who flagged me down on my first trip to the university and, stepping into the road, asked, 'What is it?' 'A car,' said I, to which he replied, 'Get it off my foot.' In those days the traffic through the centre of the city was controlled by a policeman sitting in a glass box, glued to a television monitor. Cars coming up over Framwellgate Bridge and turning up on to Palace Green had to circumnavigate this obstacle. The car being so low on the ground he never knew that I and my Lotus were there, and so I had to reach up and knock on the window in order to be let through, followed by expletives. Cruellest of all was Sister Holland's query, 'You're not taking him home in that?' As if ready for my reply, 'Well, if he doesn't he will have to walk,' she produced a knitted bonnet to protect him from the elements and the strange behaviour of his Dad.

Even then, deep down, I knew that the Lotus must eventually go, to be replaced by something more like a family saloon that would protect us from the northern winters. The turning point came when, on returning home from an Extra Mural class one autumnal night, I had real problems because, sitting almost at headlight level, the only way I could see over their glare on the thick fog was to kneel up on one leg. I borrowed a walking stick to work the accelerator and limped home. Then, to cap it all, a few nights later I eased past a large lorry on the A1 and found myself up to my waist in melting slush. I took it out for a final run up the A69 towards Otterburn and did four circuits over the bumps put there by the Romans, long before flying Lotuses were invented. A much more sensible Vauxhall van took its place.

My first bout of practice at being a Dad soon came to an end as I rushed off to join the expedition in Spain, so setting a pattern of which I am completely ashamed.

Doctor's orders suggested that we should wait a while before trying for another baby of our own and so we were finally vetted for adoption and passed with flying colours. Almost at the same time we were offered joint moral tutorships at the newly built St Aiden's College, designed by Sir Basil Spence no less. The offer was made by the Principal, Dame Enid Russel Smith, and it came with a natty little bungalow, 1 Windmill Hill, which enjoyed one of the best views out across the heritage skyline of the city. I always said that Sir Basil must be very good at cathedrals and colleges but he wasn't very good at bungalows, for the only window that looked in the direction of what was to become a World Heritage Site, was the loo. To add insult to injustice, when I was sitting on the lavatory, I was facing in exactly the wrong direction. My father had decided to take early retirement from Boots and they bought our bungalow at Witton Grove and came to live in the north-east.

Going to see a baby that may become a new member of your family is a strange experience. The adoption papers gave adequate details, warts and all, but when you first make eye contact something very special happens. We were going to have that experience in all six times, and only on one occasion did we turn to each other and say no, all the other times it was an immediate yes. Neither of us can explain why, but that's the truth. Some people might be tempted to say, 'How lucky, why should they have been allowed to adopt so many?' Our only excuse is that it was much easier back then: there were many more babies crying out to find families.

We took Rufus – then three years old – with us and set off in our Vauxhall van, discussing potential names en route. By the time we had arrived the favourite was Abigail. Left in her presence we all said 'yes' and then, while taking turns to have a cuddle, we discovered two tortoises in the room, the female of the pair having Henrietta inscribed across her shell, and that is how we got a Henry instead of an Abigail. I think she was just as pleased as we were and settled down in Windmill Hill with our pet white rabbit who lived in a cage from which it escaped to breed profusely with the grey wild ones in the college grounds, giving our young family and tutees an object lesson in Mendelian genetics.

Women's colleges and moral tutors may seem a somewhat archaic concept in this day and age but, whatever its shortcomings, the system worked. For many of the students this was their first time away from home and some needed more than a shoulder to cry on. The more worldly came and drank our sherry and passed the time of day, whenever it was convenient. However every year, for one or two, I like to think that being able to be part of our family helped them get through their three years as undergraduates. Tutees also provided an endless stream of baby-sitters, so Rosemary could keep her academic interests up to date by teaching at the local Tech, and part-time at Durham School.

After the trauma of two more miscarriages we were invited to go and see Brighid and immediately fell in love, bringing her home not to Windmill Hill but to Observatory House. Dame Enid had retired as Principal, leaving a great void in both the college and the university. Her cigar-smoking replacement, Irene Hindmarsh, though as different as blue Stilton and Brie, was a great success. She came complete with her Mum, and therefore needed something a bit more commodious than the Principal's flat. So, she took over Number One and we were offered Observatory House, a rambling property with a large wrap-around garden tucked between Windmill Hill and Observatory Hill.

This was a great place in which to raise our now multicultural family. I use that word rather than 'multinational' for all our family were born in Britain. Although it was possible to adopt children from other countries, the process was long and could be very painful, with proceedings falling through even after you had met the child. We had already had the trauma of such an adoption in Britain. Sam had become part of our family when his genetic mum and dad decided to get married and, naturally, he went to live with them. We were all broken hearted, that first-sight bond was much stronger than either of us had ever imagined and that included the children.

There was one problem with Observatory House. Its walls were thin and hence our heating bills were enormous. We could understand why no Professor of Astronomy ever came to take up residence. The fact that it had nine bedrooms not only compounded the heating bill but also set us on the road back to what had now become known in family circles as 'The Church of England Building Society', for Rufus was demanding a little brother.

Our next addition was a baby boy of Asian origins. We greeted him with an immediate 'yes', but had to wait several weeks while Eoghain got over a bout of jaundice compounded with eczema. The homecoming was a day of great jubilation, marred only by the fact that he soon caught chicken pox which, together with his eczema, turned him into a mass of weeping itchiness. Only the spots were weeping, however, Eoghain just sat and smiled and smiled and smiled until the bout was all over, and to this day he is the most laid back member of our family.

With so many spare bedrooms, we took tutees and students as lodgers, swelling our family of adoptive uncles and aunties and helping to pay the heating bills. However there was a sort of niggle in the back of our minds: shouldn't we become house owners once more? So it was that we began to scan the local market. Finding a nice medium-sized Georgian number way out in the country, we took a look and even went and made a bid. Sadly our maximum was not nearly large enough to secure the prize, so went back home with our tails very much between our dented egos. Next day my phone rang in the department and a voice at the other end said, 'We hear you are interested in buying a house near Hamsterley. We live in the one next door and are just about to put it on the market, would you be interested?' We went round like a shot, and moved in a few months later.

It was and still is a fabulous family home, not really big enough, but what a place to grow up in, set in a crook of the Bedburn Beck, with what I then thought was a bit of almost natural deciduous forest filling most of a large garden. This included an orchard, vegetable patch and two lawns, part of it in the shadow of a five-storey mill that was in a very poor state of repair. All this was at the gateway to the local Forestry Commission Plantation, with forest trails, bridle tracks and a local riding school run by Judy Dennis. What more could two young girls and two rapidly growing boys want?

The first weekend in our new home was a voyage of very special discovery. We all took to the beck and, though cold, it made for great swimming – a bit hazardous because the bottom of the pools consisted of all sorts of bits and pieces of scrap iron, horseshoes, springs, cogs, broken tools and the like, all welded together by aeons of rust. There were great screams as Rufus and Henry disappeared into a secret passage in the riverbank. The entrance was too narrow for my shoulders, so I had to do with a second-hand account of what was there. 'Large lumps of wood' came the muffled cry. Weekends became a mixture of get the homework done as quickly as possible and on with the excavations. The first thing we discovered was the remains of a spade mill, driven in its prime by an overshot waterwheel. Where the gigantic hammer had been, there were the rusted remains of perhaps the last hay spade it ever stamped out. The excavation carries on in fits and starts to this day. At the moment we are removing the ash and clinker from the steam engine era and somewhere, we believe, are the remains of the Bishop of Durham's Iron Bloomery, dating to 1408.

Iseabal Hannah – always known thereafter as Hannah – with a mass of somewhat unruly black curls came to live with us at Bedburn two years later, in 1978, and we all lived there happily ever after – well at least until careers called them away to distant places. Many family discussions about adopting more children took place over the years, with really heavy campaigning for a Chinese brother or sister – 'Why not one of each?' When we asked 'Why?' the immediate answer was, 'Well we haven't got one of those.' Despite all this, family size has remained at seven, the two of us plus five on some days exasperating but on most days fantastic kids.

The largest total of family pets at any one time was 134, mostly guinea pigs and rabbits but including horses, sorry ponies, a lamb, two chinchillas, a gerbil, seven cats, Mum's Aylesbury and Muscovy ducks, chickens, bantams, guinea fowl, a budgie, assorted goldfish and shubunkins, and an annual crop of baby rooks that fall out of their nests in a high wind. I forgot to tell you that the garden is blessed with a large rookery. We eat the chicken and duck eggs, but all their mortal remains are given a decent burial in the garden, although as a conservationist I draw a line at wooden crosses for them all.

My Mum was there at Hannah's christening and so saw the family in its complete form. I wish she had been with us when Brighid would have made her a Great Granny, but that was not to be. The night Mum died was the worst of my life. The whole of County Durham was wrapped in thick fog and I was in a very deep sleep when the phone rang and our doctor broke the news. I had thought I had prepared myself – one day it had to happen – but I evidently hadn't convinced my lachrymal glands. I suddenly understood the meaning of 'floods of tears'. They soaked the bed and the car all the way to Durham. The doctor had waited with Dad until I arrived and we sat together, each enveloped in our own grief. Mum had, as usual, cleaned the house from end to end, and on returning home from a shopping trip, sat down and became an angel. A very special memorial service, held at Sutton Baptist Church, was made a little more bearable when the minister quoted a passage from the Bible: 'As you climb the Golden Stairs you see Angels ascending and descending'.

The smell of lavender always reminds me of my Granny, and the telephone reminds me of my parents, for they were always there at the other end, eager to have a chat. To this day I will rush towards the telephone intent on sharing any news – 'I must tell Mum and Dad' – and then I turn back, bereft of the comfort of their voices. Voices are strange things, a unique trademark, and I still hear their voices in my dreams and nightmares. But for the presence of Rosemary and the family, I don't think I could bear those moments of despair. Families are very special things and apart from all the Bellamys and 'Other Mother', I must record my great debt to two other wonderful ladies: little Edith Mordue and big Edith Coverdale who have, over the years, been towers of strength in both household and family matters. Without them life would have been much more of a problem.

Rosemary and I are still happily ensconced in the Mill House and the children come to stay whenever they can. Christmas is a particularly special time – and I still firmly believe in Father Christmas. After all, I look more like him every year. When we are tucked up in bed after midnight communion in Hamsterley church, stockings overflowing with fascinating things, collected by Rosemary over the year, are placed at the foot of each bed. Then, after breakfast, the main presents are opened around the tree. Christmas dinner is completed in time to listen to the Queen's speech.

The Mill House dining table can accommodate twelve at a pinch, with the cats and the dog waiting in hope beneath. Lengthy discussions before Christmas are just as important as notes up the chimney, for they decide what the main dish is to be. My favourite always was pork, but now that it doesn't have the crackling it used to, I'll settle for a goose, not that I get my way that often. Stuffing, I never did like, but the crackly bacon, roast potatoes, parsnips, mince pies and plum pudding, wow, what would Christmas dinner be like if any one of them was left out?

Games have changed with the years but we still play Monopoly with great zest and then it's time for tea: jelly, junket or blancmange are old faithfuls, although Angel Delight has edged itself into pole position in more recent years, then home-made Christmas cake and crackers, just like we used to have back home in Cheam. Times may change but family traditions and rituals must go on for ever.

14 SCREAMING FROM MY IVORY TOWER

MEANWHILE, BACK TO 1967. David John had just completed his base line surveys of the seaweeds around the coasts of Cornwall, when the impossible happened. The *Torrey Canyon* super tanker struck rocks off the Lizard and foundered, sending massive oil slicks towards the holiday coast. Pictures of oiled birds crowded the pages of broadsheets and tabloids alike, and the local fishermen and the tourist industry were adamant that something had to be done and quick. In an attempt to burn off some of the oil, 161 bombs, sixteen rockets and 3,200 gallons of napalm were hurled at the remains of the stricken ship, while £16 million was spent on pouring any old detergent on the beaches and rocky shores.

The media, hungry for an expert in marine pollution, dragged me screaming from my ivory tower and demanded good council. Here the scene gets a little confused as both BBC and ITV, in the guise of Yorkshire and Tyne Tees Television, claim my discovery: I was certainly interviewed on a number of beaches along the north-east coast, all of them polluted by sewage and all besmirched with oil provided by kind permission of the tankers which were in those days allowed to flush their empty tanks into the sea. John Craven, then a rookie reporter for BBC

North East, stood me on a concrete pipe that was discharging raw sewage into the sea not far from Redcar: 'Tell us about the problems of marine pollution.' As the pipe was encrusted with *Mytillus edulis*, the common edible mussel, my reply went something like this: 'You see what's coming out of the end of that pipe, it may be shhhhh, you know what, to you and me, but to a mussel, that's cordon blue cookery.' Evidently people in high places were watching and legend has it that Paul Fox, then head of YTV, saw the clip and said, 'Sign him up.'

Amongst all the mayhem of media hype, I had the audacity to suggest that, as my team had detailed pre-pollution data, perhaps we should be financed to go back and check out the damage in Cornwall. The immediate response was, send your data to the Marine Laboratory at Plymouth, they will do the resurvey. Then I probably made my next real career mistake. In the politest of terms I said, 'Stuff it.' Unfortunately, this displeased Sir Solly Zuckerman, who was the government's chief science adviser, not a man to be crossed. Fortunately I had made my remark within the earshot of the press, who came to my rescue in the guise of several articles by Angela Croome. These prompted several true British citizens to offer finance. All we needed was some £800 so, while we were waiting for officialdom to make up its mind, I borrowed it out of my current research grant and got on with the job before the crucial evidence was washed away.

It was all hands to the pumps as the whole team, including the Bellamy family, camped in Sennen Cove, ready to carry out the resurvey. I think it was at that juncture that Rosemary got an inkling of what family life was going to be like from then on. The sun was hot and the work progressed rapidly, the whole team diving twice a day, returning to shore with kelp plants for full analysis on the beach. As our suntans turned from painful red to sand burned brown, the data made it clear that, apart from the birds, the real damage had been done below high tide mark in those areas that had been subjected to detergents. The rocky shores that had been left to their own devices recovered remarkably quickly. A brief resurvey later in the year confirmed our findings, and a paper on our work was hurriedly submitted to *Nature* and was published the following week on 23 December 1967: 'Effects of

Pollution from the *Torrey Canyon* on Littoral and Sublittoral Ecosystems' by D.J. Bellamy, P.H. Clarke, D.M. John, D. Jones and A. Whittick, Departments of Botany and Engineering Science, University of Durham, and T. Darke, Glencoe, Porthcothan. Tom Darke was a Cornishman, and it was his local knowledge that made the rapid resurvey possible.

This period of work gave a boost to all our careers. David John, after working in a number of African universities is now at the Natural History Museum in London and travels the world studying seaweeds. Alan Whittick went off to Newfoundland, where he is on the staff of the university. Dai Jones, after a career that spanned Canada, is now an environmental consultant based near Vancouver.

Marine pollution was all of a sudden part of the big agenda. I found myself invited to lecture all over the place and became a founder member of the Royal Society's Marine Pollution Discussion Group. It is an awe inspiring thing to turn up by invitation, at the portals of the world's most prestigious scientific society, let alone to be asked immediately what your travel expenses are and to be paid in cash, on the spot, out of a tin box. The discussions were of great interest and showed just how little anyone had even thought about the problem, let alone done any real research on it. Incredulity was rife, how could a single land based species ever have any real effect on the oceans, which cover five-sevenths of this ill-named planet? Members from the navy and the medical profession gave testimony about the then widely held opinion that you could never catch anything nasty just by swimming in the sea. One piece of conflicting research told of a whole group of soldiers who had been ordered to demonstrate their swimming prowess in a marine bathing pool. Sadly, it was polluted with some very nasty sewage and the number of men that went down with cholera was directly correlated with the number of lengths they had swum. However, it was rapidly pointed out that dilution made open sea bathing a safe pastime. I can guess what Surfers against Sewage would say to such statements in the light of another thirty years of experience.

I pointed out the fact that the Second World War had inadvertently been a gigantic experiment (although one I didn't seek a grant to repeat) in which hundreds of ships and planes, full of toxic chemicals, had gone down in what we now call the Irish Fish Box. I also pointed out the fact that some of the best dive and sport fishing sites were around wrecks, and that despite all the pollution and seismic upheaval, those wartime years had seen a remarkable recovery of the fish stocks in the area. All this hinted that it was not going to be easy to sort out the effects of overfishing from pollution.

Several research projects followed as we spread our fins, monitoring the health of the oceans. We even got tied up with a dental school in a search for mussels, not for eating but the object being to be able to use the chemical which holds mussels fast on wet rocks to do the same for fillings.

Of all the people I ever teamed up with, Andrea Pfister is the most unlikely. I have a very untidy will-o-the-wisp sort of mind, but for Andrea every fact has a pigeonhole and whatever the question, the messenger pigeons fly out in ordered rank, providing you with an answer that leaves you saying, 'I wish I could do that.' Andrea is also a great gadget master. Swiss Italian by extraction, he discovered me in Santa Maria De Castellabate at a workshop organised by Pietro Dhorn, the latest member of the family line that had, with Charles Darwin's blessing, founded the Stazione Zoologica in Naples. The workshop was on planning and running underwater national parks, and a very diverse crew of students, teachers and divers turned up. My team came down with our by then ageing Zodiac and Jim Barnes as dive leader. Andrea came with all the latest dive gear and looked not unlike a Christmas tree in Oscar Gugen's Dive Shop.

It was here that I not only got the taste for Italian food but also learned that Leonardo Da Vinci himself had suggested 'that a model of the Mediterranean should be made, showing all the inputs of water from the rivers and the outflow through the straits of Gibraltar', all this 'in order to be able to trace the source and the fate of the pollutants' that even then persuaded rich Romans it was better to take their holidays on the Atlantic coast of Spain, where large tides twice a day kept the beaches clean. Here we were in the second half of the twentieth century, a couple of years after James Watson had sat in the zoological station at Naples, deliberating on his part of the classic paper on the basic structure of DNA, yet Europe was still without a model which would allow real decisions to be made about the problems of pollution in an almost tideless sea.

The workshop was a rattling success. The results of our deliberations and Pietro Dhorn's power of rhetoric even persuaded the local fishermen that, when a night's fuel costs more than the market value of the fish they catch, it really is time to get off the road to ruin – not only for themselves but for the future of their families and the fisheries upon which their ancestors had depended. The only reason that they could even contemplate doing this was that our 'mad' idea offered them another way of making a living: our argument was that they should set the area up as a marine park and let the fishers earn a living as wardens and guides. Then, when the fish stocks had recovered, they could continue to fish in time honoured ways to feed their families and the growing numbers of tourists. We were of course dreamers, and our dreams included working holidays for sport fishermen, and even for people to come and learn how to make the traditional fishing boats that were still constructed with axe and adze right there on the beach. Rosemary and I even looked at a disused fisherman's cottage with an enormous mulberry tree and dreamed of living and working in the park. In hindsight, it would have been a good investment as the whole area is now packed with hotels. The dream was swallowed up by the course of local politics. The party that agreed to consider the matter lost power and the fishers left out in the cold went off the boil and continued to overfish the area, using dynamite when the fish were too small to make any other method viable.

My next major marine pollution summons was to a meeting at the headquarters of the United Nations, Food and Agriculture Organisation (FAO) in Rome, where I found myself in the company of Arthur Bourne from the Central Office of Information. I had already met Arthur when he introduced me to Kit Peddlar, a world expert in the human retina and mastermind behind the television series *Doom Watch*, a sort of environmental *Quatermass*. These were the first television programmes that opened the eyes of the British public to the potential horrors of mucking about with the environment, especially in the absence of real information on the effects of novel chemicals, let alone novel, untested ideas. A classic in the series concerned the release of engineered bacteria that digested all the plastic in a transatlantic airliner. I can well remember our first meeting at a bistro somewhere in London where I first ate pigeon and drank good French wine. Kit drove a yellow Lotus and I was impressed. Our discussions ranged from the setting up of a global village down in London's decaying docklands to the possibility of projects in the Cameroons that would save what little was left of the rain forest by letting the local people live on in harmony on their land. The rationale behind the idea was simple, the right sort of tourism, with people paying to go and stay in their villages where they could eat real, yes, organic food. Sadly, finding no support in Britain for his research into his global village or his computer model of the human retina, Kit took himself off to Canada.

Listening to all the rhetoric at my first meeting as part of a committee at the FAO, I was appalled at what I saw as a lack of reality in their deliberations. 'How,' I asked at question time, 'can we plan to continue to pollute the sea when we do nothing to curtail overfishing?' I might have got away with that but I added, 'And surely we should say something about the population explosion.' The Vatican newspaper interviewed me, and it was the first time I was asked the question, 'What do you fear most for the world?' My answer, as it has been ever since, was: 'An exploding population with exploding material desires'. The main attack on my effrontery came from the contingent from our own Ministry of Agriculture Fisheries and Food: 'You can't behave like that at an international meeting, this could be the end of your career.' I suppose in some ways it was, if I had desired a life as a career biologist caught up in an interminable round of costly international conferences. Arthur Bourne roared back to the UK to collect some vital data and with a little bit of filibustering we did get something about population included in the conference deliberations.

It was at this conference that I first came face to face with the difference between pure scientists and career scientists; please note I do not say 'pure and applied' for there are career scientists on both sides of that particular divide. I think my allegiance to pure science stems back to my physics master at school. Streak Lorimer was very tall and thin with a biting tongue. As my mathematics left a lot to be desired, I was not very good at physics, but all the definitions, which we were expected to keep in copperplate in a special notebook, fascinated me. I can't honestly say that I can still remember many of them but one has stuck in my mind: 'The centre of gravity is the point of application of the resultant of all the parallel forces of gravity acting upon the individual particles which comprise the body.' I wrote it down and scratched my head, I didn't understand. With some temerity I went and asked him to explain please. He did just that, with diagrams and stories of Newton's apple and the *Principia*, explaining again and again that once you had definitions and laws that could be shown to work, then, as a scientist, you were honour bound to tell the truth within the bounds of those laws.

What with my Christian upbringing and scientific ethics à la Streak I was skewered, and have tried always to stick with pure science. Indeed, as I write, I can reach up and hold a copy (sadly only a facsimile) of the *Principia* in my hands. The university library had a copy of the original locked away in the rare books section, and though my knowledge of Latin, apart from the binomials of plants and animals, was nil, I used to go and leaf through its pages when I was particularly worried about something. Such contact with a real piece of history somehow helped, and I could console myself with the fact that my tribulations were trivial compared with those of Copernicus, Galileo and Newton.

Common sense warned that if people were producing the pollutants and if population pressure and mismanagement were causing the over-fishing, then surely it was a losing battle and hence a total waste of money if we didn't do something about the root cause. That is why I finally bowed out of the field of marine pollution research and refused another grant to carry on programmes of *a posteori* monitoring. Why not just stop people using the sea as a general dustbin, or at least demand that they tell us what, where and how much of what, they are putting in? It was as I emerged from a very murky Tees estuary that I found someone on a boat labelled ICI who was seeking answers to similar questions. I am sure that it was this encounter with someone on the 'opposite side' which helped sow the seed that, thanks to David Shreeve, germinated fifteen years later into the Conservation Foundation. The sole object of this was to publicise the good news stories of industry and conservation working together to right the environmental wrongs of the past and set a programme towards zero emissions, for the sake of all our futures; good news extolling the virtues of the work of a new partnership of industry and conservation that helped make the Tees estuary part of a living river once again.

Phytosociology, peatlands, marine pollution, summers in the high Arctic and winters diving in the Indian Ocean: was I becoming a polymath or a catastrophe in the making? I often said to myself, for God's sake, stick to one subject and sort your ideas out. Well deep down I was trying, but every next telephone call, letter or even tutorial brought new, exciting challenges. However, I did co-author a paper, reproduced in full in Appendix 3, which was the result of a student tutorial that started in its appointed hour before lunch, spilled over into the New Inn, occupied the whole afternoon and continued into the early hours of the next day. To anyone except the purest of mathematicians, thermodynamics is perhaps the murkiest of waters in which to dabble, but I make no apologies for including this missive to *Nature* in 1968. It was the most important paper I ever managed to get published. It may seem to the uninitiated to contain scientific gobbledygook, but it convinced me that the succession of plant communities on any piece of land is simply and elegantly a continuation of the process of organic evolution. Life, even if it is a unique product of the Earth, has to obey the laws of the universe, laws laid down at the moment of or in the act of creation. As a Christian and a scientist I found this revelation a much more tenable idea than that of a God setting out to create each species separately.

I can only apologise if I offend any of my readers. The fact is that the more my privileged life style has allowed me to understand the perfection of the plants and animals (let alone the intricate checks and balances that typify all living systems of which they and we are a part), the more difficult it has been for me to see any real difference between evolution and creation. What is more, the difference between the world's religions and religious philosophies appear just as blurred.

I cannot tell you what the reaction of the scientific commune was to the paper, for, as far as I can ascertain, the only written remark came from one of its referees who intimated that 'there was no need to publish this paper as it contained nothing new'. Fortunately, the editorial board of *Nature* begged to differ.

15 MEANWHILE, BACK ON THE BOGS

DESPITE ALL THE hype of marine pollution, peat bogs always were and always will be my major passion. So it was that I teamed up with Tom Pritchard, who had landed the job as regional officer of the Nature Conservancy Council in the west Midlands. It was in his offices, housed in the stable block of Attingham Park, that Project Telma was dreamed up, and it was in that great house that an international meeting of peatland experts first met to discuss what could be done about the world's rapidly disappearing peat bogs.

Everybody who was anybody in the peatland world turned up for three days of hectic workshop sessions. One member, who had more to say than most (everyone thought he was my elder brother), was in fact Professor Bill Radforth of the Muskeg Research Institute in the Maritimes of eastern Canada. Muskeg is the word used by the first people of Canada for any area covered with peat. Among Bill's talents was air photo interpretation and the classification of the muskegs of that real cool slab of real estate which boasts some 30 per cent of the peat of the world – second only to Russia with, believe it or not, little old Ireland coming third. The Emerald Isle was well represented at the meeting by Father J.J. Moore of the University of Dublin, a phytosociologist and one of the most charismatic lecturers I ever had the pleasure to hear.

At the end of the meeting Bill Radforth invited Tom and me to go on a lecture tour of Canada to meet all the peatniks in Winnipeg, Waterloo, Toronto, Arcadia, Newfoundland and Nova Scotia. At each stopover we met old friends and made new acquaintances.

Jennifer Walker, the world expert on *Phragmites australis*, hadn't changed much since her London days where she did her PhD on one of the world's most widespread and important wetland plants. She still called it friggy frag, with a Joyce Grenfell type giggle. Tom and I booked in to an expensive hotel, the rooms of which had sealed windows and were so hot that I couldn't get any sleep, so we soon moved in with Jennifer. This was evidently not the done thing – a female member of staff, putting up two male colleagues – so a stentorian rap at the door revealed the college authorities, checking us out.

Field trips to look at the winter-bound muskegs that lined Lake Winnepegosis found me driving a very snazzy snow-mobile, with Tom on a little sledge hitched on the back. Though very noisy, it was a lot of fun and the only way to get about over the frozen lakes and bogs. Neither of us were experts either at skidooing nor at reading the muskeg terrain, and I almost wrote Tom off as we shot over a very steep peat bank. The university had a wonderful field station that looked not unlike the ski hotel in *White Christmas*. It was here that, amongst other things, we discussed the role of *Phragmites* in stripping minerals from flowing waters during the first stages of peat formation. Driving back to the freeway, through great herds of white tailed deer, the lack of deep snowdrifts brought us face to face with the conundrum that although very little rain or snow falls this far from the coast, wetlands are everywhere. The answer is that there are long, cold winters and a very flat terrain with permafrost lurking just below the surface of that enormous landscape; during the summer the permafrost melts, keeping the terrain saturated enough for peat formation. The fact is that if you chose your route, you would be able to walk, clear across Canada, on muskeg all the way.

Waterloo brought me back into contact with John Morton who had

TOP LEFT: Winifred May Green.
Before she was my mum

TOP RIGHT: Self, 1933

BELOW: Mum, G and me, 1935

ABOVE: Gervais and me
BELOW LEFT: My first school photo
BELOW RIGHT: Me and my gran

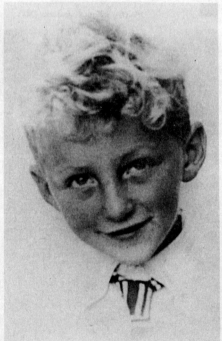

TOP LEFT: Gervais, Dad, Mum, me and Granny, Cheam, 1935

RIGHT: Spring Pond Cottage with special woodland behind

BELOW: G and me, Spring Pond Cottage, 1940

TOP LEFT: Me plus George Red Rex, garden in Cheam
TOP RIGHT: Big brother G, acting one of his many parts
BELOW: Ravenstor Youth Hostel (myself and Rosemary on step, left to right)

ABOVE: My first car, 1951

RIGHT: Rannoch Moor when I became a peatnik, 1958

BELOW: Margaret Cornish and Francis Rose

RIGHT: Francis Rose in action, 1957

Rannoch Moor, 1958

ABOVE: Mum, Dad and Rosemary,
Germany, 1958

RIGHT: Our wedding. 3rd January 1959

BELOW: Rosemary. Honeymoon in Ireland, 1959

ABOVE: Winter field trip. Ben Lawers, Scotland, 1962

LEFT AND BELOW: A Real Gone Don, 1960

ABOVE: Self and Stanislav Kulczynski
peat boring near Sczecin, 1959

RIGHT: Rosiebell, 1961

ABOVE: Raft race (left to right: Rosemary, Brian Witton, Geoff Banbury, self and Peter Pearson)
LEFT: Research team, Durham, 1964 (left to right: Jack Rielly, David John, Wendy Tickle, Alan Whittick, Peter Holland, Jenny Dodd, me and Keith Thompson)
BELOW: Operation Kelp, 1969

ABOVE: Rufus in the Lotus

ABOVE: Mum on the Maundy morning

RIGHT: Rosemary and Henrietta, Jura, 1974

BELOW: Rufus

nature

Vol 248 No 5444 March 8 1974   UK 35p USA $1.00   Macmillan Journals Limited

ABOVE: Cover of *Nature*

LEFT: *Half of Paradise*

BELOW: It's not a hammer head, honest

ABOVE: Talking to kids in Trinity College, 1984

BELOW: *Blue Peter* 50th birthday cake, on my return from prison in Australia

LEFT: Me, Dad and our first classic microscope

BELOW: Family picture (left to right: Rosemary, Hannah, Rufus, Henry, Eoghain, Brighid)

done his PhD with Professor Valentine at Durham and was now working on the flora of Manatoulin, the largest island in the world that is surrounded by fresh water. It was fascinating to see his floristic lists and the marginally sub-Arctic 'end of the ice age' communities bejewelled with birdseye primrose, very like those back home in upper Teesdale.

Arcadia University lived up to its name, a small campus set on the edge of the marshlands that had in their heyday supplied New York with all the hay needed to power a million-horse town. We stayed in a wonderful Victorian hotel, sleeping in four-posters and dining on silver plate, a real Ivy League interlude. At the end of my main lecture, a great bear of a student, dressed in somewhat dishevelled jeans, shambled up to ask me some impossible questions. His name was Ed Tyzinski and he had been a star player in American football when an in-game fracas put him in intensive care for a year, suffering from concussion. He had then been advised to go to university and use his considerable brainpower to get a degree and Arcadia had offered him a place. Ed wanted to sort of float around between the disciplines, a course of action which evidently didn't fit in with university protocol, so he had become something of an itinerant. He was a fascinating guy to talk with, his mind jumping from one subject to another but always making rational and exciting connections. So, when he asked if he could come and work with me in Durham, I jumped at the idea. It was not so easy when I found he had little in the way of academic qualifications. Still, on my return to Durham I approached the administration with his letter of application and he was accepted to read for an MSc. Uncle Ed became part of the Bellamy family before he found a house for himself and his wife in the then new town of Peterlee. Children were absolutely fascinated with him and our young son Rufus was no exception. They would play abstruse word and numbers games together for hours on end linking art and science with stories in the air.

Ed chose as his subject of research 'The Place of General Systems Theory in Biological Problems'. He was pitchforked into my small research lab, which already did its best to accommodate Jack Rieley, David Shimwell, Bert Bridgewater, Wendy Tickle, Keith Thompson,

Peter Holland and Alan Whittick. His thinking between the lines caused not a little altercation. In would come Ed with the enlightening idea of writing your phytosociological tables on rubber sheeting and stretching them over an oblate spheroid. He was of course too large to throw out, so we all had to sit down and discuss topology and evolution or some such obscure concept.

Phytosociology was perhaps another of my career mistakes. It is a technique developed across the continent of Europe which allows accurate description, naming and hence classification of vegetation. Britain, led by Sir Arthur Tansley, the first person to use the term ecosystem, had thrown the whole concept out of the window and gone its own less formal way. For some perhaps obstinate reason, I found the whole discipline fascinating and of great potential practical use. Carl Linnaeus's binomial system of giving all living things two Latin names had made it possible for natural historians the world over to talk with the same tongue. Tuxen, Braun Blanquet, and all the other continental phytosociologists in my opinion did the same for ecology.

I again found myself out on a limb, as it were, and so did all my students who based all their work on the principles of these continental schools. We all went to the annual meetings of the hierarchy of phytosociologists, which met in Reinholt Tuxen's institute near Rinteln, a small town not far from Hamelin in west Germany. There, not only did we meet all the other practitioners, but whatever our interest – be it succession, productivity, eco-physiology or just plain natural history – when it came to the specifics of vegetation, we all spoke with a common tongue. I well remember the débâcle of my first lecture to the group, which I tried to give in German. They laughed a lot.

To ensure vintage discussion, Tuxen would buy a large supply of a good local wine and we would talk away the night on subjects that ranged from the classification of medieval organ pipes and bacteriological succession during the menstrual cycle, through to the planning of the next international phytosociological excursion, one of which my team organised in Britain. Part of the planning was to engineer secretly the first meeting between Sandy Watt from Cambridge and Tuxen. At the end of the Second World War the Cambridge Botany School had leaned on the British authorities and succeeded in getting Tuxen and his institute back to work as quickly as possible. It was awesome to witness that meeting of two great minds, which we had arranged out on what little was left of the unique Breckland heaths of East Anglia. There Watt demonstrated his theories of pattern and process in vegetation and Tuxen translated it, at least for the believers, into Latin nomenclature. For me the culmination of the trip was when I was able to show the august multitude *Scheuchzeria palustris*, the Rannoch Rush, growing in Britain's only real example of *Scheuchzerietalia palustris*, that being the proper phytosociological name of the plant community I had studied during my undergraduate project. Little wonder that we all then went to the Rannoch Arms and drank the health of Tuxen in Spring Bank whisky, to me still the greatest single malt of them all. I decided there and then that I would write the definitive account of The Phytosociology of Pure Malt and am still savouring the research.

Summoned to give a paper on the conservation of peatlands at the Third International Peat Congress, held in Quebec in 1968, I found myself in the company of someone from the other side of the conservation fence: a remarkable Scotsman called Ken Whamond. Born in the Gorbals, he was then making a good living out of the extractive industries, which included digging peat from bogs around Falkirk. In an attempt to do the same the British government had acquired a bog, invested heavily in the latest equipment and failed miserably. Ken had snapped it up at a bargain price and made it work, selling the product under the name of Thistle Peat. Finding that it was money for old humus he had his eyes on as many peat bogs as he could get his drainage and peat digging equipment stuck into.

This was in the early days of the exploitation of peat for the mass horticultural industry. Multinational supermarket chains were galloping around the corner, demanding ever more massive, dedicated supplies of a whole range of what the Americans called truck vegetables and patio plants: multimillions of lettuces, cabbages, carrots, broccoli and mange tout. Everything the affluent could be pursuaded was good to eat, and of course plants and flowers to decorate their tables and instant gardens, were in ever greater demand. All the commercial growers began to use peat as a base substrate. The peat bogs of the world were in increasing danger every day.

I found myself with Ken, this larger than life character, watching the latest methods of winning peat from a series of raised bogs on the coast of New Brunswick. Giant machines were scarifying the surface of superb pristine raised bogs, scraping the loosened peat into wind-rows ready for drying and bagging for export. Gone were the turf cutters' donkeys and the back-breaking work with slanes. A group of business men came up to me and asked what area of muskeg they would need to buy in order to be able to exploit peat in a sustainable manner. My answer was, 'It all depends on how much peat you want to produce every year.' I also suggested that they asked the local people who were making their living out of this relatively new use of peat what they thought of the idea of outsiders cashing in on their resource. The latter didn't go down too well. The locals were all of good Catholic stock, their other livelihood coming from some of the world's richest lobster fisheries. We were gorged on their produce at a grand banquet laid on in our honour: as soon as you had finished one lobster another appeared on your plate. The showpiece was an individual with a single claw that weighed over two kilogrammes.

At the conference I had attempted to argue the case of Project Telma, which was trying to mobilise international co-operation in the conservation of peat bogs, but was shouted down, especially by the Russian, Finnish and Irish producers of horticultural peat, who pointed out that the real culprits were those who had decided to build chains of peat burning power stations. These were the ones who were really wasting this precious resource on a catastrophic scale. They were of course right. The low calorific value of even the best peat, and the long lines of rail tracks I had seen on my honeymoon, spreading across the peatlands of the central Irish plain, were proof positive. Common sense screamed out that it all involved short term profits and to hell with the future of the local people, let alone the local environment.

Ken and I ended up with a plan to look at all the peat bogs in Scotland that had already been ruined by forestry or other mismanagement, and see if peat extraction could be turned into a win-win situation: remove the trees, which shouldn't have been there in the first place, use the peat, and leave the bog in a viable state so that it would continue to provide a habitat for all the special plants and animals, until, some time in the distant future, the bog was again ready for exploitation. Sadly, it was going to take another thirty years of campaigning against Jiffy pots and grow-bags to get any real movement at governmental level to even think about conserving this important resource in England.

Collaboration and friendship also grew with Bill Radforth and I spent a number of field trips with him working in the high Arctic. In fact we travelled across the length and breadth of Canada, from Alert in the far north to the Maritimes in the east and to the fastest growing peats on Earth, way over in the west. I ate sturgeon and chips for the first time and came into contact with the culture of the Haida people: which involved sustainability, if it ever existed, set between the sea and the temperate rain forest that had once swathed much of the coast from Alaska clear down to California. Even then the forest was falling ever faster, to new and catastrophic methods of clear cut. Our research was being funded by the oil companies who were then busy parcelling up the terrain with seismic trails and plans for pipelines to transport the black gold down from the Arctic slope. Our output was published, where else but in *Nature*, on 18 June 1971. I also co-authored publications on the subject of peat and its conservation in the two subsequent years.

16 ISLANDS IN THE SUN

DESPITE MY WANDERINGS between the murky disciplines of marine pollution and peat bogs, I was tolerated and in some places even lauded, the greatest plaudit coming again from the Royal Society: an invitation to lead the first diving phase of their great expedition that was then laying down base line studies of Aldabra. Biologically one of the most important atolls in the Indian Ocean, this is the last natural home of the Indian Ocean giant tortoises, and plans to build a military airfield were putting it under serious threat.

The grapevine soon spread the message and I was inundated with requests to join the team, which eventually comprised: my first diving buddy and mentor Jim Barnes; Ed Drew from St Andrews, then a whizz kid in measuring the productivity of all things underwater; John Lythgoe, expert in the vision of fish; Brian Whitton, blue green algologist from Durham; Dai Jones, one of my research students, to carry all the heavy gear; and Lee Kenyon, perhaps the most unlikely member of the team.

Lee was an artist, in fact the artist who had copied all the documents for the prisoners in the famous wooden horse escape during the Second World War. A great character, he kept us enthralled with his stories.

One of the least bizarre was that of how he got into the diving game. Having seen an advert put out by Cousteau for someone to give lectures on his behalf, Lee applied for the job, saying he was a qualified diver. To his surprise he was called for an interview in the Mediterranean where Cousteau was busy excavating a wreck full of ancient amphora. Lee toddled along to the Chelsea branch of the British Sub Aqua Club and had a basic lesson in the pool before heading south for the interview. Arriving at the scene of the excavation, he was handed an aqualung and told that Cousteau was down on the wreck. So in he went for his first sea dive. En route down he found he couldn't see a thing, and on reaching the wreck he grabbed at an amphora to anchor himself. The neck broke off and both he and his anchor shot to the surface, followed by an inquisitive Cousteau. Back on the dive boat Cousteau asked, 'Was that your first dive?' 'Why?' asked Lee. 'Look in your mask,' came the reply. It was half-full of blood. Still, he got the job.

Back in the sixties Mombasa was the sort of place you had read about in history books. Its streets overflowed with locals of all shapes and sizes, with matelots of many nations checking out the brothels and more salubrious bars and restaurants in which a cross-section of humanity drank beer or sipped tea. Being somewhat short of money we boarded the good ship *Manahine* as soon as possible and made our final arrangements from there. Captain Mike was a great help and showed us much more than the ropes, including how to deter the milling hordes of maidens who offered their services as cooks, housemaids or whatever to be part of the expedition. Well-provendered, and with all the gear stowed, we were soon on our way and it was now I found I was really in charge. The Captain jokingly had said 'Where to?' to which I had jokingly answered 'Zanzibar.' Consider my surprise when I awoke with a strong smell of cloves in my cabin, at anchor off the clove capital of the world. We took in the sights of this main stop-over on the ancient Arab trading routes, then weighed anchor again, complete with a shark cage on the rear deck.

Steaming across the Indian Ocean you are made very aware of the fact that it is actually a desert, not of course for want of water, there's plenty of that, but dissolved in the surface layers of this azure pond that separates Africa from India there is little in the way of plant nutrients. This fact is made painfully obvious by the lack of fishing boats, sea birds or even floating seaweed. With little to look at except waves, the journey was a welcome respite between the end of an ultra hectic university term and jumping in at the deep end of a new research project – time to think about the problems of just how deep that end was going to be. If I had found myself taxonomically at sea in the rain forests of Sierra Leone, what chance did I have among the corals of the Indian Ocean? No friendly locals would be there to give a helpful name or two, and what about the audacity of a phytosociologist studying coral? I consoled myself with the fact that, although they were animals, corals behaved like plants and most of them stayed fixed to their own appointed spot.

All too soon the call of 'Dolphins ahead' brought me to my senses; work was about to begin. Cetaceans, boobies and sargassum told us, long before the trace on the scanners flicked upwards, that the shallower sea ahead was rich in life – and there was Aldabra, a speck on the horizon. Atolls, as Charles Darwin had shown, are polo-mint islands with holes in the middle, each appliquéd on the top of sea-mounts which cause upwelling of deep water containing just enough nutrients to support an amazing variety of life, much of which is in the construction and carbon sequestration business. Coral is made of a complex form of calcium carbonate, and the carbon comes from the seawater and the atmosphere. When the reefs are alive and growing they soak up carbon dioxide from the global greenhouse and store it out of harm's way.

Landing our gear on an island made of coral limestone, eroded into razor sharp bits that would make even a great white shark gnash its teeth with envy, was going to be a problem especially as we had deflatable boats. If it hadn't have been for the skill of the locals, we would never have made it. They launched their wooden pirogue and, with nothing more than oars, navigated the only passage through that part of the reef. Once safely on land we were formally introduced to the Seychellois (who were at the time running the fishery on the atoll) by the current manager Archange Michael: there was Big Harry, who always had a smile on his face, while Thomas was small and wiry, a great performer both in a fishing boat and on the fiddle; then there was an Adonis of a man, rippling with muscles and about to become a father. I had been warned of the fact and had had some preliminary instructions about midwifery. The members of the departing phase of the expedition also warned me that there was some resentment between Adonis and the rest of the group and we should regard him as Baddy Number One. I was handed the .22 rifle and shown where the cartridges were kept.

Sure enough, that night Adonis turned up and made me understand that I should follow him to his hut. There I was given palm wine scooped out of an old 50-gallon oil drum that was fermenting away under the overhang of the roof. Sheer bravado made me knock it back in one. My tin mug refilled, I was shown into the hut where his young wife was great with child while his twin girl toddlers were fast asleep on the mud floor. Pidgin and gesticulations let me know that his wife would like some gin, and that I would be needed at the birth that he intimated was imminent. Thank goodness Harry's wife was not far away, and it was she who assured all of us that the baby would not come that night. We all shared some London Dry out of a half-empty bottle I had found in my bedroom and parted on the best of terms. I can't say that I slept well because I had an awful foreboding of what might happen if something went wrong at the birth.

From that point our daily routine got into gear: up early with a pre-breakfast dive, then, observing the six-hour rule, surveying of the land vegetation occupied my time, before taking to the depths once again in the afternoon.

As I had the key both to the fish store and the first-aid chest, mid-morning coffee was surgery time. Cases ranged from hangovers – and when induced by coconut wine they can be bad – to burns and wounds. Wounds were mainly accidents and fights, which included the ancient art of biting. My little red book told me that in the pecking order of infection, human bites can be the worst because they can carry human diseases, but, armed with good old iodine and with penicillin to hand, I had no trouble. When patients turned up with a chunk bitten out of their arm, leg or penis, I did what I could and enquired what they had used to stop the bleeding. I was shown a mixture of plants that included

Moringa and aloe, which grew in abundance around all the huts. Another medicine, gin, seemed to work wonders too.

Another form of 'bite' soon became the bane of the divers, despite the liberal application of mercurochrome to each and every little scratch. Of course corals don't really bite and most of them can't sting us, but they are very abrasive and each cut appears to get more than its fair share of coral reef chemicals, each part of an armamentarium of novel proteins, enzymes and antibiotics which seem to do little to boost the average diver's immunogenic system. So, after a couple of weeks, instead of healing, coral 'bites' start to fall to pieces. Saturday night became antibiotic night, good old main-line penicillin. Since no one's injection technique was above the reproach of the others, you soon learned to do it yourself.

There were two other ways of curing this particular ill. The least popular was to stop diving, or, for those with time on their hands and air in their tanks, you could join the local underwater NHS. Just like the one back home this all too often required a good deal of hanging about, queuing up at a 'cleaner station' along with assorted fish of all shapes and sizes. When it came to your turn you let the cleaner-fish and shrimps give you the once over. You always tended to wait your turn with patience as the other patients could include large carnivorous fish. There were no copies of *Country Life* to while away the time, but with your underwater notebook to hand you could carry on with your research while waiting. What's more, as the assorted theatre staff chewed away all the rotting tissue, not only did it tickle but it left you with a clean wound, well on its way to healing. Whether the cleaners carry their own oral antibiotics with them, I do not know, but the amount of research that has since been done by pharmaceutical giants on reef organisms makes me sure they do.

Christmas was a joyous occasion with Lee decorating the church with cut out figures of all the characters of Christmas portrayed with key faces from the island community, a cardboard Oberammergau in which everyone had a part. We also made presents for all the children using the bands meant for ringing the birds strung into necklaces. Soon after these festivities, the main supply ship arrived from the Seychelles and Baddy Number One, complete with family current and still to be, departed for Mahe. The whole island, including me, breathed a sigh of relief as the ship got under sail. Evidently the baby was born before it disappeared over the horizon.

The sigh of relief, at least for me, didn't last long because as soon as the boat was out of sight a group of the locals turned up to inform me that the cook, who had served the last expedition, had not died of natural causes but had been poisoned by Baddy Number One. A delegation took me to the place where the bottle that had contained the poison had been hidden. It was formaldehyde stolen from the chemical store. In the face of all the accusations and so-called evidence, I had to spend hours taking down the verbal statements in pidgin, recording them in English, and having them retranslated and read back to the informer before he signed them. The evidence to hand was then sent by radio to the police in Mahe who sent out a party to exhume the body. It was not a nice thing to have to be part of at any time, let alone in the tropics; it was a messy business and we never did hear the end of that particular saga.

For me the best dives of all were in Grande Passe and Johnny Channel, the main connections between the lagoon and the open sea. They and the lesser channels were the places where big fish could always be found in plenty, holding station in the strongest of currents and virtually being force-fed on a never ending stream of smaller fry. At the mouth of the main channel were a series of underwater sand dunes that appeared to change their positions slightly every day, their crests boiling with sand whipped up by the pulse of the currents. On an incoming tide all you had to do was drop in and ride the roller coaster of the current. When the speed was just right, you could dive into the boiling crest of the dunes and in effect get a good sand blasting, much better than washing before going to bed. If you judged it wrong you could come to an abrupt halt. The most exciting thing was to emerge on the other side to be faced by the local shark pack, waiting for their meal. It was while amusing ourselves in this way that we realised that these currents could be used to our advantage, cutting both the time and the expenditure of muscle power and hence of air. The recorder floated backwards while his buddy guided him around coral heads and other obstacles that might have caused catastrophe.

It was on one such current assisted survey that we saw, down below us, the shadowy bulk of great bastions of reef rock separated by deep channels. Further work indicated that these were the reefs that had formed around Aldabra when world sea levels were much lower, probably during the last ice age. The thought of what would have been in effect a part hollow tower of rock, protruding more than 100 metres above the waves, was awesome. Calculating the amount of carbon dioxide released and absorbed during such cycles of reef erosion and re-growth certainly added to our understanding of the control of the global greenhouse when that concept eventually hit the headlines.

Ed Drew's work on the uptake of carbon dioxide by corals indicated the role of reefs in not only aiding the control of levels of atmospheric carbon but also in the production of oxygen which makes the living world go round. Brian Whitton's interest in the populations of simple organisms – bacteria and blue-green algae – growing between the tides, linked up with the studies of Lyn Margulis and the eventual publication of the *Gaia Hypothesis*.

The survey at the far end of the atoll was spiced with the dubious excitement of a long sea journey in inflatable boats, wallowing through the waves and greeted by a number of sharks. These, the most exposed shores, were almost devoid of any living corals. This surprised us, for most of the textbooks then talked about the richest coral growth being on the most exposed shores, the theory being that oxygen stirred in by wave action helped the coral animals to thrive. In fact, all our research indicated that Aldabra had never read those textbooks and was growing the wrong way round, the most luxuriant reefs being along the most sheltered shores of the atoll. We consoled ourselves with the observation that Aldabra is situated within the northern limit of the hurricane belt, and perhaps this factor alone forced it to step out of line, the worst storms in a bad year trashing any corals that had got a foothold on the most exposed shores.

We also found that the black coral, *Dendrophyllia*, which was usually present only in water deeper than forty metres, could be found in abundance in the shallow water of the big reef channels. The hypothesis we put forward to explain this phenomenon was that as the channels are so well supplied with fast food, lack of competition enabled them to thrive. With so many important questions to be answered, we already began to dream of another expedition to survey atolls in more sheltered waters.

All too soon we were back in Mombasa, unloading our collections and what was left of our gear. I found that the only clothes I had were a pair of shorts and a torn Fred Perry shirt with a large red cross placed there by the port customs officer. Jim Barnes and I arrived in Heathrow, hired a car and started to drive home through flurries of snow. All went well until we ran out of petrol not far from Durham and discovered just how cold a place the north-east could be, especially after many weeks diving in the tropics. Making it home at last, the first thing I had to do was go to the garage and unearth a large cardboard box. Rosemary had allowed Rufus to stay up and I acted as a belated Father Christmas, presenting him with the pedal car that had been on his Christmas list before I went away. Then it was off to bed because I had to lecture at 9 a.m. next morning. It was back to the old routine, and what a routine it was becoming, so I will, if I may, continue the story of my exploits in the coral seas before returning to the other strings that were twanging in my bow.

The prospect of ever going back to dive in the tropics again seemed pretty remote, although I did scan the maps of the coral seas to select the perfect site in which to carry on the research. I also began to get lots of letters asking me to help other diving expeditions plan their itineraries. One of these contained a letter from two members of the RAF diving club planning a Joint Services diving expedition to a coral atoll, asking me to suggest a programme of useful research. A few days later two squadron leaders, Richard Bird and David Rickard flew in for a briefing. Over a cup of departmental coffee Dicky and Dave sat amazed as I gushed forth with a stream of hermatypic rhetoric. They shut me up in mid-gush, saying that if there was all that work to be done, then how about my coming along and helping to do it, and asking me where was the best place to go. You can guess how I felt as I blurted out 'The Chagos Archipelago!' As far as I knew no one had ever dived there before.

As with all Joint Services expeditions, which are part of the three services' programme of arduous training, ours was advertised in barracks, wardrooms and messes throughout the world, from whence applications came pouring in. The main qualifications required of each service member were at least second-class diving standard and/or a minimum of one other useful aptitude. These could range from boat handling through telecommunications and surveying to, as the *Exchange and Mart* so aptly puts it, 'what have you'. All of this took almost two years, during which time David Rickard unfortunately had to drop out as he was posted to other duties. Dicky Bird thus took over as officer in command, with Commander Alan Baldwin, OBE, RN, as deputy leader and diving officer.

While selection of the team was going on the nitty-gritty of expedition planning rolled rapidly into top gear. Equipment had to be requested and cleared from official service stores and from the diving clubs of the three services. Transport had to be organised and finance sought from various trust funds (to whom we are more than grateful). My tasks were less difficult. I had to immerse myself in all the scientific literature concerning the ecology of coral reefs and specifically that of Egmont Island, chosen as our objective because of three facts: it was part of the Chagos Archipelago which is well outside the hurricane belt, it was small enough to be adequately surveyed in the two months available and, thirdly, the only other scientists to visit it in the past had been members of the Percy Sladen expedition way back in 1915, and they had spent only a few hours on land. I then had to find a team (immediately christened the Scientificos) who could adequately cover the major range of plants, animals and ecology we were likely to find. It all may sound a doddle but I had a growing family, a full-time teaching commitment, a large contingent of research students, and a new career direction bubbling on the horizon. Life certainly never had enough time to get tedious.

Last, but most important of all, I had to go to Judge Sharp in Durham and swear an affidavit stating that I wished to become Brighid's Dad, because the adoption was imminent and I wouldn't be able to be in court.

The final team, the Magnificent Twelve plus Five, who eventually gathered in Gan on 29 October 1972 for the last leg of the journey to Egmont was as follows: Squadron Leader R. (Dicky) Bird; Commander Alan Baldwin, deputy leader; Major Don Phillips, RE, survey; Wing Commander Doug Macleod, surgeon; Lieutenant Graham Stoddart-Stones, Sub-Mariner, stores; Fleet Chief Petty Officer Arty Shaw, dive engineer; Staff Sergeant Ray Perren, camp engineer and cinematography; Chief Petty Officer Jeff Arnold, dive engineer; Sergeant Paddy McCauley, marine craft; Sergeant Ian Purvis, communications and records; Chief Technician Dave Woolf, communications; Corporal Brian Richards, photography; Dave Bellamy, ecologist; George Russell, algologist; Mont Hirons, ornithologist; Ted Hinton-Clifton, zoologist; Jim Barnes, diving technician, photography and my diving buddy. To be among the first to do anything at any time in the history of exploration is a many splendoured thing. To be able to do it on the scale of the first underwater base line survey of an enormous atoll, in the mid-twentieth century is almost beyond comprehension.

The reefs were everything we dreamed of and they too hadn't read the textbooks for the most luxurious coral growth was always found in the most sheltered waters. The other end of the Egmont atoll, immediately christened Shark Alley, provided us with some of our most spectacular diving. Perhaps the most memorable led to the discovery of the wreck of the *El Maren* that had struck the atoll on her maiden voyage back in the early 1920s. The wreck provided extra evidence that corals thrive best in sheltered waters, for the lee side of her hulk was covered in coral. Diving in this artificial reef was like being in a can packed with sardines of an immense diversity of shapes and sizes, and in the shallow water we denizens of the land could see their full range of the colours of the rainbow.

It was at this juncture that I received a radio message to inform me that the legalities of adopting Brighid had gone through. I still have the scrap of paper with the message scribbled by Dave Woolf, rubbing in the fact that once again I was absent at a crucially important time in the life of my family.

The vegetation of the island, which had been a copra farm for many years, was recovering and the few native species that were left were reasserting their presence. Sadly, it was a silent forest, for the density of rats was sufficient to ensure few nesting birds – and a regulation trim if you slept with your head too close to the mosquito net. Rats were everywhere, descendants of those accidentally introduced by visiting boats, as they have been on just about every island on Earth. This was a great disappointment especially to Mont, who nevertheless recorded fifty species of bird that dropped their visiting cards, including three that were doing their best to settle in.

As if to taunt our ornithologist, every morning and evening we caught glimpses of legions of birds on the move way out to sea, pointing to the fact that somewhere north of us there were rat free islands where they could nest in peace. The survey both on land and under the water was carried out with military precision and, of course, posed more questions than it answered.

We just had to go back and just two years later, on 18 January 1975, my forty-second birthday, we anchored off Eagle Island, our home base for another magical stay. The task to hand was even more monumental than that of the first expedition: to survey as many of the other islands of the Chagos Bank as possible. If it hadn't been for Warren Blake and *The Four Friends* it would have been impossible.

Warren, brother of Peter Blake who was destined to take the Americas Cup away from America, had been born with salt in his veins and the strength of well-trimmed canvas pulling him to life at sea. His story up to the time I met him would fill several books and his wife Tue from Vietnam is one of the strongest yet gentlest people I have ever met. Not the best of sailors, she was Warren's constant companion and brought a sense of great decorum to our all-male expedition, so we all ended up with white bits among the brown. *The Four Friends*, a 76-foot ketch, was to serve as transport and a dive base between islands, and work began in earnest.

The journeys between islands were not without their problems. Carrying all petrol for the outboard motors made cooking on the ketch a verboten operation. This had a silver lining for Tue's way with fish, raw, straight out of the sea and spiced the Vietnamese way, made for exciting and ultra healthy eating. Tue staked out her claim to the space upfront, close to the place where the giant inflatable life raft was stowed. One memorable day, running before the wind with lee rail under, the black mass of the inflatable rose up like a tethered whale on the foredeck – pandemonium, not only to re-stow it but where was Tue? She was nowhere to be found, so turning into the wind, we did our best to follow our wake, scanning the mess of water for a life jacket. No luck. Eventually some bright spark went and looked in the captain's cabin, and there was Tue, fast asleep.

Eagle Island was covered with coconuts and infested with rats and so, like Egmont, almost devoid of nesting birds. The same was true of all the larger islands that had borne the brunt of the copra industry, which had done its best to plant coconuts on every scrap of land above high tide mark. However, on the smallest ones, where rats hadn't jumped ship, there were teeming populations of birds.

Two other factors also became obvious. On the biggest copra islands, which had been vacated only a few years before, there were still signs of the vibrant village communities that had developed there: homes, a school, swings and everywhere the saddest graffiti I have ever read, farewell-to-paradise notes scrawled in pidgin, saying that they didn't want to go back to Mahe. I stood in what had been the manager's house, taking the first freshwater shower I had had for weeks and cried my eyes out. To us Mahe and the Seychelles are paradise, allowing us to escape for a few days from an overcrowded world, but to them those same islands meant a routine struggle for survival, set against the affluence of the then developing boom of package holiday makers. What more could anyone ask for than a palm-thatched hut on Eagle Island, by an unpolluted tropical beach, fish fresh from the sea and fruit and veg grown in your own garden plots – real family life spent pottering about in the garden, or going fishing, all day in paradise. I cried a lot more as I thought of Rosemary back at home with Rufus then eight, Henrietta 4, Brighid 3, and adoption procedures on the way for Eoghain. Again I had had to visit Judge Sharp before I left.

A quarter of a century on I get mad when I hear world politicians talking about the two billion plus people who are still attempting to live off their own land in village communities, as poor – so poor that they must be given aid to become part of our throw-away society, a society in which unemployment is rife and where the rich talk of 'quality time', which they spend with their families, covering their gardens with decking, sunbathing by the pool or perhaps even just going fishing.

The other fact that became obvious was that, in the absence of management, the islands were in the process of self-rehabilitation. The palms were beginning to die and the tropical shrubs and trees, some of which had probably been members of the original forest were taking over. For the rest of the expedition and for the rest of my life I have talked about the potential of rehabilitating those parts of the world already ruined by the wrong sort of development, and removing all feral plants and animals. The challenge was there, get rid of the rats and Chagos would become one of the most important bird reserves in the Indian Ocean – and an island paradise once again, which with proper management of fishing and possibly tourism could again become the home of people earning their own living. I was therefore glad when, early in the new millennium, the people were given permission to return to their islands, and live in great hope that their livelihood will be developed in the right way.

Meanwhile, underwater everything was going like clockwork. The pattern of coral growth revealed on Aldabra was repeated on every island: the most sheltered shores were always flanked by a vibrant living reef while the most exposed were almost bare of living coral. The black coral was found in shallow water only in reef channels where high densities of sharks always joined us on the dive. Only once in the whole dive programme did they almost lose their cool, and it happened with BBC television cameras taking down the evidence. 'An Island called Danger' was the only documentary I ever made with the Wildlife team from Bristol for, as you will see, I was destined to do most of my work with Auntie Beeb's Department of Adult Education based in London.

Deep down everyone knew that to complete the job we must dive, survey and film the reef channel which showed up on the scanners midway between the islands of Danger and Sea Cow, a long way from any dry land and hence fraught with problems and spiced with danger. *The Four Friends* was loaded and off we motored. By the time the ketch was on station, the wind was beginning to whip up the white horses. Three inflatables were launched and three dive teams were put down from the Zodiacs, which were anchored exactly where the echo sounder had pinpointed the edge of the channel.

The first team in included Peter Crawford and the underwater camera wielded by Ray Pringle Scott. After their requisite time they surfaced, shouting excitedly about big fish, but it was our turn next and we didn't wait to listen. I was to go in with Alan Baldwin, Dave Young, Tom Peake and Adrian Lane, with Stan Stanley standing by in the dive boat. When our turn came we plummeted over into a somewhat murky sea and headed off down the shot line to the bottom, which was at around sixty feet. There were a number of sharks motoring about, so we mounted a shark guard and, checking that the anchor weight was well wedged, started the routine survey.

Having completed the work, the team swam to the edge of the drop and peered longingly down into the whiteness of the channel proper. If only we had the time and the air! But we hadn't, and so we turned reluctantly back to our heap of coral sacks stacked by the anchor. I hadn't finned more than a couple of strokes when I sensed excitement in the water. Turning, I saw a knot of three of my buddies all gesticulating at an immense grouper which had swum up out of the channel. It was gigantic, how much it weighed I couldn't even start to guess. It took no notice at all of our excited interest, swimming slowly past the knot of divers, opening and closing its mouth in a very fishy way.

No sooner had this fabulous fish vanished into the gloom than another, just as large if not larger, swam into view. The second was a hump head wrasse, and looked more grotesque and hence much more menacing than the first. Beside these two monsters the flurry of sharks was almost forgotten in the excitement of those few spectacular moments.

We arrived back at the pile of coral sacks and were ready to ascend the anchor rope, but it had gone. We looked around and could see no sign of the sinker – the inflatable had probably dragged its anchor while we were away on the edge of the channel. Collecting the precious sacks, we followed the instructions in the dive rulebook to the letter: bunch and keep close together during the ascent, then, when close to the surface, send one man up to look for the boat.

We hovered in mid-water and Alan Baldwin went up to look for the boat. It all seemed much longer than it actually was until he rejoined us, signalling that there was no boat in sight. Was it just my imagination, or were the sharks behaving in a different way? Could it be that these giant fish could sense the fact that we were in trouble and hence vulnerable to attack? For the first time in my diving career I felt really worried that we were about to be attacked. Evidently so did the others, for the shark guards unscrewed the safety catches on their bangsticks and we all bunched much closer together. Rising to the surface, we inflated our life jackets. I had often jokingly said that I would rather end my days being eaten by a shark than being run over by a Mini, but I was beginning to wonder what the first bite would be like, would I drown or bleed to death? I had always had a terrible dread of drowning.

All that was visible at water level were the waves rolling in, apparently from every point of the compass, and looking down there were the sharks. Our dive boat was nowhere to be seen, but there, between the waves, was the top of a mast of *The Four Friends*, metronoming high above the water. Panic was setting in: could they see us in the water? Fortunately, realising our predicament, Warren Blake was up at the crosstrees and his sharp eyes picked us out in the mess of waves. In next to no time our dive boat was alongside and we heaved ourselves thankfully out of the sea.

In the time that had elapsed since the start of our dive, conditions had worsened and the gigantic swell, together with a surface current, had whipped our dive boat away. With no point of reference against which to judge their position, the boat handlers had been oblivious of the fact. The dive leader decided that conditions were too bad to continue work. It had been a fitting end to our expedition, which was now complete. What a place, what a dive and what fish!

During our trip, we had been lucky enough to spot an Abbott's booby which was then confined as a breeding bird to Christmas Island (Lat. 10°30'S, Long. 105°40'E) in the eastern Indian Ocean. It was once known to nest on Assumption Island but has not attempted to nest there since 1930, owing to gross interference by man. On Christmas Island it nests in tall trees some distance from the sea, and despite sensible and well-enforced conservation laws its numbers were then declining. The reasons for this decline are obscure and may be linked with increased human pressure, but more likely due to the build-up of the island's frigate populations. Whatever the exact reason, here is a species in need of new nesting sites. Its presence around Eagle Island is indeed exciting and there are certainly a number of areas of broad-leaved forest which would appear ideal for the establishment of a new nesting colony. If the rats were controlled it might just be possible that the Abbott's booby would be able to take up residence before all the nesting real estate was occupied by the more local bird populations.

Little did we know then that we were among the favoured few who, given the power of underwater vision and the freedom of the seas by Cousteau and Gagnan, would witness such things – coral reefs, admittedly not in their pristine glory for they had already been changed by human intervention, but reefs still teaming with myriad life, with all parts of the food chain: producers, consumers, top carnivores, decomposers and recyclers, still more or less intact. Our work with amateur divers had shown that the balance of life in the seas around Britain was in places grotesquely out of kilter, and that in some places total collapse was not far away. From that time on, the war on the Earth and the life-giving sea escalated out of all proportion. Mother Earth might have been able to handle the needs of the exploding human population, but she couldn't cope with the greed of rampant short-term profiteering. Holes in the ozone layer were about to be discovered, the concept of global warming was about to replace our fears of a nuclear winter. Despite ever more dire warnings by groups like Greenpeace, Friends of the Earth and WWF, overgrazing, overfishing and over exploitation of all key resources on land and sea escalated out of control.

Every time I return to my old diving grounds with the new age of marine biologists, I enjoy their enthusiasm for what they see. Oblivious to the bleached, dead coral heads, they emit great plumes of bubbles as they say, 'Look at the colour of that coral, the size of that shoal of fish. Wow, look, a shark.' Yes, it still is magic, but only those lucky few who goggled in the early days really saw it as it was when the 'wow' factor was six feet high. I was privileged to be amongst that number, a privilege that still drives me relentlessly along the campaigning road. I know what it was like and what it could be like again, if only the world would come to its senses before that teeming biodiversity is lost forever.

Sadly, there are still rats on the islands of the Chagos Bank, and even more sadly, El Niño has recently done its worst, but one day I will go back with the new breed of goggling volunteers spawned by groups like Coral Cay, and with the local people, whose resource it was in the first place, we will nurse it back into life.

17 BY ROYAL COMMAND

IN 1972 I WAS awarded the Duke of Edinburgh's Prize for Underwater Research. Unfortunately I couldn't make the date and had to send one of those complex 'I am Sir your most obedient servant' sort of refusal letters. This was my first Royal Command and I really got it in the neck from my Mum for saying no, despite the fact that I had checked it all out in *Debrett's Book of Etiquette*.

Having been asked to present a paper at the Fourth World Congress on Underwater Activities in Stockholm in 1975, I arrived there a little late after a hectic summer: a field trip to Europe as usual, changing planes in Copenhagen where Rosemary came out to meet me and bring my arctic gear, then it was off to Canada for a bit of consultancy work in the furthest north before returning to Stockholm to give my lecture and attend a special dinner. Thanks to Rosemary I had my evening dress with me and was all ready to go. Unfortunately, Hans Hass, who was meant to do the honours at the opening ceremony was incapacitated and failed to turn up, so I was substituted and found myself in at the deep end without a lounge suit and tie for lunch with the Crown Prince.

A quick whip round among the other members of the BSAC hierarchy who were in attendance came up with a number of pieces of wet clothing, even several lounge suits, but none that came anywhere near my size. Unfortunately, my evening dress had satin lapels, all the rage in the 1950s when it had been bespoked for me by the Co-op, but it was going to have to do. Borrowing a tie from Bernard Betts, I slunk into the reception and tried to keep in the darkest bits of the room. The food was fabulous, mainly fish, with the biggest smoked eel I have ever seen laid down the centre of the table. Having eaten much more than my fill and chatted to all and sundry, I thought I had got away with it when along came the Mayor of Stockholm, with whose wife I was in animated conversation. He simply said, 'The Crown Prince is waiting.'

My satin lapels were about to go on royal show and there was no dodging the fact, for there round the table were three occupied chairs, and one other, for me. Thank goodness the Crown Prince was a keen scuba diver, so much so that he had broken court protocol and learned to dive with a sport club. I found myself enthusing over our next Joint Services expedition scheduled for 1978. I even found myself asking, 'Why don't you join us? You will never have a better chance of diving with sharks.' I was hurried away and politely informed that the Crown Prince had his duties to see to, and he dived with the Swedish Navy.

The following year, 1976, a letter came inviting Rosemary and me to a Garden Party at Buckingham Palace. Dresses, hats and gloves were bought and a suit was hired. I was working at Thames Television in Euston Road and it was there that we got all geared up and I asked them to call me a cab. As it arrived I stepped in and said in my most grandiose way, 'Buckingham Palace please'. Back came the reply, 'You bxxxxxx, Dave, now I'm going to get stuck in that bloody great queue.' Great it was, and the party was a fantastic affair. The cucumber sandwiches were divine, without a curl at any edge, and the tea was Earl Grey, just like in the storybooks. We saw the Queen and the Prince of Wales and spent as long as we could beating the bounds of the chamomile lawn and stalking the herbaceous borders which were overflowing with regimented colour. The bits most guests didn't bother to visit, around the compost heaps, were overflowing with weeds.

There and then, I decided to ask permission to write a book about the Queen's hidden weeds. Her Majesty graciously gave her permission, and

I teamed up with one of Britain's leading botanical artists, Marjorie Lyon. Thanks in great part to the results of an ongoing survey by the South London Entomological and Natural History Society, the book was published in 1984. The title was *The Queen's Hidden Garden*, and Port Meirion, no less, brought out a set of tableware incorporating some of Marjorie's sixty-four paintings.

The penultimate chapter of the book is about a personal dream of mine, a dream that did come true. I have never lost my love of the ballet and perhaps my deepest regret, is that I rarely get to a performance, so, although the series 'Bellamy on the Ballet' hasn't yet come to fruition, when the tenth anniversary of the West Midlands Youth Ballet loomed upon the horizon I wrote this chapter, which became the story of a ballet called *Heritage*. I even commissioned Malcolm Williamson, Master of the Queen's Music to write the score. He is an amazing man, who made me understand the complexity of modern music, and his rapport with the young dancers was total magic. An Australian, he was also a great supporter of the Tasmanian Wilderness Society in their fight to stop the despoliation of a World Heritage Site.

This is my ballet:

HERITAGE
(A Ballet in Three Acts)

Set along the Great Border of the Gardens of Buckingham Palace

ANIMALIA
THE CREEPY CRAWLIES – BUTTERFLIES AND MOTHS

Holly Blue *(Celastrina argiolus)*
Large White *(Pieris brassicae)*
Swallow-tailed Moth *(Ourapteryx sambucaria)*
White Ermine *(Spilosoma lubricipeda)*
The Herald *(Scolopteryx libatrix)*
Garden Tiger *(Arctia caja)*
Red Admiral *(Vanessa atalanta)*

PLANTAE

THE QUEEN'S FLOWERS

Camellia 'Elizabeth'

Sweet-scented Stock

Delphinium 'Royalist'

Rose 'Queen Elizabeth'

Regal Lily

THE QUEEN'S WEEDS

Holly

Shepherd's Purse

Privet

Dandelion

Dock

Willow

PERSONAE

The Monarch

Garden Party Goers

Synopsis

THE FAIRY STORY WHICH CAME TRUE

ACT I

It is a warm, dry, wilting day, and the caterpillars are hungry – oh, so hungry. They approach the flowers growing in the Great Border and enquire if they may feed from their leaves. The flowers rebuke them, saying, 'No! We are the Queen's and we are ready for the Royal Garden Party. We are far too important to be eaten by mere insects, nasty creepy crawlies.'

ACT II

It is evening on the same day in a less well-kept corner of the flowerbed. The caterpillars are now desperate, for without food they will die. Each in turn asks one of the weeds for sustenance, which is willingly given. A Red Admiral butterfly joins the party, asking no more than a place in which to lay her tiny green egg. She tries each weed in turn, but none will suffice, for her life cycle can only be completed on a Stinging Nettle, all of which have been banished from the garden. Heartbroken, she dies.

ACT III

It is the day of the Garden Party. The Monarch and his guests arrive to be enthralled by the beauty of Holly Blue, Large White, Swallow-tailed Moth, White Ermine, The Herald and Garden Tiger – two butterflies and four moths appearing in all their summer glory as they cast away their caterpillar coats while dancing on the breeze.

On 6 July 1985 my dream came true as I stood with Malcolm, Phyllis Kempster (director of the Company and choreographer of, yes, my ballet), to take the final curtain call with all the dancers. I still haven't come down to earth. I get that same thrill every time I open a school or community wildlife garden (and I must have opened many hundreds in my time), for I know that that heritage of metamorphosis can be put back into every corner of the Earth, if only we care enough.

It was some years later that I was invited to dinner at Buckingham Palace. We turned up dead on time along with about 1,000 others. Ushered into the Palace, we were given what looked like dance cards, that turned out to be a list of selected palace treasures on display for the guests. So, apart from spotting everyone who was anyone, there was a lot to keep us occupied. The court page had said that the Queen, Prince Philip and the Duke and Duchess of Kent would be there.

Standing, admiring the pictures in a first edition of Audubon's *Birds Of America*, I was somewhat surprised to be tapped on the shoulder, not by Rosemary but by a very beautiful young lady who said, 'It's nice to see a familiar face.' Puzzled, I thought that she must be some ex-tutee whose name I had forgotten and started chatting away. The young lady certainly appeared to know a lot about me and my family, so I thought I had got my identification right and warmed to the occasion. Seeing Rosemary looking somewhat worried, I double-checked my identification. I had been talking to the most famous face in the world. Well, you don't expect the Princess of Wales to slap you on the back, do you? Changing tack somewhat, we talked of everything from ballet to the problems of the Third World, and then she went her way with a strange question: 'Have you eaten?' 'Not yet,' said I. Her reply was, 'The food's awful,' and she floated away across the room. We never did find the food, there were so many people to meet, and when the official party closed with 'Carriages at One a.m.', our party continued all the way back up the M1 with all the more impecunious members of the great and the good who lived up north, keeping themselves going with coffee at the service stations.

Another meeting with Lady Di did entail food. She was opening a new exhibition at the Natural History Museum. At the reception we were all given one of those little plates with a plastic wine glass holder on the side, not the easiest thing to manipulate at the best of times, but almost impossible when the canapés include oysters on the shell. Etiquette demanded that most people said no, but all the marine biologists present were making sure that none went to waste. I was about to devour my sixth, or was it my seventh when there she was, smiling that lovely smile and saying, 'Difficult things to eat in public, aren't they?' What a sense of humour, and what a dreadful waste of the life of one of the world's great campaigners.

18 'IM ON TELLY

THE TRUTH OF the matter was that for those first ten years at Durham, learning and teaching were in complete symbiosis. I don't think I really taught anyone anything. Together my students and I shared the excitement of surfing the web of knowledge. All I can do is hope that I inspired them to hang on in there. Two students who attended those memorable, at least for me, tutorials were Burt (Peter) Bridgewater and John Laughton. Burt is now Directeur of the 'Division des sciences ecologiques' at UNESCO in Paris, and John Laughton FRS, is head of the National Environment Research Council in London. Little did I know it then, but I was about to face a much larger classroom.

How it happened, I am not quite sure, but I found myself at the BBC Department of Further Education watching a film called *Meersee Biologie*. My German was rudimentary, but that couldn't spoil the underwater pictures, which were fantastic. At that time we were all being thrilled by the camerawork of the Cousteau team, diving in exotic places, but here were pictures of great beauty and excitement taken not in tropical climes but right in our own backyard, the cold North Sea. The commentary, though teutonically correct, left a lot to be desired and when asked to comment I said 'Fantastic film, but someone needs to put fire in the belly of "das ist ein anderers fisch, das ist sehr interessant".'

To my surprise I found myself in front of a camera, wading into the sea, complete with aqualung, and flopping into what was obviously very shallow water, a television debut that made me a laughing stock in BSAC circles. Never fear, this was my launch into the world of natural history on television as script rewriter and linkman in a series called *Life in our Sea*.

It was easy to be popular back in those days of only a few channels, when the viewers didn't have much choice and so stayed tuned in to your programme, week after week after week. There were also decent budgets to spend even when working for Adult and, as it became, Further, then Continuing Education. Crews consisted of producer, director, PA, camera, assistant camera, sound and even assistant sound and there was the potential of world travel. What is more the FE department was full of great characters with expertise on everything under, above and around the sun including the then nascent world of hard disks and software. I had, of course, long been a great fan of David Attenborough whose team from the then developing Bristol stable has done more than any other to open the eyes of the world to the wonders of the animal kingdom. I had dreamed that one day, when television was in full colour, someone would do the same for the plants. All of a sudden the ball was in my court and with the FE team behind me it started to happen and fast.

Despite the opening scene, *Life in our Sea* was a great success, except that when I saw myself on the screen, I couldn't understand why people would want to watch. I had always hated hearing my recorded voice, but to tell you the truth, with picture added as well it made me feel more than a little queasy, further convincing me that I must suffer from some special sort of autism. In consequence four things became part of my psyche. As academic botany was my career, I would try never to get up tight about television. Teaching had always been fun and television would be no different. I would never watch one of my programmes, once it was out of the commentary room, and I would not collect either tapes or reviews. Whether they were covert decisions, I don't know, but that is what happened.

Two years later, in 1972, *Bellamy on Botany*, hit the screens, a television series all of my own, written and presented by me: the formula for a swollen head if ever there was one. It was produced by David Cordingly and directed by one of the most creative guys I have ever known, Michael Weatherley, aided in later series by Anna Jackson, a linguist with Icelandic origins, an eye for beauty and a deep love and knowledge of the world of homespun crafts. Mike was an engineer who did his PhD on the physics of shunt wound motors. He always boasted that variable speed electric motors were in part thanks to him. He was a great raconteur with an immense knowledge and love of music, especially opera and ballet, so it wasn't long before we dreamed that one day we would collaborate to make 'Bellamy on the Ballet', an extravaganza which would follow the training of a young girl and boy through their first years in dance, and end up with all our favourite routines choreographed for a full sports camera crew operated by top dancers. All this would include freeze frame animation, allowing the skin to be stripped from the dancer to demonstrate muscles, ligaments and bones at work – the physiology of dance, a 100 per cent fit human body trained to do things it really shouldn't. Back in those days of two channels and a BBC that believed in Further Education, it could have happened, and so I discovered the West Midlands Ballet Company as the potential source of the two young dancers. Sadly, as you have already heard, it was never to be, but there were other great things ahead for the Bellamy–Weatherley Team.

Filming *Victoria amazonica*, which grows to perfection each year in the glasshouse at the Botanic Garden in Edinburgh caused not a little consternation. Mike was already spread-eagled with the camera high on the roof when he discovered that his head was not for heights and had to be inched down to safety. Meanwhile, I was swimming in the tank, waiting to demonstrate exactly why the tray-shaped leaves of this gigantic plant didn't fill up with rainwater and sink. Cameras rolled, I was ready to intone, 'Aren't plants marvellous things?', when a worried looking member of staff rushed up to enquire as to my health. A member of the public had reported from below that someone was drowning in the water lily tank, which had a glass viewing panel.

Crews changed but one of our regulars became David Jackson camera with Dennis Cartwright sound. Though based in Manchester, they were on secondment to Further Education. Dennis, though an excellent recordist, lived up to his namesake, a real menace. For a start he always fixed my microphone on with gaffer tape, well known for its sticky tenacity, so by the end of our many encounters my hairy chest had, to use a botanical term, become glabrous, a very painful process.

A flit through a list of our programmes reveals some of the Cartwright Saga. 'In the mire' saw us deep in Sweat mere in Shropshire, trying to get a top shot of the vegetation. David, complete with Arriflex, climbed on Dennis's shoulders and I lifted the two of them on to mine to stagger off through the peaty swamp. Action! All went according to plan until the wet peat beneath my feet gave way, causing me to sink up to my waist as sound and camera slowly toppled forward in an unplanned crash zoom with a watery end.

Peat boring on Din Moss in Scotland for 'Deeper in the Mire' found us out in the open, with six metres of metal borer sticking out of the peat, just as we were enveloped in a freak thunderstorm. Raised bogs may be one of the rarest types of vegetation in the world, but they are very inconvenient places to find yourself in or rather on, with lightning in the offing. Removing the borer and covering the equipment, we all did our best to keep as low a profile as possible. Not an easy thing to do when the peat is sodden, as it should be, with water. The storm passed quickly without mishap. Dennis was wearing what appeared to be a wetsuit top, but the rest of us were soaked and we all retreated to the very upmarket Ednam House Hotel in Kelso where we had been booked in for the night. After checking-in, amongst all the fishing baskets and freshly caught salmon, Dennis started to strip off in the centre of the foyer. Calling the porter in best Cartwright manner, he said 'Grab hold of this', which the porter did, helping to peel off the wetsuit and then ushering what looked like an overweight Amazon dolphin (which are pink) politely but firmly towards the grand staircase.

Fan mail began pouring in and, of all the letters I ever received, the one from Connie Lewcock I treasured most. Connie had watched the programme 'The Kingdom of Canute' from a hospital bed where she was awaiting an operation the next day. I had enthused about *Parnassia palustris* growing in the wet bits between the great sand dunes that protect so much of the coast of Holland. It had long been my favourite plant because not only does it have the most perfect flower, white with a coronet of golden staminodes, but it also, like me, enjoys partial immersion in water. Connie confessed that it was also her favourite flower and that the sight of it had helped her through the operation, speeding her to health. I wrote back and said that when she was fully recovered I would take her on a trip to see the plant.

So it was that, on a fine summer's morning, I collected Connie from her little house in Newcastle and headed up across the Pennines to Nenthead where *Parnassia* grew in profusion. Connie was a magical companion, a one-time suffragette, she had married a Labour activist and told me of the trials and tribulations of life in the mining communities early in the last century. The strength of her character was immense and all her stories were told with a twinkle in her eyes, especially the one in which, to show the solidarity of the Votes for Women activists, she was given the job of blowing up Durham Cathedral. Heeding the advice of her mining friends, that there wasn't enough explosive in the whole of the Durham coalfields to do the job, she settled on blowing up the University Observatory instead. Having learned the tricks of the explosive trade, she camped out in the nearby field to check the staff in and out of the building, so that she didn't hurt anyone, and got ready to make her point with a bang. A young miner unknowingly came to the rescue of the building – he made advances to young Connie, who upped and returned home.

We arrived at the site, parked on the road and, arm in arm, strolled along the bank of a small stream through drifts of our favourite plant. She was astounded at how many there were and asked me why. I pointed out the fact that the stream was hemmed in with spoil heaps from the days of lead mining and that only very special plants like *Parnassia* could tolerate the high levels of lead in the soil. She pressed me on the point and I did my best to explain the intricacies of evolution and competition in the plant kingdom, which seizes every opportunity by overcoming even the most difficult problems. The same is of course true of humanity

– out of adversity comes strength. Connie had first seen the plant growing at the mouth of Crimdon Dene where many a mining family spent their precious holidays and where part of the real Labour movement had its very special roots.

We sat together on the bank, listened to the rushing waters of the burn and drank in the now unpolluted air as Connie told me that she was going to write her life story. Sadly, all good things have to come to an end and Connie had to be home to cook supper for her son, a much respected caretaker at the local school. He was waiting at the door and ushered us into the narrow hallway of her tiny house where a most beautiful poster of those suffragette days still evoked wide vistas for a better future. 'What will you call your autobiography?' I asked, 'Some Cats Scratch' came the answer, as I bid this amazing lady farewell. A few days later I received through the post a little book, her own copy of *The Wild Garland* by S. Waring, published in 1841, a thank you from Connie. I opened the marked page and read, 'The Grass of Parnassus', a sonnet. The book has pride of place in my library, sharing shelf space along with Alfred Russell Wallace, Charles Darwin and a copy of my next paper, published in *Nature* on 19 April 1969: *Status of the Teesdale Rarities* by D.J. Bellamy, P.Bridgewater, C. Marshall and W.M. Tickle. All are mementoes of the process of creative evolution of which humankind is a part. Out of sweetness there came forth strength.

Offers of television work came thick and fast and so did offers of advertising. Looking back, perhaps I should have upheld my image of the real gone don and slipped out of university into a life in the media, especially as it was in that year that *Nature* added its own fantastic accolade to my career – the cover of the 8 March 1974 edition bearing a photograph of a young lady in a grass skirt being chased by me with a lawn mower, proving that science was fun in a programme called 'Carry on Cutting'. This was part of the series which also had me jumping up and down on the surface of Chartley Moss in Staffordshire, making mature pine trees sway wildly. The object of the exercise was to prove that I was standing on the surface of a floating bog. It must have worked, for to this day a whole generation of viewers don't say, ''ere, you're 'im on telly,' but ''ere, you're the bloke who made the trees sway about.'

At the time I don't think I even thought about leaving; for better or worse I had become a workaholic. There were twenty-four hours in every day and each year brought me a new crop of undergraduates to keep me up to date in the fast moving world of plant ecology. If there was some aspect of the world's ecology that I wanted to see, my new Fairy Godmother, TV, waved her magic wand and off I went. The list of all the series of programmes I made is in Appendix 4 and I think is pretty impressive; as you can see, it includes programmes made with many different television companies.

The list of speech days, sports days, school plays and Nine Lessons and Carols I attended was equally impressive, for at one time we had five different children at five different schools. However, I must admit that the list Rosemary attended made mine pale into insignificance. This she bore with a smile on her face, but my media popularity meant that holidays, family outings to the cinema, museums or even journeys on trains were always shared by autograph hunters.

Apart from the family, the other thing that suffered was my research. I had to drop out from the next expedition to the Chagos Bank. My place was taken by Charles Sheppard, who is today at the University of Warwick from which he edits the *Marine Pollution Bulletin* and does consultancy work all over the coral seas.

Mike Parsons, who worked with me on the ecology of the Soil Association's Organic Farm, went on to a distinguished career in tropical agronomy and has now returned to Britain from teaching in South Africa. His colleague, Abdullah Basahy from Saudi Arabia, arrived in Durham one autumn and I took him up on the high fells for a day's work on the productivity of heather moor. I was in fact stripping down all Peter Holland's enclosures, ready for transport back to home base. It was hard work and freezing cold and Abdullah almost passed out, not because of the inclemency of the weather but because he was fasting for Ramadan. For the next few years I joined in, and found that it was the best way to keep my mind focused on the haves and have nots of the world.

The following day I went back up on the fells and loaded all the stakes and wire up on to the Haflinger. It was one of those beautiful cold days with a cloudless duck-egg-blue sky. I stood on the summit of Little Fell, looking down over the High Dale and the compass of the best grouse moor in the world, and sensed change on the horizon. As I turned, all the sheep that had been spread out across the fell turned and walked with me down the slope. I picked up the last ungainly load and carried it, balanced on my head, back towards the vehicle. Instead of following the track I struck off across the heather, a stupid thing to do for I was soon in trouble as I stepped into a deep bog pool, sinking down to my waist. With a heave, I threw my load off – an act which pushed me down even further into the grip of the peat. I won't say that thoughts flew through my head about becoming a twentieth-century Bog Man, preserved forever in the peat, but I was more than a bit worried. Rescue, thank goodness, was at hand in the form of a large stand of very ancient heather. Well into its senescent phase of growth, its ageing fronds dangled down within my reach. Grabbing it like a long lost friend I pulled myself free from the mire with a sucking plop. Gathering up a piece of the heather and my load, I regained the track and made my way down hill. By the time I reached the Haflinger my clothes were frozen and it was snowing hard. I counted the annual rings in a cross section of that heather stalk, revealing that it was forty-eight years of age, and the widest ring was in 1932 the year before I was born and the season before the record grouse bag was made on that or any moor. Somehow the grouse had known there would be a good crop of heather in 1933 and had staked out large numbers of small territories the previous autumn, providing a record harvest for the glorious twelfth.

John Waughman, whose parents were stall holders in the East End of London, had joined my team and was attempting to link the disciplines of phytosociology, productivity and phytochemistry. His special interest was nitrogen balance in bogs and fens. He was also a dab hand at statistical analysis of data of all kinds and dragged me screaming from Kulczynski Squares into the realms of multivariate analysis in which my last PhD student also became adept: Brian Wheeler was a genius and I owe both him and John a great debt of gratitude, for they helped to hold the ecology research up as I rushed around the world. Brian is now an ageing whizz kid working out of Sheffield University, with a research record that makes me very envious. Then there were all the students on the MSc in Ecology course that was run jointly by the departments of botany and zoology, and I still meet them and my undergraduates all over the world. I would at this point like to thank them all for teaching me so much, and I apologise for the fact that, although I still count myself to be a good taxonomist, I am not very good at putting names to human faces.

It was great fun being part of the in-house team of *Don't Ask Me*, Yorkshire Television's flagship programme that popularised science in the early seventies. The dangers of standing on the same platform with the flying arms of Magnus Pike and having to handle a multitude of animals in a studio situation were ameliorated by the presence of Dr Miriam Stoppard. Between the three of us we would endeavour to answer questions – many of which we would really have liked to avoid – before a studio audience. Terrifying, yes, but with the full weight of a production team and the special effects of a large sound studio, it was great fun trying. It must have been great fun for the audience too, for the series ran for a number of years and the studio audiences were queuing up every week.

On two occasions Miriam's medical credentials certainly came in handy. The question 'How long before the birth should an expectant mum keep going to work?' was answered without a pause: a very pregnant Miriam was sitting in a comfy chair from which the baby to be provided the answer, for it kicked the script off her lap and was born next day. The other occasion was a little scarier – at least for me. To answer the seemingly simple question 'Why do we say, crocodile tears?' the team had borrowed a crocodile from the zoo, and the script demanded that I would open its jaws so that Miriam could massage its lachrymal glands from within and make it weep. This was supposed to demonstrate that, as crocodiles had such flat heads, chewing their favourite meal massaged their lachrymal glands, producing a flood of tears. With me lying on top of the croc, everything went well, until having withdrawn her arm, Miriam was answering the question. While I was listening to the answer, the crafty croc temporarily relaxed his jaw muscles, putting me off my guard for a moment. Then he snapped them shut with my arm inside – mayhem and blood everywhere. Although I didn't get the kiss of life from Miriam she rendered first-aid and I was carted off to Leeds Infirmary which was crowded with the evening's crop of closing-time casualties – not the best place, when asked the cause of injury, to answer 'bitten by a crocodile'.

Insurance was always a problem, and when I was asked to make what turned out to be my most prestigious series, *Botanic Man*, I was sent off to Harley Street for a thorough going over. Zooming up several storeys in a very plush lift, I was introduced to the consultant who asked me for the forms from the insurance company. These I had left in the car, so off I went to get them. As the lift was otherwise occupied, I went down and back up the stairs at high speed. The first test was heartbeat and blood pressure and both went off the scale. After a nice cup of tea during which we discussed the proposed filming itinerary, the consultant congratulated me on my fitness and off I went, documents in hand. Mind you he did give me the let out clause, saying that even with such a good bill of health, I could walk out of the building and drop down dead. Perhaps I wasn't as fit as he had said or perhaps it was the ultra hectic schedule I outlined, for I was told that each part of my anatomy was to be insured by a different company. I would love to know which bits they thought more valuable or more vulnerable.

Jeremy Isaacs found the budget, the team was led by Randall Beatty and the locations were researched by Martyn Day, with links to the education department, with which I was also making the schools series *It's Life* and *It's More Life*, supplied by Michael Feldman. During the course of the research and the programme making we went round the world four times. The main trouble was that with all that foreign travel everyone wanted a slice of the action, so it was intimated that a different crew would film each programme. We dug our heels in, pointing out that if we were going to make a series worthy of the respect we thought it deserved then we needed continuity throughout the production.

Randall took the brunt of the acrimony and common sense won the day. And wow! a BAFTA award. It was the eventual result for this story of evolution from an ecologist's-eye view. *Botanic Man* not only sustained large audiences throughout its run (for one glorious week it beat *The Muppets* to the number one slot in London) and was shown all over the world, it also brought me the Richard Dimbleby Award, the year after Alan Whicker got it. In fact he flew in to hand it over to me in 1978.

The university had given me two years' unpaid leave to complete this mammoth project and as I walked out of the editing suite at Thames Television, having put the final touches to the last episode, I was greeted by the whole production team in the foyer. In the corner was a large wooden crate in which they told me was my diving gear. As I stepped forward to take a look, out jumped Eamon Andrews, the red *This Is Your Life* book clasped in his hands. Rosemary had managed to keep this a complete secret and as I had left home that morning a team of helpers had moved in to get the family down to London for the programme. It was a wonderful experience and great to see so many old friends and colleagues. The last surprise before I was handed the book was Rosemary's mum carrying in Eoghain, then three years of age, in her arms. He gave the final tribute: 'Dad you're brilliant.'

Despite promising myself that I'd spend more time at home, enjoying being a dad, I was off next morning early to fly to Sydney where Mike Weatherly was waiting to start filming *Up a Gum Tree*, the nature of Australia in four parts. Landing somewhat disorientated, I was whisked away to Bondi Beach and handed a long surfboard. Thirty minutes of instruction by the guy who had recently put Prince Charles through his surfing paces and I was supposed to stand up on the thing and, stepping off it on to the beach, introduce my new series. I wasn't as good a pupil as HRH, so my landing was not quite as regal. However, it sufficed, and we all took off to put the nature of Oz in the can.

Australia is an amazing place and it probably has more real characters per square mile than any other country on earth. A sequence in the pub at Marble Bar, reputed to be the hottest place in Australia, brought me into painful contact with a local. It was about take twelve of a sequence in which I was trying to catch a glass of beer, slid western style down the length of the bar. Unfortunately their narrow bottomed lager glasses don't balance as well as a good old beer mug and the guy behind me kept butting in with the same question. In consequence much ice cold Swan Lager went to waste. At last the glass ended up in my hand, there was no interruption, I turned triumphantly to camera and let out a yell of pain. My flailing arm had effectively stubbed out his fag. We drank each other's health in what by then was slightly tepid lager, set the shot up again and, at last, put it in the stubby. It was a wrap and the day's shoot ended up with a party, much of which took place on the hot tin roof of the Iron Rails pub. Then we went on our way, the best of friends in the sweltering heat of a perfect night, with the Southern Cross pointing the way to the next location.

The flora of Western Australia is one of the richest in the world and with the help of many locals we were able to dip into its diversity. One of these was Eric Newby, a local farmer who lived near Mangimup and was doing an MSc with an ex-student of mine, Peter Bridgewater, who was then working at one of Perth's great uni's. Eric's knowledge of the local flora was incredible and he led us through the floristic intricacies of the local heathland that not only thrives on fire but also protects some of the oldest soils in the world from erosion. Soils that contain so little in the way of micronutrients that, in order to coax a crop from this inhospitable land, a would-be farmer must bear the expense of the world's strangest fertilisers, containing things like copper, zinc and molybdenum.

A short walk with Eric anywhere among the lantern hakeas (triffid-like plants that appear to grow on no minerals at all) revealed a dozen different carnivorous plants and hundreds of shrubs, many in full flower, including a number new to science. He pointed out the many signs of overexploitation of the countryside: abandoned farms, soils held together only by a crust of salt and many just blowing away on the wind. Why, one was forced to ask, were these treasure houses of unique plants being sacrificed to grow winter wheat, when overproduction of the same crop was then being burned in Britain? Local jobs and making money for shareholders by selling fertilisers and tractors were the local and the international answer. Rampant short-termism was even then the cancer that was killing the natural world upon which we all depend.

It was the same with the local forests that sported some of the world's most sought after timbers. Karri, Jarrah and Mari were being clear felled, some to make way for plantations of, in comparison, very low value Monterey Pine, originally imported from California. The official reason was again, of course, provision of local jobs and the fact that pine trees grow faster than gums, arguments put forward again and again across the world. I could in some ways stomach the former but not the latter, for the gums are among the fastest growing trees on earth.

Some people still do try to do something about it. In 1999 campaigners stood guard around a stand of trees in the aptly named Styx Valley of Tasmania. To make their point and highlight their plea for help to a world about to celebrate the last Christmas of the millennium, they decorated the tallest specimen with Christmas lights. *Eucalyptus regnans* is a gentle green giant, the tallest hardwood tree left standing on Earth, a beacon of hope for the world's oldgrowth forests about to be trashed for wood chips. Sadly, the pictures of this, the ultimate Christmas tree, though e-mailed around the world, didn't make it into many papers.

The golden yellow blooms of the Western Australian Christmas tree, in actual fact a parasite growing on the roots of other plants, warned us that the festive season was not far away and that a holiday was scheduled in the middle of filming. Off I went to Tullamarine airport to meet my family who had flown in to spend Christmas and New Year with Dad. Our dream of Christmas dinner on the beach at Lorne was not to be. Rain stopped play, but it didn't dampen the spirit of the occasion, for after a dinner of turkey and plum duff we trampolined on the beach and built sandcastles in the rain. Then it was on to Alice Springs to film this famous outback community. Here we were the guests of the Machonochy family, Dr John, his wife Aija and two young sons. My children thought they had found heaven, sitting all day half in and half out of the pool, eating ice cream and strawberries. New Year's Eve saw us all at Uluru, then still known as Ayers Rock, not the place to climb in the heat of the day but a wonderful backdrop for seeing the New Year in with a jeroboam of Australian Champagne.

Palm Valley provided me with one of the most magical nights of my life. After having fried an egg on the rock in the heat of the day for the benefit of the cameras, I stayed the night sleeping out under the Southern Cross and the panoply of stars we town dwellers rarely get a chance to see. My sole companion was the sound engineer with his fantastic array of recording gear, transported across the world, especially for this occasion. The silence almost hurt, amplifying the slightest noise, and when a duck splashed, it sounded like force 10 on the Richter scale. There was no need for an alarm clock, for long before dawn lifted the eyelid of the southern world, the denizens of the valley started to wake up. The first sounds were like the rustle of falling leaves, but when collated and amplified they metamorphosed into the gentle stirrings of frogs and the staccato marching of the myriad legs of insects, spiders and millipedes: a unique shuffling symphony, by kind permission of the very special diversity of this very special place, all going about their early morning business.

In Brisbane, I said my fond farewells to the family, after an outing to see Disney's film *Candle Shoe,* which so amused Eoghain that we couldn't stop his paroxysms of very noisy mirth. Carrying the cases from the hotel the next morning I found him in deep conversation with the taxi driver. 'Has that young fella really been to all the places he tells me about?' the driver asked. 'I guess so,' I answered. 'Blimey sport,' came the response, 'I have never been out of Brisbane. How is it back home?'

That was a question I was asking myself: how was it going to be back home and back to my full-time post at the university? Offers of more television, programmes and advertising were coming in thick and fast. The more programmes I made the more of the world was at my finger tips opening up new horizons and filling my personal data banks with more ideas for more research and ever more programmes. The sad thing was that I was watching a world being torn to pieces by the globalization of greed and here was my chance of getting it over to the big unwashed world wide audience who knew me as ''im on telly' in an ever increasing number of languages. Perhaps this was the time for radical change. The opportunity and the invitation were there.

1980 THE CAMPAIGNING
DECADES ONGOING

19 BOLTING THE DOOR

Sir Arthur Norman, KBE, DFC,

Chairman, World Wildlife Fund, UK,
requests the pleasure of the company of

Dr David Bellamy
at the launch of the World Conservation Strategy
in the presence of
HRH The Duke of Edinburgh, KG, KT,
President, World Wildlife Fund – UK
in the Princess Anne Theatre
British Academy of Film and Television Arts,
195 Piccadilly, London W1
on Wednesday, 5 March 1980, at 11.30 am for 12 noon prompt

I had long been a supporter of WWF, both as a member of Council and
as a Trustee, and was being asked to support various new causes by the

week. The conservation scene was hotting up, with both Friends of the Earth and Greenpeace doing great things on the campaigning trails. UNESCO's list of World Heritage Sites (those areas of the world that were considered of great importance to humankind, in terms of their biology and/or their culture) was published: a galaxy of amazing places like Mount Everest, California's giant redwoods and Durham Cathedral, that were from then on under international protection. That was of course, if the owner-occupying government were not under pressure not to have them listed, and if any money would ever be forthcoming for their proper management. The same was true of programmes that were meant to afford protection for the world's most important wetlands, aimed at slowing the trade in endangered animals and plants. It is easy to make lists and promises but they all need money if they are to be implemented, and the begging bowls of conservation were getting ever more numerous.

A list of some of the groups and campaigns with which I became associated in name or as patron, vice president or president can be found in Appendix 5. The record number was over sixty such requests in one week. Even back in the early eighties, I was having to apologise for the fact that I could in probability only become a paper tiger, my name appended to a letter of support or appearing on their headed note paper. Even then it often took many hours on the phone, to find out if I was dealing with a just cause, in the real ethic of conservation, or simply another 'Not In My Backyarder'. My time was no longer my own, and with two television series to complete and several more in the pipeline, I began to cut back on my university research programmes.

I must admit that I was very lucky as my fame on television must certainly have got up the noses of part of the academic body, yet in the main they, or at least the real botanists, seemed to accept it. George Cansdale, Peter Scott, Armand and Michaela Dennis, Hans and Lotte Hass, Gerry Durrell, Jacques Cousteau and David Attenborough had already done great things for the cause of zoology. However, botany was still regarded by some as a pastime for young ladies to pursue until marriage. Apparently, when I hit the screen, up to my waist in what Lenny Henry much later christened compost corner, the numbers signing on for botany courses at university took a turn for the better, so my antics were tolerated.

The reasons for my finally saying goodbye to life as a full-time academic were many. My twenty-two years at Durham had been fascinating. Every year a new crop of some of the brightest potential biologists in the country were there, eager to share ideas – that is what I believe to be the true essence of university, and all I can do is hope that I helped a few undergraduates to look back on their time at Durham with satisfaction, likewise those who attained an MSc in Ecology and the twenty-nine graduates who chose me to help guide their research aspirations. I know all the latter and many of the former got good meaningful jobs, for I keep contact with some and meet many others on my travels.

It was the most difficult decision I ever had to make: to give up the annual crop of stimulus and that job with a pension of which my parents were so proud. The truth of the matter was that the botany department and the university were changing out of all recognition. A hard commercial edge was creeping in as management began to usurp wisdom. As I type these words the 'top' administrative staff of a number of universities, who find themselves earning salaries more handsome than mere professors, are challenging age-old statutes and taking on that very title for themselves. It's worth noting that the definition for the title 'professor' extends to include 'that assumed by charlatans, quacks, dancing masters etc.' I believe it was one of the Huxleys who said, 'If you want your child to excel in academia, christen them Professor.'

To name names would be ludicrous so I will summarise my reasons for saying goodbye to academia in the following excerpt from a joint paper with Alastair McIntosh. This we presented to a packed hall in Edinburgh when like-minded academics and many students were trying to save the oldest green think tank in Britain from closure.

In the year 387 BC, 482 years before the writing of the *Apocalypse,* Plato established the first university; it was called the 'Academy' (from which we get the word academic) and it was visited by Socrates. Most of what we know about Socrates is from Plato's writings. Socrates saw that philosophy is essentially about life. In his comment 'we are discussing no small matter, but how we ought to live' (Republic VIII 352d), he showed that he shared a common concern with mankind today.

Today the highest award given by our universities is a doctorate in philosophy – a teaching qualification in *philosophia*, literally the love of the goddess of wisdom. When we speak of academic excellence today, we are drawing on the tradition of the Greek word *orete*, meaning all round virtue or excellence.

Socrates' own relationship with nature is a telling one, reflecting the ambivalent attitude towards learning from nature apparent in so many academics today, yet Socrates had the humility and the wisdom in the end to admit the narrowness of this view. Plato portrays this beautifully in the *Phaedo*. Phaedrus meets Socrates wandering barefoot in Athens, persuades him to leave the town and the pair wander out to a grove by a river. Once there, Socrates is overwhelmed by such a delightful resting place. Chastising himself for having been unaware of what nature had to offer to the thinker, Socrates begs forgiveness for having presumed that nature could not teach anything to a lover of learning. Filled with inspiration, he then goes on to show that the endeavour to know love is the central motivation and goal of the philosopher. Without love there is no wisdom, only dry learning. Socrates concludes his dialogue with Phaedrus by thanking the spirits of nature for having inspired him with lofty thoughts. It is perhaps in this context that we should weigh up Plato's decision to locate the Academy, the first university, not amongst the spires and towers of the town but outside the city, in a wooded grove.

What of modern universities and education? In our experience, nearly every university around the world today is becoming a groveless academy. Car parks grow where trees once stood. Playing fields are sold off to be supermarket lots. Life is filtered and packaged into virtual reality. We are in danger of producing graduates more comfortable with the computer than in relating to a living community, either of people or of nature. If it continues down this track, the modern Academy, the university, will become a betrayal of philosophy because young minds are being deprived of the insights of the ancients within the very institutions that were founded on their wisdom. At his capital trial, when charged with teaching subversive views to the youth of Athens, Socrates said in his defence, 'If, in your annoyance, you will finish me off with a single slap, then you will go on sleeping until the end of your days, unless God, in his care for you, sends someone to take my place.'

World conservation needs the ethics of the Academy more than ever before. We must not allow philosophy to be failed. The cause of world conservation needs to become more than just a source of business, of research grants and consultancies, to our universities. Instead, it should be their most important raison d'être, for the earth itself hangs in the balance.

The other reason I wanted to leave was that at that point jobs in ecology were not thick on the ground. What was the use of me bringing any more overtrained students into a jobless market. I could make my living from the media and my university salary could be used to give two up and coming youngsters a job at the bottom of the ladder. When it came to the crunch the way the whole thing was being handled by the administration was in my opinion a disgrace and so I made my decision and left in just one day. On arriving home I gathered the family together and told them the news. The immediate answer I got from Eoghain, then six years of age, was 'What about your pension Dad?' That did it; I knew I had made the right decision.

*

My dream was to be my own boss, the head of Botanical Enterprises Publications Limited, to make my own decision as to when I would work and what I would work on, to be able to spend more time with the family. I soon found out that any such dream is in reality but a daymare in disguise, especially for Rosemary. Home becomes an office, the daily post and now faxes and e-mails grow in volume, the phone never stops ringing and, with my ever more hectic travel schedule, it all fell on one person's shoulders. Thank God these shoulders were and are still of the strongest mould. As well as a part-time teaching post at Choristers School, a Tutorship at St Aidan's College and looking after a family of five at different schools spread across the country, Rosemary now had to bear the load of accountancy, including that most abominable of all taxes, VAT. She also ensured that I had packed my bags properly and then put up with my deep jet lag on my return home. Only once did I think divorce proceedings might be in the offing, but more of that later.

I was out in the big wide world without a job and without a pension. All the sensible things that my upbringing had drummed into me were gone. The challenge was immense, not only was university changing but so was television. Gone were the two-channel days when it was easy to be popular while family viewing was being usurped by a multiplicity of choice. Game shows and soaps washed documentary slots away as programming based on the common denominator of audience numbers began to amuse family audiences to death.

I had for some years been working with Harry Green at BBC North East on a series of local natural history programmes called *Looks Natural*. Harry had been part of the dynamic team that put Mike Neville on our screens as anchor man for our local news output *Look North*. These programmes were done on a shoestring budget, but took us all over the north, digging up stories and basically enjoying ourselves. The very first programme started right at the top of the region, on Cross Fell; at least it was meant to, but a heavy fall of snow allowed us to get only as far as the radar station on Little Dunn Fell, where Harry, I, cameraman and a young sound man called Eric Woodward, on his first assignment, stood shivering among enormous snowdrifts. His first words to me were, 'Why aye bonny lad, it's cold,' and since that day I have always known him as Bonny Lad. Apart from the fact that the editor thought we had shot it in black-and-white, the programme must have been well received for we went on to make a lot more, during which I teamed up with many local characters. We were always short of money and, mainly because of my hectic life style, short of time. Once, at the end of a very long day doing an ecological classification of the English Lakes, I was standing above Buttermere, trying to explain the problems of eutrophication, the enrichment of lakes by fertilisers draining down off the farms. We had by that time run out of light, so the final piece to camera was delivered in the beam of the headlights of the camera car.

Perhaps it was that experience on Little Dunn Fell, but I suddenly realised that the story of all the special plants of Upper Teesdale was in fact the legacy of four great seasons: the Great Winter of the Great Ice Age; the Great Spring and the return of the plants and animals from the warmer south; the Great Summer, when hunters and gatherers, and then neolithic, bronze and iron age farmers and craftsmen, made a good living from the dale; and the fullness of the Great Autumn, when mining, quarrying and well-run shooting estates kept families and communities living in the dale. The cycle of the great seasons posed the question, 'What next?' as the inane Common Agricultural Policy was doing its best to wreak havoc on the flora, the fauna and the local communities.

One of the local characters was a very talented artist called Sheila Mackey who lived in a most amazing house in Shotley Bridge that was always full of children, animals and tobacco smoke. We teamed up and my concept was turned into a book, lavishly illustrated by Sheila, called *The Great Seasons*. As the Queen Mother, herself a Bowes-Lyon, had spent some of her childhood in the dale, and as it was her eightieth birthday, I plucked up courage and wrote asking her to consider writing a foreword to the book. No answer was the stern reply until, just before publication, I received a letter apologising that my request had been lost amongst all her birthday cards and saying that she would be delighted to give the book her blessing.

The book was accompanied by four documentaries. Filming not only took us all over the dale but also to Iceland to film the ice age sequences.

Harry and Bonny Lad were of course there and our cameraman was David Cox, one of the most talented I ever had the pleasure of working with. I only once saw Harry getting ruffled and that was during the filming of a scene in which I was washed away by melt waters through an ice bound landscape. The shot was fine, on the fourth take, but I was suffering from hypothermia – as I also was when I emerged from a lake carrying a huge lump of ice and turning to camera said, 'A baby iceberg, just what I always wanted.'

Suffering for the cause of putting a point over almost became a Bellamy trademark, and never more so than in the two series *Bellamy's Backyard* and *Seaside Safaris*, although in these the viewers never saw the agonies through which I went. My life-long interest in microscopes had not waned and Dad and I had built up quite a collection of fantastic instruments. I had really become hooked when watching pond life projected on to the screen, 'all alive-oh' by John Clegg, curator of Haslemere Education Museum. My dream was to be miniaturised down, so that I could wander through the microscopic world and explain the wonders that are present right in your own backyard. This all happened long before the wonders of computer animation, but with a team led by Mike Weatherley and Paul Kriwaczek, using mirrors and front axial projection, everything became possible. However, it necessitated me hanging like Peter Pan on a flying wire in a blue studio for days on end, all the while watching the action of the creepy crawlies on a micro-projector screen and reacting 'mirror image wise' to their every movement.

The worst sequences of all were when I had to appear to fly Superman-like over the camera. For these shots the relative comfort of the counterbalanced flying wire was replaced by a plastic breastplate, which exactly fitted my upper torso. I had to lie upon this contraption trying to look happy, while keeping both my head, trunk, arms and legs held up with no support other than my muscles. Still, it worked, and some of the effects were convincing enough for me to be asked by fans young and old, 'How did you do that?' The first shot of the first series was perhaps the most ambitious for the camera started on a high crane above the house, tracking across the local landscape and down on to the patio. Then, all in one continuous move it focused on a wiggling earthworm, from behind which I stepped to begin the commentary. My favourite sequence was the one where a freak rainstorm washed me off the roof, along the gutter and down into the garden pond, where I was caught in a jam jar by a small boy.

Fortunately, the stand-up comedians found my voice and mannerisms irresistible, and so helped to keep me at least in the public ear. As far as I know, it all started with Willy Rushton sitting in a wetsuit enthusing about the 'weely amazin' contents of a tea bag he had just fished out of a canal. Benny Hill got a stern letter from my Mum about having the audacity to use her son's voice to tell a risqué joke. Then everyone was doing it, including almost 400 children at one of my niece's schools when I was planting a tree. There is no doubt in my mind that Lenny Henry was the best, for one day on walking into the house I heard what I thought was my voice blaring from the television in the front room. On turning the corner I could see it definitely wasn't me. What a performer! At the height of the take-off-David-Bellamy phase I was travelling down the A1 in my car when the local radio announced an 'imitate David Bellamy' contest. I stopped at the next filling station, got on the phone, and under the name of Fred Smith entered the competition. I was a bit miffed when, almost at my destination, they announced the result. I had come third. I consoled myself with the fact that if others could make a living on the box, imitating me, then surely my future was assured.

One of the main hazards of being ''im on the Telly' is the perennial April Fool's shorty you agree to make. Like the Lirpa Loof: no guessing what that means backwards, but there it was for all to see, an official label on a cage in London Zoo. Inside the cage was a diminutive actor wearing a wonderfully crafted fur bodysuit, playing the part of this unique (first time on show anywhere in the world) animal, a Primate related to the legendary Big Foot, that had just been discovered in the Himalayas and given to the Zoo as a gift from the People of China. Well that's the story the Esther Rantzen team had dreamed up, and there was I, ready to tell the world all about it when a little hand slipped into mine, as a voice said, 'David, is it really real?' Looking down, I saw a pair of very appealing young eyes looking into mine. I bent down and whispered, 'Well, you stand just over there and watch, and after I have finished you tell me.' I did my piece to camera with the Lirpa Loof imitating my every action. Bending down once more I asked, 'What do you think?' 'It's not real,' she said, 'There is someone inside.' 'Are you sure?' 'Yes, it didn't close its mouth.' My new little friend was of course absolutely right. She was very observant – everything else worked perfectly, it even had clouds of mist appearing from its mouth into the cold morning air. I said, 'Please let it be our secret, it's April Fool's day tomorrow.' 'Yes,' she answered and off she went. She must have kept her mouth shut, for it certainly fooled all the extra visitors and even an Australian camera crew that turned up to film it.

That old adage of 'never work with children or animals' is still catching me out to this day. *The Gene Machine*, another Yorkshire winner, had me in the studio every week with an audience and a giraffe borrowed from Bellevue Zoo, who helped me introduce the programme. To get our heads on the same level I had a special camera and a seat on a telescopic boom. If you have ever wondered why giraffes can browse happily on very prickly trees, I can tell you. They salivate a lot. I got covered with the stuff as my co-presenter helped me introduce all the thorny problems of genetics: like, 'How do you tell the sex of a chromosome?' 'Pull its genes down!'

More recently, I was caught on the hop when asked to preview the film *Free Willy* with an audience of about 800 youngsters. We all watched with rapt intent and some of them, like me, cried a lot. During question time, which mainly revolved around why Willy had not been released back into the sea, I found myself with my back up against the wall. I did my best to explain that it wasn't a matter of just letting it loose once more into the marine environment. Willy had to be trained little by little and then released into a protected area where other killer whales would not come and attack him. In the midst of all this another little girl put up her hand and asked, 'How do whales make babies?' Ready for that one, I countered with, 'Whales are mammals and they make babies in the same way that your Mum and Dad made you.' I breathed a sigh of relief, until on the way out she cornered me and said, 'No David, how does the daddy whale make it go up and down, he doesn't have hips does he?' A spark of inspiration saved my day, 'Well, think about it, the waves do the trick.' I then escaped as quickly as I could.

20 CATHEDRALS, POPULATION AND HOHOBA BEANS

On 18 March 1981 I was in attendance at a service of thanksgiving to mark the centenary of the Church of England Children's Society where I was to give the address. Of all the cathedrals I have had the honour to speak in, the one in Liverpool is not the best for, despite a PA system, you tend to hear your previous sentence re-echoing around its cavernous interior. Perhaps that's what gave the Beatles some of their inspiration. Sitting there as the good and faithful came with their gifts to say thank you and further support the Society which had provided four of our family, I pondered upon the famous painting 'When did you last see your Father?'

Despite being of Baptist stock, Dad was a cathedral and parish church freak, and whenever he travelled around the country John Betjeman's book on the subject would go with him. He, or whenever I was with him, we, would pop in for a prayer and an ogle at the antiquities. We both had favourites which changed over the years. As far as cathedrals are concerned, Southwell in Nottingham is my favourite. For a start it looks completely out of place in an English country town, almost as if transposed from the Spanish mesetas; this, despite the fact that when built the Master Builders were fresh from medieval building school, a fact borne out by the form and lavish decoration of the main building. To me the most amazing thing about this particular sacred space is the chapter house that was completed some 300 years later. By this time the descendants of those first builders had so absorbed the local scene that the internal decoration is a harvest festival of creation as displayed by the Nottinghamshire countryside, wrought in stone. At the time, when global warming was an act of God, not of mammon, Southwell was the southern gateway to the great vineyards of the Bishopric of York. A look inside the chapter house lends weight to this supposition for there are bunches of grapes entwined with local plants and animals that are common today.

Just up the road from the minster dwells a remarkable family of artists by the name of Measures: David, Christine and their two children, Simon and Sally. Christine does remarkable paintings of the cathedral, while David, like the descendants of those medieval stonemasons, makes depictions of the countryside of Nottingham in paint entwined with detailed notes. Each is a delight to see, and as you scan the symbiosis of words and images you too can touch the sanctity of creation. David is not only an artist but also an entomologist of great repute. I first met this gentle duo when David brought his class from Trent Polytechnic up to Durham, to join my students on a marine field trip along the highly polluted coast near Hartlepool. I reciprocated by taking some of my students down to Nottingham to study the architecture of urban decline in Hyson Green. There, art and science combined to ask what vandal had seen fit to destroy the community of little terraced houses that had served the lace workers so well, replacing them with the monstrosity of high rise that was already falling into graffitied decay?

It was a renaissance of a weekend for all concerned and certainly gave my campaigning a new slant. It got me interested in urban ecology and led me to become part of what I like to call the miracle of Salford. Tower blocks had been blighting both landscape and lives for some time, driving families to despair and some to suicide. Motorcars were parked bumper to bumper along both sides of what had been tree lined playgrounds, where skipping and hopscotch whiled away the school holidays and would-be Don Bradmans practised for the Ashes. Neighbourly contact had been rapidly whittled down to almost nil as people rushed to or from work each day. The dream of vertical village communities with wall to wall fitted kick-about playgrounds had become the nightmare of broken lifts and never cleaned stinking stairwells.

Salford had some of the worst blocks, cut off from the outside world by a mayhem of spaghetti raceways. When I first visited Apple Tree Court it was in an awful state, a ghetto of despair, well laced with empty flats and burned out cars, a place to get away from not to be a part of. Then Canon Wyatt turned up on the scene, a new vicar for St Joseph's with a vision in his heart. His once elegant Victorian church was as much a ruin as the lives of many of his parishioners. Yet when it was under threat of demolition they begged for a reprieve, saying that the church was the only real thing they had left in the sad landscape of their lives. The house of God was saved and, with much hard work, was returned to its former glory. The churchyard was transformed into a garden of hope and inspiration. At last the people had something to call their own and very soon it became the centre of a vibrant community with fair trading in secondhand clothes and furniture.

My small part in this story came about when one of their main open spaces came under the threat of development as a car park and I was asked to join them in their cause of common sense. All I really did was walk around the area with my mind wide open and say, 'Wow! If anyone is foolish enough to start to destroy this oasis of spirituality I will come and chain myself to a tree.' Common sense *did* prevail and I have been asked back on a number of occasions to celebrate the opening of yet more gardens – vegetable, water, cottage, Japanese – and even a sun room conservatory. Each one was the dream of one of these high rise parishioners, brought into being by a hardworking band of down to earth angels. No wonder there is a waiting list of people hoping to move in when an apartment falls empty.

My most recent visit was to take a group of bishops to see the miracle for themselves, part of a meeting of all the 120 bishops and suffragan bishops to discuss the role of the church in matters environmental. I arrived very early, to be greeted by a crowd of clothes-, furniture-, and paper-recyclers all hard at work. Whisked inside for a cup of tea, I was sitting between two very young ladies watching the telly, when in came a besuited man, saying: 'I am the Bishop of Carlisle's driver, have we come to the right place?' 'Yes,' said I, 'You're a little early, how about a cup of tea?' Enter Canon Wyatt some ten minutes later to find the bishop sitting with his granddaughter and little friend, watching *Sabrina the Teenage Witch*. God moves in mysterious ways, his wonders to perform. It was a wonderful, mind opening day, ending with evensong in the echoing magnificence of Liverpool Cathedral.

When it comes to speaking in cathedrals, Lincoln is my favourite. It was there that I made my debut for Population Concern, a non-governmental organisation (NGO) which concerns itself with the subject of Paul Erlich's 1971 bestseller, *The Population Bomb*. Its mission is to answer the call of women and men across the world for access to modern methods of reproductive health care and small-is-beautiful job opportunity. Before these bigoted days of political correctness we used to call it family planning. I joined its ranks in 1974, which had been styled World Population Year, when its work was masterminded by Eric McGraw, and I became President under the legendary Mani Rowley. She and Octavia Hill, Petra Kelly, Whangeri Matthai and Sylvia Earl rank as my all time heroines.

For the past twenty years I have attended their annual workshops entitled 'Planet Without a Plan', and talked to houses, often cathedrals, packed with sixth formers about their hopes and fears for their future. For me, the most memorable was the first one we held in Belfast. There, during question time, a young lady came to the front and turning to me said, 'David Bellamy, half of us here are Catholics and half are Protestants and we aren't fighting. Who are these awful people who want to cause trouble?' It was at this meeting that I was also first asked the question, 'How can you come and preach to us when you have a large family yourself?' My answer – 'Well four of them are adopted' –

quelled the disapproval a little, but back came the rejoinder, 'But you have had the pleasure of a large family, haven't you?' I still have no real answer for that. All I can do by way of recompense is return to that memorable centenary celebration that echoed around the great void of Liverpool Cathedral, and offer the moment when Mike Lyddiard sang a song and invited everyone to join in the chorus:

> Oh, they're everybody's children
> They need a helping hand,
> A shoulder to cry on,
> Someone who understands;
> Home's where love is all around
> And happiness is free,
> They're everybody's children
> And they need you and me.

Of all the causes I have supported, that of Population Concern has been most successful, not due to me but thanks to an immense band of dedicated thinkers and workers.

Italy now ranks among the world leaders in family planning, one-child families being the accepted norm. If you had asked me only ten years ago whether that would have been possible, my answer would have been an emphatic 'no', not because of Catholic dogma but because the vast majority of Italian men are potty about families and babies. One reason it has happened is that, with each new generation, the Italian laws of land inheritance, which demand an equal share out between all children, rub home the fact that small families make economic sense. Also, it is now true to say that wherever women have access to education and modern reproductive health care they are bravely grasping the straw of family planning. These are the brightest of lights at the end of my darkest tunnels of environmental concern. *Every* child must be a *wanted* child and one that can live out its life in a peaceful world.

Sadly, the arena of family planning is not the most peaceful in which to campaign and some of our meetings were to say the least somewhat fraught. Of all the anti Population Concern letters I have ever received, the most annoying came from Glenys Kinnock. Her letter castigated me for having pictures of three males, Prince Philip, the Archbishop of York and myself at the head of our annual report. This was my answer.

Dear Mrs Kinnock,

Many thanks for your letter regarding Population Concern's annual report. I too share your concern about the status of Women in the world and was indeed the first male member of the Mrs Pankhurst Society at Bedford College, London.

We really do do our best at headquarters where we employ only one full time male, in a staff of 18. Also as you note we are doing well among our list of vice presidents. Sadly we haven't quite managed a female Archbishop yet and I don't really want to have a sex change at my time in life.

I trust you and your husband are making equal efforts to balance the gender books in the European Parliament.

I didn't get an answer.

Despite the fact that I had taken on the cloak of an itinerant botanist, I was fortunately still in vogue with the powers that be; so much so that I was invited to go to Sydney to act as anchor man for the publicity of The XIII International Botanical Congress. Dad had by that time retired and decided to come along to have a look at the other end of the world. We were put up in the tall hotel at the top of King's Cross. Dad was rather curious about the young ladies who were wont to hang around the area, so I reminded him of our Iceland experience and got on with the job of explaining to the media, the importance of botany: 'Wiv'out plants, mate, you can't have yer kangeroos, let alone yer fizzy beer.'

The opening took place in the then new Opera House and was an impressive affair. As we all poured out down the steps it was very easy to feel part of the phytosociology of the science of botany. Everybody who was somebody was there, as was everyone who had aspirations in that direction. I took the press to the large rock outcrop, which stands opposite the main entrance and did my best to interest them in the colony of *Psilotum nudum*, which still grows there. I enthused about the fact that this rather scruffy little plant was not unlike the first plants that ever managed to grow on land and that we should look after everything that was still in its natural state in Australia and across the world, although unfortunately to little avail. What impressed them most was that on our return to our hotel one of the bevy of biodiverse young ladies congregated near the door asked, 'How's the conference going Dave?' I was evidently getting the message across to *some* of the masses out there and so I was taken along by the *Australian*, a broadsheet no less, to be photographed, very appropriately sitting beside the fountain shaped like a dandelion clock. I did point out that the sculptor had got it a bit wrong, for it was not depicted as a perfect Fibonacci series, but that didn't appear in the article. Well you can't win 'em all.

After the congress, Dad and I were whisked off in a private plane to a shareholders' meeting of a company that was growing Hohoba, a magic bean from Mexico that produces what is to all intents and purposes a substitute for sperm whale oil. I was amazed by the fact that all the shareholders, most of whom were oldsters, gathered round thanking me for the fact that they were now set for a prosperous old age. Then I found out that they were, without any reference to me let alone permission from anyone, using edited clips from a sequence on Hohoba lifted from *Botanic Man*, and were expecting me to endorse some of their preposterous claims. Dad and I did a runner.

The message about the importance of plants in all their diversity was beginning to get through but, as in all things, especially where there is money to be made, the charlatans were waiting in the wings to make a killing.

21 LIFE BEGINS AT FIFTY

Back in the early eighties, Australia along with New Zealand led the world in conservation, especially at the NGO level. Australia had the Dynamic Wilderness Society headed by Bob Brown and New Zealand had the Native Forests Action Group led by Guy Salmon. Not only were they the kings of direct peaceful action, but they were attempting to get legislation locked into the laws of their respective realms to protect what habitats they still had left in a pristine state.

Great strides forward were made, with the then Prime Minister, Malcolm Fraser, playing a key part in the eventual moratorium on whaling and the blocking of sand mining on Fraser Island, and also in the protection of some key areas of wilderness under the banner of World Heritage. Back then it seemed as if that part of the world might be coming to its senses, conservation-wise. Sadly, that was not to be.

Thanks to the popularity of my television programmes down under, I was in constant demand to back the various causes they were fighting. Of course I agreed. The most famous to which I was ever asked to lend my support was the campaign to stop the building of the Gordon-below-Franklin Dam in Tasmania. This was the latest extension of a gigantic hydroelectric scheme that had already engulfed Lake Pedder, said by many people, including HRH The Duke of Edinburgh, to be one of the most beautiful lakes in the world. I, along with another 2,612 people, joined the blockade, which obtained a reprieve for Tasmania's last free river and the pristine wilderness that was once home to the first Tasmanian people who were brutally sent to the wall of extinction by white settlers late in the 1800s. It was also home to the now mythical beast, the Thyalacine or Tasmanian Tiger, the last one of which died in Hobart Zoo in the year of my birth.

I had already disgraced myself in support of this cause while at a fund-raiser for another, the RSPB. It was a concert of Beatles' music played by the London Philharmonic at the Albert Hall in the presence of the Queen, Prince Philip and Paul McCartney. I was compering the show with Joan Collins. At a moment which appeared appropriate to me I turned to the Royal Box and pleaded that 'several thousand of your Commonwealth subjects are standing between bulldozers and a potential Site of World Heritage, the memory of which has greatly inspired your husband.' I reckon that it was the best speech I ever made – not so the organisers, or my family who were waiting in the wings to be presented to the Queen. The latter never happened, and I received one of those 'Her Britannic Majesty cannot interfere with matters of state' sort of letters: officially scolding but unofficially supportive, so I am still soldiering on.

The truth was that Tasmania didn't need any more hydropower, however cheap, but the authorities were going to sell it in an attempt to attract industry to their shores. I was one of 1,272 people arrested and one of the 447 people who refused bail and went to prison. The only difference between me and the others was that I was a household name and so became the show piece, gaoled on my fiftieth birthday.

Of all the causes I have ever been asked to support this was the best researched and ethically the most just of them all. For me this was it, right against wrong, common sense against the stupidity of vested interests. It was a battle that must be won and its success put firmly in the public psyche, so I wrote to the key public figures in conservation and asked them to join me on the picket line, to show solidarity for wilderness and everything it contained and stood for. The only response I got was from

Spike Milligan who sent me £200 towards my fare. (Bless you Spike.)

The operation was carried out with all the precision of a military manoeuvre. Two land-based groups, many of whom had slept out overnight, moved in towards the bulldozer chanting 'No Dams'. Two water-based flotillas of duckies (tiny inflatable boats) created ordered mayhem in front of the landing barges. One film crew, complete with decoy 'David Bellamy', approached Warner's Landing from one direction, and another, with the real me, came in from another. I was thus able to step off the boat right in front of the bulldozer and the waiting cameras. When a police officer arrested me I knew that my journey across the world had been worthwhile. All that the members of the Wilderness Society had worked for so long to achieve was now ready to be flashed to news programmes the world over.

It was the most uplifting thing I have ever been part of, working alongside such a broad cross-section of society peacefully demonstrating in quite inhospitable conditions against the destruction of something they didn't own but they all believed in. It was then my firm belief that civilisation could only be advanced by such action. Sadly, though inspiringly, the same is true today.

As I could write volumes about my time on the blockade and in Risdon gaol it is difficult to choose the best anecdotes but here goes. On the morning scheduled for my arrest I was woken very early, first by a pademelon who hopped in for a 'G'day', and then by a young lady reporter who shoved a microphone into my tent. As I opened my mouth to speak, she enquired 'What's that on your lip?' Feeling around with my tongue I answered, 'A couple of land leeches having their breakfast, I think.' She disappeared rapidly. A tall, young, Joyce-Grenfell-type lady, dressed immaculately in tweeds and an elegant handbag with the words I'm Myrtle Please Save Me embroidered for all to see, told me that she could no longer stand life in the camp and had asked Bob Brown if she could be arrested that day. He had agreed and she wanted assurance that she was properly dressed for the occasion. There were many real heroes and heroines like her, each doing their bit for the living world. I was proud to stand alongside them.

Bob Brown was the unassailable presence who really made it all happen, a quiet genius of a man who had the essence of the native bush running through his veins, a young GP out of Launceston, a white-fella who had tested his endurance along the white water sharps and flats of this still intact aboriginal songline, when in eighteen days he ran the full length of the river in a rubber duckie.

I first met Bob when he took me by helicopter to see the river system for myself. We landed on a sandbank and stood together in its waters, sheltered from the outside world by high banks and cliffs in part covered with huon pines, many in excess of 2,000 years old. The waters are deep golden-brown, coloured by the humic acids that continuously leach out from the pristine soils, each a biochemical fingerprint of the post-glacial history of this place. He told me of the Kutakina caves where the first Tasmanian people had set the furthest-south record for survival of humankind during this the latest cold snap.

All of a sudden the waters began to rise, covering the sandbank. This was no natural flash flood but an attempt by the hydro board to flush us out. They had opened up the sluices on one of their dams high on the catchment. We ran for the helicopter, to be whisked away, but en route to it Bob stopped to pick up two matchsticks that had been deposited on the gravel, such was the measure of the man and his respect for pristine wilderness.

After the arrest our group was taken by police launch to Straun, then by bus to Queenstown where we met the verbal wrath of some local people – and who could blame them for they had been told again and again that we were taking their jobs from them: a welter of jobs during the construction, but they didn't realise there would be precious few for the rest of the life of the dam. In court, as I was the star suspect, I was among the first on the stand. There, under the instruction of one of our lawyers, Lincoln Siliakus, I pleaded guilty to trespass and refused bail. Off I was taken to the lock up in the police station and waited all day as the rest of the batch of 'law breakers' were tried, sentenced and then locked up with me. Things were getting a bit crowded when around 5.30 p.m. a policeman came in and, asking if we would like to see the arrests on television, wheeled a set into the cell. There we were, as all the world had seen, in glorious technicolor.

I was thankful that my Mum had been in heaven for over five years, so she wouldn't have to explain it all to the neighbours. I was also very sad that I had spoilt my father's special day, for he was at that point getting married. After Mum's death he had moved back down to Sutton to live with G and renew worship at Sutton Baptist and Crown Road Mission, taking communion with those of his old friends who had not yet climbed the golden stairs. Not long before I left for Australia he had asked me, 'What would you say if I told you I was going to get married again?' Though somewhat taken aback, my answer was 'Great news, who's the lucky lady?' The lady in question was Jesse who had been a great friend of my Mum and a stalwart of the church in Sutton. I missed the ceremony, but I did send them a telegram: 'Sorry I can't be with you in person, I have gone straight to Gaol, and though I passed Go, I didn't ask for bail!'

When the last of us had been dealt with we were loaded into a bus and taken right across the island to Risdon Gaol near Hobart. At the witching hour of midnight a female fellow prisoner presented me with a biscuit surmounted by a candle and the busload of green felons sang 'Happy Birthday'.

On arrival at Risdon the ladies were taken into their part of the prison and we were told to line up, ready to be checked in. I was worried about how I would feel being locked up in a cell and so stood last in the line. When it came to my turn to be officially booked, the warder handed me a potted plant and said 'Here sport, will you identify that for my missus, please?' I was now a sentenced man and in prison. I knew I could get out by asking for bail and promising that I wouldn't go back into the National Park again, but when the cell door clanged shut I panicked. I have always been claustrophobic. Perhaps it was because of the sight of people trapped under fallen buildings during the war, or the problems Mum and I had shared at my birth. Whatever the real reason, my terror of confined spaces had always been a problem, so much so that when I was about fourteen, I had decided to put myself to the ultimate test. We were camping on the coast of South Wales, and there was a sea cave which filled with water at high tide. I waited, shivering at the thought, and when the tide was well and truly high I took the deepest of breaths and in I went. Despite the sting of the salt it was eyes open all the way. It was only about ten yards, and I knew that I could swim the length of the big pool at Cheam under water, but that light at the end of my chosen tunnel of terror seemed too far away. My lungs were bursting, I was sweating and yet I had goose pimples, when I surfaced ten yards clear of the submerged stretch. The noise of turning keys brought on that same cold sweat panic; my immediate thought was what happens if the place catches on fire? I could see a metal loo, a bed with a bare light above it and a space in the wall in which there had once been a radio – thank goodness there was nothing to catch fire. So I said my prayers and wondered what Rosemary and the kids were doing.

The answer was that they were under siege from the media in our home, half a world away in Bedburn. When at last she did emerge to go shopping they pounced, asking her what she thought about her husband being in gaol. Her answer was 'For the first time in our married life, I know exactly where he is.' What a woman!

That day there was mayhem outside the gaol as a couple of hundred partymakers complete with cake were celebrating my birthday. A helicopter circled overhead, as naked bodies spelt out 'no dams' in the women's compound. I still had my radio mike with me but, inside a Faraday's cage with a flat battery, communication with the outside world was not possible. I really couldn't ask the authorities for a battery charger, especially as I was in gaol for campaigning against the building of a hydroelectric dam, a fact recorded by a magnificent cartoon in a newspaper which showed me being presented by the warders with a birthday cake, ablaze with electric lights connected to a gigantic cable disappearing into the distance. Communications from the outside world came pouring in by post. I apologise for the lack of answers, but as the contents of outgoing letters each had to be checked by the prison authorities, time was not on my side.

The days were spent sitting about with a motley range of characters from every walk of life, each one an individualist drawn to a common cause, and each one worth a chapter of their own. Morning roll call was a hoot. We were meant to answer our names with a polite 'Present'. 'Professor Bellamy' came the call, interrupted by an imperious cry from one of the higher echelons of the society of warders: 'The name is Bellamy, no favours here.' As the rest of us trooped off to the mess hall, the warder who had called my name whispered, 'I come from Austria and know that such titles are well earned. Please remember that as I call your name each morning I will say Professor, under my breath.' The tall public schoolboy next in line to me answered with a polished 'You rang?' and was marched off to be reprimanded for his affrontery. Some years later I pressed the check-in bell at a hotel in the middle of Melbourne and a familiar voice greeted me with: 'You rang? We were in Risdon together.' To this day, hardly a month goes past without meeting a fellow inmate.

The walk to breakfast gave us a chance of greeting the other prisoners held at Her Majesty's pleasure for a variety of heinous crimes committed against, not by, the state. I shook as many hands proffered through the bars as I could and even signed a couple of autographs before I was hurried on to cries of, 'Good on yer Dave.'

We had decided to go on hunger strike, which did a lot for my figure and sorely tempted my strength of resolve, especially on the day that a large bar of Cadbury's milk chocolate was included on the menu. To prove that starvation was our choice and was not being forced on us, we had to hold the tray of food for one minute. On handing mine back through the hatch a voice from within said, 'The boys would like to put you out over the wall tonight, do you want to go?' I explained that I really wanted to be there and declined the offer. The idea that they could have accomplished this Houdini feat was strengthened next night when, after I had been firmly locked away, three sheets of paper floated into my cell, followed by a whispered conversation that asked for help with some biochemistry questions. The voice and the scribbled questions told me that their owner was stuck with his correspondence course. 'Psst, let me have the answers back at breakfast.'

Apart from galloping claustrophobia, my other pet hate is sitting doing nothing, and that was the real problem of being trapped in prison. The compound was concrete and all you could do was sit and lean against the walls which stretched high above, framing the freedom of the sky. Lucky clouds, lucky birds. The only thing that made it bearable was the camaraderie of campaign conversation. The wilderness of the mind is one that I hope they can never destroy. I thought again of the lucky birds, but vapour trails clouded even that vision of freedom, as did the new found knowledge of ozone holes and the warming of the global greenhouse. Then there was the fact that without wild places the wild birds would have no homes in which to raise their families and so would be banished from the skies. The only birds the world would have left were urban survivors like the sparrows that nested high on those walls. I must have been musing out loud. 'For God's sake, shut up Dave,' said an ornithologist, 'We're going to win,' and he walked away to squat in a patch of sunlight further round the wall.

Many years later I was asked to visit Royal Holloway prison in London, and all this became a reality once more. Some bright spark, perhaps having seen the film *Bird Man of Alcatraz* had decided to build an aviary in the main compound and I had been asked to officiate at its opening. I arrived early and was taken to see the structure that was already alive with its own inmates. There, looking in, was a very beautiful young lady, enjoying the spectacle although evidently under some stress. I asked her, 'How long have the birds been here?' The answer came, 'I have only been here ten days and they were here when I arrived. I don't like it here, please take me home.' I asked for directions to the toilet and tried to compose myself for the ceremony.

I can't remember what I said, but a very butch inmate whose bare arms bore the self-inflicted marks of desperation stood there watching the antics of the birds. She said it all: 'Oh Dave, I am glad you are here to open the aviary and let them out. Nothing should be forced to live in a cage.' To crown it all, one of the mums in the unit that housed them and their new-born babies asked: 'You adopt kids don't you Dave? How about adopting mine? She would have a much better home with you.'

That's what is wrong with prisons, there is no sense of home or homeliness. The tables in the mess hall at Risdon were bare stainless steel, no table cloths, no curtains, no shred of compassion, just concrete, concrete, concrete and the sickly smell of pine disinfectant doing its best. It reminded us of the freedom of the slopes covered with Huon pine that were under sentence of incarceration behind a high-walled dam. Yes, we must win – not just for the sake of the wild birds, animals and flowers but for the sanity of humankind. Without wilderness there is nowhere to escape from the cuckoo's nest of battery living.

If Bob Brown had told me that my staying in Risdon would have helped the cause, I would have stayed, but a series of important meetings back in Britain called. What is more, before I left Australia, I had to complete the film *Huon Cry*, directed by Philip Lohrey, who had sold his holiday cottage in the countryside in order to raise the money to make it. So I applied for bail, signed off and, on leaving the prison, was met by the photographer who had splashed my moment of arrest all over the world's press. He was effusive about all the money that shot had made him, pressed a full pint mug into my hand and snapped a farewell picture. Despite the fact that it was cold and full of bubbles, that pint was the best I had ever tasted. However, I soon found it wasn't the most sensible thing to have done on a completely empty stomach, so we stopped the car at the nearest corner shop and bought one of those quintessential Aussie meat pies, piping hot from the grill.

Before jumping on the plane I sat among the Huon pines that still protect the banks of the Great River which flows free down to the sea. The site was just far enough from the river so that the recording would not pick up the noise of running water. It was just before dusk, after the daytime chorus of birds, bees and beetles had come to an end and before the evensong of biodiversity had got under way: the cheapest and most perfect sound stage in the world. The film was then completed with archive footage of the last Tasmanian tiger, taken in Hobart Zoo just before it died, set to the song 'Animals in the Zoo', the use of which had been kindly donated to the cause by Paul and Linda McCartney.

The flight home was uneventful, punctuated by bottles of champagne given to me by Quantas and a wildlife crew fronted by an old friend, Tony Soper, who joined the plane at Abu Dhabi to record a piece for the BBC. Arriving at the airport I felt like a movie star, for the flash bulbs were there in force and so were the news crews. Then it was off to appear on *Blue Peter*, to face the most difficult interview of my career. I had a few fleeting minutes to explain to my considerably young fan club why I had deliberately broken the law. At the end of my piece, which screened clips of the campaign and my arrest, the curtains opened and, just like on *This is Your Life*, in walked Rosemary, Hannah and Eoghain. In hindsight, it was a very brave thing for Biddy Baxter to engineer and I can only wonder why a Bristol crew hadn't bothered to cover the story live, for they had been among my invitees.

Not long after my appearance on *Blue Peter* I met Prime Minister Margaret Thatcher. Expecting a short sharp handbag attack along the lines of 'What is one of our university professors doing in gaol in Australia?' I was somewhat bemused to be told that there could be 'votes in the environment!' The Iron Lady was of course right, but sadly to this day the votes all too often bring nothing but more election promises.

Along with all the other gaol birds I duly received my full pardon from Prime Minister Bob Hawke in Australia, but the greatest thrill came when I was sitting at home and a person whom I vaguely recognised passed the kitchen window. On opening the door I found a stocky Australian, complete with regulation hat, looking more than a little embarrassed. Before I could say anything he said, 'I have come to apologise. I was one of those who gave you a hard time on the picket line in Tas. I was wrong. Now there are plenty of jobs in the tourist industry and it's a great place to bring a family up in.' With that he turned to go. I invited him in for a cup of tea and then offered to take him back to Barnard Castle, where he was staying and from which he had walked, a distance of some seven miles. 'Thanks,' he said, 'but I'll walk, it's my penance' and off he went.

Unfortunately, a new millennium has sadly seen the repeal of the statutes that protected Tasmania's last free river from empoundment. Changes in Tasmanian electoral rules now ensure that minority parties like the Greens, who held the balance of power, can never be elected again – facts made even more obscene by the news that, with the help of Britain's own national grid company, there are plans to transmit electricity to the mainland using one of the most environmentally damaging methods, a method that has fortunately been spurned by more civilised countries.

*

In that same year of 1982 I was proud to be a chosen subject, along with Douglas Fairbanks Junior, for Don McCullin's photographic exhibition 'The Strength and Sensitivity of Man'. Also, along with Cliff Richard and Viscount Tonypandy, I was honoured as one of RADAR's Men of the Year. It was at that ceremony that I met the legendary giant of good estate management, the Duke of Buccleuch and Queensberry. It was certainly in part due to that meeting, and all my contact with gamekeepers, that I was invited to become a patron of the Upland Gamekeepers' Association and a trustee of the Duke's own 'Living Landscape Trust', a great honour.

From that point on invitations to back campaigns came even thicker and faster, as many as sixty in a week, and answering them became an impossible task. I soon found out that there were a lot of charlatans out there, NIMBYs of the worst sort, so each project had to be checked out and that took time, a commodity that was becoming ever rarer. I would like to take this opportunity to apologise to all those worthy causes who didn't get a reply. I would also like to apologise to Rosemary and the family for constantly screaming down the phone, always about the same thing, 'conservation', and for missing so many family outings and celebrations.

Some of the invitations I received were easy to answer for, like the Franklin Blockade, the research had been done properly and my part in it was clear. One of these was to New Zealand and my role was to help make a film to persuade the powers that be that the felling of trees in Whirinaki Forest, not far from the tourist hot spot of Rotorua, must come to a rapid end. It was, and thank God still is, a magical place, containing pristine stands of mixed podocarps. When this was translated into words like 'The type of forests the dinosaurs used to eat' it raised interest in all but the most jaundiced tour operator. As usual, the media had honed down the argument into the prickly chestnut of wilderness against jobs. Sadly, good well-publicised examples of ecotourism creating local jobs were still over a decade away. Just to see these legendary forests was well worth the trip, but to meet and work with the equally legendary Steve King who, along with his younger brother, had halted felling in Pureora, another critically important podocarp forest, was worth a million air miles. They had perfected the ploy of camping out up in the high canopy, so making it impossible for felling to take place.

The pro-logging lobby, which included traditional Maori landowners, was not all that keen on the making of the film, and so we had to keep on the move as sequence after sequence was put in the can. At last they and some media stalwarts caught us up, and the former took me into a forest hut and locked the door. They were not in the best of moods and had a chain saw, and I must say I wondered what was going to happen next. I was firmly sat on the end of a bunk from under which they dragged a crate of beer, and a bottle was handed to me. 'Well,' came the question, 'what the hell are you doing here?' 'Trying to save your forest for your people.' 'Nobody is going to take our forest away from us.' 'Well, if you carry on like this, there won't be any left, there won't be any jobs and you will have to move on.' I went on and explained that I had walked through Whirinaki and seen the post-holes of their ancestral Marai and the pigeon traps rotting on the forest floor and asked, 'What of the future?' To my surprise they unlocked the door and told the small crowd gathered beneath the ancient trees that 'felling must come to an end'. Evening was drawing on and as we walked back through the forest the glow worms, which are in fact midge larvae that spin silken traps which act like crystal lustres, treated us to their own triumphant *son et lumière,* the *son* being supplied by the massed stridulation of other insects.

Below is part of the foreword I wrote to the book, *To Save a Forest. Whirinaki* by John Morton (who had taught Rosemary zoology at QMC) and fellow campaigners John Ogden and Tony Hughes. Above all it explains the very roots of my campaigning years, and also why, when asked – as I often am, 'What gives you the right to poke your nose into another country's affairs?' my answer is always 'Because I was asked.'

The most precious possessions of any Nation are its people and their heritage. New Zealand is at this time blessed above most other nations, by a small and prosperous population and a rich and unique heritage of pre-history and natural history. Much of that population still has its roots in the soil, for its living is made through agriculture or forestry. The people must therefore understand the real problems, which relate to long-term misuse of the environment. Key parts of that heritage are still intact, though some are under threat of despoliation and destruction. One such area, one such Heritage Landscape, is the Whirinaki Forest, about the future of which this book has been written.

Thanks to the advances of medicine, machines, robots, computers and family planning, we can look forward to a future in which everyone is adequately fed, watered, clothed and housed. A caring, sharing world community, all of whom enjoy a healthful life with much leisure time, spent in a diverse, beautiful and stable environment. I also know that this can only be accomplished by putting the broad principle of Conservation to work, now.

This of course will not happen overnight, but when the world accepts the conservation ethic and moves towards a more stable, more sustainable future, those Heritage Landscapes will attract tourists in their millions, to come to see what exists nowhere else on earth.

The civilised world stands at the brink of a momentous decision. Whether to continue down the dead-end road of the profligate use of non-renewable resources, to overfill the bellies and line the pockets of the few, or whether to listen to the growing voices of reason which counsel wiser use of all resources. I know that the former can only lead the world to conflict on an ever more massive scale, conflict which can only be to the detriment of both civilisation and life on earth. I believe that the latter is the only way that promises a meaningful future for us and for our children.

If New Zealand was cut off from world trade tomorrow, none of her population would starve, or be unable to clothe or house themselves, they would also be able to keep themselves cool in summer and warm in winter. The landscapes you already have in production would adequately provide all the food you require and much for export. I can think of few other nations on earth which share the same good fortune. This is the time for New Zealand to consolidate its good fortune.

Any temperate climate can be made to produce mutton, lamb, wool, fruit or wood, and most are much nearer the main centres of world commerce. Only New Zealand has the unique natural and Maori heritage, epitomised by the Whirinaki Forest.

This and your other Heritage Landscapes, if left intact, will continue to provide a stabilising influence on the environment of the Land of the Long White Cloud, keeping its soils productive, a place of recreation, resort and wonder for natives, settlers and visitors alike and of gainful employment for many. Here is the potential of a role model for all our futures.

Another campaign I remember well was the saga of the Hainburg Dam. Brian Jackman, then environmental correspondent to the Sunday Times came along to cover the story. Hainburg in Austria is set amongst what were even then magnificent flood plain forests of the Danube. The problem was that the Austrian Government led by the unions were planning to dam the Danube. Most of the Austrian voters were dead against the idea, their arguments ranged from the sanctity, let alone the ecological importance, of their forests to the costs both environmental and fiscal of building such a dam.

Daggers were firmly drawn, professors had given their students time off to join the picket lines. The unions were enraged and the police were not being as light-handed as perhaps they should. The whole shebang was camped out in the forest, it was a crisp cold winter night and every thing was frozen solid. The centre of attention was around the legendary and very green artist and campaigner, Hunterwasser. He sat in a bower, not unlike Gandalf from the Hobbit, surrounded by students swathed in blankets, each one with a flickering light.

Rumour had it that the union men were coming to sort the pickets out, so the camp upped and moved further into the forest where Mercedes Benz's and Audi's could not disturb. By the morning the Government had capitulated and decided that the Hainburg Dam would not go ahead. The celebrations were stupendous and the pickets were on the receiving end as excited supporters handed bottles of schnapps, champagne, and lots of food to those standing along the now reopened road. The world read all about it in the *Sunday Times*, under a picture of me and the headline 'The Jolly Green Giant'.

Campaigns come in all shapes and sizes; some like the Franklin start with a bang others sort of creep up on you often sparked off by meeting someone, out of the blue. It was in the eighties that I met seven such people. Farrel Bradbury, Ronny Cryer, Arwell Jones, David Norman, Nicholas Partridge, Peter Raines and David Shreeve.

Of all that septet of acquaintances perhaps the second on the list seemed the most unlikely candidate for a starring role in the Green Movement. Ronny was a comedian, song and dance man act and an impresario in the pantomime world. His rest-of-the-year-job was running a highly successful caravan park at Haggerston Castle between Holy Island and Berwick on the coast of Northumbria. I think he really wanted to sign me on as a straight man, the foil for his many talents in a London Production of 'Babes in the Wood'. However I found myself at the caravan park, talking to the football fans assembled in the bar, about the famous Haggerston Greys, a very beautiful conifer the genestock of which had been imported from North America and used to landscape the Castle Grounds. I can't say that it went down like a lead football because they didn't throw me out, but I thought that Ronnie's idea of natural history weekends for the happy holiday set would never work.

To my surprise, next day they were all out with me and forest ranger Brian Walker identifying the trees growing next to their holiday homes. Ronny had a local carver on hand who inscribed the names on appropriate pieces of wood that were planted beside their tree. The kids also all went home with a souvenir. Their own Family Tree, a slice of a tree trunk on which they marked their family history. Using the annual rings they could not only show the dates of family events, like births deaths and marriages but, by measuring the width of the rings find out whether it was a good or bad year for tree growth. It was at this juncture that I realized that much of my life I had spent pushing the message of conservation mainly to the converted at University and specialist groups. Here was a chance to put it across to tens of thousands of people whose annual holiday gave them their main contact with the real world of wildlife.

I next found myself down at another of Bourne Leisure's Parks, Greenacres (not far from Porth Merion on the Welsh coast), running a full blown, wildlife weekend. I can't say that the evening lecture, given as part of the Friday cabaret was a huge success, but by the Sunday many determined teams were out on the beach, putting all they have learned about the problems of life on the seashore to good practice in a Grand Sandcastle Competition.

My dream then became to put a spark of environmental friendliness into all those serried ranks of caravans that have turned so many stretches of what were among our most spectacular coastlines into an extension of Coronation Street. Today working with the British Home Parks and Holiday Homes Association, thanks in no small part to their director James Spencer, there are now annual awards for the best parks. Each one is vetted by a local member of one of the now many environmental organizations. 1999 saw 361 winning parks each doing their bit for the local environment and the local economy. For believe it or not the statistics show that on average five caravan pitches support one local job.

There is still a long way to go and we are all on very steep learning curves. Not so Ronny Cryer, I have just completed three videos for Bourne Leisure, who, now having bought up the Butlin's empire, are the largest group in Europe. The videos will make natural history weekends an integral part of family holiday life. What's more plans are in the pipeline for Parks to have their own wildlife ranger led by Julie Meles, an awesome import from Oz.

Another chance meeting that decade was with David Norman. His ancestors had migrated to Scotland from Russia back in the 1800's where they started a timber business harvesting local oak and other hardwoods. Three generations on David was still in business and proud to be Scotland's biggest importer of, shock horror, tropical hardwoods and was beginning to get a lot of agro from groups like FOE Scotland and Earth First. Thank God he was not only a tough Glaswegian with a great sense of humour but he loved his family, his workforce and understood the capabilities of the renewable resource called timber. Come hell or high water he was going to stay in business and being a small guy in the world timber trade understood the real gravity of the clear cut and to hell with the future attitude of many of the big boys. So he set about finding his resources from Well Managed forests around the world and when he had, he called a meeting with both sides to discuss the matter.

It was during this process that I was invited to give a keynote at a conference in Kuala Lumpur, which was opened by the Prime Minister Dr Mohammed Mahattir no less. During the coffee break that followed both our speeches and in the presence of the press, The President intimated that he wanted to speak to me for an hour, alone. A couple of days later a very up-market black car from the British High Commission arrived to take me to the Presidential residence. Fortunately the car was air conditioned for I was sweating, not only because I was wearing a suit but because I was going to meet a man who I knew could out gun most Prime Ministers around the world.

In he came immaculately dressed and after the formalities asked 'why is it that whenever I attempt to improve the lot of the poorer people of my country I have members of NGO, saying that I head a corrupt Government?' Leading me over to the window he swept the compass of his capital, which was even then beginning to sprout the highest of high-rise award winning office blocks and said 'before your people brought "civilization"' to these shores, all that was covered with tropical rain forest. I suggest you go back and save the last two percent of your lowland raised bogs before you come here and tell us how to manage our land'.

Good fighting stuff, my hackles were up. I had all the answers ready. Like 'all we are trying to do is ensure that you don't make the same mistakes in catchment management, as we have'. 'What about the downstream effects on your coral reefs and your fisheries?' 'What about the fires, already raging in Kalimantan?' But before I could answer he said. 'I have been following what you do and say for a long time, lets sit down and discuss the matter'. Then followed one of the most interesting hours I have ever spent. Our discussions ranged over all matters environmental, from habitat destruction through family planning to the power of television in both campaigning and education, including the problem of how are you going to keep them down in the forest once they have seen TV.

The outcome was that I thought a lot more about Obe and her people and with the help of David Norman I made a film about sustainable logging practices already under development in Peninsular Malaysia. Later and with some trepidation, I presented Dr Mahattia with a copy in the hope that if all logging were carried out using those same principles then perhaps, at least some of the forest people could continue to find a livelihood in their forests.

I also helped David Norman set up the Scottish Hardwood Charter, the aim of which was to ensure that all users of hardwood in Scotland and that included Local Authorities, developers and architects had access to supplies of timber sourced from well-managed forests and plantations. In David Norman's books, well managed meant that not only would the resource be available for harvest into perpetuity but that it would continue to employ local people, would not jeopardize other peoples livelihoods and avoid costly auditing which would cut into both on and offshore profit. It was the latter that became a stumbling block for those who were then gearing up for one of the most drawn out arguments in the history of conservation. It concerned the definition of sustainable and after the Rio Summit of sustainable development.

Peter Raines turned up one day in my office with a fantastic idea and an offer. The idea was to become one of the cutting edges of new wave conservation and ecotourism. The offer was one I couldn't refuse. The idea was called Coral Cay and was aimed at the rapidly growing band of upwardly mobile tourists who were willing to pay to work hard while on holiday. The hard work was to survey the state of the coral reefs and the inshore vegetation that helps keep them and the local fisheries in working order. The attraction was scuba diving with a purpose in exotic locations where few, if any had dived before. The original locations were along the great barrier reef that protects the coast of Belize in Central America.

The proposition was that I should give it my blessing and a bit of oomph publicity in the guise of President. Of course I said yes. It was and still is a fantastic success now operating in Honduras, the Philippines and Fiji. The survey data which costs the host country nothing except an invitation and logistic support is translated into GIS and handed over to the government for use in integrated coastal and fisheries management. It worked so well in Belize that although a non-profit making organization, surplus money helped to build a marine biological station for the local university. In the Philippines we teamed up with World Land Trust, run by John Burton at one time Director of The Fauna Preservation Society, the worlds oldest conservation group. Together they raised the seed capital to save Danjugan, one of the last islands in the Philippines that was still covered with tropical forest and surrounded by good living reefs.

We – or rather all the schools and individuals who bought shares in the project – finally bought this little bit of paradise. All the investors got was a certificate signed by me, and the feel good factor that an important bit of the world was in safer hands. Reports kept them informed of the progress of the project, which made use of the resource to teach the locals and the people from nearby islands how to run dive based tourism that doesn't cost the earth or the life giving seas that nurture and protect it.

A whole new arena of conservation endeavour was beginning to open up. Not just another round of begging bowl appeals to protect endangered plants and animals, but the creation of a hands-across the world working community helping people to make their livelihoods – doing the right thing. Any excess money goes into the Coral Cay Conservation Foundation to further this vital work.

At last in 1986, thanks to David Right and Yorkshire Television, I got a children's TV programme all of my own. It was called *Bellamy's Bugle*. In reality I shared the slot with an ultra slick lady talking computer who got me into all sorts of trouble, episode after episode. It was with David that I also made *Journey to the Centre of the World*, in which different groups of local children led me on a journey through the Holy Land to Bethlehem.

David Right and I were both on the same wavelength in many things, including the magic of Arthur Ransome's books. So together we went on another pilgrimage, this time back to my youth as I played a character not unlike Uncle Jim from *Swallows and Amazons* who was allowed to join a modern day Big Six on the Norfolk Broads. I was allowed to do all the things I have always wanted to do, including sailing one of the few remaining workhorses of this wet wonderland – a wherry nice way to travel! – and still the best way to see broadland life in all its glory. My computer has just received an e-mail telling me that the latest Harry Potter book is number one in the Children's Charts and believe it or not, over ninety years on, *Swallows and Amazons* is still weaving its magic at number four.

One of the most memorable sequences in that programme was shot high on the roof of a cottage where the viewers and I were let into the secrets of thatching by Sammy Hewitt. This was for me television at its best, an electronic Fairy God Mother, teaching me as I was being allowed to share my knowledge with other people. The broadland thatchers were then having a rough time and were forced to import reeds from Poland so that the special character of the local heritage would not be lost. The reason was lack of correct management of the great reed beds that had once kept their industry supplied. What a stupid state of affairs. As I had discussed with Jennifer Walker years before, the growth of these stalwart plants helps to strip the fertilisers out of the water, thus protecting this multimillion-pound tourist resort from the scourge of eutrophication. With proper management the reeds also maintain an open yet sheltered habitat for all the water birds the original Big Six had championed so well with direct action back in the 1920s. Among my still growing number of presidencies is that of the Association of Master

Thatchers, one of the most incongruous groups of individualists.

It was during this period that my two major campaigning series, *Turning the Tide* and *Bellamy's Bird's Eye View*, came into being. The first one, made with Tyne Tees in 1986, took the concept head on, looking at everything from the destruction of rain forests in South America to unemployment and urban renewal in Newcastle. As a framework for the series I coined the phrase 'whale friendly', WHALE being a great acronym.

W stands for Water, so I became a raindrop and for the only time in my career used a stand-in – to freefall into the head waters of the Thames. I wanted to do it myself but there was insufficient time for me to get the right parachute certificates. Once in the Thames, I became part of the pollution and eutrophication cycle, floating through all sorts of environmental adventures en route. This route included Otmoor, of *Wind in the Willows* and *Alice Through the Looking-Glass* fame. I bought the first square metre of 'Alice' meadow to make the purchase of land on which to build the M40, more difficult. Today red kites can be seen flying over the re-routed monster, a sign, one hopes, of more enlightened times ahead.

H stands for Habitat. We went to the habitats of the high Andes that had given the world the potential of the potato in all its mouth-watering diversity. We found the locals being sold highly toxic chemicals like Aldrin, needed to protect the monocultures of a few new highly productive varieties they were being forced to grow on their land. Many of them couldn't afford the chemicals, and if they could, they couldn't read the instructions, for they were in English. We also demonstrated the fact that the high-tech potato breeders of the modern world were finding it ever more difficult to source the original disease resistant gene stock from the wild. The world was then home to five billion people and perhaps as many as twenty million species of plants and animals, mainly as-yet-unnamed creepy crawlies helping to hold the habitats, and hence our living world, together.

A stands for Atmosphere, earth's own wrap-around blanket, in which science was even then discovering ozone holes and warming to the problems of the global greenhouse and acid rain. We took a close look at big dams and the myth of the 'purity' of large scale hydropower.

L stands for Life. For more and more of the world's poor people, life was becoming a hell on earth as their land was cleared for cash crops. We looked at life in the Favelas – shanty towns around Rio and Lima – and the problems of high rise and battery living nearer home.

E stands for Energy, the root of most modern day advances and the root of much of the environmental evil. This found me in a Victorian bath-tub on a low-loader, going up the A1M past the Ferrybridge power station, much to the amusement of the rush hour traffic. This was to demonstrate the fact that at the other end of every electric appliance there are the polluting problems of generation. We also looked at the latest energy-saving programmes on line in factories large and small.

Bird's Eye View, produced, directed and partly filmed by Charlie Flynn in 1988, was the last series of programmes I ever made with Yorkshire Television, for those were the days when the power of the unions had gone, leading to collapsing budgets and company makeovers. The first of the trilogy we made – there were meant to be more – concerned one of Scotland's most beautiful and important estuaries at the mouth of the Eithan, home to eider ducks and many other birds whose populations were in disarray, thanks to the downstream effects of the Common Agricultural Policy and the Common Fisheries Policy. The former resulted in the pouring of nutrients into the river, causing algal blooms which smothered the mussel beds, food source of the eiders. The latter allowed massive overfishing of capelin and sand eel, the very basis of the marine food chain upon which all fishers depend.

The second programme, 'Good morning Mr Magpie', showed how we were creating intensive magpie rearing units in our easy-to-run gardens and parks with well-mown lawns and standard trees. To add to the problem, green corridors along motorways, rail tracks and canals had become express routes for the movement of these dapper mass-murderers of baby chicks. As a balance, we talked to researchers who could find no correlation between the numbers of magpies and the decline in other garden birds, and staunch conservationists who would blame anything but their cats.

We had planned to make programmes about the problems of Canada geese in our towns, and crows and raptors in our countryside, and also about the rehabilitation of our wetlands, so that otters could once again live in all our rivers, but the money ran out. It was a very sad state of affairs for, going by the stir caused by the last of the trilogy, the message was getting through: that problems of conservation and the environment didn't just happen in the so-called Third World – they were happening right in our own backyards. What is more, their solution required some pretty harsh direct action to be taken. This third programme concerned the obvious (to those who would bother to take a look) links between well-managed, shooting estates and sustainable rural landscapes, overflowing with wildlife. The closing shot was of me enjoying a well cooked leg of pheasant and saying, 'I am a hypocrite; I couldn't shoot them myself but I am glad there are people that will pay to do it.' The programme had adequately outlined the fact that without these much-vilified, politically incorrect, blood-sports people, much more of Britain's once green and pleasant land would be taken over by the highly subsidised barley and conifer barons. The tabloids loved it: 'Bellamy is a hypocrite, how can he back shooting and claim to be a conservationist?' At least they got something right, I did say I was a hypocrite.

It was at about this time that I was asked by the Nottinghamshire Constabulary to help them launch a scheme to get potential young offenders out on the streets to clean up their graffiti and other people's rubbish. I was met at the station by the local hierarchy with swagger sticks and scrambled egg all over their immaculate uniforms, and was told that as McDonald's was financing it, the launch was at one of their outlets. It was by then too late to ask them if they knew what they were letting us in for, because there in front of us was a grinning news reporter from Granada backed by members of local Green groups, thrusting part-chewed vegeburgers in my face while intoning 'Hypocrite'. I did my best to explain the contents of the programme and of the Mac Fact Sheets displayed in the store, fact sheets that informed the customer that the company had never destroyed tropical rain forests to produce hamburgers for export, only for use in the country of origin. 'Lies, lies, greenwash lies,' shouted the picketeers, and even the reporter showed little interest in my suggestion to McDonald's which was 'If they are telling lies, why doesn't your company investigate them and prove the protesters to be liars?' I even invited the protesters and the camera crew to join in with the clean-up operation we were about to launch. It really does get difficult now that investigative journalism is about selling newsprint rather than solving problems.

I began to realise that enormous schisms were developing between and within the worlds of environment and nature conservation. The ecosmoothies of the urban sprawl were vilifying the use of plastic bottles but were eating ever more designer food, while the Barbour brigade were hunting, shooting and fishing in a countryside that was being redesigned, open plan, by the Common Agricultural Policy. Both sides were salving their consciences by filling the begging bowls of ever more organisations, many of which were perforce having to hone down their campaigns to single issues. They were forced to think more about membership and cash flow rather than the more complex matters of how to solve the problems of the species they chose to champion. The media of course followed merrily along, for bad news sells papers and air-time is subsidised by adverts.

WWF and Greenpeace had by then done a great job, the world thought it was both panda and whale friendly, yet none of these icon animals were safe, for the habitats on which they depend and which stabilise the catchments and coastlines of the world were being destroyed at an ever increasing rate. What is more, indigenous people were being usurped, not only of their intellectual property rights but of the land on which their ancestors had developed those extraspecial varieties of potatoes, beans, corn, squash, rice, wheat and all the other things fast food is made of.

In essence, we were all having to run faster, not just to stand still but to avoid losing the ground we thought we had saved. Slowly but surely the intellectual property rights of a conservation élite were translated into ever larger salaries in head offices, and less and less support for projects in the field. The feel-good factor replaced the do-good factor as more and more trustees' meetings were advised that if we were going to save the world, we had got to employ the best people, and that to attract them cost money.

Perhaps they were right, but I couldn't stomach some of the things that were going on, so I quietly but firmly distanced myself from those I felt were heading in the wrong direction. I only proffered my services when asked to by those who were really doing positive things to save the world.

22 HUNTING, SHOOTING AND FISHING

I have of course, over the years, received letters – in all no more than twenty – vilifying my stance on blood sports. Please note I do not count the cranky ones. The others I have answered with great care. I was both surprised and pleased that on making an insert for *Blue Peter* about the positive role played by gamekeepers in the conservation of our countryside, I received only one negative letter. This was in marked contrast to the first insert of the series that had me pretending to be a very sad calf in a veal crate; this brought floods of letters from distressed people and some from very angry farmers. However, even I was worried when, despite dire warnings from the hierarchy of some of the NGOs on which I serve, I decided to speak at the Countryside Rally in London. Unfortunately the rally was hijacked by the Pro Fox Hunting Lobby, for it was really about the management of a biodiverse and economically sustainable countryside. I received only nine negative letters, including one resignation of a member of one of the wildlife trusts of which I was by then president. I answered them all in great detail, some on the phone. Unfortunately I didn't have time to answer the hundreds of letters with a positive message. May I take this opportunity to say thank you all. It can get a bit lonely out there sometimes.

The contents of my replies and the oration I gave at the rally are best summarised in the speech I gave when I agreed to act as patron of the National Gamekeepers' Association:

I must first make it clear that I do not hunt, shoot or fish; indeed I, like many other people, find the whole idea of killing for pleasure abhorrent. So it will seem hypocritical that I have agreed to have anything to do with, let alone act as patron of, your Association.

Killing out of necessity is an entirely different matter. I am not a vegetarian and if my family were starving I would do anything in my power to feed them. Likewise my conscience would not stop me fighting in a just war.

Indeed, in some ways I have spent almost the past fifty years fighting in what to me is the most just war of all: the fight for the environment and all the plants and animals that not only make it such a fascinating place to be a part of but also keep it in working order.

Biodiversity exists because living things are born, grow, reproduce and die. Plants and animals compete with each other, defending their territories with pitched battles. Living sentient things are eaten and living sentient things eat each other. Mother Nature in all her biodiverse forms is red both in tooth and claw.

Humanity is set aside from that process by one sole attribute, a knowledge of right and wrong, ethics, soulship, call it what you will. We alone can learn from history, be it natural or people made, and put the things of good report into action. We alone can worry about what we do. This is a cross we have to bear thanks to the fact that we are part of the process of creative evolution or whatever you like to call it.

When any species of plant or animal moves into a territory, however large or small, others have to die; that is perhaps the only sad fact of life. Whether any of us like it or not, the dominance of people across the face of the earth has led to the destruction of the habitat of gigabillions of other living things.

Unfortunately for us, in many places we have already destroyed or so altered key natural systems, forests, wetlands, rivers, lakes, estuaries, coastlines, reefs etc. etc. that we have put our own lives, our very survival, in jeopardy. Our answer to date has been to destroy more of Mother Nature, replacing her stratagems of survival with novel chemicals and fossil fuels.

Whether we live in town or country, whether we look after a house, a garden, a store, a factory, a farm or a nature reserve, countless numbers of feral plants and animals must be constantly killed to keep us in business. We have indeed created ferals, vermin and weeds simply by trying to make a living on this planet.

The good news is that at last humanity appears to be coming to terms with the environmental problems it has created. Clear across the earth concerned people are endeavouring not only to manage landscapes in a more sustainable way, but to put as much degraded land as possible back into biodiverse working order.

To accomplish this, ferals and weeds have to be got rid of; fortunately our ethics counsel that this must be done as humanely as possible.

Although I couldn't hunt, shoot or fish, it is my considered opinion that the most important people in the countryside are well-trained gamekeepers, ghillies and their dogs. Without their vigilance, the amount of badger baiting and other unspeakable cruelty carried out by often urban hooligans, who style themselves as old style poachers, would escalate out of control. Likewise, without their continual presence and long hours of hard, skilled work, the mix of native mammals and wild birds we expect to see in our countryside would disappear. They are the real unsung heroes of conservation of this marginally still green and pleasant land.

If they were not carrying out these crucially important tasks, our cherished landscapes would degrade in an even more catastrophic manner and many of our native birds and mammals would head for the wall of extinction. Without the gamekeepers, paid for by the shootists, those same jobs would have to be done by someone else, 'men from the ministry' with poisons and untrained guns.

Those who would have these things banned willy nilly must ask themselves how many rats, mice, pigeons, starlings, and other so called vermin are exterminated every night just for their convenience: that is, in order to keep their towns habitable and the fields on which their food is grown and their waste is now disposed of in a healthy and viable condition.

If everyone refused to take part in these sadly now essential practices, then the government would have to resort to conscription of unwilling citizens to do our 'dirty' work.

It is therefore my firm belief that hunting, shooting and fishing play a vital role in the conservation of our wildlife and our countryside. However, those who take part in these practices must be the most vigilant and do everything in their power to stamp out cruelty of any sort.

Which is the crueller: a free range game bird shot in flight, or a lamb raised on the same fells, drenched with sheep dip, taken hundreds of stressful miles to a slaughter house, or a highly territorial turkey raised on an intensive farm?

Whatever your answer, these forms of countryside management must be adequately policed. Indeed I believe that, as in Sweden, everyone who takes part in or manages these pastimes should have to pass a series of tough qualifying examinations. What is more, anyone stepping out of line over any aspect of animal welfare should have his or her licence to kill revoked. These are my firm beliefs and as your patron I will stand by them. I hope you still welcome me aboard.

23 LANKAN LOVE AFFAIR

I don't know how I fell in love with Lanka. What I do know is that it was one of those places I just had to visit, so when the time was ripe, off I went on the first of several trips. It was there I found the real meaning of village life and the lessons it had to teach the self-styled First World as it number crunched its way into a new millennium. My two Lankan mentors are as different as people could be, yet each espouses his own brand of faith with the 'spirituality of people as part of nature'. They are Manik Sandrasagra and Ananda Kentish Coomaraswamy.

I don't know exactly where I first met Manik but I do know that most other people I met in Lanka warned me to handle him with great care. Nor can I remember when I first read some of Coomaraswamy's seminal lectures, but it was Manik who reintroduced me to *Sources of Wisdom*, a copy of which inscribed 'To David from Manik a Son of a Bitch, 11th Dec 1987' has a prominent place in a very special part of my library. He certainly lives up to his name and reputation: a colourful rogue, storyteller and film maker who, among many other things, claims to be the first person to put Ben Kingsley on the big screen – sadly it was in one of Manik's 'spectacular' films which was not the success that Manik thought it should be. Manik was always full of fantastic stories, coloured by his coterie of friends all of whom appeared to be well heeled and many of whom made use of recreational drugs to drive boredom from their leisure filled lives. Thank God I am one of those boring people who never has had the luxury of time on my mind let alone my hands.

Manik was an archetypal Buddha of a man, short and plumpening with age, so much so that when he went into his full lotus squat his belly button completed the porcelain illusion. Wherever we went – and over the years I travelled the length and breadth of Lanka in his company – he was greeted as a friend and mentor. Immediately hitching up his sarong he would sit on the good earth from which he wove his stories and from which the village people of Lanka had woven their own heritage of sustainability for thousands of years. As if by magic, he would quickly become surrounded by a large and appreciative audience. He was a master wordsmith, and his is the oral tradition that has kept Lanka informed of its rich heritage for countless centuries. Perhaps he should not have let this genius become clouded with the problems of the silver screen, but we all have our faults.

Ananda Coomaraswamy, half Tamil, half English, a geologist by training, became one of the world's experts on oriental art, and spent the latter part of his life working at the Boston Museum of Fine Arts in the USA. There he penned the book that ranks in the top three in my library. *Sources of Wisdom* was published in 1943, five years before the assassination of Mahatma Gandhi, who, when asked 'What is your greatest disappointment?' answered, 'The hard heartedness of the educated.'

When Coomaraswamy was born in 1877 the people of Lanka still grew all the 280 varieties of rice which had been developed by and had sustained their considerable population for more than 2,500 years. The average family was self-sufficient on the produce of an area of no more than five acres. Their life styles focused on an age-old system of irriga-tion, which, though falling into disrepair, was still in place, fed from stable catchments covered with well-managed tropical rain forests. These villages, and those fishing communities along the coast, sup-ported a diverse nation enjoying a variety of life styles, good religious tolerance, full employment in agriculture and family life, and little or no malnutrition, soil erosion or environmental pollution.

They also had holy days in plenty: a continuous round of ritual, binding each and every one of them to the bounty of Mother Earth. The root of their way of life and hence of all their religions lay in the spiritual relation between creation and humankind. This age-old relationship was maintained in Lankan terms by the worship of Skanda the forest god at Kataragama. Their system of healing was Aryurvedic, which included health education, healthy eating and family planning. This worked well before the onslaught of diseases, which followed the discovery of Serendip by the pox ridden 'civilisations' of the West.

Today all this has changed, a mere twenty-seven of their rice varieties still survive and only four are widely planted. All these are now grown in monoculture and require pampering with expensive chemicals. The old methods of polyculture, though labour intensive, at least ensured an adequate crop, for certain varieties in the portfolio of planting would either miss infection or have natural resistance to the current wave of disease. Also the year-round ritual of care weeded out any disease as soon as it struck. It was the same with pests, and the presence of native forests nearby ensured a constant supply of the many species of insect, arachnid, bird and bat that helped the farming families in their work. The fact that family planning ensured that babies were not born during the periods of sowing and harvest mirrored the 'humanity' of village life. With a planned population everyone would have a job to do.

In his book Coomaraswamy warned, 'The contentment of innumerable peoples can be destroyed in a generation by the withering touch of our (Western) civilisation. The local market is flooded by a production in quantity with which the responsible maker by art cannot compete. The vocational structure of society, with all its guild organisation and standards of workmanship is undermined. The artist is robbed of his art and forced to find himself a "job", until finally the ancient society is industrialised and reduced to the level of societies such as ours, in which business takes precedence over life.'

Unfortunately, nobody took any notice, and so what was the result? Well, today the untouchables need to be touched by the social services, if only there were any; the irrigation tanks are full of silt; mass unemployment, malnutrition and grave social unrest stalk this and many other beautiful corners of the earth.

The relentless march of Western values continues unabated, the latest threat being genetically modified crops which rely on specific herbicides and pesticides: real terminator technology for the subsistence farmers of Lanka, for they cannot afford the chemicals and yet must save some of each year's harvest as seed for the next year's sowing. Bad news too for the smallholders of Europe, for such developments put 'profitable' farming out of their reach, unless they are highly subsidised by the gullible tax payers who are fed half truths concerning the real cost of the food they eat. One can only ask what will happen to them when the rules of global governance demand that such subsidies fall into the category of trade barriers and so must stop.

I found myself at an extravaganza organised by Manik in the grounds of the Taj Samudra Hotel in Columbo where we had helped build a village compound complete with organic garden, and a mud hut to accommodate the more adventurous hotel guests. Despite the troubles, he had managed to get performers, storytellers, artists and entertainers from villages across the divided nation to perform all night to the assembled crowd. It was spectacular in the extreme and we witnessed and filmed the heritage of all that had thrilled and educated the people and the rulers of this amazing country since well before the Great Hydraulic Civilization built the vast tanks and irrigation works. Hundreds of the country's top performers danced and sang and drummed the night away. We were privileged to witness a nocturnal celebration of the spirituality of the water of life that still helps people of a diversity of religions and religious philosophies to co-exist in harmony.

For me the most elegant expression of our dependence on the natural cycles of life was by a group of women from a coastal village who performed their ancient water gathering ritual in dance. Their share of nature's bounty was the final gathering of sweet water from holes dug in the sandy beach, the last chance to use it before it was 'polluted' by the salt of the sea. Precious drops of water had fallen on the flanks of Adam's

Peak, from whence they had flowed inexorably down towards the sea, gathering mass from springs, streams and confluences as they went. Polluted by every cycle of human life, the natural pulse of living water made itself pure again as it spilled from tank to tank, and new growth of paddy in these engineered wetlands pumped in oxygen as it stripped out the added nutrients along the way, preparing the water for reuse by village after village, until it was filtered by the sand that fringed the sea. There these last-in-the-line villagers sang their special stanza of the sweet song of sustainability. Every sense we had allowed us to become part of this plainchant of creation, the slow sweep of the living meandering river, the thud thud of cloth against the dhobi stone, the gentle wash of waves upon a tropic shore. The dance was performed not for money or applause but in thanksgiving for being part of it.

Their costumes, made of cotton and silk produced on the banks of that same river and dyed with the natural colours of a herbal rainbow, shimmered in the light of the torches that lit the scene, while the scent of the fragrances they used, suffused with the sweat of their hard-working bodies, drugged each one of us into the reality of village Lanka, perhaps the last place on earth where we can still touch real humanity. Such an experience cannot be packaged for tourism of any sort, and we can only guess how much of this spirituality of creation has already been destroyed, here and around the world, by the withering touch of our civilisation. Lest we forget: when asked for his views on western civilisation, Gandhi replied, ' I think it would be a good idea.'

The most bizarre events of that long night were the performances of the Dervishes, who defied all the maxims of balance and performed feats of what can only be called magic, while in deep trance. These included various forms of ritual mutilation without a drop of blood being spilt. The rhythm of the drums and the swirl of multicoloured silk costumes were intoxicating, and on three occasions we had to drag our sound assistant back into the world of tape recorders as he tried to join in with the performance.

It was the most spiritual night I have ever spent. The village had indeed come to town, thanks to an impresario called Manik. Sadly, through fear of the deep schism that was then dividing this the most ecumenical of all nations, the town was too afraid to join in this celebration of real down to earth faith, so only a handful of us – David Gladstone, the British High Commissioner, his wife, Manik, Manik's friends and a few other stalwarts – were royally entertained. There was no trouble, and despite the lack of audience the performers were overjoyed; for most of them this was the first time they had witnessed the perfection of other sections of their country's heritage.

Despite dire warnings from a number of people, including Arthur C. Clarke himself who had settled there, I decided to finance a series of six videos about Lanka to be called *Routes of Wisdom*, in which I walked the village pathways with an open mind, from the Temple of the Tooth in Kandy, where just about every religion of the world celebrates its own brand of spirituality, to Kataragama set deep in the once sacred groves where tens of thousands of pilgrims gather every year, to revel in the munificence of Skanda and the spirituality of The Golden Bough.

Of all the films I have ever made these gave me the most satisfaction. I walked from village to village with Manik, meeting his friends and mentors along the way, eating the best of Lankan food and seeing Ayurvedic medicine in traditional village practice. On one occasion we were allowed to become part of the village community and witness the local shaman at his healing work. A village couple whose marriage was breaking up were ushered into the compound and the shaman went into the deepest trance I have ever witnessed. His whole body shook and twitched until he was exhausted. Dragging himself back to life, or so it seemed, he began to question the couple. In time the tension between them disappeared, they smiled, held hands and walked from the compound together. Once he was completely revived we asked the shaman, who spoke very good English, to enlighten us as to his healing knowledge. He had neither studied at one of Lanka's great medical schools, half of which teach Ayurvedic and half Western medicine, nor had he been apprenticed to his predecessor in the village. He told us that he had been in charge of the village tractor until one day, while at the wheel, he had fallen into a trance and crashed the precious machine into a tree. From that moment on, he found himself with a great gift and had taken on the role of village shaman. He also told us that the knowledge of what questions to ask and what medicines to prescribe only came to him in the trance, and that his assistants would then go out to collect and prepare the herbal remedies.

Each traditional village is spotlessly clean, its hard baked clay pathways brushed by those who tread that particular walk of life. The clay walls of spacious houses are plastered with pure fresh cow dung to protect them from cracking in the sun or dissolving in the rain. At intervals tiny holes provide the entrance to an intra-mural nest for the wild honeybees that provide instant sweetness on tap. Open windows are protected from the elements by an extension of the roof, thatched with palm leaves. Perhaps most important of all, gigantic clay pots, standing on rat proof legs with the entrance at the top protected by even stronger thatch, are used to store the annual crops. No architect or landscape designer could do better for beauty or practicality. Every tree and plant is integral to this design of convenience living, providing shade, spices, food or medicine right in and around your own backyard. The only aromas were wood smoke and the smell of the dishes being cooked for the next meal. It is heaven in a people-made Garden of Eden here on earth.

The experience of being part of the real life of village Lanka was worth every rupee and every second I spent on the project. However, as I had been warned, the finished videos left much to be desired; film well past its expiry date had been used and other corners of production had been cut. I look forward to completing *Routes of Wisdom* one day, for it is a story that must be told to the world before it is too late.

24 THE SAGA OF DBA

The saga of David Bellamy Associates was short and somewhat bittersweet. Brendan Quayle, an anthropologist who looked a bit like John Lennon and deep down wished he was, and a gaggle of very bright post-graduate zoologists began to lean on me for help. They were the sort of students who, in my post-doctoral days, would have walked straight into a good post in a well-established university. However, at that time such likely lads and lasses with good qualifications in all sorts of subjects were heading for life in what came to be known as Yuppy Land. This particular group wanted to enter their undoubted talents in the lists on the burgeoning fields of environmental consultancy. Lacking the necessary capital, they asked if I would lend them my name. My immediate answer was, 'No, I am getting too old for such a radical change in direction,' and I left the meeting. Halfway home, I thought 'You miserable old bugger', turned around and agreed to join them, with the proviso that I vetted all the contracts and checked the reports before they went out. My excuse was that I had built up my knowledge and reputation over many years and did not want to lose it in the proverbial mess of litigation.

They soon amassed a great team around them, including a local lass,

Rita Brownsword who, with no environmental qualifications at all, turned out to be the lynch pin of their success (like all good secretaries do). Work came rolling in and David Bellamy Associates moved into a super new building on the University Science Park. We had the expertise of the university to hand and even helped to fund some undergrad and post-graduate projects in a number of departments, thus getting an ever increasing number of contracts finished in record time.

The ones I most enjoyed brought me into contact with Peter de Savary who had more ideas in the index finger that was usually wrapped round his Havana cigar, than most people have in their whole bodies. His mind was protean, jumping from one subject to another but always looking sideways for another opening. It would be too easy to say another opportunity to make money; one of the things Peter taught me was that the sort of trees that money grows on take a hell of a lot of pruning into shape.

He had purchased Canvey Island in the Thames Estuary from the Russians, an island that came complete with a petroleum cracking plant that had been mothballed for many years and an important green corridor of some 800 acres that linked a National Nature Reserve and a Grade One Site of Special Scientific Interest. We worked with Peter to protect that area while replacing the petroleum plant with an environmentally friendly housing complex. The local authority were very keen on the plan, although the petrol heads had different ideas.

The complex deliberations were going to culminate in a public consultation with me, a conservationist, in the hot seat, answering any hostile questions. The problem was that at the appointed time I was on location in New Zealand, Rotorua to be exact. In Peter's mind this was not a problem but an opportunity for stage management. The home team and all the locals sat fog-bound on Canvey, watching me, on a giant video screen, standing in the blazing sun in front of one of the most active geysers in the world. I couldn't see my interrogators but they could see me. It was a bizarre experience, and if I didn't know that it was impossible I would swear that Peter was controlling the geyser, for every time I scored a point up went a jet of boiling water. Most Canvey locals seemed to be for the project, a new purpose-built village and a freedom to walk and ride around a nature reserve, safe forever. I did get a hard time from the petroleum lobby who didn't want their future expansion limited in any way and who, strangely, were backed by deep green voices against development of any sort, anywhere, at any time.

Bizarre as it all was, it worked and the Public Enquiry was eventually won, but the official decision was overturned by the relevant minister, combat jacket and all, and the project including the Conservation Corridor went on hold.

Hey ho, they were very exciting days, a Pandora's Box of opportunities, some lost, some gained, like the time we were asked to make a video about wind power for the then Central Electricity Generating Board. I needed a yacht, and a phone call had me sailing Peter's *Blue Arrow* down the Solent with coal-fired power stations in the background. *Power from the Wind* detailed all the pros and cons of aerogenerators and culminated with me standing in a gale in the Orkneys saying, 'Great idea, but locate them all out to sea', which is where they should be, not on our last unspoiled landscapes.

The great rifts that now divide the Green movement were beginning to raise their ugly heads: the political correctness of the party line that brings in votes and keeps the membership up and hence the begging bowls full versus the truth, the whole truth and nothing but the truth. My point of view is straightforward. Highly subsidised, chemical farming, overgrazing, overfishing, wind farms on land? Never! Motorways? Yes, but in the right place where green gain vastly compensates for any environmental damage. Culling of the right sort carried out by experts at the right time of year and for the right reasons; redevelopment when the time is ripe; picket lines backed by well-planned direct action but *never* violence or willful damage from the green side of the fence? Yes, yes, yes. I would like to blame my genes for making me a heretic but as an ecologist with Lamarckian leanings I had a deep down gut feeling that the fitness of survival depends to a great part on the environment, a fact that was going to surprise the world when the results of the human genome project were published in the next millennium.

*

Brendan Quayle's latent talent turned out to be that of a very creative film director and over those six very busy years we collaborated on no less than four television series. All were of the same ilk, celebrating the heritage landscapes of the British Isles, while putting in the cause not the boot of conservation.

The Last Wilderness featured the northern Pennines, that amazing sweep of England's highest mountains that should have been gazetted as a National Park, back in 1924, but somehow got left out. Almost bisected by the Pennine Way, this area is the ancestral stronghold of the merlin, Britain's smallest raptor, and of the black cock. They were in decline, thanks to lack of the right sort of landscape management. This series had me belayed to a rocky pinnacle on the lip of High Cup Nick, conducting Maria Callas in gale force winds as a helicopter did its best to record the scene for posterity. John Beatty, ultra fit, climber and visionary stills photographer, one of DBA's many associates, did the belaying job and took many of the photographs for the accompanying book.

The Fens of East Anglia, a wet, head-just-above-water landscape, home territory of Britain's two Iron Maidens, Boudica and Thatcher, became the subject of four episodes entitled *England's Lost Wilderness*. Almost lost to creeping drainage over two millennia and a few decades of a catastrophe called the Common Agricultural Policy, the area was in the process of being put back into more natural working order. Thanks to the total eradication of the coypu or nutria (introduced from South America as a basis for a fur industry), whose burrowings all but destroyed the dykes and so threatened the flood defences, the area was saved.

Thanks to the tenacious vision of Aitken Clark, the Broads had just become Britain's latest National Park. I was allowed to cast my eldest son Rufus in the role of me as a teenager coming face to face with the fenland wildlife as he swam, as I did, along the dykes. I was also privileged to row Phyllis Ellis the length of Wheatfen Broad, discussing the fact that thanks to the lifework of her husband, Ted, more was known about the biology of this place than was known about any other wetland in the world.

Over those years, television was changing out of all recognition, more and more channels and with hundreds of independent production units, all vying for the same pot of gold and the same prime slots. While electronic gear was making it ever easier to record the facts, it was becoming ever harder to make a living. It was the same with consultancy; there was money to be made in the environment game so new consultancies were springing up all over the place. To keep their heads above the rising waters of competition DBA took on more and more. I could no longer vet the applications, let alone the reports and a couple, to which I had said an emphatic 'no', went ahead. The one that hit the headlines concerned a housing estate and a population of amphibians. The sad thing was that I had, over the years, been helping the local group to save their treasured wildlife, which was now threatened by the development. You can guess how the media loved it, stirred by local councillors who, like the papers, didn't even bother to contact me or check the full facts before getting their loud mouth opinions in broadsheet print.

It was time for out, but before I quit Brendan decided to put DBA up for sale. The only real decision I had in its fate was that I helped select the buyers. They styled themselves PA (although even they seemed to have forgotten what the letters stood for) and were a very respected firm of business consultants. My reason for backing this choice was the picture of their founding father on the wall of their board room. He was driving a Type 35 C Bughatti, still my dream, so in my opinion he must have been a good guy. Not long after, fed up with auditing the number of rolls of toilet paper used by a would-be environmentally friendly company, or trying to flush away the taste of greenwash, rather than carrying out scoping studies of sustainable tourism in the Solomons, the original team went their own ways, Brendan to the biggest of Big Screens, the IMAX and the rest to set up The Environment Consultancy in Newcastle, where all of them including Rita, now Callander and a proud hard working mum with lots of environmental cred, are doing fine. As for the reports in the papers that said I had received in excess of £1 million for the company, please take that with the pinch of salt it deserves.

*

In hindsight, I should have taken the plunge and retired then from my ultra hectic life, but new horizons were opening up all the time and how could I turn my back on the whales, wildlife, wildflowers and wild places of this world? How could I let the memory of Obe and her people, let alone all my viewers young and old, down? Although I didn't know it at the time, very soon my first grandchild would be on the way; what sort of world would he inherit if the campaigning stopped? So I decided, for better or worse, that as long as I was being useful I would carry on campaigning.

How could I say no to an offer from the legendary Deep South Natural History team of TV New Zealand to make my first series of fifty-minute documentaries? Especially when they were to be directed by Peter Hayden, an actor and natural historian of great repute. The programmes were to celebrate the centenary of the signing of the Treaty of Waitangi, a treaty under which the Maori people had sold their sovereignty but not their lands or their resources to the Crown in the ample guise of Queen Victoria.

Of all the series I have ever taken part in, *Moa's Ark* was the greatest fun to make. The camera was wielded by Michael Lemmon of *Brideshead Revisited* fame, our researcher was Ian McGee, who went on to win an Emmy for a natural history documentary on bats, and we had Peter Johnson along, one of New Zealand's top field botanists, to keep our taxonomy up to scratch. Added to that was the fact that during the making of the films we travelled the length and breadth of New Zealand and I was honoured to be Visiting Professor in Natural Heritage Studies at Massey University during the time. There I teamed up with Brian Springett, who had been a research student at Durham during my early days. Together we worked on an outline plan for nationwide ecotourism, based on heritage trails covering all aspects of the Land of the Long White Cloud. The greatest challenge was writing the book of the series as we went. It was not unlike keeping a field notebook from a time machine which spanned the whole of evolution in this very, very special part of the world.

My favourite sequence was looking to the future as I helped a group of children from Auckland plant native trees and shrubs back on Tirri

Tirri Matangi, an island just off the coast of metro Auckland, that had already been cleared of all introduced mammals. The objective was to provide a safe haven for the Takahe, one of New Zealand's flightless birds that was then heading for extinction on the feral infested mainland. Nine years later I was proud to return and see the first Takahe chick to be reared into the freedom of this Island Ark. It had been given the name Bellamy.

It was during the nineties that tourism took over the number one slot in the business world and the concept of 'tourism that doesn't cost the Earth', or 'ecotourism', has an important role to play in future economies of every nation on earth. In 1999 the Takahe project was highly commended in the 1999 Tourism for Tomorrow Awards. At the award ceremony I presented Lord Marshall, head of British Airways and sponsor of the awards, with a life-size model Takahe which now has pride of place in the company's new head-quarters, which were built on a brownfield site and surrounded with a local nature reserve with access to all.

A three-part series called *Bellamy On Top Of the World*, found me doing the most vandalistic thing of my career, boring a hole through the ice actually at the North Pole. I know I was exactly there because we were plugged into several satellites that pinpointed our position as I sucked the giant ice lolly retrieved from the borer, savouring the flavour of a bevy of microscopic plants and animals living it up or rather down in the ice. I then shared my last bit of Kendal Mint Cake with the denizens of the deep, while soliloquising about all the atomic submarines that were then still lurking down below.

This series also produced one of the luckiest sequences of my career. We wanted to film an iceberg rolling over, so that its five-sevenths which are usually underwater was subjected to thermal shock and hence exploded. The helicopter pilot who took us in to Jacobshaven Icebrae which carves the majority of bergs in the Northern Hemisphere, told us that he had been there hundreds of times and had never seen it happen. We landed, set up the camera and as I stepped in shot to explain what we hoped was going to happen, it did. An enormous lump of ice turned turtle and exploded, right behind me. After the series I received the strangest bit of fan mail that I ever had. It came from the mother of a seven-year-old and referred to one of the opening sequences that had me adrift on an iceberg, a sequence which bore some resemblance to a then current AIDS advert. The child had asked, 'Why is David Bellamy advertising condoms?'

Paradise Ploughed, made with the Anglia team, spelt out the inanities of planting the Flow country in the far north-west of Scotland with alien conifers. For a start the patterned mires of this, the only large part of Britain that has, since the last ice age, never been completely covered by trees, are among the rarest types of vegetation in the world: much rarer than the tropical rain forests and coral reefs, the destruction of which we were rightly all hearing so much about. What is more, Britain is signatory to a number of international conventions and protocols that expect desperately poor countries to protect their special ecosystems, yet here we were, engineering tax dodges to make already rich people a little richer as they profited from covering a unique (yes, in this case that is the only word you can use) type of vegetation with straight lines of alien conifers. Please don't blame people like Terry Wogan and Cliff Richard. They were only following the advice of their tax advisers, who must have found it difficult to believe their luck. The stars became sitting targets for the media, some of whom were as guilty as the scapegoats they pilloried. The filming was a great experience. I was back on my old stamping grounds, even deeper in the mire, but this time the mire of political stupidity, not in a third world country but in one of the most magical places in the Highlands and Islands of Scotland. I was witnessing the destruction of a key part of a resource of an area in which walking, mountaineering, hunting, shooting and fishing were the main job makers and money earners. All this was happening at a time when tourism was beginning to oust petroleum from the number one slot of world industry.

The week before the shoot I had been down on the Sussex coast, opening an unofficial marine nature reserve. Taken out to sea by boat, I was expected to leap in and swim ashore where, on landing, I would do the honours. Unfortunately, no one had warned me that the tide was out and the stretch of coastline was badly polluted by sewage. Leaping overboard, I lacerated my right leg on the rocks and staggered ashore, looking more like Long John Silver than the vice president of the Marine Conservation Society, to greet the press. They loved it, almost as much as the bacteria that insinuated themselves into my wounds. Three days later, as I climbed aboard a hot air balloon to get a golden eagle's eye view of those patterned mires, my right foot looked as if it had a bad dose of mumps and was throbbing away to a beat all of its own. The flight was spectacular and the scene screamed out one question again and again: how could anyone in their right mind want to cover this ever-changing living tapestry of browns, ochres, yellows, oranges, pinks and deep burgundy reds, home of bonxies and eagles, with serried ranks of invasive conifers? We could see the great ploughs, flensing this living carpet of peat from off the face of the land, and the gangs of tree planters following in its wake. This was orchestrated vandalism in its rankest form.

A helicopter was meant to catch us up, so that I could spit air-to-air venom at the stupidity of it all, but a violent rainstorm foiled that ploy. Suddenly, we were surrounded by a skirt of water cascading from the balloon canopy, an all-enveloping rainbow hiding the carnage below from our cameras. For a short time the rain was so heavy that water made its way down through the burners, providing us with very hot showers. Drifting on a strengthening wind, we emerged from the aegis of the storm to overtake an eagle making its unhurried way back towards its eyrie.

We were by then completely lost, out in the wonder of it all, high above the deep Flow country across which I had walked as a student. Our pilot pointed out the fact that, as fuel was running low, we were going to have to land, so we started our descent towards a rocky ridge with the sea in the distance. As anchorman it was my job to leap out on touch-down and hold on as tight as I could to the basket. This I did, striking my foot against a rock – agony, then complete relief as I effectively lanced my suppurating wound. As the rest of the crew gathered up their belongings, I dangled my now throb-free foot in one of the bog pools, safe in the knowledge that acid sphagnum peat had been used for its healing powers since time immemorial. Stuffing a great wad of it in my boot, I hoisted one of the empty gas tanks on my shoulder and started on the long walk down to the nearest road.

At about the same time the saga of the Pacific yew was being enacted in the temperate rain forests of Northern California, Oregon and Washington. It was another shock, horror story in the annals of what can only be called resource-icide. The Pacific yew was never abundant, but it was there in large enough numbers for it to be regarded as a weed of no commercial value. In the ancient tradition of herbal medicine a weed is a plant whose virtues have not yet been discovered; to the woodsmen this was a tree of such little commercial value that it was felled and its remains trashed. In the late eighties researchers had found that its bark contained a complex of chemicals which they styled 'taxol', part of which they found gave significant periods of remission in several types of cancer. Perhaps the saddest part of this saga concerns a man who was found in the phytochemical laboratories of Berkley University, searching for this wonder drug for his dying mother. I can understand his hopes, for a great friend of mine, himself a GP in Britain, used taxol to treat a rare type of cancer which, being close to his heart, was inoperable. It gave him a miraculous extra nine months of active practice.

Two questions must be asked: how much of these life-giving chemicals had been lost in the rush for short-term profit, and how many other potentially useful organisms had been trashed since logging began in these wet coastal forests, let alone in the tropical rain forests we all hear so much more about?

25 A HOUSE IN TUSCANY

One of my pet hates is sitting on the beach – or anywhere for that matter – doing nothing, and so I was never the best of holiday companions. To tell you the truth, when it comes to holidays skiing became my firm favourite: there's something very active to do from sunup to sunset, and for me après ski means a large intake of fuel to provide all the energy I need to carry me through the next day and then to bed to rest my aches and pains – boring for the rest of the family, but at least they all agree that it gets graunchy old dad out of their hair after dinner.

Obergurgl in Austria is our favourite resort and it was there that we had our best all-action holidays, the fondest memories of which are of the whole family together, coming down the main drag, ready for lunch. Rufus, who excelled in cross-country at school and went on to actually enjoy taking part in marathons in the heat of Singapore, was a forthright skier who seemed to stick to the snow, on or off piste. Henrietta, the most gregarious of our family, was much the same, with a polished technique that developed over the years. Brighid, who followed her father's dreams and went to ballet school, skied like one of Walt Disney's snowflakes in *Fantasia*. Eoghain, or Yoghurt as he was then called, simply pointed his skis downhill, any hill, and off he went. On one glorious occasion, halfway down the middle slopes, he whizzed past the family, totally out of control, shot over a bump and disappeared. I don't think he was trying to do a somersault, but he did, and we found the lower half of his body sticking out of a drift, his legs looking very limp. At that moment it didn't appear funny, but once we had pulled him out he was off again and beat us all down to the hotel. As for Hannah, well, like Dad she was at that time a rugged individualist who shunned the ladies at the ski school and did it her way.

Rosemary and I sailed along behind like a stately goose and gander, gathering up the tribe as we went. If only we had started to learn to ski when we were children rather than in our forties, perhaps we could have led the way. Lunch sitting on the terrace, surrounded with piles of snow and framed by the mountain peaks, saw us all together: a family doing what families should do, enjoying a little bit of heaven.

Holidays were often tacked on the end of research, field or filming trips, each one providing special memories of one or another member of the family. A package holiday in Greece saw Hannah at her most belligerent, sitting outside the communal village bakery, immovable until she had a slice of freshly cooked bread. On the first night in Iceland, camped up the side of an extinct volcano with sleet coming in sideways, we were tucking Eoghain into his sleeping bag when he said, 'I think I would rather be in school.' That same holiday found us decorously dressed in our bathers, all swimming in a marvellous hot spring emanating from beneath a glacier. We had been there all on our own for about an hour, swimming back and forth from the cold into the hot water, when all of a sudden a tourist coach turned up to disgorge a party of extra-large mixed bathers, all stark naked who, much to the embarrassment of the kids, rushed in to join us. The only appropriate thing I could think of saying at the time was 'The whole of civilisation came rushing towards us.'

Brighid found Venice – or, come to that, any city – fascinating, but always liked the shops more than the sight seeing and loved partying, sleeping all day and enjoying a full night life. Henrietta found her dream place in a large holiday complex in the hills just outside Lima in Peru. With a number of swimming pools and lots of horses to choose from, she would disappear each day until her titian coloured head of hair would turn up for lunch or dinner on some giant horse. The trouble was, the only thing on the menu was eggs. I was away most days, researching for *Botanic Man,* and would return to the wail of, 'Not eggs *again!*'

Part of our research took us close to one of the enormous battery hen houses that provided our daily eggs. I just had to take a look in, and was appalled not only at the smell of urea but at the state of the birds in their tiny cages, many dead where they had stood all their piteous lives. An official told me that without the eggs and the chickens there would be no other source of protein for the millions of people who lived in that sprawling city. He bemoaned the fact that the anchoveta and other fish that used to keep the local population supplied with protein had gone, overfished almost to extinction, many to feed the battery hens across the world. There and then I added battery farming to my campaigning list and soon got hooked up with a wonderful charity called Chickens Lib, run by a group of farmers' wives back in Britain.

On our last day in Lima, before the family had to leave for home, we were sent to an ultra posh restaurant for a farewell family meal, paid for by Thames Television. The headwaiter looked in horror as the Bellamy clan filed in and sat down, the then very young Eoghain on Mum's lap. The waiter approached me with the menu and, waving his finger across the pages, asked if we could really afford the prices. We dined sumptuously and Eoghain ate everything that was put in front of him. By the end of the meal the whole restaurant staff were Bellamy-family fans and we trouped out, waved off by the best of friends, into a star spangled night. On arrival back at the hotel we found that Eoghain, who was fast asleep, was clutching one of the restaurant's spoons. It is still a prized family possession, named by the miscreant 'dolen poon'.

We had arrived in Lima with riots going on and fires at many street corners. The mini-bus that had picked us up from the airport was stopped a number of times by the militia, but on seeing all our assorted kids they waved us on. Going home proved to be even more difficult, not for me but for the rest of the family. I headed off on the research trail, while Martyn Day, who had to go to Bogota, accompanied the family on the first leg of their journey home. There was a long stop over, so, to fill time, he took them all to see the gold museum, not knowing that officials from a number of neighbouring administrations were arriving at the airport for a meeting. The result was that the family arrived back at the airport to find enormous security and gigantic crowds. I arrived home ten days later to tales from all the family that Mummy had used Eoghain's push chair as a battering ram to get on the plane.

It is our first family holiday together that provides memories of Rufus. He was about eighteen months old, and we were on the coast of Jugoslavia, back in those glorious days when Tito still miraculously held that diverse country together. A very young son, discovering the seaside for the first time, made sitting on the beach a tolerable experience, even for me. He crawled about, picking up pebbles and shells as he went, and at last approached the water's edge. Then, to our delight or was it horror, he carried on crawling until completely submerged. We fished him out from the crystal clear water and sat down beside a very friendly German visitor who turned out to be a judge with an enormous bunch of grapes. Rufus was offered part of the bunch, which he devoured with great exuberance and then crawled off to continue his exploration of the beach. That night great wails rent the air and nothing we could do would comfort him. The reason became plain when we changed his nappy, which contained a goodly collection of grape-sized pebbles. Two hours later he was as right as rain and we had realised that kids are really tough.

This holds true even when they are grown-up. Another holiday some twenty years on found us in Greenland where I decided to take a short sharp swim around a mini-iceberg in the bay. The local Inuits and their huskies all looked on with incredulity as we all took to the water. Rufus of course had to dive in with his spectacles on and came up without them. He was too blind to go and look for them himself, so Henry and I spent much longer in the freezer than we had meant to, searching in vain.

Rosemary was of course always there, complete with magic cream which instantly cured sunburn and every type of insect bite. She always remembered the passports and the tickets and the sun hats and the latest in pills or gadgets to fend off mal de mer. It was on one of our ski trips that we all learned just how important Mums really are. It was the last run of the day and the pistes were very icy. The whole family had gone ahead, back to the warmth of the hotel, and Rosemary and I were making our own way down the final slope. I had stopped beside our ski instructor on a particularly precipitous bend and Rosemary was coming alongside, when another skier, completely out of control, knocked her flat. I tried to help her up, but the angle of her leg and the look on her face showed that something was really wrong. Immediately the ski instructor took over and, as if by magic, she was strapped on a stretcher and we were off down to the hospital. I was told to wait outside so I shot up to the hotel to tell the kids, who were at that point all in one room causing mayhem: 'Mum's broken her leg, I am going back to the hospital. Rufus you're in charge.' Five of the whitest faces I have ever seen stared back as I rushed out of the room.

The news back at the hospital was very bad; the top of her femur had snapped off inside the hip and she had to go to a special hospital down the valley. It was already too dark for the helicopter so it was an hour away by ambulance, blue lights flashing all the way. Rosemary was very groggy, thanks to lashings of morphine, and I held her hand and wished that I was the one to go on the slab. After more x-rays a surgeon, already kitted up, came and did his best to tell me in Austrian what was going to happen. As far as I could understand the top of the femur was going to be bolted back onto its nether region using long stainless steel pins. I told Rosemary that I would stay with her, but she insisted that I go back to the children.

There was no more mayhem back at the hotel, and five even whiter children helped me plan the routine for the next six days. They would ski and I would take one of them down to the hospital – a train and a bus ride away – to keep Mum company. Eoghain said that skiing without Mum would be no fun and volunteered to accompany me on the first hospital run.

The surgeon met us with the good news that the operation had gone well and ushered us into the ward. After fond hellos, Eoghain disappeared under the bed, and there came a wail of: 'Mummy's dying!' and great floods of tears – he had found the bottle at the end of the drain tubes part-full of blood. I now had two patients on my hands. As Rosemary had slipped back into the arms of Morpheus, I took Eoghain out to find some lunch. The location didn't help much; the gasthof was a cavernous building like a medieval dungeon. Still, the chicken and chips were great and we returned to the hospital with a large bunch of flowers for Rosemary who was by then sitting up and taking nourishment.

So the pattern of the last week of the holiday was set, with most of the family out on the snow while two of us went Mummy-sitting. I was amazed at the efficiency of the whole thing. The representative of the insurance company was there, liasing with the hospital and helping us to fill in all the forms, and even offered to keep us all out for another week so that we could bring the patient back home together. The kids were overjoyed at the idea, but Rosemary was adamant: 'School is more important than looking after me,' and so I found out what it was really like to be a single-parent family and prepare them all for school.

The best holiday of all was without doubt the simplest: the Bellamys and the Bibbys, our family's best friends, two sets of parents and seven children, footloose on the Island of Tiree. There was really no need to organise anything for the sandy beaches, rocky headlands, mountains and moor provided a wealth of interest. The two dads, however, did run a treasure hunt, getting up early to hide a horde of goodies in an empty field. The problem was that, by the time the teams had followed all the clues and found the horde, the field was inhabited by a rather nasty bull. We also gave the children a challenge: a map and a small rubber boat with which to cross the island by the wettest route. They returned safely full of excitement, having discovered a recently collapsed croft complete with artefacts of a bygone age, a future excavation in the making. I can still see their faces, shining with triumph and soaked with salty rain, and I can taste the bashed neeps, the fresh lobster and of course the whisky. I crave to go back, but don't want to spoil those memories.

As the family grew up these holidays together became fewer and fewer – but I console myself that I can still look forward to the next. The best recommendation I ever had from the children I overheard when they were talking to the press after my appearance on *This Is Your Life*. They were asked what it was like to have a Dad who is always on his travels. 'Great!' came the answer. 'He's never there to tell us off, but he does take us on holiday to some super places.'

The year 1990 was momentous. At last we had paid off our mortgage, the Mill House was all our own, and so my habit of scanning the pages of *Country Life* took on an extra expectancy. There, in the back pages, amongst the bric-a-brac of Garden Furniture and Retirement Homes for Gentlefolk, were a number of tantalising adverts suggesting that you should go on a trip, indeed on several trips, to take a look at properties in France, Spain and Italy.

With most of the children away at school or university, Rosemary decided to take a look and I tagged on to the trip, hoping that instead of raising money for other people to go on working holidays and help put heritage back into biodiverse order, I could find such a project all of our own. The trouble was, I fell in love with every property we were taken to view, my favourite being a tiny medieval convent with walls about three metres thick and small cloistered rooms still sparsely furnished – one even had Mother Superior's iron bedstead with black leather boots placed beneath, as if she had just popped out in her nightie to take the night air. Too spooky and impracticable said Rosemary, and sadly she was right.

At the time, Rosemary was busy plotting a great family holiday, perhaps the last we would all enjoy together as the children were fast growing up. Plans were being laid for a walking holiday in the Pyrenees and excitement was riding high. All of a sudden the papers were full of stories regarding a large holiday development adjacent to the Costa Donana, Europe's seminal nature reserve. My documentaries were still quite popular in Spain and, as I had met the heads of the royal family when Spain won a top conservation award in 1988, I decided to send a letter begging the King to do everything in his power to stop the development, a development which threatened not only the integrity of the reserve but also its delicate water supply. For about a week my telephone and fax machine was under siege by the media, demanding an explanation of the contents of my letter which had of course been leaked. The thought of a peaceful holiday anywhere in Spain became impossible so I suggested to Rosemary that it would be best if she took the family on her own.

This went down like a lead balloon. She didn't even bother to answer as the colour drained from her face. What was more worrying was that she left me waiting for a reply for three awful days. I really did begin to think that divorce proceedings might be on the horizon. Then the morning post brought a clutch of official papers, one addressed to Mrs Shirley (her first name, given to her at the height of the Shirley Temple era) Bellamy. Thinking the worst I handed them over the breakfast table. Rosemary borrowed my butter knife, slit the envelope open and as she read the contents one of her most angelic smiles spread across her face. 'We are going to buy Fiori, no need to cancel the holiday, we will all go and camp in the vineyard,' she said.

Fiori was one of the Italian properties I had hummed and haa'd about, the last house in a village that tumbled its way down one of those Tuscan ridges. It all came with not-so-distant views of the peaks of the Apuan Alps in one direction and rolling hills, colour-washed in burnt siena and draped with chestnut woods, in the other. Why we hadn't bought it on the spot, I don't know. Perhaps it was because of the problem of how to restore the three-storey heap of stones and stop it all, especially the loo, from falling down the mountainside. The latter had been tacked high on the wall on the long-drop side of the house and in its heyday must have given its occupants one of the best views in the world.

So it was that, thanks to *Country Life*, we at last became proud owners of one of those 'country houses of great character in need of "some" renovation'. We soon found that all it really needed was a bit of love and local craftsmanship. There is nothing sadder than an empty house and Fiori was the saddest house I have ever seen, until it had a family to use that loo, enjoy the view and to be part of the communion of its neighbours who soon became part of an ever-growing family of friends. You can't just say 'hello' to village Italy; you have either got to become part of it or retreat seeking solace in fast-food pizza and pasta houses.

The late twentieth century had already done its worst in the locale, as it had across the world. Like some latterday Pied Piper it had lured the young people away to the promise of well-paid jobs in towns, all too often at the other end of the world. The result was an ageing population left behind who eventually could no longer look after their vineyards, vegetable patches or olive groves which had helped feed their families for generations. Uncared for, land that has sustained a considerable population for thousands of years begins to revert to forest which – unless it is managed well, and that is also the job of younger bodies – can only supply a certain amount of firewood, wild fruits and nuts, wild boar and venison. The Tuscan soil, scant as it is, must be tilled and the other necessities of life must be planted, watered, tended and harvested each in due season. I am sure that it is an inbred understanding of the limitations of the soil that had fed their ancestors that was, even then, moving Italy into pole position in the world stakes of family planning. The greatest culture shock to hit me in Italy was the dearth of young children, for one-child families were then becoming the accepted norm.

Brighid had produced our first grandchild on 24 November 1992 and, though christened Theo, he came to be known as Bello Bimbo by the entire village, especially by Mary, one of the oldest inhabitants who lived three doors down. Though born in America, she had returned to Tuscany as a child during the great depression, and tended the local church and upheld the age-old customs of village life. Always at work in the garden or carrying great bundles of grass and herbs to feed her many rabbits, she had the straightest of backs and the clearest of minds. The day we moved into the refurbished house, Mary arrived at the door with a bundle of sticks, kindling for our first home fire, and comfits for Theo. Theo soon learned his way around the community: quickly finding out who cooked the best pasta, who gave him the best tit-bits and of course who had the largest television set.

It was thanks in no small part to Mary and our next-door neighbours, Dante and Marta Gallini and their family, that we soon became part of a real village community. I was even allowed out with the men to take part in the annual gathering of fungi. This turned out to be a sort of vertical cross-country marathon that started in the late afternoon and ended with more than darkness falling down the mountain. Perhaps it's the fact that the weather is warm even in the winter that stirs the neighbourliness in everyone's soul. From early morning till very late at night someone is sitting outside somewhere in the village doing something, so that 'Buongiorno', becomes 'Buonasera', which easily metamorphoses into a meal or even a party. Real parties are gargantuan affairs, with everyone singing the praises of their own salami, bread, crostini, pasta, salads, vegetables, olive oil and vino, and the range of flavours woven into home-made grappa *has* to be sampled to be believed!

26 THE PROBLEMS OF SELLING YOUR IMAGE

Since I first appeared on television I have been asked to endorse many products ranging from farm chemicals to package holidays, and that's why I decided eventually to get an agent. I was fed up finding excuses which were not rude. The only thing I have never been asked to advertise is clothes for, along with Prince Charles and Patrick Moore, I have on a number of occasions been placed in the ranks of the worst-dressed men in Britain. I am also a strong advocate against the wearing of environmentally unfriendly clothes. Wearing a suit and tie means that you have too many layers of cloth between your main heat exchanger, your neck, and the air circulating around you – not the best way to protect your health, especially when in a stressful situation. After dinner speeches are absolute hell for me; that's my main reason for turning so many down every year. I once plucked up enough courage to wear a turtle-necked silk shirt under a tropical suit to a trade dinner at the Lancaster Gate Hotel. I was told that I would have to wear a tie, not an easy thing without a collar. I refused and so ate my dinner in the coffee shop. On being allowed back to give the after-dinner speech, I stood in the door to the dining room and shouted the first few lines.

The first advert I agreed to do was for the Wool Board of New Zealand at the time that synthetic carpets were beginning to hurt the wool industry. Synthetic carpets are petroleum based and petroleum is a non-renewable resource. Also, the sheep industry was in decline and needed help. My battle cry was keep the farmers and the rural communities which depend upon them down on the land and work with them, with the NGOs and with what was then among the best departments of conservation in the world to restore biodiversity. The adverts were a good way to get the facts over to those people who didn't watch the environmental programmes.

The large sound stage in the Hutt valley provided the setting for the shoot. The imagineers had built a gigantic model carpet so that I could be miniaturised and wander about in the pile, enthusing about the properties of natural wool fibre. It was an impressive model, so as soon as I could get to a phone I tried to tell Rosemary about it. I couldn't get through, which worried me, for she should have been home with the family. The enormous crew of creative and technical expertise soon swung into action, with me plastered in make-up and duly cut down to size, camera wise. Everything was going well until one sequence in which mini-Bellamy was supposed to give a flea's eye view of a large grand piano. I was meant to gaze up from amongst the carpet at a very elegant lady pianist. Unfortunately, however the cameras were angled it looked as if I was peering straight up her skirt, a situation that was made much worse by the script which had me saying, 'Wow, look at that!'

I kept ringing home to no avail over the next couple of days. Finally I got through to our best friends the Bibbys, who told me that Rosemary had been taken ill and was in intensive care with some strange virus. 'I am coming home!' I cried. As always Richard and Cynthia calmed me down, 'The crisis is over and the children are with us. There is nothing you can do; everything is going to be all right, stay put, we will keep you informed.' There was of course no way I could go home: the set and the crew were there, the studio was booked by others for the weeks ahead, and the adverts had to be done at once. You can guess how often I was on the phone, and as soon as the last line was dubbed I was on the plane.

Thank God, Rosemary was OK – and the adverts must have been a huge success for to this day, if I meet a New Zealand sheep farmer anywhere around the world, I always get offered a pint of beer. The truth of the matter is that, if I was asked to do the adverts today, I would have to say 'no' because of the environmental problems of overgrazing and sheep dip, and the fact that most synthetic fibres can now be recycled.

I then got asked to do a number of other adverts in New Zealand. The one I accepted with no qualms at all was a free one for the Department of Conservation. While making this I made my greatest sacrifice to the cause, having to have part of my beard removed. The caption was 'Old Man's Beard Must Go', and its aim was to get farmers and other landowners to remove clematis, originally imported from Britain as an ornamental plant, because it was running riot, a noxious weed smothering native forests.

I never received any negative letters regarding adverts I did in New Zealand and Australia, but the free ones I did for local zoos each solicited a crop of 'How can you say you are a greeny when you support those awful things called zoos?' I never have and never will support awful zoos, but I will campaign with all my strength to support *good* zoos. In this sad world they have become the arks of the covenant of creative evolution in which breeding populations of the world's rarest animals are held, waiting for the world to come to its senses. If that ever happens as I discussed on many occasions with Gerry Durrell, zoos will become obsolete as the descendants of the caged animals are retrained to live in the wild and so help rehabilitate the earth.

It was at about this time in my career that I found myself down at Marwell Park Zoo, upholding the credo that good zoos are good news and should not be closed down. Marwell even then was one of the better ones, busy putting the people in cages and the animals in wide open landscaped spaces. What is more, they were beginning to clock up a good record of breeding success, even amongst species that were on the endangered list. During the day I met a young man who introduced himself as David Shreeve. I say 'young' because I still don't exactly know how old he is – indeed it has become a standing joke between us, for when he slipped on ice one New Year's Eve and ended up in hospital with concussion, his first words on coming round were: 'Don't tell David Bellamy how old I am.' David Shreeve has a fantastic sense of humour which he certainly needs for we have been working together ever since. He was at that time, 1981, working with Pitney Bowes on a project that would put elm trees back into the Essex landscape, which had been ravaged by the Dutch Elm Disease. I found myself campaigning for Elms Across Essex (Margaret Thatcher planted one), Elms Across England (the Duke of Edinburgh planted one), Elms Across Europe (the European Commissioner planted one) and we even talked about, 'Elms Across the Earth'. Sitting on long journeys together, we dreamed dreams of campaigns and organisations that would turn the tide of those sad decades of destruction and get on with the job of rehabilitating landscapes and lives. Two years later Michael Heseltine, then Minister of the Environment, came to the Institute of Directors to launch one of them, the Conservation Foundation, in a blaze of publicity. The aim of the Foundation was to publicise any environmental *good* news that was coming out of the industrial sector. By then I had met several so called Captains of Industry who, apart from not being 'monsters of unfeeling greed' as portrayed by the deep environmental lobby, were in the main family men with real worries about their children's future.

After Pitney Bowes, our first major sponsor was the Ford Motor Car Company who hit on the idea of an annual award of money to fund grassroots conservation projects across Britain. This grew over the next eighteen years to include the far-flung corners of an expanding Europe. 'Anti' reaction went in waves. The first was a large poster showing a picture of human lungs and captioned, 'Any colour you like as long as it's black Ford conservation awards', this despite the fact that Ford were at that time leaders in the race for lean burn engine technology.

After helping to launch Schroeder's first ethical investment fund, I got the Foundation tied up running a similar fund for the Trustees Savings Bank. That opened up a real can of worms, with financial correspondents looking for scapegoat stories at such a daft idea, while some of the other new fund managers joined them to ask , 'What does David Bellamy know about the stock market?' I was too much of a gentleman to ask them in public what they knew about the environment.

Where are the ethics of investing in an oil company when very few of the investors or the protestors walk to the AGM? What's the real difference between the cosmetics sold in Boots and the Body Shop? Certainly the vast majority of the ingredients and many of the formulations had been tested on animals in the past, including generations of human beings. Anita Roddick did a wonderful job educating the public that in this day and age the use of animals for testing cosmetics was wrong. Boots maintained its status quo perhaps fearing that whichever way it went campaigners like those who let all the mink out of mink farms, wreaking untold mayhem among Britain's wildlife and pet cats, would have been at their throats.

I was at that time on a committee headed by Jonathon Porritt's father, working on the ethics of the use of animals in medical research. A lot of our effort was spent speeding research on the use of tissue culture and other alternatives to the use of live animals, and also ensuring that the laws covering animal experimentation were all the time being tightened and upgraded. My main reason for agreeing to be on the committee was that drugs tested on animals had helped to save the lives of my wife, myself and at least two of my children. I also feared that the research establishments who obeyed the rules would leave Britain and carry out their work in other countries where there were no laws, no controls and no hassles – work which was then giving great hope to people, and pets, with incurable diseases.

I even made a video called *Animal Rights and Human Ills* which set out the problem, focusing on the AIDS pandemic that was then threatening to engulf the world. The irony of it all for me was that one sequence was filmed in the very department at St Mary's where my brother and I had first met Lewis Edwin Holt and Alexander Fleming. The video was circulated to schools and as yet I have only received three negative letters concerning its contents.

I rapidly came to the conclusion that, like statistics, ethics were whatever anyone wanted to make of them, but lacked the let-out clause of obfuscating formulae. Eventually I left the TSB Fund Committee, which has since become one of the best performers in the field. Perhaps my opponents had been right, although a number of them and their funds have disappeared from view.

The most worrying turn of events was when the Conservation Foundation was commissioned by Shell to look into ways in which the Ogoni and other peoples of the Niger delta might overcome the many problems relating to the oil production from their ancestral lands. The following is from an article by Polly Ghazi in the *Observer* on 10 December 1995:

> David Bellamy, the TV conservationist, has incurred the wrath of Britain's green elite by refusing to withdraw from a Niger delta environmental survey funded by Shell. Jonathon Porritt, Anita Roddick, Greenpeace's Lord Melchett, and Charles Secrett of Friends of the Earth claim Mr Bellamy is being 'used' by Shell to improve its battered image after the execution of nine Ogoni activists, last month, including Ken Saro-Wiwa. They want him to withdraw the Conservation Foundation, a London-based charity of which he is a founder director, from the committee running the £3 million survey, which will investigate oil-related damage in the delta's fragile swamplands. Instead, they want his support for a broader 'independent commission of inquiry' into ecological and social problems in the delta.

I could only wonder why she hadn't bothered to contact me directly.

While some obviously thought I should resign, others in the green lobby disagreed.

A letter from Robin Pellew, Director of WWF, dated 14 December, stated:

I am concerned to read in the newspapers the calls for the Conservation Foundation to withdraw from the Niger delta environmental survey. I would urge you to continue Struan Simpson's involvement. For the survey to be effective, it is essential that independent individuals with experience of the delta remain involved. I have no doubt that you are quite capable of avoiding being 'used' by Shell, and that if they were so stupid as to try, you would know how to respond.

I replied to my critics, quoting from a letter written to the chairman of the Niger Delta Environmental Survey by Ken Saro-Wiwa, who was then in prison:

Dear Mr Onosode,

Greetings of the season and welcome back from your many trips. I'm trying to keep in touch with you through my brother, Owens. I have also been in close touch with Claude Ake who is a valued friend and a great source of intellectual and social comfort to me. I am very pleased that he and David Bellamy as well as yourself are in the Shell Survey. As I did say earlier, it's not that I have faith in Shell; my faith is in the fact that your presence will nudge Shell in the right direction, in a direction which they are probably not thinking of at this time. Claude is also from an oil producing area and is fully aware of the problems.

I expect that my brother may have briefed you on my son's trip to the US to accept the Goldman Environmental Prize on my behalf. He met Al Gore, had lunch with Ethel Kennedy and with the Environmental Response Fund, also with Bruce Babbit, US Secretary of the Interior. The point I am making is that the Ogoni people are determined to internationalise the issue as we think that Shell have really ruined the delta with the support of the military and civilian politicians from the North. Although all this is not a point of your brief, I doubt that people will be impressed if the government and Shell do not accept to pay rents and royalties to landlords and make available a fair proportion of petroleum profits tax. In addition to using 'best practice' in their environmental contracts. It is good to bear this in mind.

I understand you have been very upset about a recent film commissioned by Channel 4 in London to help highlight our cause. I think the mistake can be corrected and should be corrected. I'm asking my chaps here to get in touch with the film makers, whom I know, to make the necessary apologies and corrections. I haven't seen the film of course, nor were we consulted on any aspect of it.

I wish you God's blessings. Oh, before I end, my brother is discussing with Brian Anderson and will surely benefit by your experience and ideas. Please do remain available to him. The Ogoni are so few on the ground, there isn't enough advice around! God's love.
Ken Saro-Wiwa

And it was on the basis of this letter that rightly or wrongly I decided to continue the Conservation Foundation's presence on the NDES and answered my antagonists, whoever they were, with the following statement.

The facts of the matter are that the Foundation:
1 Raised the whole profile of the Niger delta affair, working with the TSB Ethical Investment Fund, by disinvesting in Shell.
2 Instigated the survey which was to address the social and ecological effects of the oil industry on the delta.

3 Attended all the committee meetings, pushing for complete independence, gained at the last meeting.

4 Demanded that Shell immediately begin to improve its oilfield practice and make reparations to the communities affected. Work already underway.

5 Decided to continue our work on the committee as it has the mandate of all the other peoples of the delta and I believe the backing of Ken Saro-Wiwa, as stated in his letter.

When conservation was basically about trying to put a stop to things, it was easy. But I know now that trying to make things go in the right direction is much more difficult.

At that juncture I thought I knew a lot about what was going on in conservation having been on the campaigning trail for almost a quarter of a century. However, I never fail to be amazed by the hundreds of good-news stories opened up by the Ford Conservation Awards every year. Each one is a green window revealing that, whatever the press like to think, the green renaissance is underway. Clear across Europe groups of people are getting on with the job of putting their own environmental house, or local patch, back into better working order.

Perhaps the strangest award winner of them all, which I must admit did cause some consternation in the ranks of our sponsor, was a slaughterhouse in Bavaria, which served all the farms in a small catchment area – farms that provided the meat that makes some of the best Wurst in Germany. The secret of their success in the competition was their level of landscape and animal husbandry, highlighted by the fact that when the beasts were walked down to slaughter, the lead animal went first with the farmer and his family in attendance. The resulting meat was completely stress free and, although they could not produce us firm evidence for it, this was probably one of the reasons for the quality of their sausages. The sad fact was that European rules were demanding that all small abattoirs should be closed, the excuse of the bureaucrats being that they were unsanitary – no mention of the cruelty of long stressful journeys in crowded lorries to unfamiliar locations with the likelihood of spreading disease en route, or the fact that the larger the slaughterhouse the more chance of epidemic-sized infections spread because of one slip in the rules.

An even worse piece of Eurobureaucracy was being enacted at that time, relating to the slaughter of deer bred in captivity. Without doubt the kindest way was to use a good marksman delivering the *coup de grâce* out of a closed vehicle, resulting in stress free, free range venison, a much healthier part of the human diet than an overbred bullock full of saturated fat and testosterone. Eurospeak decreed that these semi-wild terrified animals must henceforth be rounded up and carted off to a slaughterhouse. May God guide the ethics of these faceless people.

David Shreeve's ability for developing new ideas that help fund grassroots conservation, are never ending: the Community Chest with Trust House Forte; Lloyds People with the Bank; Wessex Water Mark, to name but a few. He is also great at finding new and exciting venues for award ceremonies, which has given me, and the annual crop of wide-eyed winners, the opportunity of seeing the inside of many of London's most beautiful buildings. The trouble is everywhere he and I go together, we come up with new and often preposterous ideas to ease the constant slog of fund raising.

A list of the Foundation's work to date and our latest good-news stories can be down loaded from our web site, www.conservationfoundation.co.uk. The Foundation is still a lean green machine consisting of the two Davids (the other one does all the work), Libby Symonds, a secretary and volunteers who come in when needed, which is always. Although registered as a charity we hold out no begging bowls to members. We work for our living, putting over good-news stories.

1990 To Sustainability and Beyond 2000

27 RIDING DOWN FROM RIO

The countdown decade to the new millennium saw me going back to the Beeb, a new director, John Percival and a new series called *Bellamy Rides Again:* six parts outlining the cycles of life and how the late twentieth century had done its best to throw as many spanners as possible into their works. All this was just in time for the now infamous Rio Environmental Summit of 1992, where 184 heads of state and their representatives met to discuss ways of solving the world's environmental problems.

There were of course two summits going on simultaneously. There was the official one whose allowed agenda had already been honed down by armies of civil servants and tens of thousands of hours of committee meetings since the last jamboree ten years before in Stockholm. The survival of these civil servants, like that of their current political masters, has little to do with fitness, for it is cut and dried by the short termism of political expediency. Then there was the other summit, a meeting of all the Non Governmental Organisations which could afford to send a representative. Many had their own straw vote agendas, whittled down into single issues by the short-term demands of survival in the begging bowl market place.

Rio is not the best holiday location in the world unless you want your nose well and truly rubbed in that ultimate culture shock, the ever-widening gap between rich and poor. However, it did show that clear across the world, important people were worried enough about the state of the environment to take a few days off to discuss the problem. It also showed the strength of grassroots opinion and expertise.

Perhaps as a botanist I can be forgiven for thinking that the most important decision that came out of the summit related to the world's rapidly disappearing tropical rain forest and other old-growth forests.

Five years before the Rio Summit the members of G-7 (that is the seven richest cash-flow countries in the world) had met in Italy where, to put it in their own words, they 'underlined' their 'own responsibility' toward tropical forests. In France in 1989, they again called for the 'adoption of sustainable forest management practices, the aim of which was to preserve "the scale" of the world's forests'.

The NGOs and *Decade of Destruction* film makers had done a good job, making at least someone in most parts of the world realise that the destruction of forests was threatening the Earth's atmosphere, and local catchment stability as well as the huge reservoir of its species and genetic resources.

In 1990, as the Amazon region burned, the leading industrialised nations meeting in the United States said, 'We are determined to take action to increase forests while protecting existing ones.' The following year, it was Britain's turn to play host to the G-7 plus Russia who, despite the fact that the new boy had the largest block of old-growth forest in the world within its borders, only 'remained concerned'. As I am writing this I can only look backwards in hope, while reviewing how radically their opinions have been watered down post-Rio.

At the Tokyo meeting in 1993, their members admitted that forests 'continue to be destroyed and degraded at alarming rates'. Indeed they were so alarmed that they wanted an 'international agreement' to protect forests. Nothing really happened until, five years later in Denver, they at least called on 'all countries to eliminate illegal logging'.

Back in Britain, in Birmingham to be exact, in May 1998, this trumpeting of sound bites without any meaningful commitment yielded an 'Action Programme on Forests', with a pledge to report back on progress in 2000. The world could only hope that there would be progress for the sad fact was that since the Denver summit, an area of forest the size of Germany had been destroyed.

The Group of Seven plus Russia next meet in Okinawa. I hoped we might get some sense at last, for Japan is a nation that loves her own forests. If G-7 had spent one per cent of the money their meetings had cost to date, on buying logging rights and so saving forests, the world might have had something to cheer about. Unfortunately, multinational companies from Japan and other members of the G-7 are still very active in destroying ancient forests, some inside and most outside their own borders. I wait with bated laptop to record their latest deliberations. Will the new millennium spark a radical change in attitude?

At least in Japan, a real action plan committed 'the leading industrialised nations to greater information sharing to help develop counter measures to illegal logging'. This was a plan that called on 'governments to assist in market transparency for the work of the International Tropical Timber Organisation'. Someone seems to have forgotten that the members of that particular organisation were already committed to 'sustainable management of their forests by that year', and almost every one of them is failing to implement that commitment, their excuse being that around 80 per cent of all logging in the world's old-growth forest is illegal.

I leave it to HH Sadruddin Aga Khan, who has been a tireless campaigner while working with many UN agencies over forty years, to summarise his incredulity over these axemen of the apocalypse, as he did in an excellent article in the *Herald Tribune*.

How tragic then that our political leaders are generally much better at planting ceremonial trees than they are at saving the forests of their nations. Perhaps a ban should be put on political tree planting until the forests are truly protected.

Who among our contemporary leaders will have the vision to save the world's remaining ancient forests? What greater legacy could one aspire to leave future generations than this unique natural heritage – the oldest and richest resource sustaining life on Earth?

Will Giuliano Amato, Tony Blair, Jean Chrétien, Bill Clinton, Jacques Chirac, Yoshiro Mori, Vladimir Putin and Gerhard Schroeder live up to their obligations?

My first meeting with the Aga Khan had been when I was invited to lunch with him at Claridges. I of course arrived early and took a seat in the grand entrance hall beside a stunningly beautiful lady in an absolutely gorgeous fur coat. Never one to miss an opportunity I tried to engage her in conversation regarding the cruelty of the fur trade. My attempts were in vain because she only spoke French, a subject I had never excelled in at school. Enter HH, who summed it up by enquiring, 'Why do people like wearing second-hand clothes?' We dined very well and I had no qualms about selecting bangers and bubble and squeak from the menu.

I have had the pleasure of discussing environmental matters with HH on a number of occasions, the most memorable being on two working cruises, one in the Mediterranean, the other around the Black Sea. Both were the brainchild of Maria Beckett, a visionary who drew together key ecclesiastics and ecologists from around the world and imprisoned them, in regal style, on a very-well-appointed roll on roll off ferry.

On both of the voyages our deliberations were led by the ecumenical patriarch and all the bishops of the Greek Orthodox Church, which had taken 'The Environment' as its credo for the new millennium. Our part was to discuss the problems and the potential of all the creeds, kinds and philosophies of the world putting the spirituality of creation back into their teachings and hence into their lives. To say they were magical experiences would be trite in the extreme. This was no ordinary set of environmental seminars from which you could escape when the subject matter got too boring or too controversial. We were all locked in a floating, Aladdin's Cave of knowledge and ideas, and let out for 'field trips', many of which were themselves making history, like the meetings of the patriarchs, bishops and lay people of the different branches of orthodoxy, some for the first time for centuries. All this was embellished with the splendour of mitres and bejewelled robes of office and accompanied by music and plain chant in cathedrals, shrines, amphitheatres and sacred groves, some of which predated not only all the branches of Christianity but all the monotheistic religions of the world.

Each experience was an open sesame to the next. The culmination for me being our visits to the Danube delta where we saw the plavs: enormous part floating reed beds I had first read about in the papers of Marietta Pallis in my undergraduate days. Communism, culminating in the infamous Ceaușescu regime had done its worst, draining those enormous reed swamps in an attempt to cultivate the land and replace the highly productive natural regime with chemical-drenched monocultures and fish farms. Their ploy was a miserable failure, but worse still they had destroyed what were in effect the kidneys of over one-fifth of Europe. The reeds could no longer cleanse the Danube, stripping pollutants and nutrients from its waters before they voided into the aptly named Black Sea. In consequence of this, and of blatant overfishing, the once rich fisheries, which included amongst their twenty-eight commercial species the luxury of Sevruga caviar and the everyday staple of the anchovies, were all but wiped out.

As our pilgrimage continued we appeared to be witnessing a miracle. We found more and more evidence of anchovies on sale in the local markets. It was in the Danube delta that we saw what I believe is the answer – the power of re-creation was there for all to see. Since the collapse of communism, the monocultures and fish farms had fallen into such a state of disrepair that the wetlands had, of their own accord, started to regenerate once more. The kidneys were starting to function, cleansing the water, enough at least to begin to restore the balance of the sea.

It is of course easy to point fingers of scorn at other people, but what of the cause of conservation itself – has it accomplished what it set out to do? How much money have we (I use the word 'we' because I am one of them and so am equally to blame) wasted over the past forty years on yet another meeting to talk about how to raise money for education programmes that would tell their members how they were going to save the panda or the tiger? Yet as we went into the countdown for the self-congratulatory new millennium begging bowl spree, many of the species we had been trying to save were still in danger, and many more are joining the list by the day.

The sad thing is that despite the fact that the World's Conservation Estate (that is, all the World Heritage Sites, National Parks, Nature Reserves, Protected Areas, Sanctuaries, etc. etc. etc. all rolled together) now rivals the size of the British Empire upon which the sun did eventually set – 6,034 species of animal and 6,259 species of higher plant are on the International Union for the Conservation of Nature's official endangered list. What is more those numbers – which include very few of the smaller animals and none of the smaller plants, on which the balance of all ecosystems and the viability of all soils depend – are going up by the day. If any multinational company had done as badly at reaching its goals, it would have disappeared off the face of the stock exchange.

Britain probably has more conservation groups than any other country in the world, yet since they, and that includes me, took to the campaigning road, 98 per cent of our flower rich meadows and grasslands, and many of the animals and birds that went with them, have disappeared off the face of this once multicoloured and pleasant land: all wiped out not by road building or pollution but by the Common Agricultural Policy. Likewise the seas around our 'frying tonight' isles are in disarray, not because of pollution and eutrophication, although these are having local effects, but because of the Common Fisheries Policy. In essence, overfishing of the sea and overproduction on the land, all for short-term profit for the few and all subsidised by the gullible taxpayer, have destroyed the biodiversity of Britain. Why haven't the campaigners had a go at them? The answer is that they've been focusing on easier targets like Shell, McDonald's or BP or some other well-known logo to keep up the hype of dubious success, and the begging bowls full.

Botanically, the most biodiverse bit of Britain is Kew Gardens, but it costs millions of pounds every year, just to keep it going. Biodiverse wilderness costs nothing to keep going and causes no downstream problems: that is what we should have been emphasising over all those years.

So, the much lauded concept of biodiversity that neatly sidestepped the real issue, which was and still is habitat destruction, became one of Rio's gifts to the dictionaries of the world – a new buzz word to rank alongside a new buzz concept, sustainable development. The latter soon became the scam of the nineties, simply another way for the richest people of the world to get their hands on those areas from which they were not already making money, and develop them under the banner of sustainability. The thing that really worried and still worries me is: what will be the world's reaction to the harvesting of Cetaceans, for instance, once their numbers are back to breeding sustainability?

In my book the term should have been 'sustainable redevelopment'. Sustainable redevelopment would put the world's fisheries back in the hands of local fishing communities and all fish and shell fish for the mass market would come from properly run closed-cycle farms that use no chemicals and cause no pollution or eutrophication. The fish would be fed, not on capelin and sand eels, the industrial harvesting of which destroys the base of the marine food web, but on worms or other invertebrates cultured on organic waste. Then and only then would the whales and dolphins, walruses, seals, sea lions, sea birds, and the rest of the biodiversity that keeps those all important solar-powered sea defences and production lines in repair, be able to do their all important jobs. With all marine systems back in more natural balance, the life-giving sea could continue to service the Biosphere, Gaiasphere or whatever you want to call it, sequestering carbon into long-term store, producing oxygen and recycling sulphur as only slightly acid rain.

At any other juncture in my campaigning career I would have agreed with my critics if they had said 'pie in the sky utopianism'. However, today I think that such dreams could one day become a reality, for Rio was not all bad. Of all the outputs of the Rio Summit, the concept of Agenda 21 shines out as a beacon of hope. The bureaucrats must have been listening for they hijacked the main slogan used in the Franklin Dam Campaign: 'Think Globally Act Locally'. In other words, keep yourself well informed about all the problems of the world, don't let them grind you down, and show that you really care by beginning to put *your own* houses in order.

I don't know how many Agenda 21 meetings I have had to turn down simply because of pressure of time, but it must be in the many hundreds. My diary was and is now always overfull, and the best way of keeping track was the number of days I managed to spend at home base each year. The number began to hover around twenty-five to thirty-five – especially after I took up more presidencies, and patronages. I don't count it as a day at home, if I left on the very early train before Rosemary had got out of bed and didn't return in time for our evening meal, which was always very late.

When in Britain it was back and forth on the train to meetings in London or elsewhere. The rest of the year I was on the campaign trail around the world: New Zealand, all corners of Australia, Singapore, Hong Kong, China, Indonesia, Tierra del Fuego, Brazil, Guatemala, Belize, Mexico, Russia, Italy, Belgium, Ireland and Canada all in one memorable twelve months. I became an addict of the bucket shops, and my genes that allow me to fall asleep as soon as I get into a car, train or plane still help me through a phrenetic travel schedule. For those tempted to say, 'All that travel – how can he claim to be an environmentalist?' the only answer I have is that a modern Jumbo when 70 per cent full is more fuel efficient than a company car with two up.

One of the most memorable Agenda 21 meetings I ever attended was held in Miraflores, a somewhat upmarket part of Lima in Peru. Despite the fact that Paddington Bear is usually depicted wearing a duffle coat, it rarely rains in his hometown, so dust is a real problem, especially in the shantytowns which house much of the population. Some green sparks had collected the grey water from a block of apartments; part purified it by filtration and then used it to irrigate the parkland. The result was magic – no dust and lots of people picnicking on a greensward bedecked with a multitude of flowers. In a workshop with some youngsters we calculated that if all the waste water from the city was treated in the same way, trees, grass and flowers could replace the dust storms while cutting down pollution along the coast which was a main migration route for whales.

28 THE GREEN RENAISSANCE

One of the most fateful questions I was ever asked while on a train started with a request for autographs for a young father of two children. He sat down and during our conversation we got round to politics. As the next election was well on the way, he said, 'Who are you going to vote for?' I said, 'Well, I think I am going to vote this time either for Arthur Scargill's Real Labour or for the Referendum Party.' I had always counted myself as a socialist and was now a campaigner for both bio and social diversity, so, although I was pleased that Britain was, thanks to a referendum, part of the European Economic Community, I didn't think that a federal Europe was the brightest star in the political firmament. What is more I had read many books on the subject, including those by Sir James Goldsmith. Two things I agreed with Mrs Thatcher about were, that there are votes in the environment and that we should never sell our sovereignty.

My new train acquaintance said, 'Be careful, I am a political agent for Goldsmith's Referendum Party,' and a few days later I was asked to lunch with Sir James. It was a fantastic meal, both for the food and for the conversation. I was somewhat blunt and asked him straight out why he had turned from being an environmental baddy to a born again conservationist, a Goldsmith to a Greensmith. His reply was somewhat complex, but boiled down to the simple question 'What use is the Midas touch?' He was at that time fighting what turned out to be the terminal phases of pancreatic cancer and his answers, all of which are in his two superb little books, *The Question* and *The Answer*, were straight to the point. He got up to go and before I could thank him he said, 'Will you stand in Huntingdon for the Referendum Party?' 'But that's John Major's constituency, you must be mad,' I retorted. Before we got to the door I had agreed.

Campaigning was a great experience. I knocked on doors and talked to people of every political persuasion and a lot that didn't have a clue. My main question was, 'What are your main worries about the future?' The answer was always, 'Will my children have a good job and what sort of environment will they live in?' I began to get worried that I would actually enjoy a stint as their representative in Parliament.

Looking back, perhaps this was the most misguided of my career decisions, because since then none of my ideas for television series have ever been taken up. At first I put it down to being too long in the tooth. I was old hat. However, when the BBC tried to use the axe on Julian Pettifer and then used it more firmly on Robin Page (who had been the Referendum Party candidate in the next constituency to mine) I began to wonder. Perhaps if I had kept out of the hustings, I might have become an adviser to the government on the environment. Then perhaps they would never have been allowed to go into the next election without mentioning the environment.

Despite the results of that particular train journey, I still think trains are great ways for an environmentalist to travel. When not chatting to people (who now ask with monotonous regularity, 'Why don't we see you on the telly these days?' and still ask for an autograph) I can either get through a lot of work or sit and watch the British countryside go by. Believe it or not, even from what's left of our railway system you can see almost every type of vegetation in Britain. Much of the railway is a highly protected linear nature reserve over which not even the most vehement 'right to roamers' really want to roam. That is why I don't really get that much work done during my long hours on the train – season by season there is always so much to see. I toyed with the idea of putting up some form of interpretation on the trains of what you can see from the windows, and even put the idea to British Rail before it became privatised. John Burton who heads the World Land Trust had also had similar ideas and came up with the concept of the world's longest, thinnest National Park. I toddled along to see the powers that be at, what by then was Railtrack and got some rumblings of approval: a good idea, but not a National Park, with all the red tape. I countered with the idea of the world's first National Park and Ride and handed it over, as only a President can, to The Wildlife Trusts. Four months later I was asked to launch the scheme in the East Anglian Region, where an audit of the biodiversity of the Railtrack estate had been completed and found wanting in nothing except a little bit of expert management. The programme is now being implemented and I look forward to the day when, 'The Permanent Way' takes on its new role, providing not only environmentally friendly transport, but also a linear University of the Countryside.

In the late 1990s, the whole face of conservation on the home front was changing very rapidly, thanks in part to Agenda 21, but also to a whole new breed of dynamic younger conservationists: Mark Rose, Simon Lister, Derek Moore and Jane Smart, to name but a few, young campaigners who were not content just to sit back and toe a party line but were rearing to get stuck in and make sure that their patch was in better working order.

There is no getting away from the fact that two very welcome sources of finance helped a lot. First was the Heritage Lottery Fund, a fount of money based on our innate desire to gamble. When asked about the ethics of it all, my answer was, 'Well, we are gambling with the future of the living world, never look a gift horse in the mouth.' The second was the Landfill Tax, to me a much dodgier environmental pill to swallow, especially as we all do our bit in this throw-away society. The sad truth is that each landfill, unless it is encased in granite or solid clay, is a time bomb for the future, a series of catastrophes just waiting to happen. What is more, there are a number of new techniques which can and do include co-generation of energy, well tested across the world. The sad thing is that I have as yet never met anyone who would welcome the location of a high-tech incinerator, a pyrolysis, gasification or steam reformation plant let alone a landfill or even a garbage recycling plant in their own backyard. Add to that the existence of a very strong pro-landfill mafia, out there. They exist for the simple reason that the cost of building a more environmentally friendly, state of the art plant saps the short-term profits. Thanks to the way the environment is still viewed at bureaucrat level, lining a hole in the ground, flaring off the greenhouse gas and moving on to sculptured landfill once you have run out of hole smacks more of political expediency than common sense. As I have gone down on record saying that, apart from tobacco and other drugs, there's no such thing as dirty money, its what you do with it that counts, I have to live with the fact. Beggars can't be choosers and even if some people do feel great pity for them, they never ask them advice about running business let alone the country. However, even that is beginning to change as the Wildlife Trusts, National Trust, RSPB and many others are in there lobbying for real change, and working with local, regional and even national governments to avoid the litigation loophole delaying the way to real action. Over the past twenty years, the Ford Conservation Awards have been identifying, rewarding and kick-starting the initiative of local green groups across an expanding European Ecological Union – dedicated groups of local people who are busy rehabilitating their own local environment: putting reefs, saltings, estuaries, rivers, streams, lakes, ponds, fens, bogs, water meadows, grasslands, pastures, heathland, moorland, bushlands, woodlands, forests, alps, whole islands and whole catchments back into biodiverse working order. Every one of these projects is improving both the ecology and the economy of their local landscape.

For the past decade the Tourism for Tomorrow Awards have been doing the same thing on a worldwide scale, linking such environmentally friendly endeavours to the new paymasters, the world's biggest industry, tourism. There was no getting away from the fact that tourism had long been one of the great destroyers of the sanctity of lives and landscapes, and the high-rise hooligans of the past, along with the vested interests of quick offshore profits, are still out there doing their worst. In the knowledge that it isn't going to go away, the only hope is to make all tourism environmentally friendly. As the chairperson of the international panel that makes the final decisions on awards every year, I am amazed by the range of entries that win, let alone the quality of those that make it into the final round. From mega projects like the rehabilitation of Magaluf in the Balearics, and Skyrail in Queensland that gives half a million tourists the educational experience of a lifetime through tropical rain forest, to micro projects like Chombe, a 24-hectare coral island off the coast of Zanzibar, and a caravan park in Norfolk, it's all beginning to happen.

29 Clouds on the Green Horizon

I was getting very worried about the decision taken by the member states of the European Union at OSPAR (the Oslo and Paris Commission), to recycle the oil rigs in the North Sea as they became redundant. It was going to use a lot of energy and produce massive problems of landfill and potential pollution. Had the true value of these multibillion dollar installations ever been considered? Surely they must be of use as test beds for offshore wind and wave power? What about the possibility of using the pipelines for transport of greenhouse gases from power stations for reburial from whence they came? With over thirty years of research in marine pollution behind me, I could not understand how the marine biota could possibly benefit from the recycling proposals.

I contacted as many relevant groups as I could and asked them their opinions. The result of my enquiries was much the same: 'Let sleeping sea dogs lie, that was last year's problem! Leave it alone because the decision at OSPAR has shown the world that we have won, the seas must not be regarded as dustbins.' If only they had looked beyond their begging bowls and said that they wanted to show the world that they meant business by forming the cornerstone of a partnership with the vision and the money that would put the seas back into working order.

Only Pete Wilkinson, who was by then running a hands-on environmental consultancy, rallied round and joined me in the search for missing information. The more we researched the problem, the more worried we became, for nowhere could we find details of the process by which the decision had been made. Where was the evidence? If it existed at all it was not in the public domain. In desperation on 19 July 1999 I wrote a letter to the Deputy Prime Minister, John Prescott (see Appendix 6).

A rapid reply summoned Pete and me to a meeting with the man whom, many years before, we had watched swim across the river Thames in a wetsuit to back Greenpeace's demands to halt the development of re-processing as part of Britain's atomic power programme. He appeared as nonplussed as Pete and I at the lack of firm evidence regarding the grounds on which the OSPAR decision had been made. Discussion still rumbles on, with key meetings of interested parties at the Society of Underwater Technology, but nothing has so far happened at government or industry level.

At least part of the reason why became painfully obvious while I was working with the local community of Delta near Vancouver in British Columbia. I had for a number of years thrown what weight I had behind the cause of saving Burns Bog from further despoliation by drainage, landfill and cranberry culture. I had first visited this giant raised bog – so large that it can be seen from outer space – when looking for a location for a key sequence in *Botanic Man*. It was ideal except for the noise of Fison's machines which were then at work on a massive scale, winning peat for the horticultural industry. As the noise was going to make filming difficult, we chose another location. It was therefore with great surprise that many years later I received a letter from one Eliza Olsen, asking me to help the local people with their 'Burns Bog Campaign'. I was even more amazed when Eliza and her band of eco-friendlies took me for a walk over the bog. A miracle had happened, for over the past two decades Burns Bog had begun to heal itself. Large tracts of it were back in biodiverse working order and the bog was beginning to form peat and to grow once again.

However, there is a sad twist in this tale, which may prolong and could scupper this very worthy campaign. In the interim the Canadian government had become a signatory of NAFTA, the North American Free Trade Agreement. It is an agreement (although I hesitate to use the word, for it implies that all parties were au fait with all its consequences) which simply and catastrophically means that Canada's water, and that includes the water that supplies Burns Bog, is no longer her own. All such natural resources are now readily available to any member of that parcel of rogues who are arrogant enough to look upon the world as their own patch in which to make their own short-term profit. They call themselves the World Trade Organisation, WTO for short. As I type this chapter, the World Bank is witholding support from India unless it gets on with the job of privatising its water. 'Privatising', in today's speak, means putting control and hence profit into richer people's hands. Already tribal people in Maharastra can no longer draw water from their ancient tank. Why? Because a company can pay more for this vital resource – 'if they can't drink water, let them drink coke.'

It was after Rio that the idea of carbon trading was becoming all the rage with the greens, and even some enlightened parts of the timber industry were backing the idea. I attended many meetings to discuss its potential and its problems. The idea went something like this: the more carbon a nation pours out into the global greenhouse the more tax it pays. The tax revenue collected from the rich countries would then be available to those countries who, on a per capita basis, use the least fossil fuel, to fund the replanting of their forests. As the billions of new trees grew towards maturity, they would soak up carbon dioxide from the overburdened atmosphere. This would give the Earth a breathing space and would give the rich countries time in which they could switch to alternative sources of energy and new clean green technologies like fuel cells, thus putting the global greenhouse back on 'regulo survival'. Please note that in this context, carbon tax and energy tax are synonymous and hence carbon tax could provide the dynamic, inflation-proof economy outlined by Farrel Bradbury and the other proponents of unitax. The idea of a carbon sequestration tax sweetened the pill so that when pre-election time came, even Bill Clinton was willing to sign on to the idea.

This was not a simple matter, and the pros and cons would take a lot of working out, but at least it had the potential of nudging humankind in the right direction, while creating millions of jobs across the world. My considered opinion was that it *should* happen, and that the first carbon credits should be given towards the protection of all that remains of the world's old-growth and regrowth forest and all natural vegetation and their soils. I also hoped that the protection of coral reefs might also be included in the package. Such a move would give vast areas of the world immediate protection, allowing the renaissance scenario to move into a higher gear.

Unbelievably, when the crunch came at the November 2000 Kyoto conference in The Hague, groups like WWF, FOE and Greenpeace came out *against* the idea. I must say I was flabbergasted at this new twist in green affairs and did my best to find out what had caused this turnabout. The only answer I got was 'I cannot live with letting America grow trees instead of cutting its emissions of fossil fuels.' These were the words of Dominique Voynet, the 'green' French environment minister in a deal brokered by John Prescott, a deal which in effect scuppered the Kyoto Treaty at another of its multimillion dollar, 'get it all together for ourselves' meetings.

As Robin Hanbury-Tenison put it, in an article published in the *Telegraph*, 'It was the greens not George W Bush that derailed the Kyoto Treaty.' One must also ask: if the French and, come to that, the British are really concerned about carbon emissions, why are they both doing all they can to export infernal combustion engines to the potentially vast markets of China and India? Surely a fund which would put billions of dollars into the world's poorest countries, and replant millions of hectares of tropical rain and other types of forest, must be better than a whole string of new atomic power stations or mega hydro dams?

As I was typing an article putting over my argument, to the *Geographical Magazine*, an e-mail came from an ex-student, Keith Laidlaw, who worked extensively in the panda reserves. His e-mail told me a sorry tale of deforestation, which attacked at the very roots of the conservation movement: despite all the money that has been spent on trying to save the panda, this amazing animal was still heading for extinction. One of the reasons was the increasing number of tourists who visit the area in the hope of catching a glimpse of this icon of conservation: to satiate their desires the bamboo forests on which the panda and hence the tourist trade depends were being felled at an ever-increasing rate. One starts to wonder whose icon is conning who?

Keith's idea was that instead of just paying the administration a fixed sum for every panda born in the wild, he wanted to turn the tide of destruction, to work with the locals in a more proactive way. His plan was to pay them, first to replant bamboo corridors joining the reserves and then rehabilitate the forests themselves. What a fantastic flagship project that should have been for the carbon sequestration fund: no more begging bowl appeals but at last a chance to get stuck in to the real business of wildlife. So, when Keith asked me to head up a new panda fund of course I said 'Yes'.

Despite my disappointment at all the clouds on the green horizon, at the time of my letter to John Prescott I was preparing a keynote speech to be delivered at the annual symposium of the Society of Environmental Lawyers in Australia. I have put a copy of the relevant parts of that power point presentation in Appendix 7, for I believe it shows very clearly the direction of my life's endeavours. I closed my presentation by quoting Francis Bacon's prayer, first intoned around 400 years ago, in relation to the then nascent philosophy of science and scientists. With no malice aforethought I think it is equally applicable to law and lawyers: 'Humbly we pray that this mind may be steadfast in us, and that through these hands, and the hands of others to whom thou shalt give the same spirit, thou wilt vouchsafe to endow the human family with new mercies.'

For those who are asking why I have given genetic engineering such brief mention, my answer is this. As a scientist I would have to agree that such fields of endeavour should be followed, but for the right reasons and with all the right controls. The possibilities of rogue transpoisons, mobile genetic elements or newly-created deadly viruses getting out of control is awesome and the potential result too horrible to contemplate. Consider the oil seed rape, which has put yellow stripes down the backs of so many fields. It has been engineered to require other herbicides and thrives on lots of fertiliser and pesticides, and yet Monsanto in all their glory never apprised the public of the fact that it underperforms all other varieties. The most frightening thing is that if they had not been so blatantly greedy and had selected a Third World crop, say millet, and engineered it to use less water or require less phosphate or nitrate, they might have got away with it. Think on these things. I know it is not that simple, and some will say it's Bellamy, that starry eyed optimist all over again, but I fervently hope that genetic engineering as it has been put into practice to date, is dead.

Another reason that I must look on the optimistic side of this equation is that, across the world, sustainable agricultural policies and technologies are succeeding. The annual growth rate of organic agriculture in Europe in the last decade of the last millennium averaged 25 per cent. Extrapolated forward, this would lead to 10 per cent of western European agriculture being organic by 2005, and 30 per cent by 2010. It is all part of the green renaissance; more and more ordinary people are demanding good healthy food and a safer more biodiverse environment. I still believe that when enough ordinary people articulate these demands, eventually things have to happen.

I have never been a great shopper but Christmas shopping is always a joyful chore and anyone who lives up north knows that York is one of the ideal places in which to do it. So it came to pass that Rosemary, Theo and I were doing the rounds of the ancient city when we came across a shop, new to us. It was called 'And Albert', and it was full of the most wonderful things, hand-crafted products fair-traded from real live villages around the world. For me it was an Aladdin's Cave and I became an And Albert shopaholic. I chose the most fabulous pot from Cambodia and also ended up buying the cart that carried such works of daily art from the village to the market in Nhom Pen. I just had to meet

'Albert', and anyone else that had made all this possible. His real name turned out to be David Murden and he was an unlikely cross between Mahatma Gandhi and Indiana Jones. His mission was to regain the lost ark of the covenant of the spiritual relationship that has existed between village crafts and the village environment for millennia.

Coomaraswamy had questioned why western civilisation is hell bent on destroying cultures and then erecting museums to display the beauty of their every day artefacts. And Albert is reversing the process by putting what could become priceless antiques in the hands of common men and women and, in so doing, sharing that spirituality of the purpose of living, real live aid to sustainable cultures on both sides of the rich poor divide. I have been working with him ever since.

While all this was going on the Conservation Foundation's most successful campaign, Yews For The Millennium, was moving into top gear. In actual fact it was, like many others, a celebration of the bimillennium, for the turning of 1999 did mark 2000 years of Christianity. Having, over some twenty years, helped build up a data base of all of Britain's oldest yew trees, most of which are growing in churchyards, we set about taking cuttings from all those that are estimated to be more than 2000 years old. That means that they were growing here in Britain while Christ walked the Earth. As a tribute to that fact, over 7,000 groups of people attended services of dedication in twenty-nine cathedrals, churches and other important meeting places and collected their trees, tiny as they were, to be planted in the heart of their community, each one a living link with the life and times of Jesus.

The outcome of the Yews For The Millennium project has been exciting for many people who took part asked, 'What next?' and decided to act as local environmental expediters to speed all that is best in Agenda 21 in their own communities.

In Appendix 8 is the talk I gave when we launched the yews idea in a packed Southwark Cathedral in London. I feel it is appropriate to quote it in full for it does sum up why I am the way that I am, why I feel the way that I feel and why I campaign the way that I always have and will continue to do. That is, until my family celebrate my woodland burial; then I will become a tree, perhaps a yew, and start to do something really useful.

30 Unto Us A Grandchild Is Born

I LIKE TO think that it was my dabblings in the general election that prompted the BBC to ask me to take part in a star-studded advert, the aim of which was to persuade viewers to tune in to Auntie's coverage of parliamentary proceedings. My appearance in it was simple, all I had to say was, 'to have fun and access to culture for all'. The date of the recording was the night that spanned 30 November and 1 December 1999. It had to be at night, or rather in the early hours of the morning, because the chosen location was the British Museum, where age-old protocol demands that the visitors must not be disturbed. Only a few months earlier I had done a similar all night stand for Sky at the Natural History Museum, to link a three-hour blockbuster which certainly did a lot for my street cred as it was about the evolution of *The Simpsons*. This time the subject was on a more sombre note.

'To have fun and access to culture for all', a simple statement to make but not so easy to side step its relevance, especially when made in the great hall of a museum built on the profits of an empire that had once spanned the earth, a hall whose contents tell how the discovery of the Rosetta stone allowed the hieroglyphs and hence the heritage of an earlier empire to be translated into ancient Greek and so into English.

The more I said the words, and I had to say them again and again in order to get the shot exactly right in the eyes of the camera people (there were two, a male and a female), the more I realised that they were at the very heart of the American Declaration of Independence. As I said them, riots were occurring on the streets of Seattle against the biggest act of empire building the world has ever seen, GATT, the General Agreement on Tariffs and Trade – in a world in which the richest two hundred people already had more money than the poorest two billion. Put that in figures, 200 to 2,000,000,000, and the shockingness of the situation screams out that something must be done to balance the books by putting people back into the equation of livelihood.

The shoot over, I went into the corridor where the make-up lady removed her art form, which had transformed me from a very tired 66-year-old into something about which even electronic cameras can lie. Then it was back into the reality of a December morning that came complete with mizzle in Bloomsbury Square. The clouds lifted as I walked back to the hotel past Senate House where, forty-two years before I had received the momentous news of my degree. I walked on, past the University of London Union building to dodge the traffic across Euston Square. I had a full English breakfast, and it wasn't bad, overlooking the tide of people flooding up from the underground: environmentally friendly people, one hoped, dodging the traffic jams already building on the Euston Road. Then I jumped in a taxi to go to my next engagement.

As we turned across the front of the White House Hotel, the taxi swerved as a red car, complete with one of those overdressed ageing yuppies plus partner, crossed lanes to jump the queue. Realising that he was heading in the wrong direction he then braked hard and tried to reverse, roaring abuse out of the window. My taxi performed one of those turning feats which only London black cabs can perform and drew up beside the red car. A war of words ensued and the objectionable little man, verging on road rage, challenged my driver to a fight 'any place any time'. 'I got to drop this important geezer off in Kensington; follow me and then I'll sort you out,' came the taxi driver's reply. It was Cockney courtesy at its best, he had a job to do and he didn't even say 'old' geezer.

I was thrilled – I had never been called a geezer before. Off we went, minus the red car, weaving our way through a London all decked out with Christmas lights.

He took me to the Natural History Museum for the AGM of Plantlife. I had missed last year's, and so had presented my presidential address on video, my last words of which had been, 'I promise that I will be there in person in 1999, our tenth anniversary.' So I was.

It is great to have something to celebrate, and in ten years Plantlife has grown from what some said was a new blot on an already overfull landscape of environmental NGOs into a dynamic force that has really put plants on to the map of conservation. Jane Smart, its director – hard working mum of two little girls, aptly named Lilly and Poppy – has really made her mark on the national and international conservation scene. She is the leader of a group who don't just attend meetings and talk about the problems, but get on with the job of conservation at the peat face, helping more and more people to change the way they do things. This is a trend that seems to be catching, as the following advertisement, which appeared in several major broadsheets on 3 December, amply testifies.

APPEAL TO THE CITIZENS OF THE WORLD

The Parliament of the Republic and Canton of Geneva is opposed to any attempt to increase the power of the World Trade Organisation (WTO) within the framework of the new round of negotiations now envisaged.

As the democratically elected representative of the people, the Geneva Parliament is extremely concerned by the loss of power of the public authorities arising from the growing liberalisation of the world economy.

The final agreement of the Uruguay Round signed in Marrakesh in 1994 and the establishment of the WTO were both presented at the time as an opportunity to ensure the well being of the peoples of the member countries of the WTO through the development of trade. Today, however, it cannot be ignored that the WTO has failed on this count. What we are witnessing instead is a concentration of 'well-being' which benefits only a minority, while poverty continues to rise in the poorest countries and among the member states of the OECD. Faced with the growing instability of the markets, especially in the financial sector, the collapse of national economies and rising inequalities between and within countries, the time has come for a pause, at the very least, in this destructive process so that we can take stock of the policies conducted especially by the WTO, the IMF and the World Bank. Moreover, the agreements already concluded have seriously undermined the ability of communities to protect themselves against the social and environmental consequences which are now appearing. All the more urgent then is the need to call in question the policy pursued thus far.

The Parliament of the Republic and Canton of Geneva is opposed to all new negotiations designed to bring about liberalisation, especially where the aim is to extend the authority of the WTO to new sectors such as investment, competition and other services (leading ultimately to the privatisation of health and education in particular). The Parliament is also strongly opposed to the TRIPS (Trade-Related Aspects of Intellectual Property Rights) Agreement.

For these reasons, the Parliament of the Republic and Canton of Geneva wishes to add its voice to the appeal launched by 1800 NGOs world-wide for a moratorium on all new negotiations to extend the powers and scope of action of the WTO. The Parliament further calls for a review of the political, social, environmental and economic impacts of the existing WTO agreements to be conducted, from outside the organisation, by an impartial institution, which will duly consult the movements representative of civil society.

At last! A canton in one of the richest and most revered economies in the world was agreeing with the essence of everything that Edward Bellamy had written in times past and it was now time, surely, to change our ways of doing certain things. They were not alone. Over the last few years of the millennium more and more very wealthy people were either worried by the environmental problems that were pushing up their insurance premiums or, like Jimmy Goldsmith, they were having pangs of conscience. I was getting more and more requests to help some of their number find and purchase tracts of biodiverse landcape. Worried? Of course I was. What was their rationale? I started checking them out and decided that if they would work with a bona fide conservation group, and if they would sign up binding agreements as to the future of their investment it could be all systems go. Here was another chance, another part of the green renaissance that could help fast track the replacement of www.beggingbowl.com by www.wildlifebiz.org. That is why I am still an optimist and will carry on campaigning, even if I am sometimes on a lonely high wire.

One thing I will never forget is what I was doing at the dawn of the new millennium. I was head cook and bottle washer for a brand new hotel set high in the Haute Savoy region of France. No I hadn't decided to cash in on the high wages offered to tempt people to work on that auspicious night.

The saga had started about three years earlier when we helped Henrietta and husband Martin to purchase a sixteenth-century heap of stones, 1,500 metres above sea level, not far from Val d'Isère. To my untrained eye it looked like a demolition job, but seeing what Martin had already done on similar heaps at higher altitudes, we believed it could be ready for Christmastide 1999 and the millennium jollifications. Indeed it was fully booked: an English family with five children, two French couples and a party of four from Sweden.

Everything was on time until the early summer of 1999. Just when the hotel drains were going in, Martin ended up in hospital with medical drains in his arm, thanks to a bad dose of builder's elbow, a sort of tennis elbow with a vengeance. The happy news that Henrietta was pregnant certainly complicated the issue, and had Grand Mum very worried when Henry answered the phone from high on the roof where she was putting finishing touches to the tiles. There was a frantic work load but by October things were coming on apace, and the scans showed that the baby was a boy. Theo got excited that his first cousin had metamorphosed from 'it' into 'him', and when the name was announced we all looked forward to meeting Joshua sometime in early February.

Joshua, however, had a mind of his own and decided he wanted to see what the twentieth century was like, so off went Granny to take some of the workload off mum and try to make him hang in there a little longer. Floors and bathrooms were still being tiled and doors were being hung, but they were confident they were going to make it. So, countdown to the grand opening was started with 10 days to go, as Granny returned to Britain for the gathering of the rest of the Bellamy clan for Christmas. It was an almost white one and as usual we all over ate and drank not a little. The most hard-worked labour-saving device was the telephone which kept us up to date with avant and après ski and le bébé. A flood in one of the hotel's bathrooms was bad enough, but the total failure of the electrician and plumber to wire the main boiler signalled catastrophe. Friends rallied around and the latest condensing boiler, eco-friendly of course, sailed into action under jury rig just in time for the return of the skiers on Christmas Day.

Sighs of relief came from all gathered around the festive tables in England and France, but the biggest came from Joshua. So determined was he to join the Boxing Day festivities that he landed Henrietta, his personal solar powered intensive care unit, in the local hospital. Mayhem reigned again, but was alleviated by Martin's cousins who had dropped in for a week in the snow. Then a call for help hit Bedburn next day as Henrietta was moved to the big maternity unit in Chambéry, two hours plus away by ambulance down the valley.

All plans for the big party in Weardale were dropped as Granny, Grandad and Theo packed their bags and headed St Bernard like to the rescue, arriving on the evening of 28 December. The flight was OK but the weather in the Loire Valley was still getting over a bout of 160 kph winds and new snow covered parts of the motorway. The petrol gauge showed almost empty as we swung into the forecourt of the last station before home. It was shut. In a flurry of snow we shot up the hairpins, fingers crossed, towards St Foy. Splutter splutter, cough cough – we were going to be stuck out in the snow – but, no – we kangarooed round the last bend, to be welcomed by a sign strung across the road that said 2000 in green lights. The car sighed its last as Martin scrunched it into a snowdrift fifty metres away from our night's lodging in the spare room of the friendly plumber who had saved the situation by working on Christmas Day to rig the boiler.

Not only did he have a spare gallon of petrol but also some great red wine, and as Martin headed up the last twenty hairpins to Chalet Chevalier we turned into a fold-out bed, surrounded by computers and all the other paraphernalia of running the busy office of a busy plumber who doubles as a star turn singer at the local hotel gigs.

With two days to the new millennium, Martin turned up bright and early to collect us, and the bread needed to feed the ravening hordes before they left for the pistes. Fortune would have it that the last four guests, who had just driven for twenty-four hours, all the way from Sweden, arrived early. This was not the best thing to happen as the English party were only just on their way home and it was change over time in the bottom apartment. The leavers had done all they could to make the job easy, but my respect for chambermaids grew by the minute as floors were hoovered, baths and tiles cleaned, beds stripped and towels arranged.

The dress rehearsal on the thirtieth came all too quickly, with happy skiers returning for vin chaud, coffee and Christmas cake. Then it happened, no hot water, the boiler had packed up, and there were twenty tired skiers all demanding baths or showers. A quick look at the boiler highlighted the problem – no cowl on the exhaust chimney; the pilot light had blown out. Thank God it was an English boiler and with the help of Lieutenant Commander Cousin Dion it was soon roaring away. Soon there were shrieks of joy from all the bathrooms, and then the meal was a great success, boding well for millennium night.

With the last reveller off to bed, we climbed the snow-covered steps up to Danielle's place, where we had been offered the gîte for the night, Hotel Chevalier being full to overflowing. The light of our torch revealed the door to a low totally rustic room with a roaring fire in a well-cracked shamrock shaped cast iron stove. The bed, which filled almost half of the room, was covered with what looked like a sheepskin, although contact revealed that it was made of some form of man-made fibre. Theo who had been doing medieval history at school backed off with the exclamation, 'That's the sort of bed that gave people the plague.' After some deep discussion we all climbed in, and the next thing we knew it was the morning of Millennium Eve. The fire had long since gone out and room temperature was well below zero.

Having despatched Martin to see the still-expectant mum far away in Chambéry – Joshua had changed his mind – the Bellamy team swung into action. Chambermaiding was already second nature, but the big meal needed a lot of planning. Starters, salami, crostini and pickles, soup, asparagus, salmon, potatoes, haricots, Thom, Beauforte, St Marcellin – and Blue Stilton to add the Royal English touch – a gigantic salad like the one I used to make for the students on the field trips, apple pie – a present from our neighbours – coffee and chocolates, all had to be ready.

Time flew until 16.00 hours when the boiler should have cut in. Silence. I was on my own, with basic plumbing skills from half a century ago and lots of theory concerning boiler control systems from the adverts. I slid on my bottom down the backway to the boiler house. Pilot light on, all systems go, I turned the starter knob – a cold silence. Out in the gas store it was all too obvious. There was a smell of propane and both of the big cylinders were empty. What do you do at five past four on Millennium Eve, 1,500 metres up a mountain, and you are out of gas? Answer: pinch one from the kitchen. Thank God there was a spare.

The kitchen was seething with activity as the first round of fireworks in Val d'Isère, Bourg, Mirabelle, Les Arc and all ski stations north, south, east and west lit up the sky. Salmon on, vegetables in, it was all going like olive oiled clockwork. Martin turned up with good news from Chambéry: Joshua was still in captivity and mother was bored but doing fine. There was no sign of the guests – of course they had all stayed to watch the fireworks. How do you slow down grilled salmon? Well, we did our best as in they trailed, ready for a bath. 'Non, non, le repas est immédiatement,' we begged, so they sat down, and by the time the coffee and biscuits were devoured they were in such a good mood that they took the 'Please go easy on the water' almost with a smile. There was sufficient water to satisfy some and they all emerged as the dancing began. We had the champagne and nibbles at the ready.

Then it happened; the telephone rang. Martin answered and a look of amazement came over his face. Josh had had his way, just seeing the light of 1999. He was only 1.75 kilos but both baby and Mum were doing fine. A 21-gun salute of champagne corks rent the air as neighbours dropped in for a bye-bye millennium and hello-baby party, both premature by about ninety minutes.

Little did we know, but over in Singapore another grandchild had just been conceived, Robin Eden by name. She happened in a new millennium and that's another story.

The millennium was something very special, but an everyday event such as a baby being born rubs home the fact that each one of us is but part of the story of the human genome which has been going on for at least 3.6 billion years. So it was that with bated laptop, I awaited the result of the human genome project. The results were surprising in the extreme and certainly didn't help the cause of genetic engineering one iota. It had been given so much hype that the peer reviewers, who would turn a blind eye to anything which their paymasters didn't want to appear in print, had to sit back and see the ultimate cat let out of the bag. In the words of Craig Venter, one of the superstars of the Celera genomics team, 'one gene leads to many different proteins that can change once they are produced.' In effect, genetic determinism is officially dead, a fact that knocked off a lot more than the smiles on the faces of gullible investors.

When Sir Bob May, President of the Royal Society, rose to his feet to sum up the Welcome Trust's celebration of the human genome project, he expressed dismay at the 'First-World centredness of the project' and said that 'the extent to which anthropocentrism has dominated the proceedings is shocking'. He was scathing in his criticism of the panel, and said he 'had expected much more'. He also said that they had 'singularly failed to grasp the most important implication of the findings of the human genome project'. He pointed out how close we are genetically to a nematode worm, reminding us of our interconnectedness to the rest of the living realm.

The great news is that the whole world can keep a watching brief on developments in these murky fields by tuning in to www.i-sis.org. What is more, my wish of more than two decades ago has come true: Beverley Williams, now Goodger, has joined the team and is busy putting www.wildlifebiz.org on line to spread the good news of the green renaissance. See you there.

APPENDICES

APPENDIX 1

Preface to *Sylva: The Tree in Britain* by Archie Miles

Sylva more precious than gold. You hold in your hand a very precious thing; it started its life as a tree growing free in one of the forests of the world.

Throughout its first life it soaked up carbon dioxide from an overheating global greenhouse. Producing the purest of oxygen as a by-product of its growing pains. Evaporating water it cooled its ambience, exhaling fluffy white sunshade clouds. Clouds, which move on the wind to protect other places and recycle the water they contain, bringing life to landscapes further from the coast.

Its leaves, twigs and seeds fell to earth, feeding a myriad worms, insects, arthropods, fungi and bacteria which together make mor (rich organic humus), binding the soil to hold minerals and water on the catchment and recycling nutrient, all in the service of generations to come. Birds and mammals hunted, browsed and raised their young within the ombrage of strong branches, protected from but celebrating the changing of the seasons. Shielding the earth from the icy winds of winter, the canopy kept the forest floor clear of snow so that frosts could penetrate deep, cleansing and rejuvenating the rich soils. Spring and the rising of the sap saw leaves burst into bud as new roots made their way through the soil, binding it together and holding it ever safer from erosion. While the pulpit of branches held up to heaven gave vantage points for feathered choristers to sing their songs of love and hymns of praise.

The heat of summer, ameliorated by the canopy, witnessed the acrobatics of myriad inchworms dangling on silken threads, well-gorged acrobats spinning their cocoons of metamorphosis. The rivers draining from the forest still ran sweet and cool, even in the driest of summers, thanks to the magic of the forest, which stores and releases last season's rain.

Lamas tide is a very special season that pertains only to trees. This is the time when they produce a new crop of leaves as they prepare a harvest home for themselves and all that live among them or come to visit.

Autumn washes the stains of a job well done from the face of the earth. As leaves show their true colours garnering the forest with a host of fruits, nuts and seeds enough to see another winter through.

All this you hold in your hand, treasure it for its origins and the wisdom inscribed upon its pages. When like its author you have gained respect for the trees of the Earth upon which they grow, do all you can to safeguard the little that is left of the wildwoods of our planet. Without those wildwoods and all the genetic stock they contain and conserve there is no chance of helping those who are heaven bent on rehabilitating this our planet, which is in a sorry state of repair.

This is a leviathan of a book as majestic as the Ents of *The Lord of the Rings*; this is your chance to share in the sense and sensibility of the trees marching with Tolkein's army to reclaim the world.

David Bellamy
Bedburn 1999

APPENDIX 2

Review of *Gerald Durrell: The Biography* by Douglas Botting

The last time I visited Gerry's Zoo was in the summer of 1998, the occasion to launch a fund raising film festival with the screening of *Baraka*. To quote the programme notes 'an extraordinary visual odyssey concerning the passionate and destructive relationship between people and this vibrant living planet'.

I had of course seen the film before and had been uplifted by and humbled beneath its spectacle, to see it in the open air in such a special place was awesome indeed.

It was not the best of Jersey summer nights, warm but with more than a hint of rain in the air. I was glad when the first drops came for they helped hide my tears, shed not only for the scenes of man's stupidity to man and to the living planet upon which we all depend, but because something seemed to be missing from Les Augres.

The scents and the sense (and it is without doubt one of the most common sensible places in the world) of the Zoo were all around us. Musk sweet from the plains of Africa, the restful restlessness of Orangs in the Bornean forest and the call of the Pink Pigeon echoing the sadness of extinction on Dodo Island. Most poignant of all were the memories of Jambo, patriarch of Jersey's lowland gorillas who, by standing guard over an unconscious child that had fallen into the enclosure, perhaps did as much for the cause of zoos and conservation as Gerry did himself.

All this and so much more, living shadows in the Jersey mist but something was missing, the man who made it all possible.

Those lucky enough to have met him will know what I mean. Jacquie, Lee and all the other members of his devoted team who had helped build, launch and keep his dream ark afloat, deserve all the praise they can get. But without the burning passion, irascible nature and sense of humour that was Gerry Durrell it would never have happened. Without the Jersey Wildlife Preservation Trust the world would be an even sadder, less sustainable and hence more dangerous place than it is today. Conservation is not a simple concept of just saving endangered species, it must take people into consideration as well.

The most memorable dinner I ever had the pleasure to attend was with Gerry and HRH Princess Anne before the opening of the Sixth World Conference on Animal Breeding. Both are great raconteurs and though stories revolved around everything under the sun and quite a lot beyond they centred on the problem of how to save the wildlife and the children of the world. It was here that I came to realise the depth of Gerry's understanding of world ecology and of the Princess Royal's dedication to both causes. In a world run the wrong way, the sad truth is that the more children that are saved the less room there is in which wildlife can survive. In a world run sustainably there must be room for both.

The party for the Zoo's coming of age was another great occasion with all Gerry's friends performing in the great Jersey Auditorium a celebration of and a fund-raiser for his endeavour. The high spot of the evening, his entrance on the stage, supported by two children dressed as what else but dodos, said it all. If only the Jersey Trust had been set up a few centuries earlier perhaps the dodo and so many now extinct animals would still be here to enthral, entertain, educate and support us in the struggle for our own survival. I was privileged to play a small part in the evening championing the cause of plants, before I sang 'Mud

Mud Glorious Mud' with Isla St Clair who looked not unlike a gorgeous hippopotamus. No I am not being rude for although our item was billed as a duet it was in actual fact a trio, for Isla produced a baby next day.

We all remember who put the scorpions in the matchbox, the water snakes in the bath. Who showed the world that, that 'bloody boy', 'the most ignorant boy in the school', loved animals more than anything else. We all enjoyed the *Bafut Beagles*, *My Family and other Animals* and all those other wonderful paperbacks, but how about those magical snippets of poetry.

> A voluptuous young mink called Saranne
> Said 'I've thought of an excellent plan
> If we had a reversal
> Of what's universal
> Then I could be wearing a man.'

Well this is your chance to rediscover the man who for over sixty years exasperated and fascinated his friends and his fans, giving hope to generations that there was a future for animals, plants and people, as long as we learn to share the wonder of this living planet.

Douglas Botting is to be congratulated; he has done a magnificent job, the complex story of a complex person, wrinkles and all. Only two questions remain unanswered. Why did so many other small boys visit Corfu and swat rather than swot insects and why this champion of the cause of conservation was never given the Knighthood he so well deserved?

Lest we forget, both Attenborough and Durrell started their writing and television careers as hunters of game, each bagging many trophies. Images of animals living in their natural state, caught on film or video, perhaps for the last time, the live ones doomed to live in captivity for the rest of their lives. Zoo Quest became Zoo Check; bad zoos must be closed down, but good zoos need our support, for in Durrell's eyes these cages of despair took on a new meaning. They became zoological gardens of hope. The only real hope we have got of putting the world back into biodiverse working order.

Some still argue that it is but a vain hope, Gerry's dream can never work, 5,000 species of vertebrate are doomed to extinction. I challenge them to go and see for themselves. Gerry's vision has come true; Les Augres has become the University of the Living World. There you will find students of every colour, creed and kind learning not only humility within the process of creative evolution but the practice of captive breeding and release back into the wild.

We can only pray that he was right, so that one day, when the world has come to its senses, the doors of Gerry's Ark and all the other good zoos he has spawned across the world will be opened, their animals set free to help us learn to live in peace and harmony as part of a truly civilised vibrant living earth. It's got to work for man cannot survive alone on this planet.

Baraka drew to its climax, the final chapter from apocalypse to revelation a revelation of understanding that can save the world. The rain had stopped and as we walked out through the summer night there was no need for tears, Gerry was still there, not in person but an all-enveloping presence of hope for all our futures. Sir Gerry Durrell of Les Augres and the Living World. The world salutes you and all the animals say thank you too.

Appendix 3

Paper in *Nature*, 26th June 1968

Application of the Second Law
Of Thermodynamics and Le Chatelier's Principle
to the Developing Ecosystem
by
David J. Bellamy and Peter H. Clarke
Departments of Botany and Engineering Science,
University of Durham

'Living organisms (biota) and their non-living (abiotic) environment are inseparably interrelated and interact on each other. Any area of nature that includes living organisms and non-living substances interacting to produce an exchange of materials between the living (biotic) and the non-living (abiotic) parts is an ecosystem' (modified after Odum). The driving force which causes this exchange is the energy incident on the given area. That part of the energy which is fixed by the photosynthetic biomass is either used by the respiring biomass or is stored in chemical form as standing crop, extra cellular produce, humus or peat.

The localised storage of energy within the system brings about the process of succession, which may be defined as a linked change of the biotic and abiotic components of the ecosystem. Succession passes through several stages to a complex, highly ordered, state, in which the stored (ordered) energy of the system remains at a quasi-constant level. In this state in unit time an amount of energy equal to that fixed by the process of photosynthesis is used in the maintenance of the ecosystem, an equal amount of energy being lost from the system by heat transfer.

Kelvin summarised the Second Law of Thermodynamics in his concept of the degradation of energy, 'owing to the irreversible processes of nature the availability of energy to do work decreases'.

Consider the ecosystem and the incident energy falling on it. The incident energy is both the driving force of the ecosystem and of succession. A pioneer ecosystem has a small biomass and fixes, stores and respires (degrades) only a small proportion of the incident energy. While there is energy reaching the ecosystem which is not fixed by the process of photosynthesis, there is the possibility of an increase in the efficiency of the system to fix this energy. All the time there is energy fixed but not utilised in the process of respiration, this energy is stored by the ecosystem and succession occurs. Succession passes through a series of states in which an increasing amount of the incident energy is degraded until a state is reached in which, in unit time, an amount of energy equal to that fixed is used (degraded) in the maintenance of the ecosystem. This state can be termed 'climax'. The ceiling level of energy degradation will be determined by the environmental factors limiting the system, and the state of evolution of the biota, in respect to these factors.

It would therefore seem that the Second Law infers that succession should occur; the system should tend towards a state of maximum degradation of the energy associated with it. The more generalised statement of the Second Law by Clausius, 'entropie strebt einem maximum zu' (entropy is a measure of the non-availability of energy to do useful work), lends weight to this idea.

Classical thermodynamics can, however, only be applied to

equilibrium states. Considering the seral ecosystem and the incident energy, equilibrium states only exist before development has started and again once it has reached climax. During the intervening period of development the ecosystem undergoes an irreversible change. De Groots uses generalised classical thermodynamics to consider irreversible processes. In his formulation of Le Chatelier's principle, he states that if an irreversible system is perturbed, that is, if one of its characteristic parameters is changed, then the system undergoes such a transformation as to oppose the change. In the seral ecosystem the parameter in question is the degradation of incident light energy, which is tending to increase. The ecosystem responds by storing energy in ordered chemical form; this stored energy brings about succession.

It may therefore be concluded that the Second Law infers that succession should occur and that the localised build-up of energy in the biomass is caused by the opposing force suggested by Le Chatelier.

Appendix 4

Television Series

Life in Our Sea, BBC, 1970.
Bellamy on Botany, BBC, 1973.
Bellamy's Britain, BBC, 1975.
Bellamy's Europe, BBC, 1977.
Botanic Man, ITV, 1979.
An Island Called Danger, BBC.
Up a Gum Tree, BBC.
Don't Ask Me, ITV.
It's Life, ITV.
It's More Life, ITV.
The Gene Machine, ITV, 1980.
Backyard Safari, BBC, 1981.
The Great Seasons, BBC, 1982.
Bellamy's New World, BBC, 1983.
You Can't See The Wood, BBC, 1984.
Seaside Safari, BBC, 1985.
The End of the Rainbow Show, ITV, 1986.

Bellamy's Bugle, ITV, 1986.
Turning the Tide, ITV, 1986.
Bellamy's Birds' Eye View, ITV, 1988.
Moa's Ark, TVNZ, 1990.
Swallow, ITV.
Bellamy on top of the World, ITV.
Paradise Ploughed, ITV.
Bellamy Rides Again, BBC.
The Owl and the Woodsman, ITV.
Journey to the Centre of the World, ITV.
Wheat Today What Tomorrow?, (Video).
England's Lost Wilderness, ITV, 1991.
England's Last Wilderness, ITV, 1992.
Routes of Wisdom, ITV, 1993.
The Peak, ITV.
Bellamy's Border Raids, ITV.
Bellamy's Singapore, STV.
Blooming Bellamy, BBC, 1994; 1995.
A Knotty Problem (Video).
Inserts for *Blue Peter*, BBC.
Honey Gatherers, MTV, 1996.
Westwatch, ITV.
Rockdust, (Video).
Turning Points, BBC.
Upstream with Bellamy, Radio BBC, 1997.
World of the Reef, (CD Rom).

Appendix 5

Groups and Campaigns

President

Bat Conservation Trust
British Homes and Holiday Parks Association
British Camping and Caravanning Club of Great Britain
British Institute Of Cleaning Science
British Naturalists Association
Buchan Countryside Group
Conservation Foundation London
Conservation Volunteers Ireland
Coral Cay Conservation Ltd
Galapagos Conservation Trust
Marine Conservation Society Australia
National Association For Environmental Education
National Council of Master Thatchers Associations
Plant Life
Population Concern

Seaham Environmental Association
Watch
Vale Royal Environmental Network
Wildlife Trusts Partnership
Youth Hostels Association

Vice President

Arboricultural Association
British Trust for Conservation Volunteers
Countrywide Holidays Association
Cotswold Water Park
Marine Conservation Society
Meddaset
Flora and Fauna International

A Selection of Trustee Chair and Patronages

Arbory Trust
British Chelonian Group
British Homeopathic Association
British Sub Aqua Club
Chongololo Club Zambia
Festival of The Countryside Wales
Institute of Complimentary Medicine
John Ray Trust
Living Landscape Trust
New Zealand Native Forest Restoration Trust
Royal Environmental Health Association of Scotland
Padi Aware
St Werburgh's City Farm
Southport Flower Show
Troy Trust
West Midlands Youth Ballet
Young Peoples Trust for the Environment and Nature

APPENDIX 6

Letter to John Prescott 19 July 1999

Dear Mr Prescott,

> Renewable energy/Ospar and funding opportunities

This is the fifth letter I have written to you on the above subject. I also discussed the matter when you telephoned me in Singapore seeking my advice on coral reefs and global warming. I received no acknowledgement of that advice nor a reply to any of my letters. I hope this letter prompts a response.

I find myself in a state of despair over two issues of great environmental importance, both with their own needs and deficiencies but each capable of solving the other's problem. Consider this: the oil industry is required by the Ospar decision to spend $20 billion to remove millions of tons of steel from the ocean. This is in environmental terms a meaningless act for the platforms to be removed have no demonstrable deleterious impact on the ocean or its biota. In fact, there is much evidence to suggest that such structures are the only places where our beleaguered fish stocks can find some respite from the profligacies of the Common Fisheries Policy. What is more, the Ospar agreement, incredibly, has not been based on any credible impact assessment: it was, as we all know, a political decision, not an environmental one.

At the same time, the funding needs of renewable energy – something to which you are committed both individually and from a government perspective – are enormous. Conferences are being held to discuss possible sources for the investment needed to finance wind, wave and solar power projects. The industry, which could revitalise our shipyards, needs billions in investment.

Research we have carried out has shown that the oil industry would not be opposed to seeing the $20 billion it is required to spend on removing redundant platforms used in a more positive and meaningful way. Nor would at least some sections of the green movement. Yet there seems to be a bureaucratic impasse, which prevents the senseless spending of money in one area being re-directed to another, more effective and profitable area.

Sadly, the $20 billion is only the tip of a very large iceberg, for when the oil industry begins to publicly discuss the options for dealing with seabed platform spoil or cuttings, the same misguided voices will doubtless demand they are removed. The cost and environmental consequences of that operation can only be guessed at. Unless there is strong evidence that toxins released from these deposits are already entering the food chain, it would surely be better to leave them undisturbed rather than stir up the potential for real trouble.

Such massive sums of money as the oil industry is planning to spend on recycling platforms would surely be better spent in getting this country on its renewable energy feet quickly, rather than being frittered away in order to appease some of the greens and do little in terms of dealing with the perennial and intractable environmental issues we face.

The way out of this unholy mess is two fold: we must discuss the implications of Ospar openly with all interested parties and I would urge you to call a meeting of the key players, greens, government and oil companies (but no more than six or seven people) to put these issues on the table and to find a sensible common approach. Secondly, as a supporting effort to that meeting or as a possible outcome, there must be a thorough and exhaustive study commissioned from an independent body to look at best environmental practice in dealing with the redundant platform issue.

Of course, this should have taken place before the Ospar decision was taken, but a retroactive study will be just as valuable in the longer run.

There must be a political solution to the twin problems we have of wasting enormous amounts of money on spurious 'clean seabed' issues and the need for large amounts of investment in renewables quickly in order to remove our dependence on fossil fuels and the environmental consequences of that dependence at the earliest possible time.

I look forward to your early reply and I fervently hope that you will give serious consideration to the matters raised in this letter.

Appendix 7

An Environmentalist's Vision of the Future

A statement from the Australian Commission for the Future perhaps best summarises what I believe both my keynote and this symposium is all about: 'The future is not some place we are going to, but one we are creating. The paths to it are not found but made. The making of these pathways changes both the maker and the destination.'

This statement is no more or no less than an extension of the Songline Philosophy of the Aboriginal people, the original human settlers of this great land, a philosophy that helped them develop the resources of their island continent over a period of at least 50,000 years.

We now know that the process which turned a lifeless planet into the living Earth as we have come to know it, took at least 3.6 billion years, a process of gradual change, that made it ever more possible for more complex forms of life to carve their niche within an ever more complex biosphere.

Biodiversity is both the stuff and the spice of life. Biodiversity exists because living things are born, grow, reproduce, excrete and die. Plants and animals compete with each other, defending their territories with pitched battles. Living sentient things are eaten and living sentient things eat each other. Mother Nature in all her biodiverse forms is red in tooth and claw.

Humanity is set aside from that process by one sole attribute, knowledge of right and wrong, ethics, spirituality, call it what you will. We alone can learn from history, be it natural or people made, and put the things of good report into action. We alone can worry about what we do. We alone can formulate laws and train lawyers. This is a cross we have to bear thanks to the fact that we are part of the process of creation, evolution or whatever you like to call it.

The Law of the Biosphere is elegant in its simplicity. Only the fittest survive in the struggle for existence. If *Homo sapiens sapiens* wants to survive, we have got to change the ways we have been doing things since long before Plato established the world's first university, the remains of which were recently discovered under a parking lot in the grid-locked tourist destination that is called Athens, where air pollution often makes life, let alone healthy relaxation, intolerable.

In the year 387 BC, 480 plus years before the writing of the *Apocalypse*, Plato established the first university. It was called 'The Academy', from which we get the word academic. Socrates visited the Academy. Most of what we know about Socrates is from Plato's writings. Socrates saw that philosophy is essentially about life. In his comment 'we are discussing no small matter, but how we ought to live', he showed that he shared a common concern with the conveners of this symposium.

We can see from Plato's *Timaeus* and *Critias* how Greek debate was conducted within the framework of an understanding of ecological history. The *Critias* refers to the detrimental effects of felling the thick woods of prehistoric Greece. The rich soft soil had all run away, leaving the land wasted and the springs and streams dried up. Plato goes on to describe how the great oaken beams in disused temples are the only records of the springs of the gods who were once worshipped in those places. This bears out what science has now proved about the effects of deforestation. What is more, insurance agencies across the world are today rightfully questioning claims relating to floods caused by profligate catchment mismanagement.

In 1776 it was written: 'We hold these truths to be self evident, that all men are created equal, that they are endowed by their creator with certain inalienable rights, that among these are life, liberty and the pursuit of happiness.' In the original draft of the American Declaration of Independence, Jefferson had instead ended the sentence with the word 'wealth'. Why he made the amendment, and how long it took him, we shall never know. We can only surmise that as a farmer and a statesman, even 150 years before the dust bowls first shattered the American Dream, he knew there were limitations 'to nature and to nature's god'. I use his own words.

In 1836, when Charles Darwin visited Australia, he wrote, 'I had formerly imagined that Australia would rise to be as grand and powerful a country as North America, but now it appears to me that such future grandeur is problematical. Pasture is everywhere so thin that settlers have already pushed too far into the interior; moreover the country further inland becomes extremely poor, therefore so far as I can see, Australia must ultimately depend on being the centre of commerce for the Southern Hemisphere.'

'Shades of Malthusian scepticism' you may well say; however a submission to Australia's House of Representatives by CSIRO (one of the world's leading scientific agencies) in June 1994 backed up Darwin's conclusions. 'Australia can carry its present population in an economically, environmentally and socially sustainable way, only if the Nation is prepared to change the way it does things.' It then goes on to outline a programme of research and redevelopment, the best I have ever seen exemplifying all the principles of Agenda 21 (that revolutionary proposal that came out of the Rio Environmental Summit), a programme which includes increasing the efficiency and international competitiveness of your cities as centres of environmentally benign commercial activity. The ball for really positive change was then firmly in the court of Australia and its aid programmes.

Data collated by Earth Watch in the run up to the new millennium highlighted the following facts. The past decade has unleashed a torrent of capital unprecedented in history, but most of the world's population has seen little impact on their day to day lives. Thirty per cent of today's households still survive on less than $1 a day. In consequence if you add up all the wealth of the world's poorest 2 billion people it matches the combined wealth of the world's 200 richest people. Governance in such a world appears to be becoming increasingly difficult. The vast majority of the poor are women, and usually women with children. Women do 67 per cent of the world's work; earn 10 per cent of the world's pay and own 1 per cent of the world's property. Thirty-five thousand of these women's children die of hunger every day. That is 12.8 million every year.

The skewness of the wealth distribution is highlighted by the fact that if a sustainable energy budget was to be shared equally by the current world population of 6 billion (only 200 years ago it was a mere 1 billion), there would be no meat, no dairy products (hooray say the vegans), only five litres of hot water per person per day, no fridges, no space heating, no air conditioning, no air travel, no new housing developments, no overseas imports etc. etc., for an overall energy consumption of 45 petajoules.

Two-thirds of living species will be extinct in the next 100 years due to the destruction of the environment, caused by people. The oceans too are under siege, with vast dead zones where oxygenated water and life are scarce. The largest dead zone is not in the Third World but in the Gulf of Mexico, whose waters are polluted by the Mississippi River. A century ago an armada of local fishers harvested 20 million bushels of oysters from the margins of Chesapeake Bay, which covers 165,000 sq. kilometres. The oysters not only provided nutritious food, they also helped keep the waters of the bay clean by their filtration. Gross overfishing and two oyster diseases slashed the population of filter feeders down to a mere one per cent of its former glory, thus exacerbating the problems of pollution emanating from the 15 million people of six states who now live on the catchment.

The good news is that, thanks to teams of scientists and an army of volunteer citizens, three-dimensional reefs are being constructed, new homes for the army of filter feeding molluscs, while redundant oil rigs are being developed as artificial reefs to speed recovery of fish stocks in the Gulf of Mexico.

There is little doubt in my mind that the green renaissance is under starter's orders. Across the world, people are worried about what the future holds for their children and grandchildren, and insurance companies are worried about much more than their bottom lines when paying out claims for floods caused by profligate catchment mismanagement. So what is my vision of the future?

The best news of all is that all indicators point to a scenario in which the human population will stabilise in the year 2050 at around 10 billion. The problem then is not only how to service their needs but also how to keep them happy.

The bad news is that the best studies carried out to date show that in order to produce all their needs and sequester all their wastes, the average citizen living in the First World requires the equivalent of 4.5 hectares of good soil. Without technology the world population should then be no more than 1 billion.

In consequence a new brand of really civil engineering is going to have to take the strain. Fortunately, on 30 June 2000, the British Institution of Civil Engineers and the American Society of Civil Engineers signed an agreement to work together for the good of humanity and the environment. Despite the fact that the media didn't even bother to cover the event, it was one hell of a leap in the right direction for humankind.

My vision for the future is this. Every child will be a wanted child, and one for whom the Earth can provide a fulfilling life. All areas of land that have been ruined by profligate mismanagement will be returned to their 'natural' state as soon as possible as part of worldwide integrated catchment and coastal management. Riverside wetlands, water meadows and forests will be put back in place to control erosion, ease flooding and strip excess nutrients from the rivers and carbon dioxide from the overheated global greenhouse. All unproductive soils will be put back to native heath and woodland. All steep slopes will be protected by native vegetation, which is not under threat of logging, overgrazing or unplanned fire.

All native forest, woodlands, savannah, scrub, heathland, grasslands, wetlands, mountain pastures and moorland that are left will be gazetted and managed as habitat reserves and hence gene bank reserves into perpetuity, reserves that will continue to supply the wealth of natural genestock for an ethically regulated plant and animal breeding industry, which recognises and rewards intellectual property rights. These will be locked in with buffer zones of native vegetation, which will be locked in with sustainably grazed and harvested crops of native species. In essence one third of each type of landscape will be put back into 'natural' working order.

The other two-thirds of selected catchments will be developed for sustainable agriculture, forestry and building infrastructure; the latter will be planned to be contained by law within no more than 10 per cent of any but certainly not of every catchment area.

Production of staple foods will be concentrated in those areas of the world best suited to their husbandry (which, apart from rice, should not include irrigation), using a mix of the best available crop varieties, always using integrated crop management and organic production wherever possible.

Semi organic orchards will be producing fruit. Planning will be well advanced to ensure that all truck farm crops (soft fruit and vegetables) will be produced using green grow technology (hydroponics and aeroponics) which close both the water and the nutrient cycles. All animal production will be free range and free from steroids or other booster chemicals. World fisheries, electronically regulated to sustainable catches, will be rapidly replaced by fish and shell fish farms, that are fed on the byproducts of horticulture and via plankton farms that will themselves strip nutrients from the products of our effluent society. All such farms will then be on closed cycles in relation to nutrients and water. The ultimate aim will be to slowly wind down the need to harvest the wild stocks of any marine organisms, leaving the seas unsullied to perform their natural functions of carbon sequestration, oxygen production and to play their vital part in the water and nutrient cycles. Wind, solar and fuel cell powered cruise ships of many sizes will ply the ocean as the mainstay of the international tourist trade.

There will be vibrant cities of various sizes, each multicultural yet each maintaining its cultural roots, and each producing at least 70 per cent of its own food within its hinterland, in part by recycling its many organic wastes. Each city will be united as complexes of 'village' communities governed through subsidiarity. A large proportion of the rural population will live in well-serviced villages that are not threatened with loss of their schools, post offices and shops. Their inhabitants will engage in food production, diversified by high-tech cottage industries and country pursuits and 'ecotourism', that is, nature conservation, walking, riding, hunting, shooting and fishing. Such countryside pursuits will pay for catchment and landscape management, the control of ferals and the governance of the rural areas.

Large tourist complexes, Disney Lands, Sun Cities, Center Parcs, will all be as close to large conurbations as possible to cut down the necessity of travel for the bulk of their visitors. Each one will be built on rehabilitated land and, wherever possible, locked in by large areas returned to native vegetation.

If you are tempted to say that this is pie in the sky, and it could never happen, then think on this. Not a million miles away from this room, a public demonstration recently demanded the cessation of logging in the States' old-growth forest. Groups of local volunteers led by the Men of the Trees of Western Australia are hard at work planting millions of trees – the right trees in the right place to help return man-made salt desert to productive agriculture once again. A programme of sustainable plantations orchestrated by the States conservation body, Calm, is already stripping nutrients out of 120,000 hectares of abandoned farmlands, thus protecting downstream and inshore fisheries from the problems of eutrophication. Western Australia has some of the best-regulated fisheries in the world, and Rotness Island is a jewel in the crown of sustainable tourism.

Meanwhile, all across Australia, Earth Sanctuaries is busy buying up 1 per cent of the landmass and rehabilitating it back to a more natural state. In order to do this the company which was recently floated on the stock market has bought breeding stock of marsupials from the well-managed reserves of Western Australia's department of Conservation and Land Management, and successfully reintroduced them back into other States in which they were deemed extinct.

There are plenty of similar good-news stories from around the world, but good news rarely makes the headlines. Sadly, there is of course much catastrophic news which *does* get reported: one reason why so many people are worried enough to start to do something about it themselves, even taking the law into their own hands.

Among the best news is the fact that during the last two decades, microcredit disbursed by NGOs to poor working people with little or no collateral, loans which get them started in their own small businesses, have demonstrated that: (1) The poor will repay loans. Repayment rates on such loans are in the 95 to 98 per cent range; (2) The poor will pay market rates of interest on these loans; (3) Organisations making these loans can reach large numbers of people; (4) Money gets invested in small businesses, creates new jobs and increases the income of the client, who spends the increased income on more food and education for her children, better housing and better medical care, and uses some of it in support of community projects. 'A microloan, instead of being a hand out, becomes a way out.' So says Charles L. Dokmo of the International Fund for Agricultural Development.

The fund's aim is to tap some of the wealth on Wall Street to reach 100 million people with microcredit. That will require a loan fund of around $20 billion – an enormous sum, but it is only 0.2 per cent of the $10 trillion growth in US stock market capitalisation in the past decade. It is a figure that is about half as much as Greenpeace and the European Union are forcing oil companies to spend on recycling redundant oil rigs out of the North Sea, with no benefit either to the marine environment or to the beleaguered fish stocks and the local fishers.

Despite what the vested interests of the past would lead the world to believe, the environment is high on the agenda of many people and an increasing number of the companies for which they work. The Green Renaissance is accelerating very fast. Of these things I am sure. How the laws of the land and the sea could be redrafted or redefined to accelerate the Renaissance is outside my sphere of expertise. However, it is my considered opinion that the consequences of continuing down the Dark Age route are too horrible to contemplate.

I will, however, make what I hope are relevant comments on some of the topics of the papers about to be laid before you:

Landfill solves nothing but the immediate problem of how to sweep the waste produced by the throwaway society under what at first sight appears to be a convenient carpet. Each landfill or sculptured landfill site represents a catastrophe waiting to happen; those catastrophes are already happening and not only just in the developing world. It has long been my considered opinion that high tech incinerators are a better option. However, now even that road is obsolete for gasification and steam-reforming techniques can turn our carbon wastes into hydrogen, alcohol (both of which are energy sources for fuel cells), distilled water and fertiliser with no flue and no flue gases to worry about.

There is a popular Turkish saying, 'Iraq has oil, we have water. Let them drink their oil.' It is being said with monotonous regularity that the next world war will be fought over the planet's dwindling supply of water, water that is sweet enough to drink and is not so full of fertiliser that it exacerbates the many problems of eutrophication. Eutrophication is one of the main problems facing humankind.

Duty of care legislation must take all such downstream effects into consideration, that's why I believe that carbon taxes must be implemented as quickly as possible, and be enjoined with good catchment management taxes in the not too far distant future. This would then speed integrated catchment and coastal management. Likewise overfishing is an important factor in the eutrophication of shallow marine waters for, instead of the nutrients being held long-term in large fish, they go into short-term cycle. The complications of the jurisprudence of the biosphere are many and intricate and we still have a lot to learn.

I am often asked what is my greatest worry. My answer is always the same: 'the development of a cheap safe source of energy before society is ready to face up to the implications'. I was recently in Lucerne to celebrate the evolution of the fuel cell. I quote from the programme of that celebration, 'Fuel Cells: A Key to a Sustainable Energy Future', where I wrote:

> Science has been my mistress for more than half a century and one of her many products, television, has been my fairy godmother for the past thirty. Thanks to them both I have circumnavigated the world more than 150 times, riding high on the horsepower of the apocalypse. I have seen the terrible problems caused by the misapplication of science and technology yet I can, with my hand on my heart, say that all those problems can be solved by the correct application of science and technology – a key part of which is the fuel cell.
>
> As the new millennium approached I was privileged to drive a prototype car powered by a fuel cell. At the end of my test run I lay down and made as if to drink the water emanating from its tail pipe, and turning to the press, said, 'Science has done it, at last a safe source of mobile energy: good news for all those who suffer from particulate diesel fever, good news for those against global greenhouse, good news for those worried about acid rain and nitrate eutrophication, good news for the dwindling stocks of fossil fuels which can now be conserved for use as raw materials of our plaster-chemical future. But why is my shining automobile always stuck in other people's traffic? Why am I always demanding new motorways, more parking lots, but of course, never in my own back yard?'

One must ask, is society ready to make wise use of such truly miraculous advances in the heritage of science and technology?

APPENDIX 8

Talk given at Southwark Cathedral, 1999

'Consider the lilies of the field, how they grow. They toil not, neither do they spin, and yet I say to you that Solomon in all his glory was not arrayed like one of these.'

The message I have been asked to convey today is for me encapsulated in this verse from the Bible. Though cast in God's image, humanity must be humble before creation.

We now know that the process, which turned a lifeless planet into the living Earth as we have come to know it, took at least 3.6 billion years, a process of gradual change that worked God's purpose out, making it ever more possible for more complex forms of life to discover their role within creation.

In the fullness of time, complex organisms that had the ability to sense the spirituality of existence could walk upon this Earth, this Garden of Eden. There they discovered the soul within and around them, the sense of right and wrong, the mystery of God's image, the majesty of Soulship, the potential only we have, the cross only we have to bear within creation.

The time fast approaches when we celebrate 2,000 years of Christianity, 2,000 years during which a growing band of people across the world have attempted to base their way of life, ethics, spirituality, call it what you will, on what little we know about the life of Christ: born in Bethlehem of Judea, brought up in Nazareth as part of a craftsperson's family, campaigner, teacher, master, prophet, martyr, Son of God.

Half a millennium before his birth, over a period of no more than 120 years, five great thinkers living in different parts of the world had come to remarkably similar conclusions regarding people and the living world upon which we all depend and of which we are a part. They were Zarathustra, Deutero-Isaiah, Gautama Siddhartha, known as the Buddha, Confucius and Pythagoras, and, despite the fact that they never met and in all probability had no knowledge of each other's teachings, they each came to the same conclusion concerning the relationship between people and creation. They came to the realisation that 'each individual human being had it within them to attain a direct personal relationship with the ultimate spiritual reality that lay behind the universe in which they find themselves'.

It was from this realisation that evolved the great spiritual philosophies of the world: Brahmanism, Buddhism, Christianity, Islam, Judaism, Taoism, Zoroastrianism, in all their diverse forms.

Like all other manifestations of creative evolution, these philosophies came into being in isolation, developing in response to local conditions. Again like all other products of creative evolution, as they increased the territory over which they chose to hold sway, they came into conflict with their neighbours, a state in which sadly they remain to this day.

Territoriality usually concerns the annexation of specific resources: water and food, good hunting or fishing grounds, good soil, a place to live in peace and prosperity. In the case of a philosophy the resource is human minds. Perhaps that is the forbidden fruit of every Eden.

It is an awesome thought that all these forms of one basic philosophy of life, all these expressions of spirituality, have become corporitised into the para-national warring factions that have come to be regarded as separate religions.

As we approach AD 2000 we may hear much talk about ecumenism, the sharing of spirituality, but conversion is still the battle cry of most of the religions and most of the branches of those religions. Their aim, though couched in terms of salvation for the world, is really about more power to the specific beliefs, corporate dogma of that specific branch, eventual world domination, domination bathed in the blood of one crusade after another, crusades now policed by the so-called United Nations.

Sadly, there is no getting away from the fact that religion is causing severe unrest and social dislocation across the world. It appears to have lost its way, or for those of us who believe in one true spiritual being, the devil is making a highly successful take over bid.

If the Messiah, the Son of God or Mohammed returned to earth in the year 2000 he would not only shudder at the unholy mess that has been perpetrated in his name, he would also find the moneylenders hard at work, especially in the temples of creation.

Over half of the world's population are still attempting to live in villages, growing their own food and fuel from their own lands. As Sir James Goldsmith said before his death, 'They do not figure in the so called global economy for there is no way that stock exchanges can benefit from their existence.'

The same is of course not true of their lands, so as an excuse to get them out of the sustainable life cycle and into the unsustainable job cycle, they are persuaded to grow so called cash crops on their land: cash for the shareholders of the multinationals and starvation for those who don't get a paid job as a grease monkey, part-time worker in the packing factory or security guard.

I challenge any member of any religion who has any sense of the abiding spirituality of creation within their souls to find solace in a world in which the rich get richer at the expense of the poor getting poorer; a world where every day the richest one-third of the so called human population throw away more resources than the poorest two-thirds have access to; a world in which every day 100,000 people die prematurely of malnutrition and environmental pollution as a similar number are forced to leave their homelands and head for the promise of the throw away society, a long march to cities that are not paved with gold but engulfed in end of the road shanty towns.

It is tempting to think that it is just a passing phenomenon of the developing world – but why are thousands of young men sleeping rough on the streets of Britain's towns and cities, and why did 500 of them commit suicide last year?

Why? Well, I can only conclude that it is because we are losing touch with the spirituality of creation, replacing it with the arrogance of self-importance, so much so that one in ten of all the plants and animals – which like us are a product of creation and upon which our past, present and future depends – are facing extinction.

Two thousand years since the birth of Christ – what better time to admit our shortcomings and absolve our many sins of the past by becoming part of the true spirituality of creative evolution? The way ahead is to take up the cross of Soulship, the only way to work God's purpose out and move the living world towards a sustainable future.